Regional Currency Areas in Financial Globalization

Regional Currency Areas in Financial Globalization

A Survey of Current Issues

Edited by

Patrick Artus

Chief Economist, CDC IXIS (Caisse des Dépôts et Consignations' Investment Bank), France

André Cartapanis

University of the Mediterranean, France

Florence Legros

University of Paris-Dauphine, France

Edward Elgar

Cheltenham, UK • Northampton, MA, USA

Published by
Edward Elgar Publishing Limited
Glensanda House
Montpellier Parade
Cheltenham
Glos GL50 1UA
UK

Edward Elgar Publishing, Inc.
136 West Street
Suite 202
Northampton
Massachusetts 01060
USA

A catalogue record for this book
is available from the British Library

ISBN 1 84376 690 6

Printed and bound in Great Britain by MPG Books Ltd, Bodmin, Cornwall

Contents

Contributors

Michel Aglietta, CEPII, FORUM, University of Paris X-Nanterre

Jean-Pierre Allégret, GATE, University of Lyon II

Patrick Artus, CDC IXIS, Paris

Camille Baulant, CEPII, University of Angers

Agnès Bénassy-Quéré, CEPII, THEMA, University of Paris X-Nanterre

Marie-Noëlle Cales, GATE, University of Lyon II

André Cartapanis, CEFI, University of Mediterranean, Aix-Marseille II

Benoît Cœuré, French Ministry of Economics and Finance

Vincent Dropsy, California State University, Fullerton

Jean-Jacques Durand, CREM, University of Rennes I

Hubert Escaith, ECLAC, Santiago

Pierre Faure, CEFI, ERUDITE, University of Paris XII

Christian Ghymers, European Commission, Brussels

Daniel Goyeau, CRIEF-MOFIB, University of Poitiers

John Hawkins, Department of the Treasury, Australia

Alain Jousten, CEPR, IZA, University of Liège

Marc Klau, Bank for International Settlements, Basel

Pierre Laurent, CDC IXIS, Paris

Florence Legros, University of Paris-Dauphine

Jacques Léonard, CRIEF-MOFIB, University of Poitiers

Olivier Manioc, LEAD, University of French West Indies and Guyana

Luis Miotti, CEPN, University of Paris XIII

Sandra Moatti, CPR Asset Management, Paris

Jean-Gabriel Montauban, LEAD, University of French West Indies and Guyana

Nathalie Payelle, CREM, University of Rennes I

Dominique Pépin, CRIEF-MOFIB, University of Poitiers

Dominique Plihon, CEPN, University of Paris XIII

Carlos Quenan, CEPN, University of Paris III

Rogerio Studart, Inter American Development Bank, Washington

Jérôme Teïletche, CDC IXIS, Paris

Virginie Traclet, CREM, University of Rennes I

Preface

On 26 and 27 March 2002 an international colloquium was held in Santiago, Chile on the following theme: Towards Regional Currency Areas. Gathering around 100 participants, academics, central bankers, representatives of the main international financial institutions (IMF, ECB, OECD, BIS, ECLAC and so forth), in the prestigious backdrop of ECLAC's Raùl Prebisch Conference Room, this colloquium was organized by Fondation de la Caisse des Dépôts et Consignations, CEFI (UMR 6126, CNRS-University of the Mediterranean, Aix-Marseille II), CEPII, ECLAC and *Revue Economique.* Nearly 60 contributions were presented and many themes were dealt with: exchange rate regimes and optimal currency area theory, exchange rate regimes in emerging countries, international capital markets and regional currency areas, the experience of the creation of the EMU and the euro, exchange rate regimes in Central and Eastern Europe, Asia and Latin America, dollarization, the coordination of macroeconomic policies in the presence of regional currency areas and so on.

Combined with the publication of a special issue of *Revue Economique, Macroeconomics of Exchange-Rate Regimes* (**54** (5), September 2003), this book was edited by Patrick Artus, André Cartapanis and Florence Legros. It offers a selection of the interventions dedicated to the stakes and challenges associated with projects of regional currency areas against the backdrop of financial globalization.

Regional currency areas and international financial architecture in financial globalization: an introduction

Patrick Artus, André Cartapanis and Florence Legros

THE CHALLENGES ARISING FROM FINANCIAL GLOBALIZATION

Theoretically, the globalization of financial markets is likely to generate an efficient allocation of resources on a worldwide scale. In addition to the advantages already provided by international specialization, one has to add the possibility of transferring financing capacity to economies suffering from a shortfall in savings, and also of smoothing over time the lack of adjustment between savings and investment triggered in each country by the overriding need to develop infrastructure, specific demographic features, the life cycle of households or the state of public finances. In an increasingly uncertain world, financial innovation also gives rise to possibilities of hedging and transferring risks that did not exist in the past.

But simultaneously international capital movements can lead to greater fragility and chronic instability in international financial markets. In a context of asymmetry of information and short-sightedness in decision-making, the decisions with respect to portfolio reallocation by international investors in the asset markets and the brutal discontinuation of loans extended by international banks can respond to herd-like rationality, endogenous changes in expectations reflecting swings in perceived insecurity, without any significant deterioration in macroeconomic fundamentals. Such episodes are likely to disrupt the determination of asset prices and the allocation of savings on an international scale, triggering crises and leading to huge social costs. Thus the 1990s saw a rash of currency crises, with wild fluctuations in exchange rates, along with massive losses of currency reserves and reflected by a steep devaluation or the floating of a currency which had been pegged until then, or by a severe and sudden depreciation when they were in a situation of dirty float. The currency crises of the 1980s and 1990s are estimated to have created cumulative deficits in output, relative to the long-run trend, ranging from 4 per cent to 7 per cent, and twin crises, combining banking and currency crises, resulting in losses in production of around 15 per cent. The magnitude of these shocks is explained by the size of the capital inflows and outflows. During the Asia crisis of 1997, net capital outflows from the five worst-hit countries, that is Thailand, Malaysia, Indonesia, the Philippines and South Korea, thus exceeded US$100 billion, or about 10 per cent of their aggregate GDP, in a few months.

Against this backdrop, the official doctrine justifying the liberalization on a vast scale of capital markets, once presented as a prerequisite for the economic development of emerging countries, according to the yardstick of the Washington consensus, now seems far more tentative. There is no irrefutable empirical evidence of a positive link between the international financial integration of developing economies and their growth rate. Conversely, volatility of macroeconomic performances and vulnerability to crises have increased significantly. Faced with the experience of massive capital inflows and outflows creating pro-cyclical and disruptive effects, one can consider that there is no longer any neo-liberal Washington consensus. The triumph of the market and financial globalization certainly does not mean that states must withdraw from the international financial arena. All the initiatives adopted by the international community for the last ten years, including central banks, the BIS and the IMF, refer to the principle of international capital mobility, while acknowledging furthermore the need for an institutional infrastructure capable of correcting the inherent flaws of international financial markets. But how can this be achieved?

WITH THE NEW INTERNATIONAL FINANCIAL ARCHITECTURE, A NEW BRETTON WOODS IS NOT ON THE AGENDA

Everybody admits that it is politically unrealistic to want to build a new international monetary and financial system by drawing on supposedly cast-iron rules, which international institutions benefiting from widespread transfers of competences would be in charge of enforcing. This is why the reforms known as the new international financial architecture, sketched out in June 1999 under the aegis of the G7 and implemented since then by the IMF, are not aimed at leading to a new Bretton Woods – that is the reconstruction of a monetary and financial system on a global scale – but less ambitiously seek to improve the functioning of financial markets, especially in emerging countries. This purpose in principle encompasses four objectives: improve transparency and access to information; modernize the prudential regulation of financial institutions; reinforce the role of existing financial international institutions and reform their modes of intervention to meet the challenges of market instability more adequately; correct the system of incentives that shapes decision-making in the private sector and ensure the private sector shoulders an appropriate share of the burden during a crisis.

The question of exchange rate regimes – and one needs to keep in mind that this was at the core of the Bretton Woods system – therefore is not explicitly mentioned in the agenda of the new architecture. Nevertheless the repetition of international financial crises throughout the 1990s and 2000s cannot be dissociated from the options adopted in terms of exchange rate regimes: stepping up the target zone system, in Europe in the run-up to EMU and the creation of the euro; pegging to the dollar in many emerging economies such as Mexico or Thailand; the setting up of a currency board in the case of Argentina. As is well known, these choices led to a string of severe crises, in 1992–93, in 1995, in 1997 and in 2002. Hence the renewed relevance of the Mundell triangle of incompatibility.

THE CHOICE OF AN EXCHANGE RATE REGIME: CORNER SOLUTIONS OR INTERMEDIATE REGIMES?

Economists have recently rediscovered a principle set out by Mundell as early as the 1960s: only corner solutions, that is pure flexible exchange rates or hard pegs, such as dollarization or a currency board, would be durably sustainable in a context of high capital mobility and, conversely, intrinsic fragility allegedly characterizes intermediate exchange rate regimes.

But this stance does not enjoy unanimous backing. It is often argued that intermediate regimes not only can remain, but also offer real advantages for emerging economies by combining the virtues of exchange rate stability, notably from the viewpoint of monetary discipline, without creating dangerous irreversible situations as illustrated by the meltdown of Argentina's currency board. It can even be argued that no exchange rate regime is optimal in absolute terms, as the optimal choice could prove to be different not only according to country but also according to the period for any one country. A currency float can be the best solution for more developed countries or for the most highly integrated economic zones, and therefore between the dollar, euro and yen zones. Exchange rate fixity can prove to be preferable for small economies, which are very open to the exterior or where hyperinflation prevails. Intermediate regimes can respond to the diversity of mixed situations. All the more so, as adopting a fixed exchange rate regime, typically when joining a currency area, can generate significant modifications in *ex ante* choice parameters, be it the degree of external openness, the weight of intra-zone trade or the correlation of cycles within a currency area.

However debates about the choice of an exchange rate regime and the consequences it can entail have changed in nature to some extent, if they are compared with the post-Second World War debates about the respective pros and cons of fixed and flexible exchange rates. One no longer seeks to assess the advantages and the drawbacks of each exchange rate regime on the scale of the international monetary system, with either option to be applied to all economies, by preferring the question of external adjustment, and absorption of imbalances in current account balances. On the contrary one now looks with respect to each national economy, or even at a regional level, at the type of exchange rate regime that seems to be the best choice, from the viewpoint of the efficiency of overall macroeconomic steering as well as in reference to the sustainability of the regime in a context of financial globalization. The range of possible options has widened substantially. Regarding flexible exchange rates, one draws a distinction between pure floats and dirty floats. With regard to fixed exchange rates, extreme solutions can be adopted: a currency board, dollarization (or euro-ization), creation of a currency area and so on. But one can also envision the implementation of a whole range of intermediate regimes: target zone-like fluctuation bands, pegged to a central nominal or real parity; crawling pegs; pegs that are more or less adjustable to a key currency or a basket of currencies; and so on. As a result, fresh analyses have enabled the criteria to be used to choose an exchange rate regime to be fine-tuned.

NEW CRITERIA TO MAKE CHOICES AMONG THE VARIOUS EXCHANGE RATE REGIMES

The specialized literature dedicated to exchange rate regimes and regional currency areas rapidly became a cottage industry in the late 1990s. But even if we were to restrict our study to corner solutions, we could not talk about the supposed theoretical superiority of either regime, and the situation we face resembles more a trade-off between the costs and the advantages of both. At the same time the criteria drawn upon to choose an exchange rate regime must now factor in the new deal that consists of financial globalization. We will now look at both sides of the argument in more detail.

Fixed exchange rates present the advantage of reducing uncertainty and therefore the currency risks weighing on international trade or international transfers of savings, lowering risk premiums and the cost of access to international capital markets, ensuring a credible anchoring for monetary policy, reducing spreads on an international scale, opposing the monetary financing of budgetary imbalances, preventing competitive depreciation policies, and so on. Simultaneously some drawbacks are inevitable: the credibility of the commitment in favour of fixed exchange rates is fragile and the triggering of a currency crisis can prove to be very expensive; monetary policy gets to depend significantly on the options taken by the country it has pegged its currency to; the economy becomes very sensitive to external shocks, but also to real shocks of domestic origin; there can be an overvaluation of the exchange rate likely to generate a deterioration in external trade and an unsustainable rise in unemployment; and so on.

The following characteristics are found on the plus side for flexible exchange rates: the independence of monetary policy, the neutralization of external shocks or real shocks thanks to changes in exchange rates, but also the absorption of effects on external competitiveness from an acceleration in inflation. Among the drawbacks note the risk of imported inflation, the contraction in international trade or transfers of savings when there is significant currency volatility, the risk of competitive depreciation policies developing within a given regional area, even the lack of incentive to implement adjustment policies or structural reforms.

In the past few years however, new theoretical arguments have completed the debate. Some authors operate within a political economy of exchange rate regimes and examine the political cost of macroeconomic adjustments according to the exchange regime that has been chosen. Others favour what they call the 'fear of floating,' in other words the counterproductive effects of floating when there is large external indebtedness denominated in currencies. As for the proponents of intermediate regimes, they draw on a whole range of criteria stemming notably from the theory of optimal currency areas to justify possibly choosing such a regime: degree of openness and magnitude of domestic or external shocks, whether symmetrical or asymmetrical; internal mobility of factors; degree of transmission of exchange rates to domestic prices; significance of credibility effects; aversion to inflation; and so on.

Apparently however this debate made progress via the discussion of the empirical experience of exchange rate regimes, notably in the 1990s. The question of the choice of an exchange rate regime inevitably suffered from interferences as a result of the high number of currency crises, among European countries firstly, in the early 1990s, and subsequently in emerging countries. The debate about the determinants of exchange rate regimes therefore cannot be dissociated from financial liberalization and the wild swings in capital movements in Asian or Latin American emerging countries. It has to be widened to the question of the vulnerability of fixed or target zone exchange rates. For the choice of an exchange rate regime, *de jure* or *de facto*, undoubtedly depends on normative criteria such as an optimal currency area (mobility of factors, degree of openness, indexation of wages and so on) or the preference function of policy-makers. But it also relates to financial factors that have to do with the sustainability of the regime or the lack of sustainability of the exchange rate regime that prevailed earlier, until a crisis imposed a change. For emerging countries, this macro-financial dimension (external indebtedness, exposure to the spreading of speculative outbreaks, relative weight of direct investment and banking or portfolio flows, volatility of capital movements, recent experiences of currency crises and so on) can prove to be decisive in terms of the credibility of a fluctuation band, such as a target zone.

But globalization, from the point of view of international trade as well as with regard to savings flows, has gone hand in hand with an intensification of regional relations, and this leads to the question of exchange rate regimes being widened to the analysis of regional currency areas.

BEYOND EXCHANGE RATE REGIMES, THE RENEWED RELEVANCE OF REGIONAL CURRENCY AREAS

Once more, it is primarily on the basis of the experience of the 1990s that the relevance of regional currency areas within emerging countries has been reasserted.

The example of the European Monetary Union and the creation of the euro have given rise to new projects. This is the case of the strategy envisioned for ASEAN countries within the framework of the Chiang Mai initiative: these economies could indeed choose an intermediate exchange rate regime, such as a target zone, in the prospect of eventually joining a future Asian regional currency area. This is also a hypothesis looked at by some Mercosur countries, Brazil and Argentina notably, which are thinking about a similar model.

But these initiatives result above all from the lessons drawn from the systemic crises that hit these countries in the second half of the 1990s. One merely needs to keep in mind the role played by the way the Thai crisis spread throughout the region to all of South-East Asia in 1997 or how stock market volatility spread within the South American continent in the autumn of 1998, and even more strikingly, think about the effects induced by the floating and the depreciation in the Brazilian real on the sustainability of Argentina's currency board. At a theoretical level, in the most recent models, systemic currency crises punish a widespread lack of coordination, as the taking into account of the excessive risks accumulated in some countries could result in mounting fragility in the neighbouring countries, regardless of their own situation at a macroeconomic level or with respect to their external financial commitments. If a local shock occurs, expectations can spread mistrust with respect to other currencies, in the direction of other economies, under the form of transfers of volatility or changes in asset prices, according to various channels of contagion: readjustment of all international portfolios (assets or banking debts) when uncertainty becomes widespread and consequently triggers pure contagion: spillover effects linked to trade or financial interdependences at a regional scale, or in response to a common creditor, and so on.

If the risk of a currency crisis depends not only on the weaknesses of a national economy but also, and even first and foremost, on the perception held by international investors about the situation of neighbouring countries, then the debate about the choice of an exchange rate regime turns into a discussion about regional currency unions, about their pros and cons, and about the criteria that each candidate must comply with to join this area.

The theory of optimal currency areas proposes an uncompromising vision of a fixed exchange rate system, since the purpose consists not only in designing a system of irrevocably fixed exchange rates but also in transferring to the currency areas sovereign responsibility for monetary policy and the exchange rate policy with the rest of the world. Hence the high number of question marks about the convergence criteria required *ex ante*, but also about the degree of freedom and the *ex post* mode of economic policy coordination insofar as the currency area entails some kind of budgetary federalism that preserves national prerogatives in this field. From such a point of view, it is not certain that the theories of optimal currency areas *à la* Mundell or *à la* Kenen are currently the most robust in terms of answering these questions. On the one hand, the European Monetary Union was made up by a group of countries that did not meet the theoretical criteria of an optimal money area – whether with respect to the mobility of factors or to real wage flexibility. On the other hand each emerging country of a given regional zone, in Asia, Latin America or the Caribbean, presents specific attributes with regard to the degree of liberalization of financial markets or the relative weight of various modes of external financing (direct investment, sovereign debt, portfolio investment on the stock markets) and is therefore exposed to specific financial vulnerabilities. These are all phenomena that the theoreticians of optimal currency areas have deliberately neglected, but that one should however take into account to ascertain the financial sustainability of a regional currency area.

Thus the implementation of real regional currency areas in response to globalization and financial instability in emerging or transition countries seems premature. This then brings us back to the optimality and the vulnerability of intermediate exchange rate regimes within a regional zone, and raises many questions about common pegging, the forms of cooperation and/or coordination required at a macroeconomic or macrofinancial level, the leeway for exchange rate flexibility within a regional target zone, and so forth.

THE SANTIAGO COLLOQUIUM AND THE QUESTION OF REGIONAL CURRENCY AREAS IN THE CONTEXT OF FINANCIAL GLOBALIZATION

Such is the historical and analytical environment in which the international colloquium Towards Regional Currency Areas was held in Santiago, Chile on 26 and 27 March 2002. During the colloquium, a great number of themes relative to regional currency areas were dealt with: exchange rate regimes and optimal currency areas theory, exchange rate regimes in emerging countries, international capital markets and regional currency areas, the experience of the creation of the EMU and the euro, exchange rate regimes in Central and Eastern Europe, Asia and Latin America, dollarization, the coordination of macroeconomic policies in the presence of regional currency areas, and so on.

This book offers a selection of interventions dealing with the key issues and challenges of regional currency area projects in the context of financial globalization.

The interventions focus on the three central questions and the answers offered are presented in the three parts that make up the book:

- What effects can be expected from the creation of regional currency areas on the efficiency and the stability of international financial markets?
- In view of recent experiences, how have emerging countries chosen their exchange rate regimes or the currency they have pegged their exchange rate to (dollar, euro and so on)? What result can be already drawn, notably from the point of view of effects on the regional integration of each zone?
- What are the implications of choices of exchange rate regimes in terms of economic policy, within a monetary union, as in Europe, as well as with regard to international coordination?

INTERNATIONAL FINANCIAL MARKETS AND REGIONAL CURRENCY AREAS

The first chapter in this book tackles the issue of the determinants and effects of the creation of regional currency areas: 'Financial market aspects of regional currency areas' is by John Hawkins and Marc Klau. After reviewing the favourable conditions and factors in terms of the creation of a currency area, they highlight the following point. While the euro zone and the issue of dollarization in several countries rekindled the debate, the question of the impact on financial markets is not new but lacks a clear answer, because there is not a long enough track record. The authors thus propose an analysis of the impact of the creation of a currency area on the financial markets of the countries they study. Their conclusion is quite mixed: probably, the creation of a currency area is a factor of stability and efficiency for financial markets. Nevertheless it is in no case a sufficient condition and is absolutely not a remedy for the 'original sin' of some countries, unable to raise capital in the international markets.

If, as the following chapter, 'Currency regimes and the process of regional financial integration of the emerging countries', tells us, belonging to a currency area implied a degree of homogeneity between countries, there would simply be an arbitrage between assets of major currency areas and, little by little, integration of emerging countries. This is precisely this 'distance from integration' that Daniel Goyeau, Jacques Léonard and Dominique Pépin measure, showing the weight of what they call 'geographical proximity' in contrast with 'monetary proximity'. The authors show that integration is generally more geographical then monetary, and this conclusion is confirmed by many other chapters in this book.

The impact of what they call 'social remoteness' is measured in the analysis of Alain Jousten and Florence Legros, 'Pensions and savings in a monetary union: an analysis of capital flows'. The question consists in understanding what are the implications of a currency area for the flow of savings between two countries hit by the same demographic shock but with very different retirement systems. Their chapter helps us to understand how the savings rate, and therefore capital movements between countries of the same economic union, could be changed by the demographic shock, and therefore how the weight of the demographic shock is shared between countries. Apparently countries with a regime of voluntary pension funds may have to bear a heavier demographic burden when they belong to a currency area than if they are not members of such a union; this burden entails a notably larger financial risk that could weigh on the holders of pension funds.

The chapter by Pierre Laurent and Jérôme Teïletche, 'Emerging sovereign bond markets: a view from the extremes' confirms the preponderance of geographical proximity in the financial integration between emerging countries. The authors draw upon a deliberately statistical approach to measure the risk inherent to emerging bonds from two angles: the usual, univariate approach and a more original one, a so-called multivariate approach, which takes into account contagion at an international level of shocks that affect emerging markets. While several well-known characteristics (heterogeneity of the term 'emerging countries', the nonetheless riskier feature of such assets, the decline in the risk of contagion since 1999) are reviewed, the method used by the authors, Extreme Value Theory – in other words, the failure of a normal distribution law to describe such financial assets – allows the authors to reveal a greater likelihood of a crash than a boom, and above all highlight the weight of geographical proximity in the combined risk of a crash. Geographical proximity would therefore be a factor of symmetry of shocks, and accordingly an element to be taken into account in order to determine the opportunity of creating a currency area. As much as the results it provides, the method used itself deserves further research: it is clearly extremely promising with respect to risk analysis, notably multivariate risk.

EXCHANGE RATE REGIMES AND REGIONAL CURRENCY AREAS IN EMERGING COUNTRIES

The purpose of the chapter written by André Cartapanis and Vincent Dropsy, 'Financial vulnerability and exchange rate regimes in Latin American and Asian emerging countries: towards new criteria?', is twofold: on the one hand it seeks to build indicators of exchange rate regimes that factor in not only the official regime – *de jure* exchange rate regime – but also the actual regime – *de facto* regime – while on the other hand it tries to explain why these *de facto* regimes diverge from *de jure* regimes. For whereas *de jure* exchange rate regimes are designed to integrate the countries considered within currency areas, the *de facto* regimes are often designed to achieve a transition into these zones. The authors thus propose an analysis of the dynamics of exchange rate regimes that takes into account this convergence process. They show that the usual definition of optimal currency areas is not sufficiently precise to explain why an exchange rate regime is chosen, and one needs to take into account several additional variables to understand satisfactorily the choice of an exchange rate regime; notably, whereas financial depth argues in favour of exchange rate flexibility, international capital mobility would call for fixed exchange rates and foreign direct investment would not be a significant variable. The authors show that moreover there is effectively convergence between exchange rate regimes towards their level of long-term equilibrium.

The following chapter by Luis Miotti, Dominique Plihon and Carlos Quenan, 'The dollar, the euro and exchange rate regimes in Latin America', also deals with the determination of the gap between *de facto* and *de jure* regimes, and attention is paid specifically to Latin America. The study concludes like the previous one on the importance of financial factors when rewriting the history of currency areas. For instance the history of the euro is illuminating with respect to this point as well as the importance of the period of transition towards an equilibrium exchange rate. Can this lesson bear fruit for Latin American countries? The statistical studies carried out show a significant proximity to the dollar zone, not only for Mexico as is often argued, but for all South American countries. A peg to the dollar is therefore natural. But pegging one's currency just to the dollar is a debatable, although simple, decision: policy is made more transparent, the market can test more easily the credibility of policies, and so on; but the relatively diversified structure (compared with Mexico's) of trade in most countries in Latin America could justify adopting a basket of currencies including the euro.

De facto peg or intermediate exchange rate regime with regional cooperation? This is the question posed by Agnès Bénassy-Quéré and Benoît Cœuré in 'Big and small currencies: the regional connection'. The following point has often been made theoretically: corner solutions are often preferable to intermediate solutions; empirically, *de facto* regimes sometimes diverge markedly from *de jure* regimes – stabilization of the regime because of the fear of floating, for example. The authors argue that debates about the optimal regime neglect the regional dimension and highlight the weight of geographic factors, emphasizing the difference between the sharing of a currency by a region (currency union with a supranational central bank) and the adoption of a peg currency (with a national central bank external to the region considered, for example in the event of dollarization). This geographical weight is therefore found for small currencies. Nonetheless the economies concerned can have an interest in regional cooperation around a peg to a basket of currencies rather than a corner solution.

'Regional integration and the issue of choosing an appropriate exchange rate regime in Latin America', by Hubert Escaith, Christian Ghymers and Rogerio Studart, also emphasizes the problems met in defining a peg for Latin American countries. They explore the two solutions proposed in the previous chapter: should one prefer a peg or a currency area? In other words, a foreign central bank or a regional central bank? Their answer is that – although Latin America is far from representing an optimal currency area – the latter solution could be preferable. On the one hand, it would give a common institution to the region and therefore probably a reason to cooperate with respect to shared macroeconomic targets. This is the argument of political economy based on the idea that centralized decision-making improves decisions. On the other hand, globalization develops a risk of strain on the financial markets and therefore enhances the attractiveness of the regional zone. Naturally these arguments point to the desirability of reinforcing the regional dimension that becomes no longer just a geographical but also an economic argument, with the purpose of providing an incentive for macroeconomic stabilization.

A regional rationale also provides the basis for the questions about the opportunity of a currency area in CARICOM (the Caribbean Community and Common Market, created in 1973) in 'Is a monetary union in CARICOM desirable?', by Olivier Manioc and Jean-Gabriel Montauban. The answer to this question raises two other problems. The first is: has regional trade integration been effective – in other words, is the region likely to become an optimal currency area? The second is: will trade be facilitated by the creation of such a currency area? Can cooperation be achieved between these countries? The authors answer the first question negatively: the goods produced are more substitutable than complementary and the potential of trade, in all likelihood, has already been achieved. They answer the second question by arguing that apparently differences in cycles between countries, and accordingly differences in terms of optimal cyclical reactions, also lead to a negative answer.

REGIONAL CURRENCY AREAS AND ECONOMIC POLICY

The first chapter in Part III, 'Exchange rate regimes in the route to EMU', by Michel Aglietta, Camille Baulant and Sandra Moatti, seeks to describe the transition of Eastern European countries and the slow move by these economies towards the euro. It also highlights, as the previous contribution did, real factors. The point highlighted by the authors is the diversity of paths followed by Central and Eastern European countries to move in this direction. These diverging approaches are correlated to the specific domestic conditions of countries: state of financial markets naturally, but also the level of inflation required for technological catching-up by countries and, notably, corporate borrowing requirements, the level of public expenditures needed for catching up in the fields of health, welfare, and so on. They thus establish a real need for soft and differentiated convergences to avoid endangering growth in the countries they study.

If foreign direct investment has no more than an indeterminate relationship with the choice of an exchange rate regime, as was already demonstrated in the chapter by André Cartapanis and Vincent Dropsy, the volume of foreign direct investment and, accordingly, that of induced employment hinges to a great extent on the tax system adopted by the various countries of a same currency area. In this chapter, 'Can the free-rider behaviour of small countries offset the profligacy spending bias of large countries in the euro zone?', Patrick Artus examines the case of two countries in the same zone, different in terms of their size and their priorities on government expenditure, as the large country has a greater preference for government expenditure, just as is the case in the euro zone. The question then consists in ascertaining whether it is necessary to choose tax cooperation in the money area or if, on the contrary, tax competition is necessary to force the large country to change over to a more reasonable and less detrimental behaviour. In his model, Patrick Artus shows that the greater the difference in size between countries, the more any move of capital from the large country to the small one will have a major impact for the small country and a negligible one for its large partner. As a result, coordination of tax policies leads to higher taxes in the small country and thus a decline in its well-being. Asymmetrical coordination – in which large countries weight more than small ones – would therefore provide an incentive for spending while reducing well-being in small countries. Conversely a policy of tax competition increases well-being in the small country without however correcting the large country's profligacy. The most common practice in the euro zone, that is asymmetrical coordination, is therefore probably the worst of the three options.

Pierre Faure's chapter, 'Comparing monetary and fiscal policies in Europe and in the United States: a strategic analysis', seeks to assess the degree of coordination of European policies. One idea is that the decentralization of budgetary and tax decisions means the European Central Bank enjoys even greater freedom of action and, by contrast, the fact there is a single central bank facing a high number of budgetary decision-makers loosens the links between the central banker and regional policy-makers. Compared with the situation in the United States, Europe's situation tends to change substantially strategic interdependences between decision-makers and therefore the results of the economic policies implemented. Insofar as cooperation exists between a subset of players, this hardens the position of the others. Accordingly, budgetary federalism is efficient only if there is cooperation between tax and budgetary authorities. Moreover the structure of European government means that appointing a hawkish governor of the European Central Bank is detrimental for the entire world, as it gives rise to a lack of coordination within the euro zone and also at an external level.

While the credibility of monetary policies has fuelled an abundant literature, the same point does not hold for the credibility of fiscal policies. The chapter written by Jean-Pierre Allégret and Marie-Noëlle Cales, 'Fiscal policy and war of attrition: the case of Latin American countries', deals with this point, and more precisely with reference to the case of Latin America. The authors show that if South American authorities have been led to implement extremely restrictive fiscal policies since the 1990s, this was because their previous behaviour had often been lax and they had to win back credibility, even though the cost of these adjustments in terms of growth was high. Seeking to achieve credibility thus implies – as is the case for monetary policy – a conservative fiscal policy that ends to avoid the inflationary bias, but which is reflected by some indifference to the real implications of the policy pursued.

Obviously these two characteristics often lead economists to criticize the monetary policy conducted in the euro zone. Jean-Jacques Durand, Nathalie Payelle and Virginie Traclet, in the last chapter of the book, 'Are there benefits to a monetary policy rule in the EMU?', look back at the recent past by asking what effects the disappearance of pre-EMU rules had – and, notably, of the McCullum Rule since it prevailed under a modified form before the appearance of the European Central Bank. From the experience of three major countries, France, Germany and Italy, it would seem that maintaining such a rule would have led to at least comparable results to those that have been obtained. This justifies maintaining such a rule in the EMU, because of the expected gains in terms of transparency and credibility.

All in all, proximity between economies is an important factor for the implementation and the success of a regional currency area. But this proximity must be geographical, and therefore trade-related, as well as financial. More generally speaking, proximity means one has to consider the models of economic development followed by member countries: weight of the state, homogeneity of tax provisions, type of external financing and insertion within financial globalization. The chapters gathered in this book thus make it possible to study in greater depth the conditions required for the creation of regional currency areas among emerging countries, but also their impact on a possible convergence of institutions or growth regimes.

PART I

International financial markets and regional currency areas

1. Financial market aspects of regional currency areas

John Hawkins and Marc Klau[1]

INTRODUCTION

The concept of regional currency areas (RCAs) has gained adherents since the successful launch of the euro.[2] Previously, the establishment of common currencies had mostly followed political integration, such as the unification of Italy in the early 1860s, the United States in 1789 and Germany in 1990. RCAs between independent countries have been rarer; current examples are the euro area, the two CFA zones in Africa and the Eastern Caribbean Currency Area. (Appendix A also lists some historical examples such as the Latin Monetary Union and the Scandinavian Currency Union.) But now a number of governments in Africa and the Middle East have announced plans to form regional currency areas and the idea has been discussed in many other parts of the world (see Appendix B). While the euro area is too recent to be a basis for strong conclusions, the RCAs in West and Central Africa (with one change of parity – a devaluation in 1994) and the Caribbean have all been operating for over half a century now. This record of stability is in marked contrast to many unilateral exchange rate pegs. When RCAs have been dissolved, it has usually been due to war (which ended the Latin and Scandinavian monetary unions) and change of political status (which led to separate currencies being adopted fairly quickly in the states which had formerly shared the currencies of Czechoslovakia, the USSR and Yugoslavia).[3]

RCAs usually accompany other regional integration initiatives, and so are often dominated by political considerations. But there are also economic reasons why many countries, especially smaller ones, may wish to band together. Removing exchange rate variation between the members is likely to boost trade and capital flows between them.[4] In addition a more stable effective exchange rate should reduce volatility in consumer price indices. In many cases such considerations outweigh any possible advantages of using an independent monetary policy to offset idiosyncratic external shocks.[5]

Theoretical support for supranational currencies goes back at least to John Stuart Mill[6] but the recent literature starts with Mundell (1961).

At one extreme, the desirability of conducting an independent monetary policy for stabilization purposes might lead to a huge number of floating currencies – one for every city and town. At the other extreme, transactions convenience would imply a single currency for the world. Mundell sought a balance by suggesting that an optimal currency region is one where factors are highly mobile within the region but relatively immobile in terms of moving outside the region.

In subsequent work, the main criteria suggested have been the similarity of shocks and business cycles, trade links or similarities, wage and price flexibility and the extent of risk-sharing, especially through fiscal transfers: see Kang and Wang (2002) and Mongelli (2002) for recent summaries. A currency union may be more workable for economies at similar stages of development; they would find it easier to agree on goals (such as inflation targets) as well as on practical aspects such as the denomination at which coins give way to notes. An important point, first raised in Mundell's original article, is that the criteria are to some extent endogenous. Joining an RCA may itself alter the characteristics of an economy. Hawkins and Masson (2003) elaborate on these arguments and summarize empirical tests of them.

DOES FORMING AN RCA AID IN DEVELOPING FINANCIAL MARKETS?

The literature discussed above is overwhelmingly concerned with implications for the real economy. The implications for the development of financial markets have been relatively neglected. This is despite it being cited as an advantage by some proponents of RCAs. For example, Yam (1999) commented that, as a long-term possibility, an RCA in Asia 'would create larger and more liquid markets that are less susceptible to manipulation'. Al-Jasser and Al-Hamidy (2003) expect the planned RCA in the Gulf to integrate and deepen financial markets. The Eastern Caribbean Central Bank aspires to create a 'single financial space' within its RCA and has acted to broaden and deepen financial markets. For example it is working on developing an integrated primary and secondary regional bond market. Within Europe the Lamfalussy Group has examined ways of moving towards a more integrated financial market within the euro area.

A larger financial market will have more scope for specialized financial institutions. It also allows institutions to diversify credit risk without incurring foreign exchange risk. Joining an RCA is likely to increase pressures for a more homogenous trading structure and standard contracts in financial markets.

In Europe many of these gains are being reaped following the introduction of the euro. Investors in fixed income markets are focusing more on the characteristics of individual borrowers than the nationality of the issuer: see Barth et al. (2002) and Galati and Tsatsaronis (2001). Similarly, prices in European equity markets increasingly reflect risk factors specific to industrial sectors rather than individual countries. Borrowers have benefited from easier access to a larger investor base. Nonetheless markets to some extent remain segmented because of national differences. For example diverging market practices, arising partly from differing legal and taxation frameworks, are impeding development of pan-European collateral arrangements in money markets. National prestige can also prove an impediment. Rivalries and regulatory incompatibilities continue to impede creation of a pan-European equity trading platform.

In emerging economies, financial markets appear to have benefited less from RCAs. In Africa the CFA franc zone has segmented banking systems and only rudimentary regional financial markets; see Masson and Pattillo (2004).[7] Some countries' wish to foster 'their' financial market can impede regional initiatives.

As there are too few examples of longstanding RCAs, the rest of this chapter addresses the question of their likely impact on financial markets by examining the extent to which larger financial markets tend to operate better.

Foreign Exchange Markets

A small foreign exchange market may be more volatile and less efficient. A single large transaction is more likely to affect the exchange rate. Less innocently, it may be more vulnerable to speculators. An apparently conflicting conclusion is reached by Galati (2001), who reports that most empirical studies tend to find a positive association over time between trading volumes and price volatility. Galati surmises that this may be due to both being driven by the arrival of new information. In this case, it may still be consistent with larger markets being less volatile, other things being equal.

Unsurprisingly, larger currency regions tend to be more liquid. So when Portugal joined the EMU, it went from having a currency involved in 0.2 per cent of global foreign exchange trades to one used in 38 per cent of global trades. But the effect is non-linear; the US dollar and, to a lesser extent, the euro are far more heavily traded than the shares of their respective economies in world GDP would suggest. Among medium-sized economies the relationship between economic size and foreign exchange turnover is not strong (Figure 1.1).

Larger markets would be expected to be more efficient and benefit from economies of scale (and this would be compounded if larger markets are

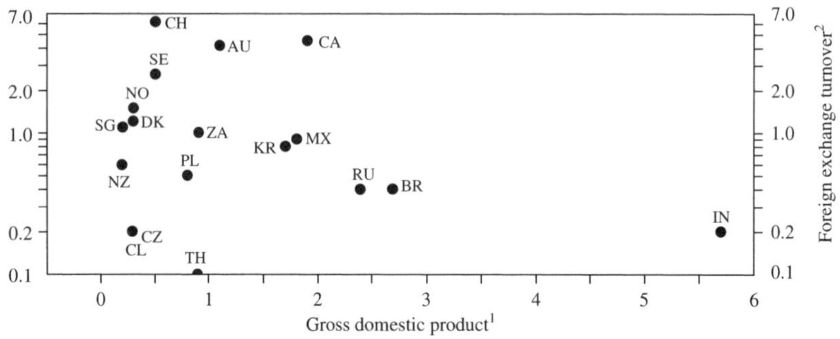

Notes: AR = Argentina; AU = Australia; BR = Brazil; CA = Canada; CL = Chile; CZ = Czech Republic; DK = Denmark; XM= Euro area; FR = France; DE = Germany; HK = Hong Kong SAR; HU = Hungary; IN = India; IL = Israel; IT = Italy; JP = Japan; KR = Korea; MY = Malaysia; MX = Mexico; NZ = New Zealand; NO = Norway; PE = Peru; PL = Poland; RU = Russia; SG = Singapore; ZA = South Africa; SE = Sweden; CH = Switzerland; TH = Thailand; TR = Turkey; GB = United Kingdom; US = United States.
1. As a percentage of world GDP in 2002.
2. Turnover measured in April 2001; log scale.

Sources: IMF; BIS.

Figure 1.1 Foreign exchange turnover and GDP

also less volatile). Transaction costs (bid–ask spreads) are lower in markets with more turnover (Figure 1.2).

Figure 1.3 and 1.4 compare two measures of exchange rate volatility to the size of the market in the currency. The measures capture short- and long-term volatility respectively.[8] Figure 1.3 measures volatility against whichever of the US dollar or euro is regarded as more important to the particular economy. Figure 1.4 is based on medium-term deviations of the real effective exchange rate from its trend, which are likely to impose a greater burden on the real economy than do the daily fluctuations. A bivariate relationship cannot be observed in the graphs, suggesting that other factors are more important than the size of the market in determining the volatility of currencies. This is consistent with the results of Galati and Tsatsaronis (2001) who found that the introduction of the euro had not substantially affected volatility, spreads, trading volumes and liquidity in foreign exchange markets.

Interbank Money Markets

Interbank interest rates are likely to be less volatile when the money market is larger and more liquid (Figure 1.5). In the euro area, the bid–ask spreads

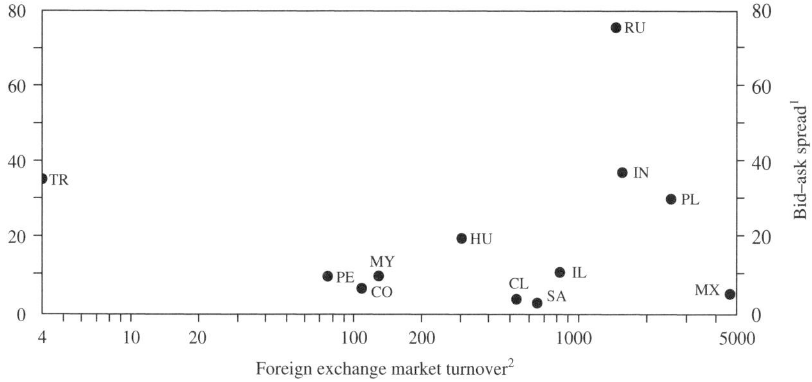

Notes:
1. In basis points.
2. End of 2002; in billions of US dollars; log scale.

Source: National data.

Figure 1.2 *Foreign exchange rate turnover versus bid–ask spread in spot market*

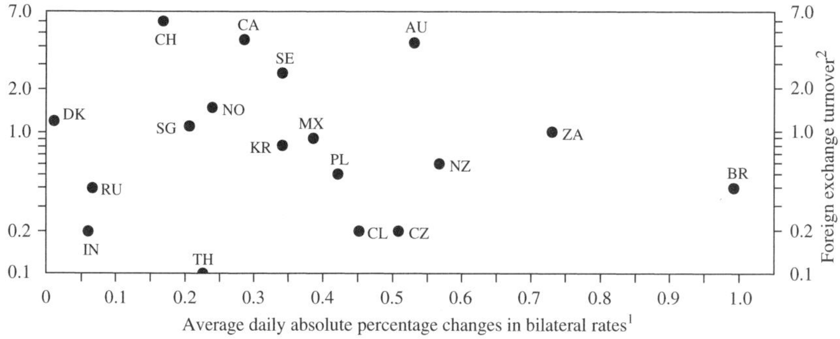

Notes:
1. Calculated over the period 2001–2002.
2. Turnover measured in April 2001; log scale.

Sources: IMF; BIS.

Figure 1.3 *Foreign exchange turnover and daily changes in exchange rates*

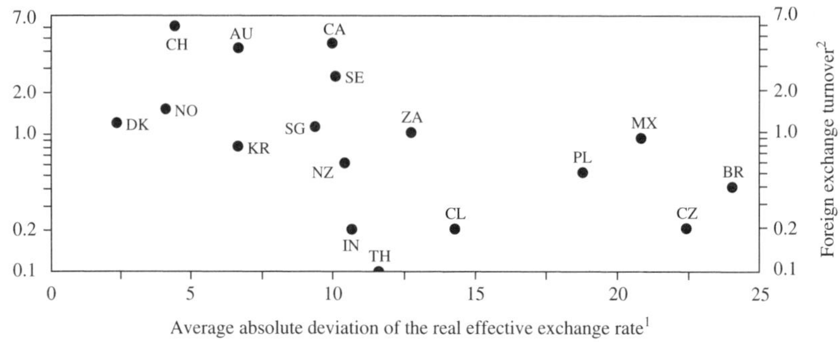

Notes:
1. Absolute deviation of the real effective exchange rate from a 5-year centred moving average, average over 1990–2002; for the Czech Republic and Poland deviation from a 3-year average, average over 1995–2002.
2. Turnover measured in April 2001; log scale.

Sources: IMF; BIS.

Figure 1.4 Foreign exchange turnover and real effective exchange rates

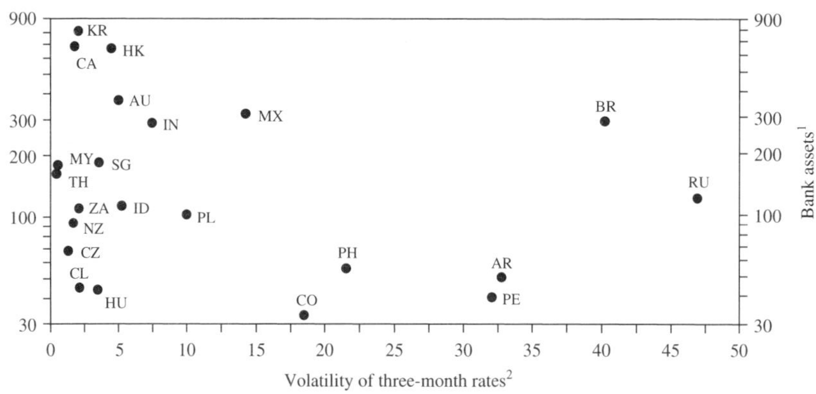

Notes:
1. End of 2002; in billions of US dollars.
2. Average absolute daily change; in basis points; January 1999 – latest.

Sources: IMF; Bloomberg; national data.

Figure 1.5 Bank assets versus volatility of three-month rates

in the three-month deposit market narrowed from around 14 basis points in 1996 to under nine basis points following the introduction of the euro. This brought the average spread from above those found in the United States and Japan to below them. It was also notable that by 2000 the spreads were identical across the different countries within the area, whereas there had been significant dispersion when the countries had separate, albeit linked, currencies; see Galati and Tsataronis (2001) and Sántillan et al. (2000).

Central banks generally like low volatility in short-term interest rates. As medium-term interest rates reflect expectations of future movements in short-term rates, central banks gain more influence over medium-term rates if changes in target overnight rates are reflected clearly. More orderly market conditions may make the transmission mechanism quicker and more predictable. And it should assist in the quest for financial stability by making it easier for financial institutions to assess and manage risks. Excessive volatility in money markets may feed uncertainty about economic fundamentals and adversely affect the overall reputation of the central bank; see Bartolini and Prati (2003). Interest volatility is seen as a symptom of misallocation of liquidity among banks and uncertainty about monetary policy. Many of these considerations apply even under rules-based monetary regimes like modern-day currency boards; see Hong Kong Monetary Authority (1994) and Meredith (1999).[9]

Volatility in short-term interest rates would be more of a concern if it were associated with volatility in bank lending rates, as this could cause greater volatility in real activity. Morton and Wood (1993) did find that economies with the least volatile overnight rates also have the least volatile three-month rates. Figure 1.6 gives a recent cross-country comparison. There appears to be some correlation but it is not strong.

Another argument for forming an RCA is that development of a money market may be impeded in small economies if one or two banks dominate the banking system; Mohanty (2002). This problem however is not unique to small countries. In the average emerging economy, the share of the top five banks in the total assets of the banking system is around 60 per cent; see Hawkins and Mihaljek (2001).

Domestic Banking Markets

A World Bank report (2001) highlights the issue of small banking systems. It notes that over 200 million people live in 60 countries where the total assets of the banking system are less than US$1 billion – about the size of a single one of the smaller banks in the world's top 1000. The authors argue that small banking systems underperform. They suffer from a concentration of risks, cannot exploit economies of scale in payment systems and other

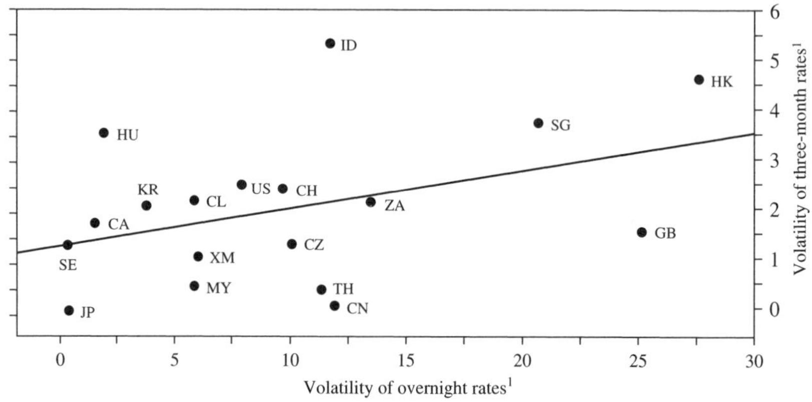

Notes:
1. Average absolute daily change; in basis points; January 1999 – latest.

Sources: Bloomberg; national data.

Figure 1.6 Volatility of overnight versus three-month rates

areas, and competitive pressure is low. One indication of this is that smaller banking systems tend to charge larger spreads (Figure 1.7). Furthermore, regulation and supervision of small systems are disproportionately costly. For further empirical evidence on these issues, see Bossone and Lee (2002).

Developing regional banking systems is likely to be easier within an RCA. For example, the two RCAs in Africa have established supranational banking supervisory agencies. However in practice such gains do not appear to have been fully realized, perhaps because the development of an integrated banking system depends on many factors other than the use of a common currency. For instance van Beek et al. (2000) find that domestic financial institutions in the Eastern Caribbean Currency Union often restrict their activities to their home country. This tendency is reinforced by restrictions on foreign ownership (even by companies from other member countries), different tax arrangements for non-members, and prohibitions on residents' purchase of foreign currency securities or real estate abroad. Even in Europe, few of the bank mergers since currency union have been cross-border.

Domestic Bond Markets

The potential benefits of a domestic bond market may not be realizable for small countries as the small market could limit the feasible range of

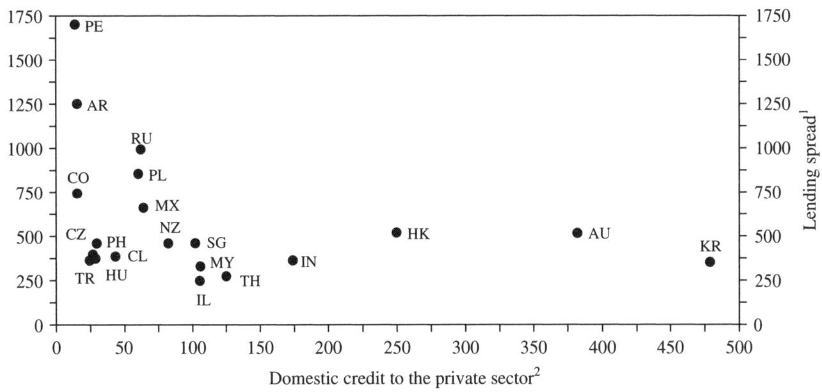

Notes:
1. In basis points.
2. End of 2002; in billions of US dollars.

Sources: IMF; national data.

Figure 1.7 Credit to the private sector versus bank lending spread

marketable instruments and their effective tradability; see Turner and Van't dack (1996). Much of the infrastructure needed to develop a liquid bond market (such as trading and settlement systems) requires a minimum turnover in order to function smoothly and cost-effectively.

A second argument could be that the small number of market players and the dominance of a few players may reduce competition in the bond market and distort yields. Concentration ratios in the non-bank financial sector are often even higher. Even without explicit collusion, this is likely to lead to less efficient markets.

Larger bond markets do tend to be more liquid; see Inoue (1999) and Figure 1.8. McCauley and Remolona (2000) suggest that sustaining a very liquid government bond market may not be easy below a size threshold of around US$100–200 billion. But size is clearly not the only important influence.[10]

This suggests that having a regional market within an RCA may give better outcomes. European experience suggests that bond markets became deeper after the adoption of a common market and currency.

International Banking and Bond Markets

The currencies of small economies attract much less international attention and investment than do those of larger currency areas. For this

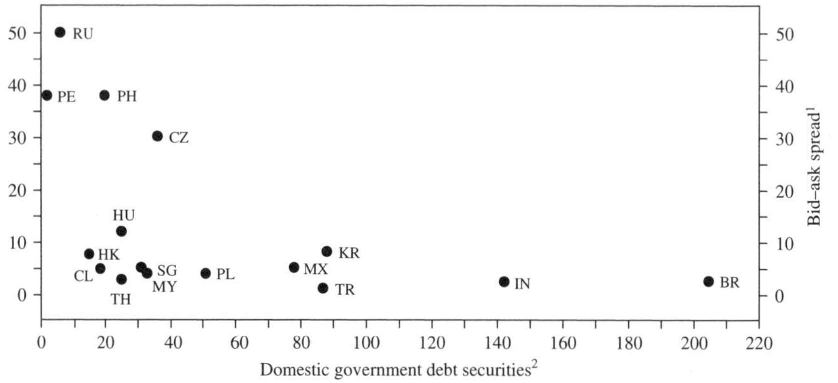

Notes:
1. In basis points.
2. End of 2002; among outstanding; in billions of US dollars.

Sources: BIS; national data.

Figure 1.8 Domestic government debt securities versus bid–ask spread in bond markets

reason there is a liquidity premium to be paid, in addition to any perceived greater currency risk. Table 1.1 shows the average spread for euro members narrowed markedly after they joined the euro zone (much of the narrowing occurred after the announcement that they would join). From having a median spread about twice that of non-members, their spreads are now similar.

A phenomenon of emerging economies highlighted by Eichengreen and Hausmann (1999) and Hausmann (1999), which they term 'original sin', is the difficulty some of these economies encounter in issuing bonds or borrowing from international banks in their domestic currency. This has led to a severe structural defect in the banking systems of many emerging economies. Either their banks borrow in foreign currency and lend in domestic currency, and so have a large exposure to exchange rate fluctuations, or they lend in foreign currency and face a large credit risk (as in the event of a large devaluation, borrowers with largely domestic revenues default). See Hawkins and Turner (2000) for a further discussion. Goldstein and Turner (2004) argue that Hausmann underplays the extent to which good policy can gradually allow long-term domestic currency markets to develop.

One factor deterring international lenders from lending in the domestic currency (apart from a general lack of confidence in macroeconomic

Table 1.1 Bond spread above Germany (average spread for 10-year government bonds; basis points)

	1990–94	Jan 1995–Apr 1998	May 1998–Dec 1999	Jan 2000–Dec 2001	Jan 2002–Aug 2003
Euro members					
Austria	18	14	18	28	14
Belgium	90	32	24	33	17
Finland	288	95	24	23	15
France	63	22	10	14	7
Greece	1588	498[1]	498[1]	67	29
Ireland	111	96	23	23	17
Italy	462	296	26	35	23
Netherlands	12	−2	11	15	9
Portugal	360	234	29	36	17
Spain	354	234	26	29	13
median	***200***	***96***	***24***	***29***	***16***
Non-members					
Denmark	112	93	41	33	26
Norway	124	44	103	120	142
Sweden	274	190	45	21	53
Switzerland	−192	−195	−142	−138	−152
United Kingdom	115	151	72	14	25
median	***115***	***93***	***72***	***21***	***26***

Note:
1. April 1998 is when the countries to join the euro were selected. The exception was Greece, which joined later and so an average for 1995–99 is used for both periods.

management) may be the small size of domestic markets. Bordo and Flandreau (2001) find that during both the eras of globalization at the beginning and the end of the 20th century, financially developed countries could issue sovereign debt in their own currency. Financial development may be more likely in small countries if they join together into a common currency area. The evidence for medium-sized economies suggests this effect is swamped by other factors (Figure 1.9).

Equity Markets

Forming an RCA makes it easier to have a regional stock market, such as those in the West African and East Caribbean RCAs. A larger equity market is likely to be more attractive to international fund managers. Given

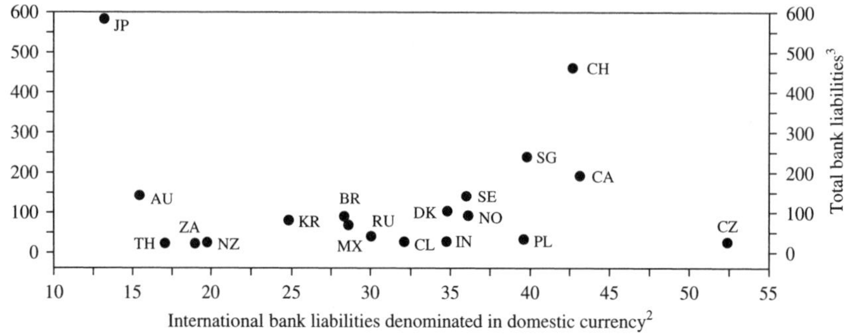

Notes:
1. To BIS reporting banks.
2. As a percentage of total bank liabilities in 2002.
3. Total bank liabilities in billions of US dollars in 2002.

Source: BIS.

Figure 1.9 International bank liabilities[1]

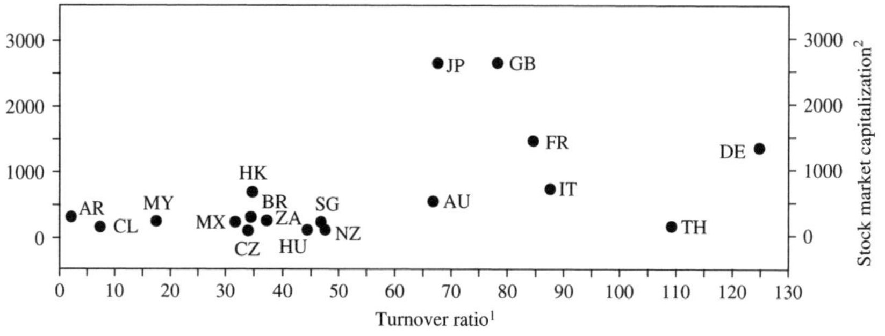

Notes:
1. 2001; in per cent.
2. 2001; in billions of US dollars.

Source: IFC.

Figure 1.10 Stock market capitalization and turnover ratio

that domestic investors tend to have a home currency bias, it allows for greater diversification in portfolios.

Market size is unsurprisingly associated with higher turnover. Of more interest is that turnover appears to rise more than proportionately (Figure 1.10). Explicit trading costs are lower as economies of scale in

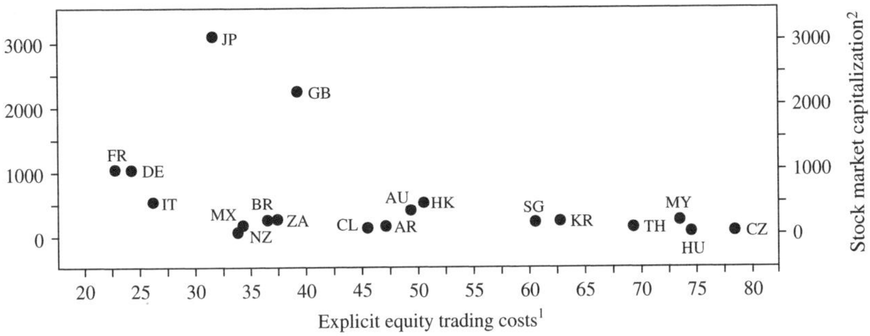

Notes:
1. Average over the period Sept. 1996–Dec. 1998; in basis points; explicit costs include commissions and fees.
2. Average over the period 1995–2001; in billions of US dollars.

Source: IFC.

Figure 1.11 Stock market capitalization and explicit equity trading costs

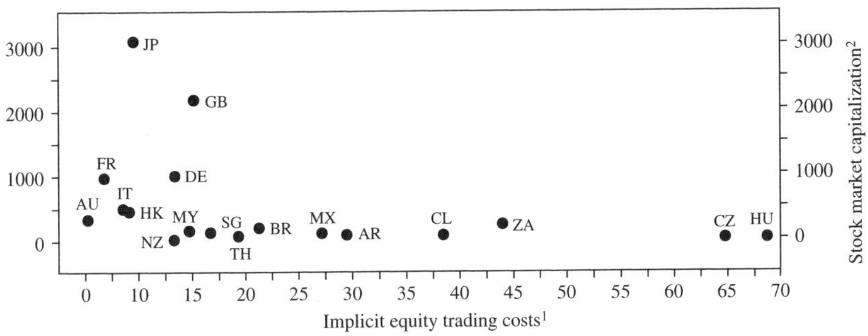

Notes:
1. Average over the period Sept. 1996–Dec. 1998; in basis points; implicit costs are computed by comparing the trade price to a benchmark price on the day of the trade.
2. Average over the period 1995–2001; in billions of US dollars.

Source: IFC.

Figure 1.12 Stock market capitalization and implicit equity trading costs

physical processing are reaped (Figure 1.11). Implicit trading costs are lower as there is more competition and greater liquidity (Figure 1.12).

However achieving these benefits is not always easy. Few companies are listed on the West African stock market and trading is infrequent. The

Central African countries have a project to establish a regional stock market in Libreville, Gabon, but the Cameroonian authorities, with the region's largest economy, have chosen to proceed with their own stock exchange, in Douala. Given the small number of actual and potential transactions, competition between the two exchanges is likely to hinder the establishment of a true regional financial market.

CONCLUSION

The small number of RCAs makes it hard to draw conclusions about their effect on financial markets. However the evidence presented in this chapter suggests that while forming a regional currency area would aid in developing financial markets, it is only one, certainly not a sufficient, factor in their development.

APPENDIX A: REGIONAL CURRENCY AREAS

Some examples of independent countries sharing a common currency are:

European Monetary Union (1999–)

Austria, Belgium, Finland, France, Germany, Greece (joined in 2001), Ireland, Italy, Luxembourg, the Netherlands, Portugal and Spain adopted a single currency, the euro, in 1999, although euro notes and coins were only introduced in 2002. See Strauss-Kahn (2003).

Eastern Caribbean Currency Area (1950–)

Anguilla (UK territory, joined 1987), Antigua and Barbuda, Dominica, Grenada (joined 1968), Montserrat (UK territory), St Kitts and Nevis, St Lucia and St Vincent and the Grenadines. Some former members left the area to establish their own currencies: Trinidad and Tobago in 1962, Guyana in 1965 and Barbados in 1972. The Eastern Caribbean dollar is pegged to the US dollar. See van Beek et al. (2000).

Central African Economic and Monetary Community, CAEMC (1945–)

Cameroon, Central African Republic, Chad, Republic of Congo, Equatorial Guinea (joined 1985) and Gabon. Their common central bank is the Bank of the States of Central Africa and the common currency is the *franc de la coopération financière en Afrique centrale*. Originally created as a colonial currency in 1945, it was retained after independence. It has been pegged to the French franc, and now the euro, throughout this period, but was devalued by half in 1994. At least 65 per cent of central bank reserves are held with the French Treasury, which guarantees its convertibility into euros. Equatorial Guinea is the only member that is not a former French colony. See Masson and Pattillo (2004).

West African Economic and Monetary Union, WAEMU (1945–)

Benin, Burkina Faso, Côte d'Ivoire, Guinea-Bissau (joined in 1997), Mali (left in 1962 but rejoined in 1984), Niger, Senegal and Togo. (São Tomé and Príncipe may be joining soon.) Their common central bank is the Central Bank of West African States and their common currency is the *franc de la communauté financière d'Afrique*. Originally created as a colonial currency in 1945, it was retained after independence. Both the Central African and West African currencies are commonly called the 'CFA franc' but are not legal tender in the other region. In theory they could have different values but in practice they have always been the same. See Banny (2002) and Masson and Pattillo (2004) for further information.

East African Currency Board (1963–72)

Kenya, Tanzania and Uganda operated a joint currency board after independence in 1961–63, essentially continuing colonial currency arrangements that had been in place since 1919. The divergence between the socialist path taken by Tanzania, the capitalist path in Kenya and the tyranny in Uganda placed the joint currency under stress and they established separate currencies. Cohen (1998) and Masson and Pattillo (2004) provide more information.

Latin Monetary Union (1865–1914)

Belgium, Bulgaria, France, Greece (joined in 1868), Italy and Switzerland formed a monetary union, initially for a 15-year period, but subsequently renewed.[11] It provided for the circulation of gold and silver coins (at a fixed parity) throughout the union by all members, the coins being identical in size and weight but with national designs, and acceptable as legal tender. The union ended with the First World War. See Bordo and Jonung (1999), de Cecco (1992), Einaudi (2002) and Henriksen and Kærgård (1995) for further discussion. Flandreau and Maurel (2001) are sceptical on whether this union added anything to the gold standard arrangements.

Scandinavian Currency Union (1873–1913)

Denmark, Norway (joined in 1875) and Sweden formed a monetary union when they adopted the gold standard (but note that the latter two were also in a political union until 1905) and a common unit, the krona. But they continued to issue their own notes and coins. At the outbreak of the First World War they all abandoned both the gold standard and the currency union. See Bergman (1999) and de Vanessy (2003) for further information.

German and Austro-Prussian Monetary Unions (1838–67)

Baden, Bavaria, Frankfurt, Hesse, Nassau Saxe-Meiningen (joined later), Schwarzburg-Rudolstadt (joined later) and Württemberg agreed on a monetary union with the northern states adopting the thaler and the southern states the florin with a fixed rate of exchange. All states agreed to issue silver coins in proportion to their population which were legal tender throughout the union. The 1857 treaty between Austria and the German member states fixed the exchange rate between the Austrian currency and the German currencies and members agreed to withdraw non-convertible notes. After the Battle of Sadowa, Bismarck issued a decree dissolving the union, and its formal dissolution occurred through a treaty signed in 1867. See de Cecco (1992) and de Vanessy (2003) for more details.

Earlier Monetary Unions (1379–1814)

Monetary unions such as the Hanseatic Monetary League and the Monetary Federation of the Rhine were negotiated when money was essentially coinage and its value was determined by the value of its gold or silver content. The monetary unions largely consisted of standardizing the coins. See Einaudi (2002). There was a long-running monetary union involving paper currency until around 1750 between Connecticut, Massachusetts Bay, New Hampshire and Rhode Island; see Graboyes (1990).

APPENDIX B: PROPOSED REGIONAL CURRENCY AREAS

Some of the most notable proposed future RCAs are listed here. Some are now the declared aim of governments while others are academic conjectures.

Greater Europe

Many Eastern European countries have recently joined or are keen to join the European Union and the euro area: Bulgaria, Cyprus, Czech Republic, Estonia, Hungary, Latvia, Lithuania, Malta, Poland, Romania, Slovakia, Slovenia and Turkey. They will be expected to participate in ERM II for at least two years in order to fulfil convergence criteria before joining the euro area.

There are also discussions about a regional currency for Belarus, Kazakhstan, Russia and Ukraine by 2011; see Marchenko (2003).

Africa

The Economic Community of West African States (ECOWAS), which includes the members of the West African Economic and Monetary Union (see Appendix A) plus the Gambia, Ghana, Guinea, Liberia, Nigeria and Sierra Leone, declared its intention to form a broader monetary union in April 2000. This had been stated as a goal of ECOWAS since its formation in 1975 and is intended to accompany a broader integration process. A West African Monetary Institute (WAMI) was established in 2000 as a precursor to a regional central bank. The current plan is for a monetary union of all the Anglophone ECOWAS countries in 2005, followed by a later merger with the WEAMU countries. See Masson and Pattillo (2004), Ojo (2003) and Ukpong (2002) for further discussion.

In 1999 Kenya, Tanzania and Uganda signed a treaty forming an economic bloc and laying grounds for a monetary union, which would be essentially reviving their former currency union. See Guillaume and Stasavage (2000) and Mkenda (2001).

Alesina et al. (2002) report that 11 members of the Southern African Development Community are debating whether to form a monetary union, possibly centred on the rand. See van Zyl (2003).

The African Union (successor to the Organization of African Unity) has recently reaffirmed the aim of a common African currency based on first establishing RCAs in various African regions. The Association of African Central Bank Governors at its August 2003 meeting declared they would aim at a single currency by 2021. See Masson and Pattillo (2004) and Ojo (2003) for further details.

Arabian Gulf

The Gulf Cooperation Council, comprising Bahrain, Kuwait, Oman, Qatar, Saudi Arabia and the United Arab Emirates, was founded in 1981 and one of its initial goals was to move towards a common currency. The successful launch of the euro invigorated these aspirations and the Council announced in early 2002 a customs union by 2003 (brought forward from 2005) and a plan for a common currency by 2010. A new currency, possibly to be called the Gulf dinar, will be established. As an interim step, all member currencies will be pegged to the US dollar. A committee of central bank governors, and a technical committee of central bankers, is working on the project. All the countries currently have pegs to the US dollar and oil or related products account for 70–80 per cent of revenue in all of them. See Abed et al. (2003), Jadresic (2002) and Laabas and Limam (2002) for further information.

Latin America

The Mercosur countries (Argentina, Brazil, Paraguay and Uruguay, with Bolivia and Chile as associate members). In 1997, Argentina's then president Carlos Menem proposed such a currency union in the indefinite future. At the Mercosur presidential summit in 2002, the idea of a Monetary Institute of Mercosur as an embryonic central bank was informally discussed. With Argentina and Brazil having been forced off their exchange rate pegs in the last couple of years, the idea may gain more support. See Eichengreen (1998) and Fratianni and Hauskrecht (2002) for academic support for the idea that an RCA would support the push for deeper integration within Mercosur, Ferrari-Filho (2002) for a critique, and Belke and Gros (2002) for a further discussion.

The Andean Community's (Bolivia, Colombia, Ecuador, Peru and Venezuela) 1969 agreement called for 'harmonization of exchange rate, monetary, financial and fiscal policies', and set some convergence criteria but no firms plan for establishing an RCA. See Temprano Arroyo (2002).

The Central American Common Market countries (Costa Rica, El Salvador, Guatemala, Honduras and Nicaragua) have as a medium-term goal a monetary union, but some members have recently adopted the US dollar.

Caribbean

CARICOM agreed in 1992 that its eight members which are currently not part of the ECCB area (Bahamas, Barbados, Belize, Guyana, Haiti, Jamaica, Suriname and Trinidad and Tobago) should join it to form a Caribbean-wide single currency, but it has not been implemented. See Manioc and Montauban (Chapter 9 in this volume) and Worrell (2003).

North America

Canada, Mexico and the United States are members of the trade group NAFTA. Given the high proportion of Canada and Mexico's trade with the United States, a NAFTA dollar or 'Amero' has been proposed by some Canadian academics such as Grubel (1999). See also Robson and Laidler (2002).

Asia

In December 1998, ASEAN (Brunei, Cambodia, Indonesia, Laos, Malaysia, Myanmar, the Philippines, Singapore, Thailand and Vietnam) leaders endorsed a project to study the feasibility of a common ASEAN currency, and a task force of central bank officials led by Bank Negara Malaysia was established in August 2000. The head of the Hong Kong Monetary Authority raised the possibility of a wider common Asian currency in Yam (1999), albeit in the distant future. The idea has also been discussed by academics such as Kim and Ryou (2001) and Mundell (2003) and in a paper commissioned from Bayoumi and Mauro (1999). One factor favouring an RCA in Asia is that the countries have diversified trading partners so there is no obvious candidate currency to which to link. Kang and Wang (2002) provide a recent overview.

South Pacific

Brash (2000), Grimes and Holmes (2000) and Coleman (2001) provide a discussion of suggestions for Australia and New Zealand to adopt an 'Anzac dollar'. The latter two studies note that half the New Zealand public and the majority of NZ business leaders support a monetary union. New Zealand prime minister Helen Clark regards the idea as worth considering. However given that the Australian economy is seven times as large as that of New Zealand, it may be more realistic to think in terms of New Zealand adopting the Australian dollar. The topic of a currency union is little discussed in Australia and the advantages there would probably not outweigh the costs of introducing a new currency. The five small Pacific nations currently using either the Australian or NZ dollar could also join, as could Fiji, Papua New Guinea, the Solomon Islands and Vanuatu, for which Australia is the largest trading partner; see de Brouwer (2000).

NOTES

1. The views expressed are those of the authors and not necessarily shared by the BIS. This chapter draws on some joint work with Paul Masson. Thanks also to Corrinne Ho, Elmar Koch and Tom Minić for helpful comments.
2. Rogoff (2002) goes so far as to suggest that the world is heading towards just two or three major currency regions in the long term.
3. This is not always the case: Norway's independence from Sweden in 1905 and Ireland's from the United Kingdom in the 1920s were not accompanied by the establishment of separate currencies until much later.
4. The 2002 Monterrey Consensus declaration refers to 'reduced exchange rate volatility' as 'essential to economic growth'. But it has been the subject of much disagreement in the economic literature. See Box A in Hawkins and Masson (2003).
5. The choice of an RCA rather than other forms of hard fix will in part be influenced by economic issues such as the desirability of at least being able to influence regional monetary conditions. It is also often just a matter of relative sizes; similar-sized economies such as France and Germany are more likely to form a new regional currency, but a very large economy is unlikely to modify its currency arrangements to suit a very small economy. This often leads small economies to use currency boards or unilaterally adopt another currency.
6. In 1848 he trenchantly wrote: 'so much of barbarism, however, still remains in the transactions of most civilised nations, that almost all independent countries choose to assert their nationality by having, to their own inconvenience and that of their neighbours, a peculiar currency of their own'.
7. Indeed Monga and Tchatchouang (1996) criticized the monetary union, and in particular the peg to the French franc, for having delayed financial development within these RCAs (by in effect routing transactions through Paris). Strauss-Kahn (2003) provides some contradictory evidence. The CFA franc zone members seem to have a comparable degree of financial development to their neighbours.
8. Figure 1.3 is based on daily volatility but using monthly changes gives a similar picture.
9. But there may be some reasons why eliminating volatility in overnight interest rates may not be desirable even if it were feasible. Van der Merwe (1999) says that South Africa was concerned about deterring the development of money markets. Another concern is that too little volatility may hide signals of liquidity pressures in the bank reserves market. Quick and sharp adjustments in interest rates may be necessary during crises. Arrangements to smooth interest rates in normal times should not impede this. Perhaps especially in economies with a fixed exchange rate, the authorities may want the overnight rate to react sharply to exchange rate pressures but want to insulate more crucial medium-term interest rates that have more impact on economic activity. Spörndli and Moser (1997) argue that in small open economies (in their case Switzerland) there is a case for leaving some uncertainty in financial markets. They see a fixed interest rate as possibly leading to greater volatility in the exchange rate, or even a speculative attack.
10. McCauley (2003) suggests factors such as 'holdings by government accounts and other "buy and hold" investors, the concentration of outstanding debt in benchmark issues; the industrial organisation of the dealers and construction of trading platforms; taxes; arrangement for sale and repurchase; and clearing and settlement' as also being important.
11. In 1865, France proposed extending the union to include Britain and the United States, which would probably have ended up with most of the world as members. Despite some enthusiasm at a conference, the idea faded for lack of sustained political support. See Cohen (1998, pp. 69–70).

REFERENCES

Abed, G., S. Erbas and B. Guerami (2003), 'The GCC monetary union, some considerations for the exchange rate regime', *IMF working paper*, 03/66, April.

Alesina, A., R. Barro and S. Tenreyro (2002), 'Optimal currency areas', mimeo.

Al-Jasser, M. and A. Al-Hamidy (2003), 'A common currency area for the Gulf region', *BIS Papers*, 17, September, 116–20.

Banny, C. (2002), 'The future of the Central Bank of West African states', *Central Banking*, **13** (2), November, 55–63.

Barth, M., E. Remolona and P. Wooldridge (2002), 'Changes in market functioning and central bank policy, an overview of the issues', *BIS Papers*, 12, 1–24.

Bartolini, L. and A. Prati (2003), 'The execution of monetary policy, a tale of two central banks', *Federal Reserve Bank of New York Staff Reports*, 165, April.

Bayoumi, T. and P. Mauro (1999), 'The suitability of ASEAN for a regional currency arrangement', *IMF working paper*, 99/162, December.

Belke, A. and D. Gros (2002), 'Monetary integration in the southern cone, Mercosur is not like the EU?', *Oesterreichische Nationalbank Working Paper*, 72, August.

Bergman, M. (1999), 'Do monetary unions make economic sense? Evidence from the Scandinavian Currency Union, 1873–1913', *Scandinavian Journal of Economics*, **101** (3), 363–77.

Bordo, M. and M. Flandreau (2001), 'Core, periphery, exchange rate regimes and globalization', *NBER Working Paper*, 8584, November.

Bordo, M. and L. Jonung (1999), 'The future of EMU, what does the history of monetary unions tell us?', *NBER Working Paper*, 7365, September.

Bossone, B. and J-K. Lee (2002), 'In finance, size matters', *IMF working paper*, 02/113, June.

Brash, D. (2000), 'The pros and cons of currency union, a Reserve Bank perspective', *Reserve Bank of New Zealand Bulletin*, **63** (2), June, 74–80.

Cohen, B.J. (1998), *The Geography of Money*, Ithaca, NY: Cornell University Press.

Coleman, A. (2001), 'Three perspectives on an Australasian monetary union', in D. Gruen and J. Simon (eds), *Future Directions for Monetary Policies in East Asia*, Sydney: Reserve Bank of Australia.

De Brouwer, G. (2000), 'Should Pacific island nations adopt the Australian dollar?', *Pacific Economic Bulletin*, **15** (2), November, 161–9.

De Cecco, M. (1992), 'European monetary and financial cooperation before the First World War', *Rivista di Storia Economica*, **9** (1), 55–76.

De Vanessy, X. (2003), 'Monetary unions, a historical perspective', in P. Crowley (ed.), *Before and Beyond EMU*, London: Routledge.

Eichengreen, B. (1998), 'Does Mercosur need a single currency?', *NBER working paper*, 6821, December.

Eichengreen, B. and R. Hausmann (1999), 'Exchange rates and financial fragility', *NBER Working Paper*, 7418, November.

Einaudi, L. (2002), 'The generous Utopia of yesterday can become the practical achievement of tomorrow, 1000 years of monetary union in Europe', *National Institute Economic Review*, **172**, April, 90–104.

Ferrari-Filho, F. (2002), 'A critique of the proposal for monetary union in MERCOSUR', in P. Davidson (ed.), *A Post-Keynesian Perspective on 21st Century Economic Problems*, Cheltenham, UK and Northampton, MA: Edward Elgar.

Flandreau, M. and M. Maurel (2001), 'Monetary union, trade integration and business cycles in 19th century Europe', *CEPR working paper*, 3087, November.

Fratianni, M. and A. Hauskrecht (2002), 'A centralized monetary union for Mercosur, lessons from EMU', paper presented at a conference on euro and dollarization at Frodham University, New York, 5–6 April.

Galati, G. (2001), 'Trading volumes, volatility and spreads in FX markets, evidence from emerging market countries', *BIS Papers*, 2, 197–225.

Galati, G. and K. Tsatsaronis (2001), 'The impact of the euro on Europe's financial markets', *BIS working paper*, 100, July.

Goldstein, M. and P. Turner (2004), 'Controlling currency mismatches in emerging economies, an alternative to the original sin hypothesis', Institute for International Economics, April.

Graboyes, R. (1990), 'The EMU, forerunners and durability', *Federal Reserve Bank of Richmond Economic Review*, July/August, 8–17.

Grimes, A. and F. Holmes (2000), *An ANZAC Dollar? Currency Union and Business Development*, Wellington: Institute of Policy Studies.

Grubel, H. (1999), 'The case of the Amero, the merit of creating a North American monetary union', *Critical Issues Bulletin*, Fraser Institute, September.

Guillaume, D. and D. Stasavage (2000), 'Improving policy credibility, is there a case for African monetary unions?', *World Development*, **28** (8), August, 1391–1407.

Hausmann, R. (1999), 'Should there be five currencies or one hundred and five?', *Foreign Policy*, Fall, 65–79.

Hawkins, J. and P. Masson (2003), 'Economic aspects of regional currency areas and the use of foreign currencies', *BIS Papers*, 17, September, 4–42.

Hawkins, J. and D. Mihaljek (2001), 'The banking industry in the emerging market economies, competition, consolidation and systemic stability', *BIS Papers*, 4, August, 1–44.

Hawkins, J. and P. Turner (2000), 'Managing foreign debt and liquidity risks in emerging economies, an overview', *BIS Policy Papers*, 8, September, 3–59.

Henriksen, I. and N. Kærgård (1995), 'The Scandinavian Currency Union 1875–1914', in J. Reis (ed.), *International Monetary Systems in Historical Perspective*, London: Macmillan Press, pp. 91–112.

Hong Kong Monetary Authority (1994), 'Management of interbank liquidity', *Hong Kong Monetary Authority Quarterly Bulletin*, **1**, November, 1–7.

Inoue, H. (1999), 'The structure of government securities markets in G10 countries', *CGFS Publications*, 11, May.

Jadresic, E. (2002), 'On a common currency for the GCC countries', *IMF policy discussion paper*, 02/12, December.

Kang, S. and Y. Wang (2002), 'An overview of currency union, theory and practice', in H-G. Choo and Y. Wang (eds), *Currency Union in East Asia*, Seoul: Korea Institute for International Economic Policy, pp. 11–37.

Kim, T-J. and J-W. Ryou (2001), 'The optimal currency basket and the currency bloc in Asia', *Bank of Korea Economic Papers*, **4** (1), May, 194–216.

Laabas, B. and I. Limam (2002), 'Are GCC countries ready for currency union?', Arab Planning Institute, Kuwait, April.

Marchenko, G. (2003), 'Interview', *Central Banking*, **13** (4), May, 44–9.

Masson, P. and C. Pattillo (2001), 'Monetary union in West Africa (ECOWAS), is it desirable and how could it be achieved?', *IMF Occasional Paper*, 204.

Masson, P. and C. Pattillo (2004), *The Monetary Geography of Africa*, Washington, DC: Brookings Institution Press.
McCauley, R. (2003), 'Unifying government bond markets in east Asia', unpublished paper, July.
McCauley, R. and E. Remolona (2000), 'Size and liquidity of government bond markets', *BIS Quarterly Review*, November, 52–60.
Meredith, G. (1999), 'Liquidity management under Hong Kong's currency board arrangements', paper prepared for the International Workshop on Currency Boards, Convertibility, Liquidity Management and Exit, October.
Mkenda, B. (2001), 'Is East Africa an optimal currency area?', *Göteborg University Department of Economics working paper*, 41, April.
Mohanty, M. (2002), 'Improving liquidity in government bond markets, what can be done?', *BIS Papers*, 11, June, 49–80.
Monga, C. and J-C. Tchatchouang (1996), 'Sortir du piège monétaire', *Economica*, Paris.
Mongelli, F. (2002), 'New views on the optimum currency area theory, what is EMU telling us?', *ECB Working Paper*, 138, April.
Morton, J. and P. Wood (1993), 'Interest rate operating procedures of foreign central banks', in M. Goodfriend and D. Small (eds), *Operating Procedures and the Conduct of Monetary Policy, Conference Proceedings*, Washington, DC: Federal Reserve Board.
Mundell, R.A. (1961), 'A theory of optimal currency areas', *American Economic Review*, **15** (4), September, 657–65.
Mundell, R.A. (2003), 'Prospects for an Asian currency area', *Journal of Asian Economics*, **14**, 1–10.
Ojo, M. (2003), 'Regional currency areas and use of foreign currencies, the experience of West Africa', *BIS Papers*, 17, September, 141–5.
Robson, W. and D. Laidler (2002), *No Small Change, the Awkward Economics and Politics of North American Monetary Integration*, Toronto: C.D. Howe Institute.
Rogoff, K. (2002), 'Managing the world economy', *The Economist*, 3 August.
Santillán, J., M. Bayle and C. Thygesen (2000), 'The impact of the euro on money and bond markets', *European Central Bank Occasional Papers*, 1, July.
Spörndli, E. and D. Moser (1997), 'Monetary policy operating procedures in Switzerland', *BIS Conference Papers*, 3, March, 140–5.
Strauss-Kahn, M. (2003), 'Regional currency areas, a few lessons from the experiences of the Eurosystem and the CFA franc zone', *BIS Papers*, 17, September, 43–58.
Temprano Arroyo, H. (2002), 'Prospects for subregional monetary integration in Latin America, a view from the EU', draft paper presented to the 8th Dubrovnik Economic Conference, 27–29 June.
Turner, P. and J. Van't dack (1996), 'Changing financial systems in small open economies, an overview', in *BIS Policy Papers*, 1, December, 1–57.
Ukpong, G. (2002), 'Second monetary zone in ECOWAS, issues, progress and prospects', *Central Bank of Nigeria Economic and Financial Review*, **40** (5), December.
Van Beek, F., J. Rosales, M. Zermeno, R. Randall and J. Shepherd (2000), 'The Eastern Caribbean Currency Union, institutions, performance and policy issues', *IMF Occasional Paper*, 195, July.
Van der Merwe, E. (1999), 'Monetary policy operating procedures in South Africa', *BIS Policy Papers*, 5, March, 228–57.

Van Zyl, L. (2003), 'South Africa's experience of regional currency areas and the use of foreign currencies', *BIS Papers*, 17, September, 135–40.
World Bank (2001), *Finance for Growth, Policy Choices in a Volatile World*, Oxford University Press.
Worrell, D. (2003), 'A currency union for the Caribbean', *IMF Working Paper*, 03/35, February.
Yam, J. (1999), 'Causes of and solutions to the recent financial turmoil in the Asian region', *Hong Kong Monetary Authority Quarterly Bulletin*, **18**, February, 52–60.

2. Currency regimes and the process of regional financial integration of the emerging countries

Daniel Goyeau, Jacques Léonard and Dominique Pépin

INTRODUCTION

Vis-à-vis the rising interdependency of Western financial markets, reducing a priori the potential profits of diversification of international portfolios, the development of emerging financial markets since the very beginning of the 1990s has been generally regarded as likely to offer new opportunities.

In this context, it has become traditional to structure the search for yield opportunities and the associated investments according to a logic with large geographical spread.[1] Asia, Latin America, CEECs, the Middle East.

This geographical logic of diversification never truly takes account of the heterogeneity of each of these regions, a heterogeneity which obviously concerns real factors (level of development, type of specialization, degree of opening) but also monetary factors, where exchange rate and convertibility regimes are the structuring elements.

Geographical logic consists in arbitrating large areas between one another, and would, for that reason, lead to financial integration of emerging markets, therefore with the realization of the law of single international price of risk (Goyeau et al., 1999). However such a realization requires a double continuous adjustment: that of the foreign exchange market on the one hand, that of financial markets on the other.

Also, when one is more particularly interested in the methods of diversification with respect to assets in emerging countries, one can a priori doubt the realization of the law of single price of risk insofar as the currency regimes (exchange rate and convertibility regimes) are subject to a more or less strict regulation on behalf of monetary and financial local authorities.

To simplify, by distinguishing two canonical currency regimes – a hard pegging and a soft pegging of national currency – an alternative logic with geographical logic would consist in capturing the differences in risk premia resulting from heterogeneity between the currency regimes. In other words, the lack of continuous adjustment in the case of hard pegging is likely to be at the root of a quite different pricing of risk from that associated with a soft pegging.

Consequently, the topology of emerging financial markets can be established either according to the usual criterion of geographical proximity, or according to a criterion of proximity of currency regimes. By explicitly considering the differences in currency regimes, and more specifically the differences in exchange rate regimes, the aim of this chapter is to analyse, firstly in analytical terms, the influence of proximity of currency regimes relative to that of geographical proximity in the processes of integration which are operational on emerging markets.

As for empirical evidence, we will endeavour to identify these relations, like their evolutions since the beginning of the 1990s, and this for a sample of 22 countries distributed out of four emerging geographical regions (Asia, Latin America, CEECs, the Middle East). This analysis makes it possible to establish a typology of the processes and levels of integration of emerging places: in relation with effective membership of the currency of the country to one of the two canonical currency regimes, and as compared with the typology built on a geographical basis.

MONETARY PROXIMITY VS. GEOGRAPHICAL PROXIMITY: ANALYTICAL APPROACH

It is first of all a question of defining a methodology, making it possible to quantify the influence of monetary proximity and geographical proximity in the determination of risk premiums relating to each market; we then present econometric methodology and finally we build an indicator allowing us to identify the *de facto* exchange rate regimes.

Modelling

The selected methodology is based on the use of a mixed model of evaluation, which combines international evaluation and 'regional' evaluation (monetary area or geographical area) of the assets. The importance of the regional influence in the determination of the risk premium of each emerging market can then be estimated for each monetary or geographical area.

The generic model of evaluation used is that of Adler and Dumas (1983). This international model of evaluation integrates the exchange rate risk in a sufficiently general way as to include as a particular case the former models of Solnik (1974) and Grauer et al. (1976). The exchange rate risk is a combination of pure real exchange rate risk *à la* Solnik (1974) (PPP invalidated and zero or non-stochastic inflation) and pure nominal exchange rate risk *à la* Grauer et al. (1976) (valid PPP and stochastic inflation).

In a world with L countries, Adler and Dumas (1983) show that the expected return of any asset, using as cash the currency of one of these countries,[2] is a linear function of the covariance of the return of the asset with the international market portfolio and its covariances with the L rate of inflation:

$$E(r_{it}|\Psi_{t-1}) = \lambda_{1t-1}Cov(r_{it}, \pi_{1t}|\Psi_{t-1}) + \ldots \\ + \lambda_{Lt-1}Cov(r_{it}, \pi_{Lt}|\Psi_{t-1}) + \lambda_{mt-1}Cov(r_{it}, r_{mt}|\Psi_{t-1}) \quad (2.1)$$

r_{it} indicates the excess return of the asset i, which represents the return of the country i market portfolio, compared to the nominal return of the riskless asset (that is the interest rate on cash),

r_{mt} indicates the excess return of the international market portfolio,

π_{jt} is the rate of inflation of the country j with use of the common cash to measure the price of the goods of the country j.

The parameters $\lambda_1, \ldots, \lambda_L$ indicate the unit risk premia[3] related to the exposure to various nominal risks (inflation) and the unit market risk premium.

The model described by (2.1) is the conditional version of the model of Adler and Dumas (1983), where ψ_{t-1} describes the informational set available to the investors at the end of period $t-1$ to build their expectations on returns in t. The various risk premia are subscripted by $t-1$, which means that they are entirely anticipated in $t-1$. The return of the riskless asset is itself (by definition) perfectly expected. It should be noticed that this model admits a simplified version, more usually used in practice, obtained with the additional assumption that the rates of inflation (measured in local currency) are zero or non-stochastic.[4] These assumptions are unlikely in the case of our application; the general version of the model was preferred.

The model of international integration is a model in which only the monetary risk related to the dollar matters from the point of view of investors, the risk premiums for other currencies being supposed to be zero. By more simply noting π_t the rate of inflation for the dollar, and by considering that the dollar is the cash used, the general model described by equation (2.1) becomes under these assumptions:

$$E(r_{it}|\Psi_{t-1}) = \lambda_{\pi t-1}Cov(r_{it}, \pi_t|\Psi_{t-1}) + \lambda_{mt-1}Cov(r_{it}, r_{mt}|\Psi_{t-1}) \quad (2.2)$$

The generic model (equation 2.1) can be also declined in both cases of regional monetary integration and regional geographical integration.

The model of monetary integration

In the model of monetary integration, the nominal risk related to the American dollar does not matters any more (the United States not forming part of the definite emerging areas). The model of evaluation is then reduced to a traditional CAPM, where the return of each market is proportional to its covariance with the return of the market portfolio of the area of monetary proximity. We suppose that there are two integrated emerging areas, each one defined by a given rate regime: *A* area (hard pegging) and *B* area (soft pegging).

According to whether the emerging market is supposed to belong to area *A* or *B*, there will be the various models of evaluation:

$$E(r_{it}|\Psi_{t-1}) = \lambda_{kt-1} Cov(r_{it}, r_{kt}|\Psi_{t-1}) \quad \forall k \in \{A; B\} \tag{2.3}$$

where r_{kt} indicates the return of the market portfolio of the area, $k \in \{A; B\}$.

Let us note D^i_{t-1} the dummy which indicates if market i belongs at time t to the A area or not. It is to be noted that this variable is subscripted by $t-1$ (and not by t) to indicate that it is known from investors at the end of period $t-1$. Taking into account these dummies, one can gather the two equations of the type (2.3) in only one:

$$\begin{aligned} E(r_{it}|\Psi_{t-1}) = {} & D^i_{t-1}\lambda_{At-1} Cov(r_{it}, r_{At}|\Psi_{t-1}) \\ & + (1 - D^i_{t-1})\lambda_{Bt-1} Cov(r_{it}, r_{Bt}|\Psi_{t-1}) \end{aligned} \tag{2.4}$$

The model described by (2.4) is sufficiently general to allow market i to shift from one integrated emerging area to another.

The finally adopted model is a mixed model, which combines the influence of the monetary area and the international influence in the valuation of assets. It is described by the following equation:

$$\begin{aligned} E(r_{it}|\Psi_{t-1}) = {} & \lambda_{\pi t-1} Cov(r_{it}, \pi_t|\Psi_{t-1}) + \lambda_{mt-1} Cov(r_{it}, r_{mt}|\Psi_{t-1}) \\ & + D^i_{t-1}\lambda_{At-1} Cov(r_{it}, r_{At}|\Psi_{t-1}) \\ & + (1 - D^i_{t-1})\lambda_{Bt-1} Cov(r_{it}, r_{Bt}|\Psi_{t-1}) \end{aligned} \tag{2.5}$$

This model allows for the particular case of each polar situation of regional integration (with $\lambda_{\pi t-1} = \lambda_{mt-1} = 0$) and international (with $\lambda_{At-1} = \lambda_{Bt-1} = 0$), like any situation of partial integration combining regional and international factors of valuation.

Equation (2.5) shows two components in the determination of the excess return, an international component and a regional component, respectively defined as:

$$\omega^i_t = \lambda_{\pi t-1} Cov(r_{it}, \pi_t|\Psi_{t-1}) + \lambda_{mt-1} Cov(r_{it}, r_{mt}|\Psi_{t-1}) \tag{2.6}$$

$$\kappa_t^i = D_{t-1}^i \lambda_{At-1} Cov(r_{it}, r_{At}|\Psi_{t-1}) + (1 - D_{t-1}^i)\lambda_{Bt-1} Cov(r_{it}, r_{Bt}|\Psi_{t-1}) \quad (2.7)$$

We then define an international integration rate of market i in t, noted ζ_t^i, which measures the relative importance of the international component:

$$\zeta_t^i = \frac{|\omega_t^i|}{|\kappa_t^i| + |\omega_t^i|} \quad (2.8)$$

This rate measures the share of the international influence in the determination of the unit risk premium of market i. When market i is perfectly integrated into the international market of capital, this rate is 1; when on the contrary market i is integrated into an emerging zone, it is 0. The evolution of this rate can thus be considered for each market, and be put in parallel with the evolution of the exchange rate regime of the considered country.

The geographical model of integration

The adopted model is again a mixed model which combines the geographical area influence and international influence in the valuation of assets. It is described by the following equation:

$$E(r_{it}|\Psi_{t-1}) = \lambda_{\pi t-1} Cov(r_{it}, \pi_t|\Psi_{t-1}) + \lambda_{mt-1} Cov(r_{it}, r_{mt}|\Psi_{t-1}) + \lambda_{kt-1} Cov(r_{it}, r_{kt}|\Psi_{t-1}) \quad (2.5\text{bis})$$

The excess return of the market thus depends on its covariance with the rate of inflation on the dollar, with the return of the world market portfolio, and with the excess return of the market portfolio of its regional area. λ_{kt-1} represents the unit risk premium paid for the exposure to the risk of regional market.

We define as in the preceding model an international component and a regional component in the determination of the excess return of the market return:

$$\omega_t^i = \lambda_{\pi t-1} Cov(r_{it}, \pi_t|\Psi_{t-1}) + \lambda_{mt-1} Cov(r_{it}, r_{mt}|\Psi_{t-1}) \quad (2.6\text{bis})$$

$$\kappa_t^i = \lambda_{kt-1} Cov(r_{it}, r_{kt}|\Psi_{t-1}) \quad (2.7\text{bis})$$

In the geographical case, the international integration rate of the market i in t is defined in the same way as:

$$\zeta_t^i = \frac{|\omega_t^i|}{|\kappa_t^i| + |\omega_t^i|} \quad (2.8\text{bis})$$

Econometric Methodology

There exist various manners of considering a conditional model, according to the way of modelling the conditional moments. The approach adopted here is that of Harvey (1989, 1995). The conditional expectation of the return on the assets is supposed to be a linear function of the instrumental variables which make up ψ_{t-1}:

$$E(r_{it}|\Psi_{t-1}) = \delta_{i1}\Psi_{1t-1} + \delta_{i2}\Psi_{2t-1} + \ldots + \delta_{ip}\Psi_{pt-1} = \Psi_{t-1}'\delta_i \quad (2.9)$$

We define u_{it} as the forecast error of r_{it}:

$$u_{it} = r_{it} - \Psi_{t-1}'\delta_i \quad (2.10)$$

The condition of orthogonality $E(u_{it}|\Psi_{t-1}) = 0$ implies according to the law of the reiterated expectation:

$$E(u_{it}\Psi_{t-1}) = 0_p, \text{ where } 0_p \text{ is a null vector of order } p. \quad (2.11)$$

We develop hereafter the econometric methodology concerning the model of monetary proximity. In this case, various covariances can be rewritten:

$$Cov(r_{it}, r_{mt}|\Psi_{t-1}) = E(u_{it}r_{mt}|\Psi_{t-1}) \quad (2.12)$$

$$Cov(r_{it}, \pi_t|\Psi_{t-1}) = E(u_{it}\pi_t|\Psi_{t-1}) \quad (2.13)$$

$$Cov(r_{it}, r_{kt}|\Psi_{t-1}) = E(u_{it}r_{kt}|\Psi_{t-1}) \quad \forall k \in \{A; B\} \quad (2.14)$$

Moreover, the unit risk premia are supposed to be a linear function of the instrumental variables (Dumas and Solnik, 1995):

$$\lambda_{\pi t-1} = \gamma_{\pi 1}\Psi_{1t-1} + \ldots + \gamma_{\pi p}\Psi_{pt-1} = \Psi_{t-1}'\,\gamma_\pi \quad (2.15)$$

$$\lambda_{mt-1} = \gamma_{m1}\Psi_{1t-1} + \ldots + \gamma_{mp}\Psi_{pt-1} = \Psi_{t-1}'\,\gamma_m \quad (2.16)$$

$$\lambda_{kt-1} = \gamma_{k1}\Psi_{1t-1} + \ldots + \gamma_{kp}\Psi_{pt-1} = \Psi_{t-1}'\,\gamma_k \quad \forall k \in \{A; B\} \quad (2.17)$$

Under these assumptions, (2.8) becomes:

$$\begin{aligned}\Psi_{t-1}'\,\delta_i = {} & \Psi_{t-1}'\,\gamma_\pi E(u_{it}\pi_t|\Psi_{t-1}) + \Psi_{t-1}'\,\gamma_m E(u_{it}r_{mt}|\Psi_{t-1}) \\ & + D^i_{t-1}\Psi_{t-1}'\,\gamma_A E(u_{it}r_{At}|\Psi_{t-1}) \\ & + (1 - D^i_{t-1})\Psi_{t-1}'\gamma_B E(u_{it}r_{Bt}|\Psi_{t-1})\end{aligned} \quad (2.18)$$

We define ε_{it}:

$$\begin{aligned}\varepsilon_{it} = {} & \Psi_{t-1}'\,\delta_i - \Psi_{t-1}'\,\gamma_\pi u_{it}\pi_t - \Psi_{t-1}'\,\gamma_m u_{it}r_{mt} \\ & - D^i_{t-1}\Psi_{t-1}'\,\gamma_A u_{it}r_{At} - (1 - D^i_{t-1})\Psi_{t-1}'\,\gamma_B u_{it}r_{Bt}\end{aligned} \quad (2.19)$$

Equation (2.18) is then equivalent to:

$$E[\varepsilon_{it}|\Psi_{t-1}] = 0 \tag{2.20}$$

According to the law of the reiterated expectation, equation (2.20) has as an implication:

$$E[\varepsilon_{it}\Psi_{t-1}] = 0_p \tag{2.21}$$

Having estimated the whole of the parameters – thanks to equations (2.11) and (2.21) – we draw from it the estimation for each date and each emerging market for the variable ζ_t^i:

$$\hat{\zeta}_t^i = \frac{|\hat{\omega}_t^i|}{|\hat{\kappa}_t^i| + |\hat{\omega}_t^i|}, \tag{2.22}$$

where the estimated components are defined by:

$$\hat{\omega}_t^i = \Psi_{t-1}{}' \hat{\gamma}_\pi \hat{u}_{it} \pi_t + \Psi_{t-1}{}' \hat{\gamma}_m \hat{u}_{it} r_{mt} \tag{2.23}$$

$$\hat{\kappa}_t^i = D_{t-1}^i \Psi_{t-1}{}' \hat{\gamma}_A \hat{u}_{it} r_{At} + (1 - D_{t-1}^i) \Psi_{t-1}{}' \gamma_B \hat{\hat{u}}_{it} r_{Bt} \tag{2.24}$$

The informational set Ψ_{t-1} which is supposed to help investors to build their expectations on returns in t, remains to be defined. Of course all the variables known at the beginning of the period t should be integrated in Ψ_{t-1}. With respect to the huge number of instruments which would be implied by an exhaustive census, we are led to suppose that returns depend on a reduced number of variables: the return of the nominal riskless asset, or the rate of interest on cash (noted i), since $i_t \in \Psi_{t-1}$ by definition; we add the delayed returns of the various market portfolios (monetary areas and international), in order to take account of memory effects in the series of returns of emerging markets, as well as the delayed rate of inflation on the dollar. Finally, we thus have a number of instruments equal to 5.

Taking into account the defined instruments, the forecasting model of returns can be written as:

$$E(r_{it}|\Psi_{t-1}) = \delta_1 r_{mt-1} + \delta_2 r_{At-1} + \delta_3 r_{Bt-1} + \delta_4 i_t + \delta_5 \pi_{t-1}, \tag{2.25}$$

and the risk premiums take the form:

$$\lambda_{mt-1} = \gamma_{m1} r_{mt-1} + \gamma_{m2} r_{At-1} + \gamma_{m3} r_{Bt-1} + \gamma_{m4} i_t + \gamma_{m5} \pi_{t-1} \tag{2.26}$$

$$\lambda_{At-1} = \gamma_{A1} r_{mt-1} + \gamma_{A2} r_{At-1} + \gamma_{A3} r_{Bt-1} + \gamma_{A4} i_t + \gamma_{A5} \pi_{t-1} \tag{2.27}$$

$$\lambda_{Bt-1} = \gamma_{B1} r_{mt-1} + \gamma_{B2} r_{At-1} + \gamma_{B3} r_{Bt-1} + \gamma_{B4} i_t + \gamma_{B5} \pi_{t-1} \tag{2.28}$$

$$\lambda_{\pi t-1} = \gamma_{\pi 1} r_{mt-1} + \gamma_{\pi 2} r_{At-1} + \gamma_{\pi 3} r_{Bt-1} + \gamma_{\pi 4} i_t + \gamma_{\pi 5} \pi_{t-1} \qquad (2.29)$$

With regard to the procedure of estimation, all the series not being the same length (the data relating to some emerging markets are available only starting from later dates), we used a procedure which distinguishes the estimation from the specific parameters to each market (parameters of the model of expectation) and the estimation of common parameters (parameters appearing in the unit risk premia).

Thus, the various models of anticipation were estimated by applying the method of the moments to equation (2.9), which amounts in fact to regressing each market portfolio on the various instruments, using the method of OLS. We thus draw the estimation of the parameters $\delta_{i1}, \ldots, \delta_{i5}$ for each market *i*. Starting from the estimation of these parameters, we then draw the value of the residues $\hat{u}_{it}$, which is used in the second part of the procedure.

In the second part of the procedure, it is necessary to consider the common parameters to all of the markets, that is those appearing in equations (2.22) to (2.25). For that, we apply the method of the generalized moments to equation (2.21), where the errors are replaced by the residues. The data used in this second part are those relating to the markets of which the data on returns are available since the starting date.

All the parameters of the model being estimated, we can then carry out the calculation of $\hat{\zeta}_t^i$. For each market, one thus obtains the $\hat{\zeta}_t^i$ series, which appears rather volatile. To be able to read the evolution of these series, we smooth them. To this end, we consider that each one of these series obeys the model:

$$\hat{\zeta}_t^i = a_t^i + \eta_t^i \qquad (2.30)$$

$$a_t^i = a_{t-1}^i + v_t^i \qquad (2.31)$$

where η_t^i et v_t^i indicate two white noises (null expectations) uncorrelated.

The model given by equations (2.30) and (2.31) can quite simply be estimated using the Kalman filter. The smoothed series is then given by the estimate $\hat{a}_t^i$. Since the shock η_t^i has a transitory impact (whereas the shock v_t^i has a permanent impact), the series $\hat{a}_t^i$ thus represent the initial series $\hat{\zeta}_t^i$ from which are eliminated the transitory fluctuations.

Concerning the estimation of the geographical model of proximity, the econometric methodology is identical, except for some adjustments. In this case, the instruments used are: the current value of the interest rate, the delayed value of the rate of inflation, and that of the world market portfolio, to which we add the delayed values of the various regional market portfolios (Asia, Latin America, CEECs and the Middle East).[5]

IDENTIFYING THE *DE FACTO* CURRENCY REGIMES

For obvious reasons of unavailability of the data, it is quite impossible to follow, year after year, the trace of the evolution of the convertibility regimes, country by country, and this on the whole of the period under review. The collected data are summarized in Table 2.1, which accounts for these regimes according to three degrees, and this at the level of the capital account of the countries, for the years 1996 and 2000. They nevertheless reveal a strong heterogeneity of these convertibility regimes within the

Table 2.1 Evolution of convertibility regimes

		1996	2000
Latin America	Argentina	3	3
	Brazil	2	3
	Chile	1	3
	Colombia	3	2
	Mexico	2	3
	Peru	3	3
	Venezuela	2	1
Asia	India	1	1
	Indonesia	2	1
	Korea	1	1
	Malaysia	2	1
	Pakistan	2	2
	Philippines	2	1
	Thailand	2	1
CEECs	Czech Rep.	2	3
	Hungary	2	2
	Poland	2	3
	Russia	2	2
Middle East	Egypt	3	3
	Israel	2	3
	Jordan	3	3
	Turkey	2	2

Notes:
1: low level of convertibility.
2: intermediate level of convertibility.
3: high level of convertibility.

Source: FMI.

same geographical area as well as in terms of evolution during the second half of the 1990s.

With regard to the component 'exchange rate regime' of the currency regime, the analysis that we carry out here requires us to account for the *de facto* regimes and their evolution, and not for the *de jure* regimes.[6] For the latter, the International Monetary Fund, in the new classification of 1999 (International Monetary Fund, 1999), distinguishes between seven alternative exchange rate regimes, from the most constraining agreements (monetary unions and currency boards) to the various systems of independent floating. Between the two extremes fit the multiple forms of pegging, actually most widespread with regard to the emerging countries.

Our approach of the *de facto* exchange rate regimes, in the line of work of Holden et al. (1979), Weymark (1997), Levy Yeyati and Sturzenegger (1999), Poirson (2001), considers the volatility of nominal exchange rate of the currencies of the emerging countries retained in the sample with respect to the dollar, in relation with the implicit degree of intervention of the central banks on the foreign exchange market, this being approximated by the variation of the international reserves of these countries.[7]

Consequently the indicator of exchange rate regime that we build is a continuous variable, founded on the observed movements of international reserves and of exchange rates.

More precisely, the monthly indicator of the *de facto* exchange rate regime (*ERR*) is built as the ratio of the variation (in absolute value) of the nominal exchange rate of the currency considered with respect to the dollar during one month (ΔE) to the variation (in absolute value) of the international reserves of the country for the currency considered during the same month (or ΔR), this variation being standardized by the monetary base of the previous month. Thus, for the currency of country *i*:

$$ERR_{it} = \Delta E_{it}/\Delta R_{it} = \{|E_{it} - E_{it-1}|/E_{it-1}\}/\{|R_{it} - R_{it-1}|/B_{it-1}\}$$

with:

E_{it} = nominal exchange rate with respect to the dollar in the month t
R_{it} = net international reserves, less gold, in the month t
B_{it} = monetary base in the month t.

ERR is an indicator of *de facto* flexibility of the exchange rate since if, for example, ΔR. is significant compared to ΔE, therefore if *ERR* is relatively low, that most probably gives an account of massive interventions of the monetary authorities on the foreign exchange market so as to thwart the market forces.

ERR thus takes values ranging between 0 and the infinite, its limits being associated on the one hand with absolute pegging with the reference currency ($\Delta E = 0$), on the other hand with the completely free floating with respect to this same currency ($\Delta R = 0$).

ERR is thus calculated monthly on the whole period and for all the countries considered. Then we calculate the average of the *ERR* obtained. Taking into account the fact that a majority of the countries of our sample belong to *de facto* 'intermediate' exchange rate regimes, and for simplicity, we consider that the general average of the *ERR* (for all months and all countries) acts as a threshold discriminating two types of exchange rate regimes.

This threshold enables us to identify, for each month, the exchange rate regime to which the country *de facto* belongs and to build the dummy 'exchange rate regime':[8] an ERD lower than this threshold testifies to the practice of a 'hard pegging' and conversely, an *ERR* higher than this threshold gives an account of a 'soft pegging'.

Of course, it would have been judicious to be able to completely determine the currency regimes of the countries of our sample by crossing the evolutions of the convertibility regimes and those of the exchange rate regimes. The very low frequency of the observations for the convertibility regimes, and particularly for the *de facto* policies, prevent us from doing that.

We thus assume that the degree of convertibility of the currencies, even when it is low, is never sufficient to stand in the way of capital movements tied to the international diversification of portfolios, and thus to stand in the way of the tendency to the realization of the law of the single international price of risk.

EMPIRICAL RESULTS

Monetary Proximity

We first of all calculate some simple statistics on the three benchmark portfolios (see Table 2.2):[9] the international market portfolio, the soft pegging countries market portfolio and the hard pegging countries market portfolio. The data used are the monthly excess returns compared to the American three-month Treasury Bills. The detail of the periods considered is given in the Appendix.

The soft pegging and hard pegging portfolios show an average return higher than that of the international portfolio, the difference being tiny for the hard pegging but very significant for the soft pegging portfolio. As for the standard deviations, they are higher, the difference being nevertheless much more reduced in the case of the soft pegging portfolio. The soft pegging portfolio thus dominates the hard pegging portfolio. In other

Table 2.2 Characteristics of excess returns

Portfolio	International	Soft pegging	Hard pegging
Mean (1)	0.0053	0.0099	0.0054
Standard deviation (2)	0.0400	0.0667	0.1431
Ratio (1)/(2)	0.1325	0.1484	0.0377

Table 2.3 Correlation matrix

	Soft pegging	Hard pegging	International
Soft pegging	1	0.368	0.587
Hard pegging	0.368	1	0.453
International	0.587	0.453	1

words, the law of the single international price of risk does not appear to be checked since this one depends on the exchange rate regime. If we now compare the soft pegging and international portfolios, we notice that for the same level of risk the soft pegging portfolio offers a higher return than that of the international portfolio. Over the whole period, investment in the soft pegging thus seems to have constituted a better strategy than investment in the international market portfolio.

The correlation matrix of excess returns (R) of the three portfolios (see Table 2.3) shows a relatively soft correlation between the soft pegging and hard pegging portfolios. Moreover the soft pegging portfolio is most strongly correlated with the international portfolio.

Table 2.4 accounts for the correlations between the various markets and the three benchmarks. For each market the correlation is always stronger with one of the soft or hard pegging portfolios than with the international portfolio. The importance of the 'monetary area' factor is thus indisputable even if it can sometimes be due to the weight of some markets in the soft or hard pegging portfolios.

It will be noted moreover that, for each market, the correlation of excess returns is always higher (except for Brazil) with the soft pegging portfolio. Excess returns being expressed in dollars, we can assume that this characteristic logically results from the regular, if not continuous, adjustments permitted by the weakness of the effective interventions of the local authorities on the foreign exchange markets of the countries constituting the soft pegging portfolio.

Table 2.4 Correlation table

	Soft pegging	Hard pegging	International
Asia			
India	0.449	0.285	0.025
Indonesia	0.552	0.380	0.357
Korea	0.510	0.200	0.361
Malaysia	0.630	0.257	0.445
Pakistan	0.456	0.091	0.095
Philippines	0.582	0.393	0.486
Thailand	0.633	0.362	0.464
Latin America			
Argentina	0.393	0.299	0.243
Brazil	0.355	0.604	0.342
Chile	0.581	0.339	0.314
Colombia	0.383	0.027	0.173
Mexico	0.690	0.403	0.427
Peru	0.514	0.366	0.368
Venezuela	0.347	0.172	0.218
Middle East			
Egypt	0.279	0.067	0.094
Israel	0.417	0.248	0.273
Jordan	0.168	0.116	0.121
Turkey	0.348	0.194	0.187
CEECs			
Czech Rep.	0.408	0.299	0.259
Hungary	0.589	0.503	0.486
Poland	0.403	0.331	0.332
Russia	0.698	0.492	0.532

Geographical Proximity

As previously, we calculate some simple statistics (see Table 2.5) on the five benchmark portfolios.

The Latin America and CEECs portfolios dominate the Asia and Middle East portfolios. These differences result once again in rejecting the law of the single international price of risk since this varies hugely from one geographical area to another.

We also calculate the correlation matrix (R) of excess returns of these portfolios (see Table 2.6). The correlation matrix of excess returns appears relatively homogeneous, except for the Middle East area.

Table 2.5 Characteristics of excess returns

Portfolio	Asia	Latin America	Middle East	CEECs	International
Mean (1)	0.0019	0.0182	0.0062	0.0351	0.0053
Standard deviation (2)	0.0778	0.0919	0.1046	0.1863	0.0400
Rapport (1)/(2)	0.0244	0.1980	0.0593	0.1884	0.1325

Table 2.6 Correlation matrix

	Latin America	Asia	Middle East	CEECs	International
Latin America	1	0.468	0.440	0.462	0.562
Asia	0.468	1	0.229	0.413	0.520
Middle East	0.440	0.229	1	0.307	0.286
CEECs	0.462	0.413	0.307	1	0.431
International	0.562	0.520	0.286	0.431	1

Table 2.7 presents the correlations between the various markets and the five benchmarks. With the exception of Pakistan, for each market the correlation is always harder with the portfolio of its geographical area of membership than with the others. The importance of the geographical area factor is thus checked even if it can sometimes be due to the weight of the market in the membership portfolio. This result should not surprise insofar as it reflects the usual behaviour of geographical trade-offs by international fund managers.

Relative Importance of Monetary and Geographical Proximities

Estimating expectation models

We carry out the estimation of the expectation models (equations 2.25 and 2.25bis). The expectation model for monetary proximity, as that for geographical proximity, appears more relevant for certain markets than for others (see Table 2.8), since R varies from 0.017 (Venezuela) to 0.252 (Pakistan) for the first one and from 0.030 (Brazil) to 0.252 (Colombia) for the second one.

For the model of monetary proximity, the Fisher test shows that the regression is significant with the threshold of 5 per cent for 12 markets and 10 per cent for two additional markets. The expectation model is thus overall checked for two-thirds of the markets considered.

Table 2.7 Correlation table

	Asia	Latin America	Middle East	CEECs	International
Asia					
India	0.461	0.357	0.217	0.296	0.025
Indonesia	0.692	0.446	0.215	0.402	0.492
Korea	0.697	0.230	0.031	0.180	0.352
Malaysia	0.775	0.305	0.218	0.351	0.447
Pakistan	0.331	0.366	0.289	0.250	0.095
Philippines	0.698	0.423	0.164	0.319	0.524
Thailand	0.803	0.385	0.108	0.275	0.517
Latin America					
Argentina	0.442	0.739	0.341	0.371	0.552
Brazil	0.340	0.910	0.406	0.411	0.444
Chile	0.550	0.695	0.340	0.354	0.480
Colombia	0.215	0.310	0.232	0.261	0.173
Mexico	0.395	0.832	0.374	0.396	0.504
Peru	0.302	0.639	0.263	0.229	0.368
Venezuela	0.274	0.328	0.158	0.264	0.218
Middle East					
Egypt	0.234	0.132	0.454	0.253	0.094
Israel	0.209	0.447	0.584	0.226	0.273
Jordan	0.152	0.126	0.222	0.188	0.155
Turkey	0.179	0.340	0.912	0.261	0.244
CEECs					
Czech Rep.	0.303	0.362	0.103	0.519	0.259
Hungary	0.402	0.546	0.384	0.688	0.486
Poland	0.373	0.370	0.201	0.851	0.332
Russia	0.460	0.605	0.508	0.910	0.532

For the model of geographical proximity, the same test shows that the regression is significant with the threshold of 5 per cent for eight markets and with the threshold of 10 per cent for three others. On the whole, the expectation model is validated here for half of the markets under review.

We finally note that the explanation of excess returns – using the 'monetary' model – is a priori statistically more relevant, as regards the period and the sample of countries considered, that the explanation using the 'geographical' model. However this does not suppose anything about the respective weight of the two logics in the explanation of the formation of excess returns for the various markets.

Table 2.8 Recapitulatory table: results of expectation models

	Monetary proximity		Geographical proximity	
	R^2	p-value of Fisher test	R^2	p-value of Fisher test
Asia				
India	0.152	0.010	0.178	0.007
Indonesia	0.089	0.038	0.101	0.038
Korea	0.085	0.049	0.096	0.047
Malaysia	0.118	0.008	0.124	0.011
Pakistan	0.252	0.000	0.199	0.003
Philippines	0.109	0.012	0.101	0.039
Thailand	0.089	0.038	0.081	0.105
Latin America				
Argentina	0.032	0.535	0.032	0.672
Brazil	0.026	0.645	0.030	0.698
Chile	0.124	0.006	0.091	0.062
Colombia	0.205	0.001	0.253	0.001
Mexico	0.049	0.272	0.056	0.301
Peru	0.118	0.042	0.081	0.263
Venezuela	0.018	0.896	0.025	0.891
Middle East				
Egypt	0.080	0.344	0.149	0.095
Israel	0.028	0.765	0.062	0.440
Jordan	0.076	0.078	0.073	0.147
Turkey	0.027	0.641	0.051	0.365
CEECs				
Czech Rep.	0.076	0.378	0.156	0.127
Hungary	0.129	0.097	0.098	0.448
Poland	0.116	0.046	0.202	0.005
Russia	0.167	0.031	0.178	0.071

Estimating financial integration rates

We then consider the various returns for risk in order to calculate, for each of the monetary and geographical cases and for each national market, the international integration rate (estimated forms of equations 2.8 and 2.8bis respectively). The evolution of these rates, after filtering (the curves in dotted lines represent a confidence interval of ± 2 standard deviations), is presented in Figure 2.1.

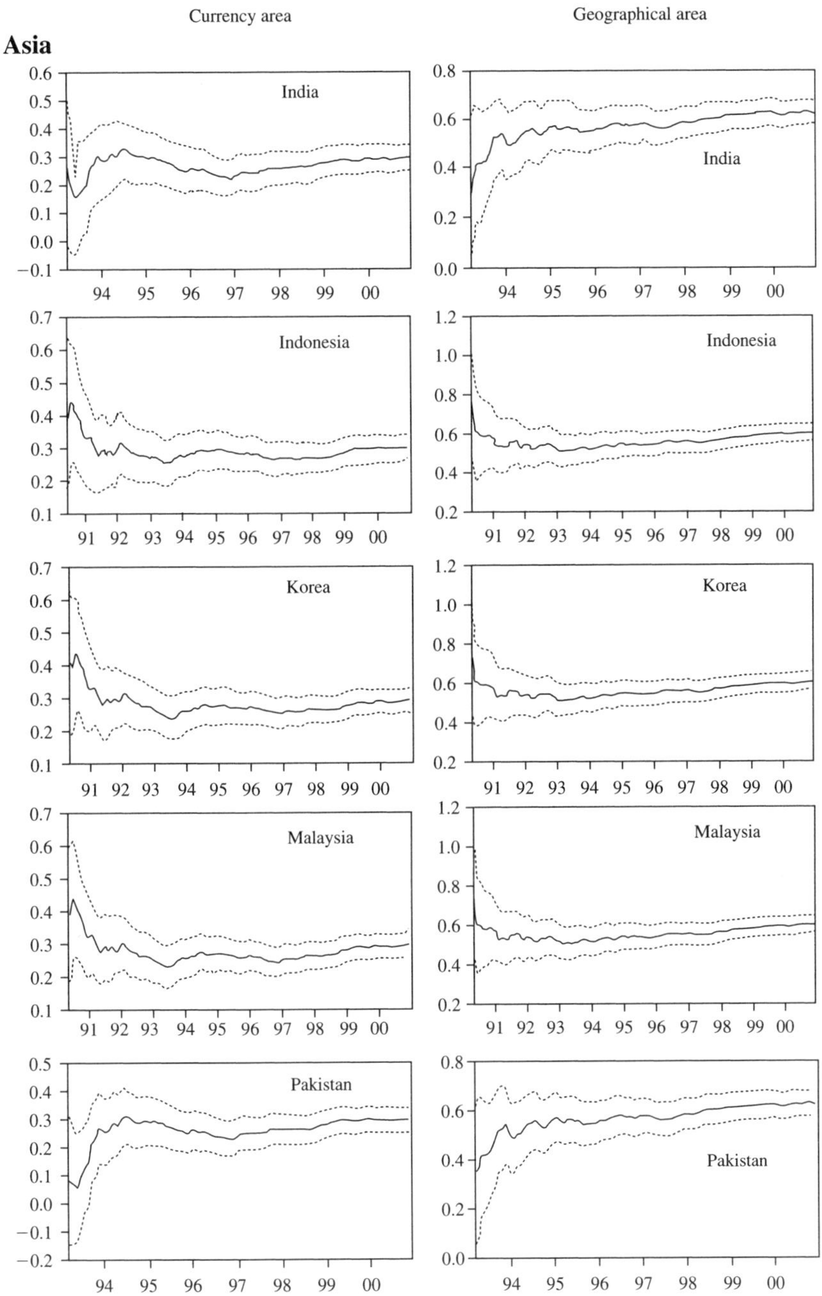

Figure 2.1 Rates of financial market integration

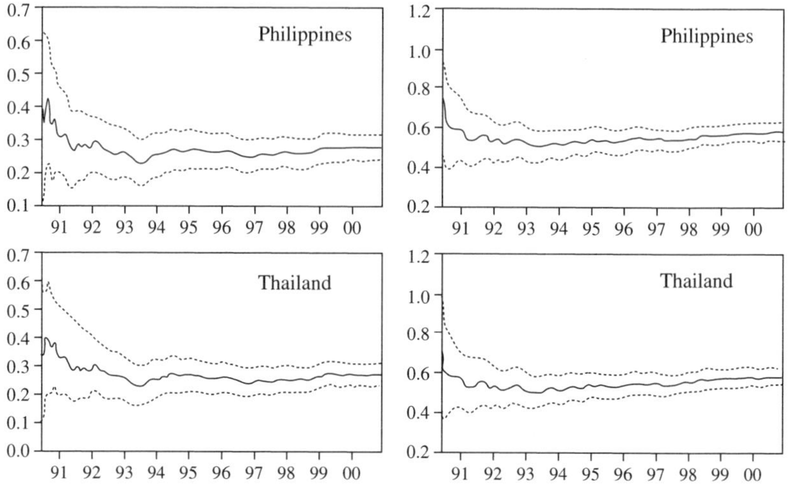

Latin America

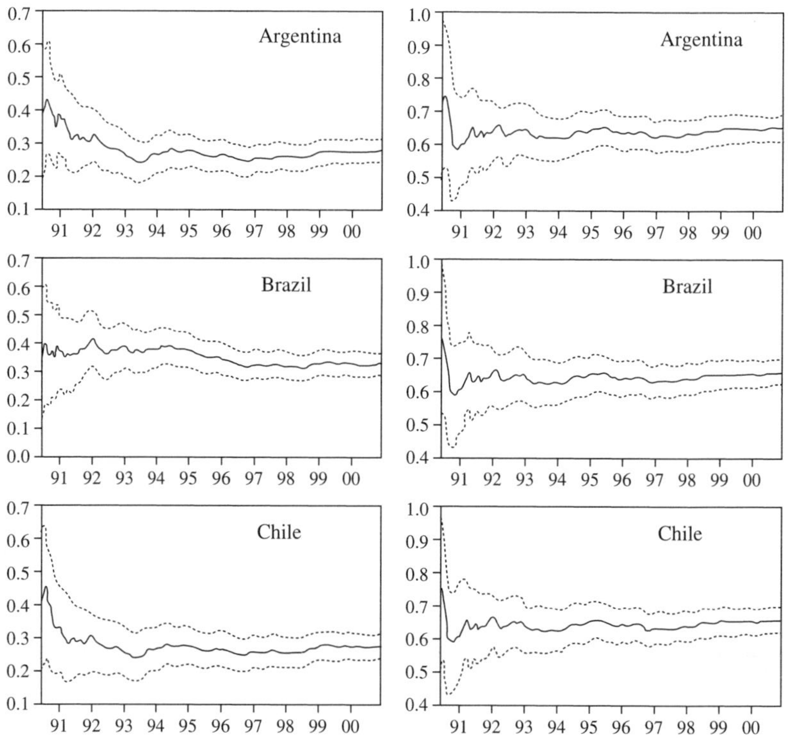

Figure 2.1 (continued)

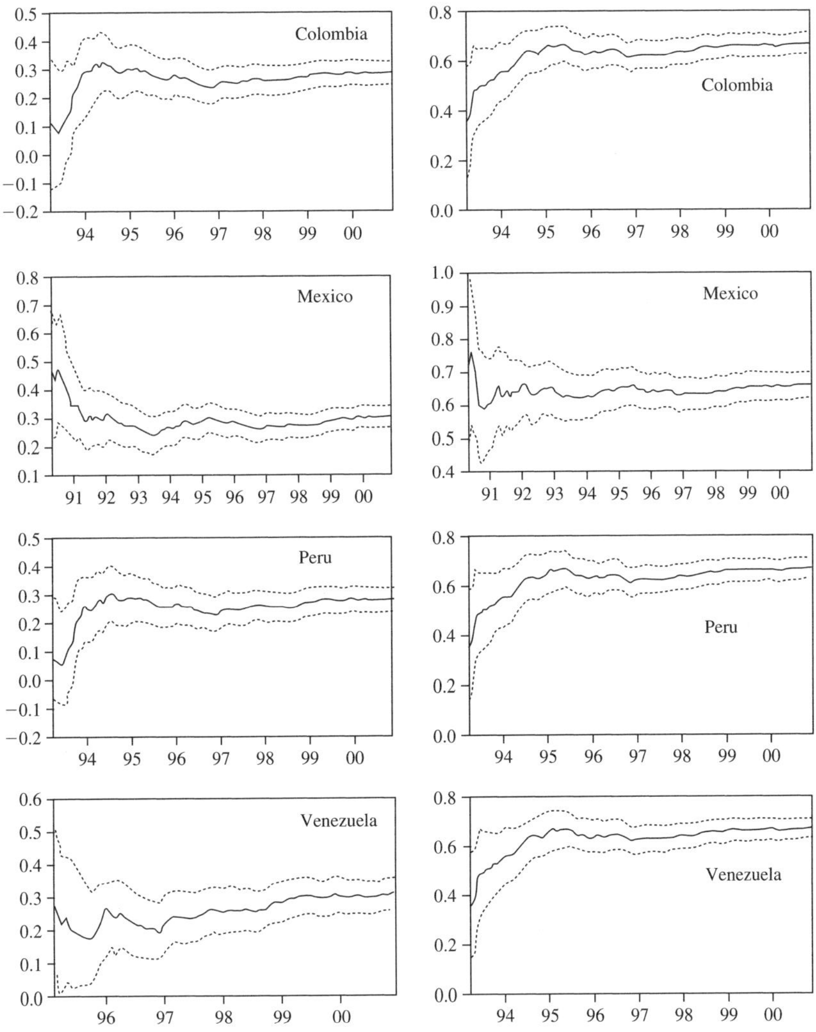

Figure 2.1 (*continued*)

Middle East

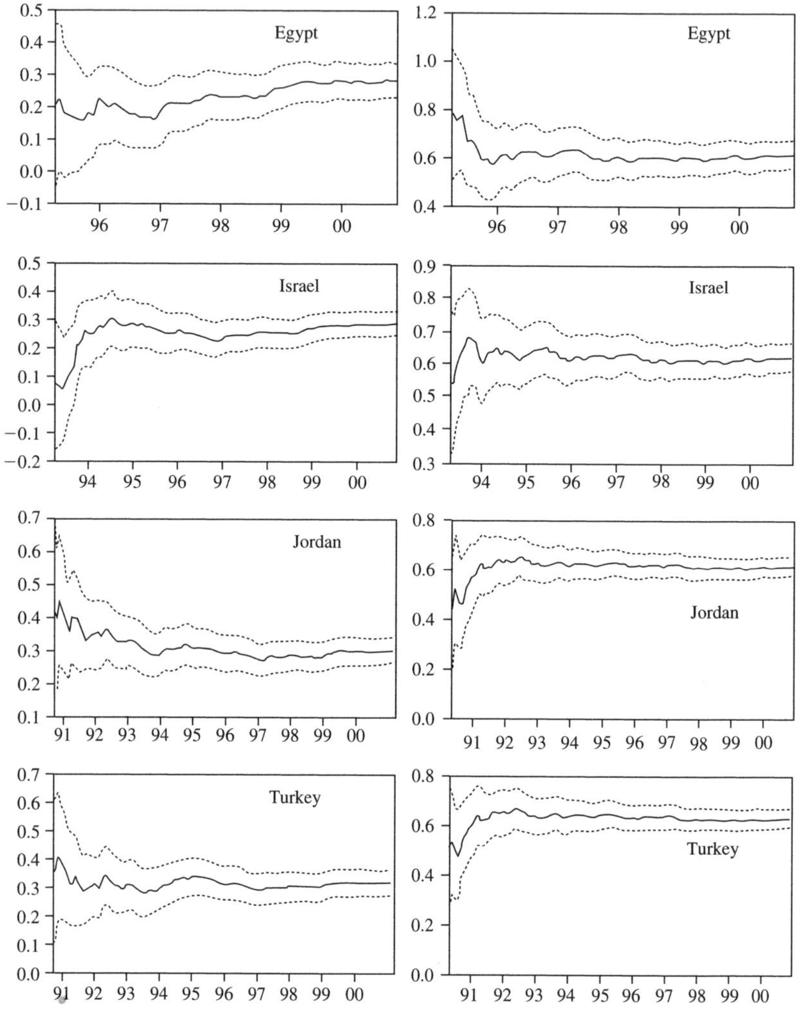

Figure 2.1 (continued)

CEECs

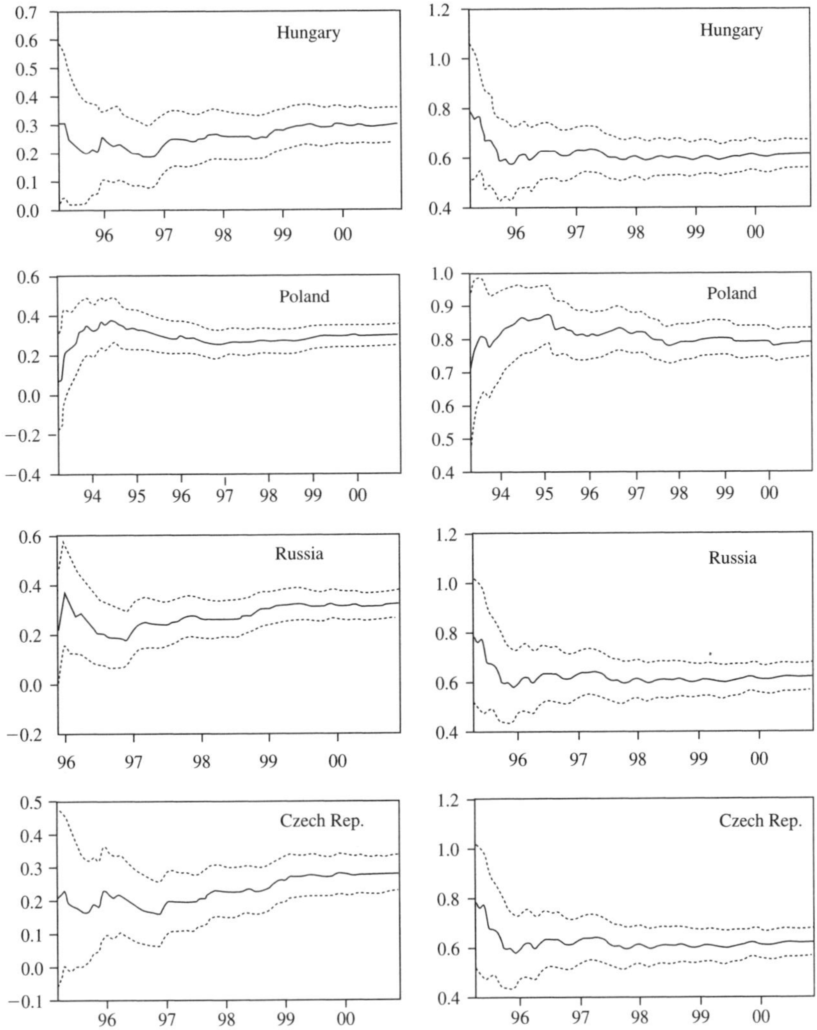

Figure 2.1 (continued)

These charts call for two main remarks:

- No particular evolution of the rate of integration, in terms of monetary proximity as well as in terms of geographical proximity, is highlighted. We quite to the contrary note a remarkable stability[10] in both cases, which goes in opposition on the one hand to some results highlighted in the economic literature and on the other hand to the idea that the trade-offs carried out by the managers of international funds should reinforce the process of international integration of the emerging financial markets.
- Whatever the national market considered, the international component appears at least twice higher in the geographical case than in the monetary one. In the monetary case, international integration rates move around a value of about 0.20 to 0.30, whereas in the geographical case they move around a value of about 0.55 to 0.65. So the monetary influence dominates very largely the geographical one in the determination of the return for risk granted by the various national markets.

CONCLUSION

The process of globalization, usually mentioned, and specially the arbitrage strategies of international funds, have not, for the moment, involved the complete integration of the emerging financial markets to the world capital market. This last is still largely segmented and reveals two quite distinct emerging monetary areas.

In addition, the choices of emerging countries differ in terms of currency regimes and this seems to have a determining influence on the trade-off strategies of the managers of international funds.

APPENDIX: STATISTICAL DATA

Asia	
India	January 1993
Indonesia	January 1990
Korea	January 1990
Malaysia	January 1990
Pakistan	January 1993
Philippines	January 1990
Thailand	January 1990

Latin America	
Argentina	January 1990
Brazil	January 1990
Chile	January 1990
Colombia	January 1993
Mexico	January 1990
Peru	January 1993
Venezuela	January 1993
Middle East	
Egypt	January 1995
Israel	January 1993
Jordan	January 1990
Turkey	January 1990
CEECs	
Czech Rep.	January 1995
Hungary	January 1995
Poland	January 1993
Russia	January 1995

Notes:
Monthly data.
Maximum period of estimate: January 1990 to December 2000.
Effective availability of the complete data, all series used.

Sources: Datastream, FIBV, IMF

NOTES

1. This diversification strategy was recently studied by Borensztein and Gelos (2000).
2. The model is invariant with respect to the choice of the cash.
3. That is to say, the premium per unit of risk, in other words the international price of risk.
4. The assumption of non-stochastic inflation is equivalent to the assumption of perfect expectation of inflation.
5. The data relating to the markets of CEECs (and thus the regional market portfolio corresponding) are unavailable on the beginning of the estimation period. Also, the delayed value of the CEECs portfolio, as an instrument in the estimation of the expectation models for the other markets, was not used. Moreover the estimation of the unit risk premium of the CEECs area had to be separated from those of the other markets.
6. Poirson (2001) notes that in 1999, among the 40 countries declaring a free or managed floating exchange rate regime, eight of them practised in fact a pegging to the dollar; conversely, some countries declaring a pegging in one form or another, actually posted a significant flexibility of their exchange rate.
7. Nevertheless it is necessary to be conscious of the limits of this method: on the one hand, the interventions of the monetary authorities necessarily are not limited to direct purchases or sales of reserves; in addition these interventions starting from the reserves of exchange can relate to the defence of several parities, in other words can be carried out with respect to several currencies and not of only one, the dollar in fact according to our

assumption. It will be noted finally that it is always perilous to distinguish the variations from the rates of exchange related to interventions of the monetary authorities of those which are due to pure exogeneous shocks.

8. The dummy 'exchange rate regime' takes value 0 for the situations of hard pegging and value 1 for the situations of soft pegging.
9. The three benchmarks are calculated like a weighted average by stock exchange capitalizations of the respective markets.
10. The apparent disturbances at the beginning of the period, whatever the country, result from statistical effects related to the technique of the Kalman filter when the series are stationary.

REFERENCES

Adler, M. and B. Dumas (1983), 'International portfolio choice and corporation finance: a synthesis', *Journal of Finance*, **38**, 925–84.

Borensztein, E.R. and R.G. Gelos (2000), 'Panic-prone pack? The behavior of emerging market mutual funds', *IMF Working Paper*, 00/198, December.

Dumas, B. and B. Solnik (1995), 'The world price of foreign exchange risk', *Journal of Finance*, **50**, 445–79.

Goyeau, D., J. Léonard and D. Pépin (1999), 'L'intégration internationale des marchés financiers: analyse et étude empirique', *Economie Appliquée*, **52** (3), 93–115.

Grauer, F.L.A., R.H. Litzenberger and R.E. Stehle (1976), 'Sharing rules and equilibrium in an international capital market under uncertainty', *Journal of Financial Economics*, **3**, 233–56.

Harvey, C.R. (1989), 'Time-varying conditional covariances in tests of asset pricing models', *Journal of Financial Economics*, **24**, 289–317.

Harvey, C.R. (1995), 'Predictable risk and return in emerging markets', *Review of Financial Studies*, **8**, Fall, 773–816.

Holden, P., M. Holden and E. Suss (1979), 'The determinants of exchange rate flexibility: an empirical investigation', *Review of Economics and Statistics*, **61**, 327–33.

Levy Yeyati, E. and F. Sturzenegger (1999), 'Classifying exchange rate regimes: deeds vs words', unpublished, Universidad Torcuato di Tella.

Poirson, H. (2001), 'How do countries choose their exchange rate regime?', *IMF Working Paper*, 01/46, April.

Solnik, B.H. (1974), 'An equilibrium model of the international capital market', *Journal of Economic Theory*, **8**, 500–524.

Weymark, D. (1997), 'Measuring the degree of exchange market intervention in a small open economy', *Journal of International Money and Finance*, **16** (1), 55–7.

3. Pensions and savings in a monetary union: an analysis of capital flows

Alain Jousten and Florence Legros[1]

INTRODUCTION

Most developed countries are undergoing a fundamental demographic transition due to the concurrent tendencies towards lower fertility rates and higher life expectancy. Both the reasons for and the consequences of this ageing process are numerous, but it will no doubt have a major impact on the way our societies are organized, in economic, social and political terms. While the economic consequences of a demographic ageing process are rather well understood in a closed-economy setting, this clearly does not hold true for more general frameworks characterized by open borders allowing for mobility of resources between countries.

The previous literature on the impact of demographic ageing in an open-economy framework has often focused on the case of different countries facing ageing processes at different times and with different intensities. The framework chosen is often one of perfect capital and/or labour mobility between the zones. This is the case for Börsch-Supan et al. (2001), Artus (2001) and the work of the INGENUE team (2001). Artus (2001) for example presents a theoretical treatment of the special case where the two regions have diametrically opposed demographic cycles. A common feature of the literature is that it heavily relies on overlapping generations models in which the world is divided into demographic zones. The international capital flows are substantial between zones, inducing a huge modification in the allocation of property rights across individuals residing in the different regions (INGENUE, 2001). On the other hand, fluctuations in the returns to capital are limited by the capital flows towards the youngest part of the world (Börsch-Supan et al., 2001) with the highest returns on capital.

The present chapter addresses a somewhat different question, namely that of understanding the macroeconomic impact of a universal and simultaneous demographic ageing process in an environment characterized by several countries forming an economic union but conducting independent pension policies. While we follow the previous authors by abstracting away from an analysis of financial risk, we innovate by considering a demographically homogeneous common economic area. More precisely, we study an economically integrated zone composed of two different countries that age at the same speed and at the same date. The demographic shock is modelled to be an exogenous and simultaneous drop in the size of their labour force. The fundamental difference between these two countries is due to their pension schemes: while the first country has a large pay-as-you-go (PAYG) pension scheme, the second one has a pension system that mainly relies on fully-funded (FF) pension funds. These assumptions can be seen as a stylized summary of Euroland reality. Countries belonging to Euroland are in an economic and monetary union, with free financial flows, identical lead interest rates and one common currency. Two broad categories of countries exist in the euro zone as can be seen from Table 3.1. Table 3.1 however also illustrates the fact that pure systems are sparse in reality: most countries have mixed schemes integrating elements of both PAYG and FF schemes, with the two extremes being Italy and the Netherlands.

Our chapter is structured as follows. The next section deals with the long-run dynamics of both countries, first considering the countries as closed economies, second considering them as financially integrated. The third section studies the transition towards a smaller size of the labour force; this short-term analysis focuses on the financial transfers between the countries. In particular it provides an answer to the following puzzle: the usual economic literacy says that the PAYG countries have a smaller saving rate than the FF countries when the economies are undercapitalized – that is, when the interest rate is greater than the wage bill growth rate – while the empirical evidence shows the opposite. The reason for this standard theoretical result is that PAYG pension contributions crowd out explicit

Table 3.1 PAYG country; closed economy

Period	Macroeconomic savings	Population	Per capita capital (from the previous period savings): k	Interest rate, wages
$T-1$	$\uparrow$	N	(K_{T-1}/N)	
T	$\downarrow$	$M<N$	$\uparrow(K_T/M)$	$r\downarrow; w\uparrow$
$T+1$		$M=M$	$\downarrow(K_{T+1}/M)$	$r\uparrow; w\downarrow$ $(r_T>r_{T-1})$ $(w_T>w_{T+1})$

retirement savings. We find that during the demographic transition period, countries of the economic union react in the same way but starting from different points if compared to a closed economy situation; this induces international capital flows. One of the linked problems is the decrease in the demand for equities, which results from the pensions funds' negative cash flows. This decrease cannot be balanced by the increase in non-pensions savings, which are not invested in equities. A way to deal with this is to increase the funded schemes contribution rates in order to push up the demand for equities. The fourth section examines the welfare effect of such a policy.

THE MODEL IN THE LONG RUN

Set-up

We start by describing the model and presenting some well-known results. We consider a representative agent model where agents live for two periods of time. When young, individuals work; they are retired when old. We denote period t wage income w_t, period t individual private savings s_t, the contribution rate to the PAYG pension scheme τ, the compulsory contribution rate to the FF system μ, the replacement rate provided by this pension scheme λ, the real interest rate r and the taxes paid by the young and by the old generation in period t, u_t and v_t respectively.

The active population N is supposed to increase at a constant rate n:

$$N_t = (1+n)^t N_0 \tag{3.1}$$

The financial equilibrium condition of the PAYG pension scheme is given by

$$\tau w_t N_t = \lambda w_{t-1} N_{t-1} \tag{3.2}$$

The production sector produces a single good using a Cobb-Douglas technology (parameter $\alpha \in]0;1[$) with constant returns to scale. The output also serves as numeraire.

$$y_t = N_t^{\alpha} K_t^{1-\alpha} \tag{3.3}$$

where K represents total capital in the economy. For reasons of simplicity, we assume full economic depreciation of the capital good used at time t. Further assuming a competitive environment and taking first derivatives of this production function, we can write the returns on capital and labour:

$$\begin{cases} 1 + r_t = (1 - \alpha)k_{i+1}^{-\alpha} \\ w_t = \alpha k_t^{1-\alpha} \end{cases} \tag{3.4}$$

w denoting the real wage, $k = K/L$ representing the degree of capital intensity in the production function and r_t being the capital yield between t and $t+1$.

We consider two countries. Country 1 is characterized by a compulsory PAYG system with contribution rate τ, but individuals have the ability to choose private savings levels s to complement their retirement income. Country 2 has a compulsory FF retirement system with contribution rate μ and complementary free private savings s.

We define the goods and services markets equilibrium (which can also be seen as the equilibrium between the supply and demand of savings):

$$N_t[s_t + \mu.w_t] = K_{t+1} \tag{3.5}$$

that is K_t disappears at the end of t; this implies, expressed in per worker terms:

$$s_t + \mu w_t = (1 + n)k_{t+1} \tag{3.6}$$

Equation (3.6) allows us to have some intuitive preview on a key result of our model: the savings variable of interest in these dynamic processes is the total savings rate in the economy ($s + \mu w$) and not the savings rate separated into the different components. If $s > 0$, a marginal change in the compulsory contribution rate μ to the FF system does not matter, as any increase in μw simply entails an equally valued drop in s, as returns to the two types of savings are totally identical.[2]

Finally, to complete the model, we define the utility function as an additively separable log-function in consumption when young (C) and old (D) with time preference rate ρ:

$$U_t = \ln(C_t) + \frac{1}{1+\rho}\ln(D_{t+1}) \tag{3.7}$$

The representative agents in the economy maximize the objective function (3.7) subject to the following resource constraint:

$$\begin{aligned} C_t + s_t &= w_t(1 - \mu - \tau) \\ D_{t+1} &= \lambda w_t + (s_t + \mu w_t)(1 + r_t) \end{aligned} \tag{3.8}$$

Individuals use the currently observed interest rate as their benchmark in the process of determining the amount of savings.[3]

Taking first-order conditions, we find the following optimality condition with respect to the savings variable:

$$(s_t + \mu w_t)(2+\rho) = (1-\tau)w_t - \frac{(1+\rho)(1+n)}{1+r_t}\tau w_{t+1} \tag{3.9}$$

or when considering the exogenous parameter λ rather than τ

$$(s_t + \mu w_t)(2+\rho) = (1-\tau)w_t - \frac{(1+\rho)}{1+r_t}\lambda w_t \tag{3.9'}$$

The Long Run

In a steady state characterized by $k_t = k_{t+1} = k$, and thus $w_t = w_{t+1} = w$, condition (3.9) allows us to make a variety of *ceterus paribus* analysis. First, consider the case of an economy characterized by a lack of capital ($r_t > n$), that occurs as soon as

$$(1-\alpha)\,k^{-\alpha} > n \tag{3.10}$$

When changing the parameters of the FF system, for example by decreasing μ, the resulting change in the private free savings rate exactly compensates for the lower compulsory savings, thus leaving national savings unchanged. Now considering an increase in the PAYG contribution rate τ, we notice that free savings drop. As PAYG contributions do not contribute to national savings, the net effect is a drop in the national savings rate. Notice however that the drop in free savings after an increase in τ is smaller than the corresponding drop in free savings after an increase in μ as the multiplier on the PAYG term is smaller than the one on the FF term:

$$1 + (1+\rho)\cdot\frac{1+n}{1+r} < 2+\rho$$

The same depressing effect of PAYG pension systems on savings also extends to the case of a dynamic inefficiency of the economy, that is, when there is excess capital pushing the return to capital below the rate of growth of the population.

Summarizing, we find that *ceterus paribus* a FF country has a higher savings rate (private and national) than a PAYG country. For an undercapitalized country, a decrease in τ increases savings, and hence helps limit the problem of insufficient capital. At the opposite, if $r<n$, an increase in PAYG is helpful to limit the over-accumulation of capital in the economy and also the problem of ever-increasing public deficits.

Economic Union

We now move away from a closed economy setting to one where these two countries are linked together through perfect capital markets, allowing seamless capital transfers between the countries, while keeping social and fiscal policy autonomy. We further assume that the other factor of production labour is immobile between countries, which is in line with the empirical observation of significantly lower mobility of labour between countries, be it for cultural, language or legal reasons.[4] Our assumption of economic integration means that the interest rates in both countries are identical as a result of the free movement of capital.

Rewriting the budget constraints for both the PAYG (country subscripted 1) and the FF country (country subscripted 2), we find:

$$\begin{cases} C_{1,t} = w_{1,t}(1-\tau_1) - s_{1,t} \\ D_{1,t+1} = \lambda_1 w_{1,t} + s_{1,t}(1+r_t) \end{cases}$$

$$\begin{cases} C_{2,t} = w_{2,t}(1-\mu_2) - s_{2,t} \\ D_{2,t+1} = (s_{2,t} + \mu_2 w_{2,t})(1+r_t) \end{cases}$$

We suppose that the initial size of the population N_0 and the population growth rates are identical between countries and that the two countries thus face exactly the same demographic prospects.

$$N_t = N_{2,t} = N_{1,t} = (1+n)^t N_0$$

The equilibrium condition of the PAYG scheme in country 1 reduces to

$$\tau_1 w_{1t} N_t = \lambda_1 w_{1,t-1} N_{t-1}$$

The equilibrium of the monetary union can be summarized by two identities. First, the interest rate identity (3.4a′) which results from perfect capital mobility and implies $K_1 = K_2$

$$\left(\frac{K_{1,t+1}}{N_t}\right)^{-\alpha} = \left(\frac{K_{2,t+1}}{N_t}\right)^{-\alpha} = 1 + r_t \qquad (3.4a')$$

Using our assumption of identical time paths of the demographic variables and writing $k = k_1 = k_2$, we can verify that the perfect mobility of capital is sufficient for avoiding labour mobility as the marginal products are equalized.

$$w_{1,t} = \alpha k_{1t}^{1-\alpha} = \alpha k_t^{1-\alpha} = \alpha k_{2,t}^{1-\alpha} = w_{2,t} \equiv w_t \tag{3.4b'}$$

Second, the condition (3.6′) on worldwide savings and investment summarizes goods market equilibrium.

$$s_{1,t} + s_{2,t} + \mu_2 . w_{2,t} = (1+n)(k_{1,t+1} + k_{2,t+1}) \tag{3.6'}$$

On a per country level, the savings and investment balances are:

$$\begin{aligned} s_{1,t} &= (1+n)k_{1,t+1} + f_{1,t+1} \quad \text{and} \\ s_{2,t} + \mu w_{2,t} &= (1+n)k_{2,t+1} + f_{2,t+1} \end{aligned} \tag{3.13}$$

where f is the monetary value of the external financial balance with $f_1 + f_2 = 0$.

We assume identical preferences across the two countries:

$$U_{1,t} = \ln(C_t) + \frac{1}{1+\rho} . \ln(D_{t+1}) \quad \text{and}$$

$$U_{2,t} = \ln(C_t) + \frac{1}{1+\rho} . \ln(D_{t+1}) \tag{3.7'}$$

Taking derivatives, it is straightforward to find an expression for national savings per worker in the two countries under our assumption of perfect capital mobility.

$$s_{1,t}(2+\rho) = (1-\tau_1)w_t - \frac{(1+\rho)(1+n)}{(1+r_t)} \tau_1 w_{t+1} \quad \text{and}$$

$$(s_{2,t} + \mu_2 w_t)(2+\rho) = w_t \tag{3.9'}$$

As in the closed economy setting, we find that the presence of a PAYG system in the monetary union lowers savings as soon as there is a lack of capital in the economy. In a steady state situation, using (3.4b′), (3.6′) and (3.9′) we derive (3.12′) and compare it with the per country economy counterpart (3.13). The expression indicates that there are international financial flows in order to equalize per capita capital between the economies, while at the same time allowing for different per capita savings levels such as defined by (3.9′):

$$s_1 + s_2 + \mu_2.w_2 = \left(2.w - \tau_1.w\left(1 + \frac{(1+\rho)(1+n)}{1+r}\right)\right).\frac{1}{2+\rho}$$
$$= 2(1+n)k \qquad (3.12')$$

For example, take the case of a situation of dynamic efficiency ($r < n$) and a world characterized by an absence of international capital flows. When country 1 decides to increase τ, *ceterus paribus*, savings clearly drop as the size of the virtual savings in the PAYG system increases, hence crowding out other forms of real savings. As a result, the external balance of country 2 will increase as country 1 now increases its borrowing abroad so as to permit equalization of wages and interest rates implied by the perfect international factor mobility. This pushes up the external financial balance. Hence intuitively, in the PAYG country, the level of per capita capital would be higher in the open economy than in the closed economy setting. This in turn implies a lower interest rate in country 1 under the regime of monetary union. The inverse obviously holds true for the FF country. Surprisingly however the general conjecture that PAYG countries should be characterized by lower private savings rates than FF countries does not seem to hold true in the real world. Often cited examples are some countries in Western Europe such as France and Belgium where private savings rates are noticeably higher than in some countries that do rely much more heavily on FF.

The above *ceterus paribus* analysis is obviously only a very partial one, as we do not consider the existence of a public sector beyond the pension system. The lack of a public sector is most striking for the FF country as it does not have an intergenerational link through the pension system, and hence might want to use the public debt process to achieve a certain degree of intergenerational redistribution. Belan and Pestieau (1999) show that it is possible to mimic the effects of a FF system by means of a PAYG system complemented by an adequate public deficit policy. Hence some of the lack of fit between real-world examples and this simple model might simply be due to the fact that we do not have a public sector in our analysis, and that some countries we would qualify as being PAYG on the basis of their pension system alone are in fact rather of the FF type when taking into account the general budget of the government. Similarly FF countries might be less so in fact as they might be running public deficits that also add to the implicit burden imposed on future generations, just like a PAYG system does. Such a different debt policy is obviously not without consequence on the international financial markets as it has an impact on equations (3.7).

SHORT-RUN ANALYSES OF A DEMOGRAPHIC TRANSITION

Another – and probably more promising – explanation for the lower aggregate private savings rates in FF countries as compared with PAYG ones runs as follows. Consider a demographic shock where the size of the active population is subject to a one-time drop in the active population from a level of N in period $T-1$ to a level of $M < N$ for all periods starting from T, and this in both countries. For simplicity, we assume that all variables are at their steady-state level in both countries and that the exogenous population growth rate n equals 0.

Two scenarios are imaginable with respect to this shock. A first possibility consists of a scenario where the generation born in $T-1$ is aware of the discrete change in the size of the population before making its savings decision in $T-1$. This possibility could be seen as the most plausible one in a representative agent model. It could be argued that the young generation of period T is the direct offspring of the young generation of period $T-1$, and hence this would imply that people are aware of their offspring when taking decisions.

A second possibility is that the shock as such is sudden and totally unexpected for individuals, such that the generation until the one born in $T-2$ makes its savings decision based on the assumption that steady-state factor returns continue to hold. In the present chapter, we follow the latter approach. The assumption is no less plausible when considering the population as being less homogeneous. On aggregate, N young individuals in $T-1$ have on aggregate M children. This does however neither imply nor necessitate that every single one of these N citizens has exactly N/M children. Pushing this idea a little further, it also means that they do not have to realize that there is an upcoming demographic shock on the aggregate. They even do not necessarily infer this information from a change of the announced replacement rate they are entitled to when retired, as the latter could potentially be the result of a totally unlinked exogenous change in the pension system.

In this rather realistic setting it is plausible that a majority of citizens ignores the exact size of the cohort of their children. Hence we assume that people make their inter-temporal choice prior to the arrival of this new information. This also means that individuals decide on savings levels prior to the arrival of the information on the shock to the population size, and thus that they are surprised by the news and exposed to the income shock induced by lower asset returns.

We successively analyse the impact on savings, wages and interest rates in a closed economy and in a monetarily integrated one. The generation born in $T-1$ is the first one to be exposed to this shock – that resembles a sudden one-off ageing process – and it is also the first one to be confronted with the consequences of the demographic changes. While young, members of this birth cohort still earn a wage that equals the steady state level ($w_{T-1} = w$) as the capital stock entering the production process was decided upon by generation $T-2$ that was still unaware of the imminent shock. Their savings are also unchanged, as information revelation only takes place after the savings decision of the first period. In the second period of their life, individuals who are born in $T-1$ face the full consequences of the shock as the PAYG replacement rate is affected by the demographic changes through the balanced-budget condition of the PAYG system.

$$M.\tau_T.w_T = N\lambda_{T-1}.w_{T-1} \tag{3.2'}$$

Similarly, people living in the FF country are not immune to the shock, as factor returns everywhere in period T are not unaffected by the demographic changes. For the PAYG country, this means that the analysis is a less trivial one than the usual purely linear relation between the parameters τ and λ.

$$\begin{cases} w_T = \alpha\left(\dfrac{K_T}{M}\right)^{1-\alpha} \\ 1 + r_T = (1-\alpha)\left(\dfrac{K_{T+1}}{M}\right)^{-\alpha} \end{cases} \tag{3.4''}$$

As far as the impact of the demographic shock on the key parameters of the PAYG system is concerned, two situations are imaginable. A first alternative (A) consists of a constant contribution rate τ and hence an endogenous adjustment of the replacement rate λ in the PAYG system. A second alternative (B) is a 'grandfathering' stipulation with respect to the replacement rate. A 'grandfathering' rule protects those people who already contributed to the system from a change in the replacement rate they were promised, on the grounds of their inability to react to the change. This type of argument is often used in pension reform discussions all across Europe, where measures are usually limited to future retirees, while keeping the entitlements of those already retired unaffected by reforms. This in turn implies an endogenous adjustment of the contribution rate τ. Notice that opting for one or the other of these two alternatives has an interpretation in terms of the structure of the pension system. The first reform is most easily thought of within the framework of a notional defined contribution system, whereas the second one closely resembles a traditional defined benefit PAYG scheme.

We first analyse the impact of the demographic shock for the PAYG country and in a second step the situation for the FF country.

PAYG Country

When people expect to be in scenario A, the direct effect of the reduction in the active population obviously has a negative impact on λ_{T-1}. The indirect effect working through the increased level of w_T however works in the opposite direction. It is straightforward to show that for our production function, the direct effect dominates at any given level of savings, and hence that λ_{T-1} is smaller than the steady-state value of λ. Hence we establish that unless grandfathering in the PAYG country is complete, individuals born in the PAYG country in $T-1$ react to the shock by increasing their savings levels, and this in anticipation of a reduction of pensions replacement rates and levels.

When individuals belonging to generation $T-1$ perceive their situation to be that of scenario B, individuals feel immune against the demographic shock and hence do not see the need for adjustments with respect to their optimal steady-state behaviour. Hence they are fully insured against the shock when scenario B prevails.[5] As we shall see below, the saving rate comes from the steady state and the per capita capital comes from the demography.

λ is supposed to be constant and the demographic shock leads to an adjustment in τ:

$$\tau_{T-1} = \frac{\lambda . w_{T-2} . N}{w_{T-1} . N} = \lambda$$

$$\tau_T = \frac{\lambda . w_{T-1} . N}{w_T . M}$$

$$\tau_{T+1} = \frac{\lambda . w_T . M}{w_{T+1} . M} = \lambda . \frac{w_T}{w_{T+1}}$$

taking into account that the steady state implies a constancy of wages, population . . . until $T-1$.

Using these expressions in the budget constraints and in the utility function, then maximizing the individuals' welfare taking into account the new constraints, provides a set of new expressions for the saving rates:

$$s_{T-2} = w_{T-2}.(1-\lambda).\frac{1}{2+\rho} - \frac{\lambda}{2+\rho}.\frac{1+\rho}{1+r_{T-2}} = s_{T-1}$$

$$= w_{T-1}(1-\lambda).\frac{1}{2+\rho} - \frac{\lambda}{2+\rho}.\frac{1+\rho}{1+r_{T-1}}$$

$$s_T = w_T\left(1 - \frac{\lambda.w_{T-1}.N}{w_T.M}\right).\frac{1}{2+\rho} - \frac{\lambda.w_{T-1}}{(2+\rho).w_T}.\frac{1+\rho}{1+r_T}$$

$$s_{T+1} = w_{T+1}\left(1 - \frac{\lambda.w_T}{w_{T+1}}\right)\frac{1}{2+\rho} - \frac{\lambda.w_T}{w_{T+1}}.\frac{1+\rho}{(2+\rho).(1+r_T)}$$

Considering the previous equations around $\lambda = 0$ leads to:

$$K_{T-1} = N.s_{T-2} = K_T$$

$$K_T = N.s_{T-1} = \frac{N}{2+\rho}.\alpha.\left(\frac{K_T}{N}\right)^{-\alpha}$$

$$K_{T+1} = M.s_T = \frac{M}{2+\rho}.\alpha.\left(\frac{K_T}{M}\right)^{-\alpha}$$

Since $M < N$, $K_{T+1} < K_T = K_{T-1}$, $k_{T+1} < k_T$ and $k_T > k_{T-1}$
This implies that: $w_T > w_{T+1}$ and $r_T > r_{T-1}$.

This implies an increase in per capita capital in period T; we shall now study the effect in the FF country but before must remark that this demographic shock is without any doubt in favour of the cohort active in t who has high wages, high pensions (mostly there because of the grandfathering policy) and high savings yield r.

FF Country

Let us write the wage received by the generation working before the demographic shock (that is in $T-1$, $T-2$, . . .):

$$w_{T-1} = \alpha.\left(\frac{K_{T-1}}{N}\right)^{1-\alpha}$$

Introducing this expression in (3.9′) with $\lambda = \tau = 0$ leads to denote that $K_T = K_{T-1}$, and provides the following results:

$$K_T^{\alpha} = \frac{\alpha}{2+\rho}N^{\alpha}$$

After the same computation and a rearrangement, we obtain:

$$K_{T+1} = \left(\frac{M}{N}\right)^{\alpha} K_T$$

This allows us to conclude that:

$$K_{T-1} = K_T > K_{T+1}; k_T > k_{T-1} \text{ and } k_{T+1} > k_T.\ r_T > r_{T-1} \text{ and } w_T > w_{T-1}.$$

Next, we consider the effects of a demographic shock in the framework of an economic union. We qualitatively discuss the features of a shock when the countries are already monetarily integrated in the steady-state situation in $T-1$, which clearly is the most relevant scenario.[6] When subjecting these economies to the demographic shock, the external imbalance of the PAYG country in period $T-1$ increases as it has a relative abundance of capital. Given the strong similarity in the economic structure of the countries, there is an incentive for savers of the PAYG country to invest their money in the FF country until there is an equalization of returns to capital all across the union. The common interest rate that is paid all across the union is higher than that of the PAYG country in the closed economy setting, while the contrary holds true for the FF country. Our model thus describes one possible theoretical model supporting the empirical evidence that PAYG countries are characterized by higher savings rates.

Saving more is an optimal strategy for the first generation affected by a demographic transition in the PAYG country, and international capital mobility allows the capital resources to find their most profitable employment. Notice that rather complex general equilibrium and distributional issues might arise between countries and between generations. For example as a consequence of the increased capital flows out of the PAYG country, period T workers in that country will find their wages reduced with respect to those paid in a closed economy setting. The opposite holds true for workers in the FF country. Hence people born in the PAYG country in period $T-1$ will react because of a lower expectation of retirement benefits (lower replacement rate) by readjusting their savings levels upwards because of expectations of lower retirement income. Thus the international capital reallocation is not without distributional consequences on an international scale.

Our discussion also shows that the largest benefit of a monetary union is to allow a smooth transition from one demographic regime to another by allowing capital to reallocate itself internationally according to its highest marginal productivity. This benefit is most obvious in period $T-1$, where the largest difference between countries exists. Interpreting the current situation in Europe as being the start of the transition period, our model would tend to indicate that the benefits of the monetary union do not

Table 3.2 FF country; closed economy

Period	Macroeconomic savings	Population	Per capita capital (from the previous period savings): k	Interest rate, wages
$T-1$	=	N		
T	↓	$M<N$	↑	$r\downarrow$; $w\uparrow$
$T+1$		$M=M$	↓	$r\uparrow$; $w\downarrow$

Table 3.3 Monetary union

Period	Capital flows	Comparison with closed economy	
		Interest rate r	Wages w
$T-1$	FF → PAYG		
T	The movement is partially reversed [PAYG → FF]	Increase in the PAYG country	Decrease in the PAYG country
$T+1$	–	*Id*	*id*

necessarily increase over time. The following Tables 3.2 and 3.3 summarize our findings.

Again, our results of large financial flows in period $T-1$ crucially hinge on the assumption that the PAYG country does not pursue an anti-cyclical fiscal policy by means of which it would increase the public debt sufficiently in period $T-1$ so as to absorb the additional private savings, hence leaving the capital stock largely unchanged.[7] This finding that an adequate fiscal policy can undo the effects of a change in the PAYG variables is not new by any standard. However while our assumption of an absence of fiscal policy, and thus implicitly of a self-imposed budgetary discipline, might not be an optimal economic policy, it still approximates the example of the European Union rather strongly.

IMPACT ON FINANCIAL MARKETS: ASSET ALLOCATION

Next we consider the question of what impact a demographic shock is likely to have on financial markets in a monetary union made up of a PAYG and a

FF country. We focus on a setting where there only exist two types of financial instruments, one-period government bonds paying a return r_t with certainty, and stocks paying a random return R_t. Uncertainty on the stock returns stem from an uncertainty on the productivity of the capital in the economy. This production function implies a complete insurance of workers against income fluctuations due to productivity shocks.

We assume that individuals' free savings are in the form of the safe assets, while compulsory savings in pension funds are entirely invested in the form of stocks. The assumption, though clearly extreme, is a rather good approximation of reality. In France, 65 per cent of private life insurance savings were made in the form of bonds, while only 25 per cent took the form of stocks. Further, a lot of private saving is done through low-risk and low-return savings accounts. Pension funds on the other hand heavily rely on stock market investments, given their generally much longer time horizon as well as their much better access to tools and instruments allowing a good diversification of risks in their portfolio. Further, Table 3.2 shows the allocation of pension investments in the Netherlands that clearly displays a bias towards investments in equity at the ages considered.

So while consumers in the PAYG country 1 face the usual PAYG balanced budget constraint, their counterparts in the FF country face uncertainty due to the random nature of the return R_t on capital. This implies that, while PAYG country households do maximize the usual expression of their utility function, for the FF the expected utility will be considered, a utility expression which is affected by the random character of the equity return.

Notice that as before, wages and interest rates are equalized between countries because of the perfect international capital mobility. Hence we have a single value of the non-risky asset yield, r.

For the PAYG country the impact will be null since the uncertainty of capital productivity has no effect on wages, replacement ratios and thus consumption and savings. However a drop of the active population from a level N in period $T-1$ to a level $M<N$ in period T still has the same positive effect on savings in $T-1$.

In the FF country, the story will be quite different: The projected consumption pathway from young to old will be changed by the uncertainty. The impact of such an uncertainty is as usual a higher savings rate which corresponds to a precautionary saving (Artus and Legros, 1999). In the FF country, there is an effective impact of uncertainty on the allocation of consumption between periods. While individuals in the PAYG country are shielded against uncertainty, the individuals in the FF country face uncertainty through the risk involved in the institutional investments of the public pension fund.

The reaction in period $T-1$ of individuals in the FF country to a drop of the active population from a level N in period $T-1$ to a level $M < N$ in period T is less trivial than the one in the PAYG country. For an unchanged level of the contribution rate μ_t to the compulsory fully funded system, individuals in the FF country still have an unchanged savings behaviour. However because all national governments are forced to keep the total of bonds outstanding unchanged under a Maastricht-style criteria, the combined demand for these bonds originating from individuals in the PAYG and the FF system has changed with respect to the previous period. Further, at this stage, the total amount of capital available to companies stays constant, as the savings of the pension funds have not changed.

This situation does obviously not represent equilibrium, as there is an implicit pressure towards higher relative prices of bonds with respect to stocks. However such an outright relative loss of value of the institutional pension assets is not in the interest of the fund, as it would produce large fluctuations in the pension income of the elderly in country 2. As a stylization of this asset market pressure, we assume that the pension fund of country 2 rationally intervenes as a sort of regulator or social planner on the financial markets to keep the interest rate r_T constant or expressed a little differently to restore the quantity equilibrium in the bond market. The pension fund operates through adjustments of the compulsory contribution level μ_{T-1} such that the demand for bonds in country 2 decreases in line with the variation in demand for fixed-income assets emanating from individuals in country 1, whose pension system cannot react. Mathematically this is equivalent to having the pension fund set the decision variable μ_{T-1} such that the level of private savings as implicitly defined by equation (3.19) exactly corresponds to the value that insures the respect of the bond market clearing condition

$$s_{2,T-1} = \frac{1}{N_{T-1}}(B_1 + B_2) - N_{T-1}s_{1,T-1} \tag{3.20}$$

where B_1 and B_2 represent the amount of public bonds available in each country, 1 and 2, respectively.

Intuitively, the pension fund will thus adjust its holdings of the risky asset if individuals in country 1 increase their savings volume as a result of a demographic shrinking process. The relative risk exposure of individuals belonging to the generation $T-1$ in country 2 will thus increase. The clear winners in the process are individuals in country 1 which take advantage of the higher capital stock at home, and hence of higher wages for their workers. The results are less clear-cut for individuals of the FF country. Their additional risk intake will to some degree be compensated by the higher returns on risky rather than on risk-free assets. However they will suffer a negative income effect as the increase in total productive capital and the decrease in the size of the labour force both lower the returns R_T.

However the decrease in the relative price of stocks is smaller than the one the individuals would have had to face if the fund had not adjusted its contribution rate and increases its asset holdings at home and abroad. The intuitive reason is that by readjusting, the fund is able to bridge some of the pricing pressure by using the additional savings to generate additional value added in the production sector.

An interesting and important remark relates to the Maastricht-style criterion that the economies have to face. The baseline assumption we have taken relies heavily on the situation the member states of the European Union currently face. Equation (3.20) shows that the dynamics of the savings and asset allocation problems would be fundamentally different if the limitation on the debt levels B_i were to be expressed in per capita terms b_i $(i = 1,2)$.

Our finding of increased pension fund investment in safe assets in period $T-1$ can obviously not be generalized to generations beyond T. Indeed from the analyses of the previous sections it is likely that individual savings will decrease, hence pushing down pension fund investment in stocks. Therefore the projections of Tables 3.2 and 3.3 are not inconsistent with our model.

CONCLUSION

Our chapter set out to study the impact of a demographic shock in a monetary union. While it is widely believed that a fully funded system provides insurance against such shocks, we show that this result does not hold true in a general setting. Indeed for the case of a monetary union with countries similar in their demographic structure, but leading different and independent policies with respect to the pensions system, we find that the FF country will bear part of the burden of the demographic transition. This result hinges on the availability of free capital flows between countries, which allow capital owners to optimally react to variations in factor returns. Our model is designed to approximate European Union reality. Hence we find some rationale for empirical observations often made. First, the first generation affected by the demographic changes displays a pattern of increased savings when young that clearly helps us understand the higher observed savings rates of PAYG countries in the European Union. Second, the role of pension funds is also highlighted. While individuals do not have the facility of access to the stock market, pension funds do. Hence they act as market regulators by investing more heavily on the stock market. In doing so they implicitly decrease the demand for bonds emanating from the FF country, and hence relax the implicit price pressure on the stock market. Hence pension funds of the FF country increase their holdings abroad, again a result empirically observed across the European Union.

APPENDIX

Main characteristics of pensions and savings for European selected countries

Countries	Pay-as-you-go				Pension funds liabilities (% of GDP, 1999)	Saving rates Average rates 1990–2001
	Replacement rates (%, 1998)			Expenditures (% of GDP, 1998)		
	Half the average wage	Average wage	Twice the average wage			
France	84	84	73	12.50	6.00	15.15
Germany	76	72	75	12.80	8.40	10.00
Netherlands	73	43	25	5.20	110	10.00
United Kingdom	72	50	35	4.40	81	5.00

The Netherlands: change in the asset allocation

Age group	2000			2050		
	Pension assets	Asset allocation per age group		Pension assets	Asset allocation per age group	
		Equities %	Non-equities %		Equities %	Non-equities %
25–29	21 518	100	0	33 180	100	0
30–34	159 516	100	0	203 399	100	0
35–39	310 876	100	0	380 847	100	0
40–44	442 292	96	4	597 863	96	4
45–49	570 012	80	20	902 020	80	20
50–54	761 294	60	40	1 309 177	60	40
55–59	713 362	40	60	1 792 411	40	60
60–64	737 922	20	80	2 095 929	20	80
65–69	715 441	0	100	2 123 877	0	100
70–74	434 973	0	100	1 523 035	0	100
75–79	192 510	0	100	1 023 279	0	100
80+	0	0	100	741 178	0	100
Total	5 059 716	2 262 226	2 797 490	12 726 194	3 834 647	8 891 548
Weighted average asset allocation		44.7%	55.3%		30.1%	69.9%

Source: Merril Lynch. The assumptions made in order to have the pension assets per age group are detailed in Mantel (2000).

Changes in asset allocation (%)

	UK		US		Netherlands		Japan	
	2000	2050	2000	2050	2000	2050	2000	2050
Equities	72	60	62	54	45	30	40	28
Non-equities	28	40	38	46	55	70	60	72

Source: Merril Lynch.

NOTES

1. Alain Jousten acknowledges financial support from the Fonds National de la Recherche Scientifique and the Fonds de la Recherche Fondamentale Collective (contract 2.4544.01). A first version of this chapter was prepared while Florence Legros was affiliated to CEPII.
2. The result does not hold true in a more general set-up with different risks attached to the two savings instruments (free private and institutionalized savings), or with a heterogeneous population instead of a representative agent.
3. This assumption is without any consequence on the steady-state results of the model.
4. As we illustrate below, this assumption is however not binding at the open-economy equilibrium of our two-country world.
5. If however, for whatever reason, the replacement rate gets adjusted *ex post*, then these individuals will bear the entire burden of the shock in the second period of their life.
6. A second possible scenario consists of an economic integration that occurs simultaneously with demographic shock. Some of the discussed results also apply to this different setting.
7. The same holds true for a so-called buffer fund, that is a partial element of capitalization in a PAYG pension system.

REFERENCES

Artus, P. (2000), 'Le placement optimal de l'épargne lorsque les pays les plus avancées connaissent un cycle démographique', *Revue d'Economie Politique*, **2**, 243–65.

Artus, P. (2001), 'Quelles politiques budgétaires dans une économie vieillissante, le cas du Japon et un peu de théorie', *Epargne et retraite, Revue d'Economie Politique*, special issue, 153–76.

Artus, P. and F. Legros (1999), *Le choix du système de retraite*, Paris: Economica.

Belan, P. and P. Pestieau (1999), 'Privatizing social security: a critical assessment', *Geneva Papers on Risk and Insurance. Issues and Practice*, **24**, 114–30.

Blanchet, D. (1990), 'Retraite par capitalisation et par répartition selon le contexte démographique: quelques résultats comparatifs', *Annales d'Economie et de Statistique*, **18**, 63–90.

Börsch-Supan, A., A. Ludwig and J. Winter (2001), 'Ageing and international capital flows', W.P. NBER 8553, October.

Equipe INGENUE (2001), 'Vieillissement démographique et transferts internationaux d'épargne: premiers enseignements du modèle INGENUE', *Epargne et retraite, Revue d'Economie Politique*, special issue, 195–214.

Mantel, J. (2000), 'Demographics and the funded pension system, ageing populations, mature pension funds and negative cash flow', Merril Lynch, 30 October.

4. Emerging sovereign bond markets: a view from the extremes

Pierre Laurent and Jérôme Teïletche*

INTRODUCTION

Over the last decade, emerging sovereign bond markets have become an important source of diversification of portfolios for global investors. According to IIF data, between 1995 and 2001 these markets received more than US$43 billion per year. If we consider only the period between 1995 and 1997 (preceding the Asian and Russian crises), more than US$65 billion per year was received. For comparison, we should note these markets received less than US$18 billion per year of buying flows for equities (US$28 billion per year between 1995 and 1997). From an economic point of view, the sovereign bond markets (including Brady bonds and Euromarkets bonds) have become a major financing channel for these countries.

In broad terms, emerging bond markets are classified as risky. This point is illustrated in Figure 4.1 where we represent the risk/return profiles obtained for several financial assets. Emerging bonds appear as the most profitable assets (the average return is the highest) but at the same time the riskiest ones. The risk involved in emerging bond markets is a crucial question, obviously for the investors in these zones but also for policy-makers. Indeed since the mid 1990s, crises in emerging markets have spread to the financial markets of industrial countries and, on occasion, they have hit the banking systems and affected cyclical developments in industrial countries. This has led policy-makers to intervene in markets (and notably central bankers) and also has led international regulators to wonder about reforms of the international financial architecture. All in all, the risks of emerging financial markets have become a prominent subject of investigation.

This naturally leads to the question of measurement of these risks. In Figure 4.1, following the standard practice, risk is estimated using the standard deviation of returns. Does the second moment of the distribution constitute an adequate measure of risks? Nothing warrantees this, as the

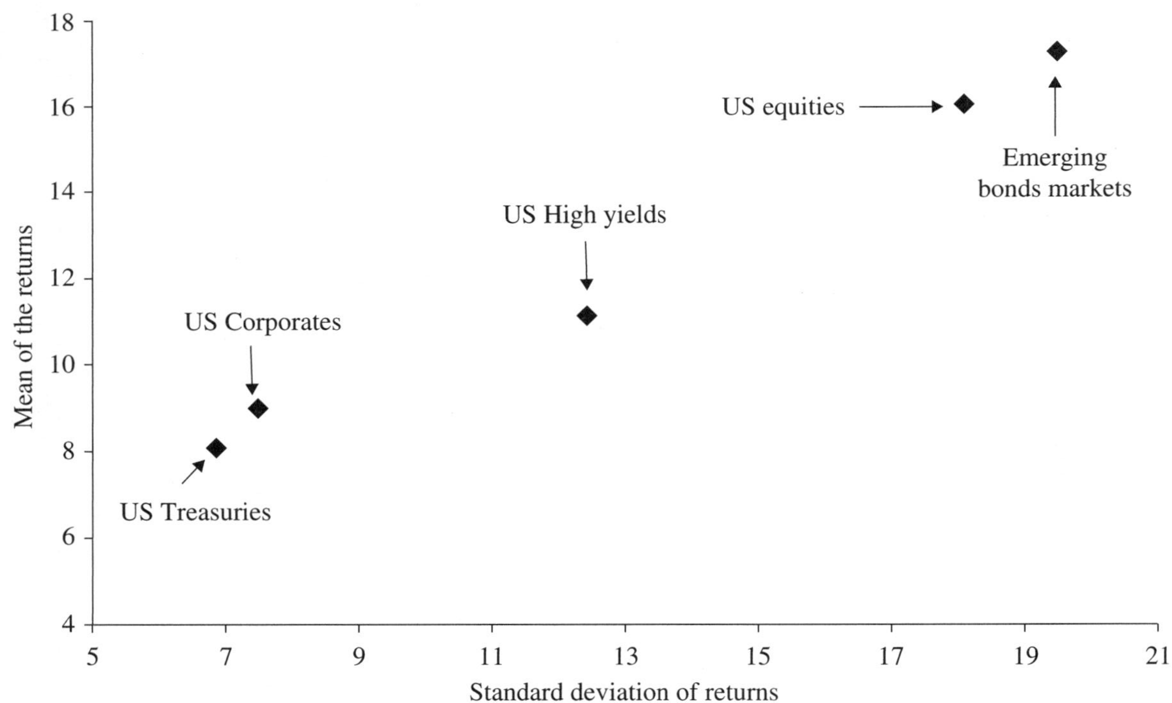

Sources: Merril Lynch, JP Morgan, MSCI, authors' computations.

Figure 4.1 Risk/return profile (as %) of yearly total returns for several financial markets (1991–2001)

experience of the EMS reminds us. It is generally acknowledged that the creation of the EMS has allowed a reduction of the volatility of the (intra-EMU) exchange rates. Indeed by constraining exchange rates to fluctuate inside margins as narrow as ±2.25%, the standard deviation of exchange rates returns has shrunk. However this result has been challenged by the findings of Koedijk et al. (1990) who have underlined the fact that while 'average' risk may have declined, 'extreme' risk has surged, extreme risk being defined as large (absolute) variations of the exchange rate. This does correspond to the way the EMS behaved in practice:[1] small fluctuations of exchange rates until a large movement induced by devaluation or revaluation of the centre of the bands. The recent experience of emerging markets points to the importance of extreme risks: while this market seems to be quiet most of the time, it has known several important crises (Mexico, Asia, Russia, Brazil, Turkey, Ecuador, Argentina). Thus there is a need for an adapted measure of these particular risks (*crashes*).

Another characteristic of the recent experience of emerging bond markets is that shocks in one country or region propagate to other countries around the world. In other words, when a crash occurs somewhere, the probability that a crash occurs elsewhere at the same time is elevated. Indeed emerging sovereign bond markets present characteristics which make them prone to contagion: they are concentrated (the ten largest issuers represent around 80% of the market) and quite narrow (in particular they are highly sensitive to international capital flows and flight-to-quality phenomena). To quantify risks in emerging markets, it thus appears crucial to be able to measure dependence in the extremes. The standard way to measure dependence is the linear or Pearson correlation. Again we may wonder whether this measure is adapted for our purposes, since correlation quantifies dependence for the whole distribution, not only the tails of the distribution (where extreme returns concentrate).

Due to these potential pitfalls in standard methods (methods which are all linked to a normal-gaussian 'vision of the world'), we need to rely on adapted tools. It is precisely the purpose of Extreme Value Theory (EVT) to analyse these extreme risks. Over the last few years, an important body of literature has proposed to apply methods drawn for EVT to financial markets returns from a univariate point of view (see among many others Longin, 1996; Koedijk et al., 1990; Lux, 2001). To our knowledge, one may find two main applications of these tools to emerging markets:[2] Jondeau and Rockinger (2000) for emerging stock markets, and Kiesel et al. (2000) for some individual bonds. In this chapter we propose a similar application to a large set of emerging benchmark indices (16 countries plus the Composite Index). Moreover we also extend the existing literature by analysing the consistency between EVT-derived measures of risks and different moments of the distribution, and by trying to identify the economic and financial determinants of extreme risks.

Multivariate applications of EVT methods are far more rare, which implies that the question of the probability of co-crashes among financial assets has largely been overlooked. In practice we know of five such studies: Poon et al. (2001) and Longin and Solnik (2001) for the stock markets of G5 countries, Hartmann et al. (2001) for the stock and bond markets of G5 countries, Straetmans (1998) and Starica (1999) for exchange rates. To our knowledge, no application to emerging bond markets has been proposed while the question of contagion in emerging markets seems ultimate. In this text, we try to fill this gap. Moreover we also extend the existing literature by trying to identify the economic and financial determinants of these extremal dependences.

The remainder of the chapter is organized as follows. In the next section, we present the methodological approach which is essentially based on the non-parametric estimators proposed by Huang (1992) and further developed in Straetmans (1998) and Hartmann et al. (2001). The third section provides details and primary analysis on the data. The following two sections present results for univariate measures of risks and multivariate measures of risks. We then report extensions to the previous analysis: analysis over subperiods, and investigation of the economic and financial determinants of extreme risks. The seventh section concludes.

FROM LINEAR CORRELATION TO EXTREME VALUE THEORY

Extreme Dependence: A Precise Definition

Let us consider the case of two markets with random returns denoted by X and Y. Suppose that one is interested in studying dependence between both markets. Most people would then estimate a standard (linear) correlation coefficient to describe such dependency or, which is the same thing, do a regression from one market's returns on the other market's returns. While this approach would seem natural, it shares a great chance to mislead its users, all the more that we want to analyse dependence in the tails of the distribution (for convincing expositions of the pitfalls of linear correlation see Embrechts et al., 1999, or Boyer et al., 1997). On the contrary, by its very nature, Extreme Value Theory (EVT) is directly adapted to this kind of question.

To motivate its use, let us introduce some notations. We denote by s the (return) threshold over which we speak of a market boom.[3] The question of dependence in the extremes does relate to quantities such as:[4]

$$\lim_{s\to\infty} \Pr\{Y>s|X>s\} \equiv \eta. \tag{4.1}$$

By definition, we have $0 \leq \eta \leq 1$. η measures the degree of asymptotic dependence, or loosely speaking the conditional probability that an extreme event, here a boom, occurs in market Y given that a comparable event has occurred in market X. If (X, Y) are perfectly dependent asymptotically (in the tails), then $\eta = 1$. On the contrary, (X, Y) are perfectly independent if $\eta = 0$ since then $\Pr\{Y > s|X > s\} = \Pr\{Y > s\}$ and $\Pr\{Y > s\}$ tends to 0 as $s \to \infty$.

While it seems quite intuitive, there exist some problems with this expression for η. Indeed unless marginal distributions of X and Y are comparable in the tails, that is $\Pr\{Y > s\} \approx \Pr\{X > s\}$, or unless raw data are transformed in such a way that the influence of marginals is removed – such as Frechet-transforms – it follows that:

$$\lim_{s\to\infty} \Pr\{Y>s|X>s\} \neq \lim_{s\to\infty} \Pr\{X>s|Y>s\},$$

if (X, Y) are asymptotically dependent. We clearly see that the asymptotic dependence differs when we change the conditioning asset while it should be invariant since it quantifies a same event. To bypass this problem, Straetmans (1998) has proposed a 'numeraire invariant' version of η, in the following way:

$$\lim_{s\to\infty} \frac{\Pr\{X>s,\ Y>s\}}{\Pr\{X>s \text{ or } Y>s\}} \equiv \eta. \tag{4.1$'$}$$

In practice we are interested in equivalent quantities but performed at finite levels of s. In other words, we are interested in the likelihood of extremal but bounded spillovers. Let κ ($\kappa = 0, 1, 2$) denote the number of simultaneous market crashes. The problem of extremal dependence between X and Y is related to the following conditional probability:

$$\lambda = \Pr(\kappa = 2|\kappa = 1) = \frac{p_1 + p_2}{p_{12}} - 1, \tag{4.2}$$

with: $p_1 = \Pr\{X>s\}$, $p_2 = \Pr\{Y>s\}$, $p_{12} = \Pr\{X>s \text{ or } Y>s\}$. λ denotes the conditional probability that a crash occurs in market Y given that a crash has occurred in market X. We see that it obviously relates to η defined in (4.1′) but here the probability is defined at finite levels of s.[5] From equation (4.2), we see that the problem of the estimation of a co-crash boils down to the estimation of three probabilities in two steps. In the first step, the univariate probabilities (p_1, p_2) are estimated. In the second step, we need to estimate the bivariate probability p_{12}.

Extreme Dependence: Theory and Estimation

To proceed with this two-step procedure, we rely on EVT methods along the lines of Straetmans (1998) or more recently of Hartmann et al. (2001). As stated in the introduction to this chapter, there exists a fairly large literature concerning probability characterizations or statistical models for univariate extremes, and also an important number of applications in finance. Here we briefly sketch the fundamental aspects of EVT applications in this context.[6] Mainly, EVT methods try to exploit the behaviour of the tails of the distribution. For financial returns, there is now extensive evidence, which history draws back at least to Mandelbrot (1963), that distributions are fat-tailed. In statistical terms this property implies that the tail of the distribution decreases very slowly (by a power law) while for other distributions it decreases exponentially (for example the normal distribution) and for others it is even bounded (for example the uniform distribution). More precisely, the defining characteristics of fat-tailed distributions is the regular variation property (where F denotes the distribution function):

$$\lim_{q\to\infty}\frac{1-F(qx)}{1-F(x)}=x^{-\alpha},\ \ x>0,\ \ \alpha>0. \tag{4.3}$$

In this case, F is said to be in the maximum domain of attraction of the Fréchet distribution which characterizes the tail behaviour of fat-tailed processes. Examples of distributions satisfying this condition are the Stable distribution, the Student-t distribution, the Pareto distribution, or the ARCH process. α is the crucial parameter: loosely speaking, it determines how fat the tails are. It also determines the number of finite moments of the distribution. Most EVT applications in univariate problems relate to the estimation of α, also called the tail index. Under the assumptions of independent observations and treating the slowly varying function as a constant for large values of X, we get the following MLE for $\gamma = 1/\alpha$:

$$\hat{\gamma}=\frac{1}{\hat{\alpha}}=\frac{1}{m}\sum_{j=0}^{m-1}\ln\left(\frac{X_{[n-j]}}{X_{[n-m]}}\right), \tag{4.4}$$

where $X_{[i]}$ denotes the ordered statistics, that is $X_{[1]}\leq X_{[2]}\leq\ldots\leq X_{[n-m]}\leq\ldots\leq X_{[n]}$. Equation (4.4) is known as the Hill (1975) estimator. The lower α (that is the larger γ), the fatter the tail of the distribution is. Asymptotically, γ is normally distributed with $\mathrm{Var}(\hat{\gamma})=\hat{\gamma}^2/m$ for m large. $X_{[n-m]}$ denotes the cut-off return above which we consider to be in the tail of the distribution. In practice, the choice of $X_{[n-m]}$, or equivalently the choice of the number m of ordered statistics considered in the tails, has serious implications for the results obtained. To summarize, we face a bias-variance trade-off: if $X_{[n-m]}$ is chosen too be too small (or equivalently, m is chosen to be too large), then we get too near the centre of the distribution and α is downward biased; on the contrary, if $X_{[n-m]}$ is chosen too be too large (or equivalently, m is chosen to be too small), then we are too far into the tails where observations are rather sparse, so that the estimator appears very volatile as results change a lot from adding or removing one observation. Here we have chosen to combine two methods to determine the value of m. The first is based on Monte Carlo simulations (see Jansen and De Vries, 1991, or Longin and Solnik, 2001). The second method is a pure graphical method, which is less precise but can be preferable to the former one in small samples (see for instance Embrechts et al., 1997 or Hartmann et al., 2001). This method consists in plotting the tail index for various levels of m and then choosing m^* in a region where the Hill estimator appears broadly constant, since in this case it resolves jointly to the problems of variance and bias.

If we get back to our purposes, we can infer excess univariate probabilities from the tail estimate, using the semi-parametric estimator proposed by De Haan et al. (1994):

$$\hat{p} = \frac{m}{n}\left(\frac{X_{[n-m]}}{q}\right)^{\hat{\alpha}}, \tag{4.5}$$

where q is a chosen quantile, satisfying the condition $q > X_{[n-m]}$. From equation (4.5), we clearly see one of the main advantage of EVT methods: the possibility to extrapolate probabilities far in the tails where observations are by nature very rare so that these probabilities are hardly estimable. In the world of finance, the industry has been revolutionized by the introduction of the VaR (Value at Risk) concept, which broadly consists in estimating the maximum loss that someone can suffer with a given probability when (s)he holds a financial asset (in statistical terms, it is simply a quantile). Armed with the tail index estimate from (4.4), VaR can be directly estimated by inverting (4.5):

$$\hat{q} = X_{[n-m]}\left(\frac{n}{m}p\right)^{-1/\hat{\alpha}}. \tag{4.6}$$

Next, we turn to the problem of estimating the joint probability p_{12} to infer the conditional probability of a co-crash λ. We need to estimate $p_{12} = \Pr\{X > s \text{ or } Y > s\}$. For this purpose, let us introduce some notations.

Suppose $F(X, Y)$ is the distribution function of the random vector (X, Y). We call:

$$D_F(u_X, u_Y) = F(F_X^{\leftarrow}(u_X), F_Y^{\leftarrow}(u_Y)), \quad 0 \le u_X, u_Y \le 1, \tag{4.7}$$

the tail dependence function of F and $F_i^{\leftarrow}(u_i) = \inf\{v \in R : F_i(v) \ge u_i\}$, $0 \le u_i \le 1$, $i = X, Y$, are the generalized inverse functions of F_X, F_Y. Through transformation (4.7), which is often called the Copula-transformation, the marginal distribution of F have been uniformized since u_X and u_Y are uniform variables defined over the [0,1] interval.

Now let us assume that there exists a function l_F such that for all $u_X, u_Y \ge 0$:

$$\lim_{t \to 0^+} t^{-1}\{1 - D_F(1 - tu_X, 1 - tu_Y)\} \text{ (exists)} = l_F(u_X, u_Y), \tag{4.8}$$

then l_F is called the Stable Tail Dependence Function (*STDF*) of F. Huang (1992) has shown that condition (4.8) holds whenever F belongs to the maximum domain of attraction of the Fréchet distribution. Its basic properties are the linear homogeneity, that is $l_F(vu_X, vu_Y) = vl_F(u_X, u_Y)$, and the fact that $l_F(u, 0) = l_F(0, u,) = u$. The STDF can be interpreted as an asymptotic dependence measure. Indeed one can show that (see Straetmans, 1998, or Embrechts et al., 2000):

$$\Pr_{t \to 0^+} (\kappa = 2 | \kappa = 1) = \frac{u_X + u_Y}{l_F(u_X, u_Y)} - 1. \tag{4.9}$$

The curvature of l_F totally determine the dependence structure between X and Y in the tail area.[7] In particular, we have the following inequality:

$$\max(u_X, u_Y) \le l_F(u_X, u_Y) \le u_X + u_Y. \tag{4.10}$$

Equality holds on the left-hand side if X and Y are completely dependent in the tail, while equality on the right-hand side obtains if X and Y are independent in the tail (in this case, we clearly see using (4.9) that the conditional probability of a co-crash is zero). All in all, the lower l_F, the higher is the probability of a co-crash.

Assuming that the univariate exceedance probabilities p_1 and p_2 are small enough (as they should be), the comparison of (4.9) and (4.2) shows that we can state that $p_{12} \approx l_F(p_1, p_2)$. Thus to estimate the conditional probability of a co-crash, we only need an estimator of the STDF. A route for this would to be specify a precise functional form using literature on copulas. In one of the few finance applications, this is for example what has been adopted by Longin and Solnik (2001) who rely on the Gumbel copula. However there exist many different copulas families and, to date, not enough work has been done in that field to retain one that seems tailor-made for economics and finance.[8] Here, following Hartmann et al. (2001) or Embrechts et al. (2000), we adopt the following non-parametric estimator:

$$\hat{l}_F(\hat{p}_1, \hat{p}_2) = \frac{n}{k}\frac{1}{n}\sum_{i=1}^{n} I\left\{X_i > X_{[n-[k\hat{p}_1]]} \quad \text{or} \quad Y_i > Y_{[n-[k\hat{p}_2]]}\right\}. \quad (4.11)$$

Basically, this estimator counts the observations which are in the tail area for at least one market, which is adapted to our purpose as we want to measure $p_{12} = \Pr\{X > s \text{ or } Y > s\}$. By definition, there are only a few observations in these cases. To increase the number of potential observations, Huang (1992) has proposed to exploit the linear homogeneity property of l_F by performing the following polar transformation of (4.11):[9]

$$\hat{p}_{12} = \hat{r}\hat{l}_F(\cos\hat{\theta}, \sin\hat{\theta}) = \frac{\hat{r}}{k}\sum_{i=1}^{n} I\left\{X_i > X_{[n-[k\cos\hat{\theta}]]} \quad \text{or} \quad Y_i > Y_{[n-[k\sin\hat{\theta}]]}\right\}, \quad (4.12)$$

where $\hat{\theta} = \arctan(\hat{p}_2/\hat{p}_1)$ and $\hat{r} = \sqrt{\hat{p}_1^2 + \hat{p}_2^2}$. The parameter k plays an equivalent role to m in the Hill estimator. In theory, it should be chosen such that k is large but k/n small.

DATA

Data comes from the composite indices computed by JP Morgan on the basis of emerging sovereign bonds (in US dollars). The first large emerging sovereign bonds were Brady bonds, issued at the beginning of the 1990s and created by titrization of previous defaulted banking debts. Due to the success of Brady bonds, several emerging countries have begun to issue debt on traditional Euromarkets, but it began to concern a widespread set of countries only in the middle of that decade. For this reason, we have chosen to concentrate on the time period covering 6 January 1995 to 4 January 2002. Returns are computed as the log difference between two consecutive observations of bonds indices. We have chosen a weekly frequency, rather than daily, since daily returns series appear very noisy and quite strongly autocorrelated. Moreover working with weekly data allows one to concentrate on more sustained crash phenomena which are assumed to have stronger effects on the real economy and financial institutions.[10]

Descriptive statistics for these returns are reported in Table 4.1. We see that on average weekly returns are positive which means that emerging bond have trended positively over the time period. This is mainly due to the

Table 4.1 Descriptive statistics for emerging bonds returns (6 January 1995–4 January 2002)

	Mean	Standard deviation	Min.	Max.	Skewness	Kurtosis	*JB*	ρ(1)	Q_R	Q_S
Composite	0.25	2.20	−17.14	7.49	−1.87*	14.92*	2377*	0.11	14.33*	30.98*
Argentina	−0.04	3.47	−25.64	9.22	−2.52*	16.91*	3336*	0.02	11.85	55.71*
Bulgaria	0.41	3.53	−29.60	13.64	−2.00*	19.25*	4274*	0.04	11.59	17.55*
Brazil	0.27	2.72	−17.50	10.45	−1.39*	10.61*	1000*	0.09	8.45	41.40*
China	0.19	0.74	−2.63	3.56	0.11	4.99*	61*	0.02	8.22	103.27*
Ecuador	0.27	4.40	−26.86	18.64	−0.80*	8.19*	449*	0.07	12.09	6.51
Korea	0.18	1.27	−11.53	6.86	−2.75*	32.36*	13 612*	0.18*	37.79*	34.45*
Morocco	0.25	2.52	−20.82	11.58	−2.22*	21.01*	5246*	0.04	15.90*	49.49*
Mexico	0.29	1.93	−11.34	6.59	−0.72*	8.38*	473*	0.06	4.37	97.80*
Nigeria	0.42	3.02	−20.01	9.29	−1.53*	11.95*	1366*	0.09	10.51	27.20*
Philippines	0.21	1.66	−9.12	8.18	−0.93*	11.13*	1060*	0.22*	24.90*	38.86*
Poland	0.29	1.51	−7.45	11.02	0.90*	15.38*	2385*	0.02	13.83	26.23*
Panama	0.39	2.56	−14.62	9.33	−0.68*	8.48*	486*	0.07	15.59*	62.78*
Peru	0.38	3.06	−15.25	11.60	−0.52*	6.78*	234*	0.08	6.29	46.51*
Russia	0.43	6.46	−54.04	37.25	−1.91*	20.36*	5362*	0.19*	34.22*	53.19*
South Africa	0.22	1.64	−10.50	14.22	−0.01	28.87*	9431*	−0.28*	35.06*	218.18*
Venezuela	0.34	3.09	−30.10	13.56	−2.53*	29.89*	11 420*	0.06	35.92*	25.28*

Notes:
The table presents descriptive statistics for weekly log composite bond returns (as %).
* denotes rejection of the null hypothesis at the 1% level of significance. *JB* denotes the Jarque-Bera statistic for the test of the null of normality.
ρ(1) denotes the first order autocorrelation.
The approximate threshold for 1% significance level is 0.13 in absolute value.
Q_R denotes the Ljung-Box statistic for the null of no autocorrelation of returns for lags 1 up to 5.
Q_S denotes the Ljung-Box statistic for the null of no autocorrelation of squared returns for lags 1 up to 5.

fact that our returns are total returns, that is they include coupons payments. The sole exception to this positiveness of the average return is Argentina, due to the crisis that this country experienced in the second part of 2001 which led it to default on its bonds. Indeed if we exclude the last year of the sample, the average return for Argentina is 0.27%.

Columns 3 to 5 reveal an interesting pattern. We clearly see that there exists some asymmetry in the returns in the sense that negative returns (*crashes*) appear more important that positive returns (*booms*). Indeed, the skewness coefficient is significant at the 1% level for 14 out of the 16 individual countries and for the composite index. To a certain extent, columns 3 and 4 show us that this skewness can be related to extreme returns since in general the minimum return is larger (in absolute terms) than the maximum return.

We also see that bond returns exhibit excess kurtosis. This result, which is standard in terms of financial returns, is generally interpreted as evidence of fat tails. While this is true in most of the cases, the excess kurtosis can also be generated by a strong concentration of returns around the centre of the distribution (that is the distribution is very peaked) without fat tails. This is one of the reasons why we need a more in-depth analysis of tail behaviour, and this is what we propose thereafter. Overall, we see that the null hypothesis of normality is easily rejected (see JB statistics).

Before turning to extreme value analysis, let us mention something about the dynamic structure of returns. We see that the hypothesis of an independent behaviour over time, which is very important in the use of extreme value tools, can be accepted with quite strong confidence (except maybe for Russia, Korea and South Africa). On the contrary the hypothesis of homoscedasticity is largely invalidated (see the Q_S statistics). It is well known that GARCH effects generate excess kurtosis. It is thus important to investigate the sensitivity of the results obtained to this heteroscedasticity (see for instance Kiesel et al., 2000, or Poon et al., 2001). To save space, the reported results are for raw returns only. Results for GARCH filtered returns are available in the working paper version of this chapter. What is important is that the main conclusions are not affected by the GARCH filtering.

UNIVARIATE RISK MEASURES

In this section, we discuss the results concerning the measures of univariate risks. The results are summarized in Tables 4.2 to 4.5.

Table 4.2 reports the estimates for the tail indices computed using the Hill formula (see equation 4.4). The table also gives information concerning the number of ordered statistics m^* used in these computations and also the way the thresholds are determined. On average, we took around 4.8% of the total

Table 4.2 Tail index estimates

	Left tail (negative return)			Right tail (positive return)			Equality test $\gamma_L = \gamma_R$	
	$\hat{\alpha}_L$	m_L^*	$X_{[n-m^*]}$	$\hat{\alpha}_R$	m_R^*	$X_{[n-m^*]}$	Stat	p-value
Composite	1.968	21 (a)	−2.973	4.062	8 (a)	3.991	1.858	0.032
Argentina	1.626	21 (a)	−4.763	2.827	14 (a)	4.516	1.592	0.056
Bulgaria	1.438	21 (b)	−3.594	3.039	21 (b)	5.068	2.183	0.015
Brazil	1.985	21 (a)	−3.624	3.773	9 (a)	4.887	1.692	0.045
China	3.185	15 (b)	−1.115	3.537	9 (a)	1.621	0.251	0.401
Ecuador	2.246	21 (b)	−6.110	2.608	21 (b)	5.818	0.482	0.315
Korea	1.369	21 (a)	−0.955	1.990	21 (a)	1.424	1.178	0.119
Morocco	1.884	21 (a)	−3.014	2.299	14 (a)	3.553	0.584	0.280
Mexico	1.746	21 (a)	−2.317	3.191	12 (b)	3.783	1.681	0.046
Nigeria	1.642	21 (a)	−3.517	4.015	12 (b)	5.480	2.381	0.009
Philippines	1.593	12 (b)	−2.605	2.630	14 (a)	2.747	1.190	0.117
Poland	1.380	13 (b)	−1.704	2.013	21 (a)	2.087	0.998	0.159
Panama	1.989	21 (a)	−3.238	2.944	14 (a)	4.546	1.145	0.126
Peru	2.396	28 (b)	−3.931	2.529	28 (b)	3.973	0.202	0.420
Russia	1.331	28 (b)	−5.958	2.596	28 (b)	6.806	2.295	0.011
South Africa	1.274	21 (b)	−1.425	1.935	21 (a)	1.815	1.307	0.096
Venezuela	1.938	31 (b)	−2.732	2.513	31 (b)	3.596	1.009	0.156

Notes:
The table presents tail estimates using the Hill estimator defined in (4.4).
m^* denotes the optimal number of returns involved in the computation which is determined using the Monte-Carlo simulation method (marked with (a)) or the graphical method (marked with (b)).
The last two columns report tail equality test, using the asymptotic approximation of γ, and its associated p-value.

observations for the right tail of the distribution and around 5.8% for the left tail. m^* varies a great deal among the countries and/or the tail considered: between 2.2% and 8.5% for the right tail, between 3.3% and 8.5% for the left tail. We also see that in about half of the cases, the value determined by the Monte Carlo simulation method has been supplanted by the graphical method. For most of these cases, the problem we have encountered with Monte Carlo results was that the values of m were too small, such that the estimator was in a region where the Hill estimator was too volatile. Comparing the results of Table 4.2 with those obtained for stock markets of industrial countries (see for example Hartmann et al., 2001, or Straetmans, 1998), one can see that the tails are much larger (α smaller) for emerging bonds. This seems to hold for both sides of the distribution. Apart from this

Table 4.3 *VaR estimates*

	$p = 0.01$			$p = 0.05$			$p = 0.95$			$p = 0.99$		
	Norm.	Emp.	EV	Norm.	Emp.	EV	Norm.	Emp.	EV	Norm.	Emp.	EV
Composite	−4.87	−6.33	−7.22	−3.37	−3.02	−3.19	3.87	3.37	3.26	5.37	4.70	4.84
Argentina	−8.10	−12.83	−13.95	−5.74	−5.20	−5.18	5.66	4.21	4.11	8.03	7.70	7.26
Bulgaria	−7.81	−11.21	−12.11	−5.40	−4.01	−3.95	6.21	5.23	5.30	8.62	8.89	9.00
Brazil	−6.06	−8.70	−8.74	−4.21	−3.77	−3.88	4.75	4.05	4.05	6.61	5.99	6.20
China	−1.52	−1.72	−1.74	−1.02	−1.03	−1.05	1.41	1.34	1.33	1.91	2.02	2.09
Ecuador	−9.97	−13.58	−13.30	−6.97	−6.19	−6.50	7.50	6.28	6.13	10.50	10.19	11.37
Korea	−2.76	−3.53	−3.42	−1.90	−1.01	−1.06	2.26	1.52	1.53	3.13	3.17	3.43
Morocco	−5.62	−8.15	−7.62	−3.90	−3.11	−3.24	4.41	3.40	3.16	6.13	6.87	6.37
Mexico	−4.20	−5.55	−6.30	−2.89	−2.37	−2.51	3.46	3.44	3.31	4.78	5.90	5.49
Nigeria	−6.60	−8.93	−10.19	−4.55	−4.17	−3.82	5.38	5.06	4.93	7.44	7.78	7.37
Philippines	−3.64	−6.29	−5.49	−2.51	−2.02	−2.00	2.94	2.63	2.48	4.06	4.74	4.58
Poland	−3.23	−4.10	−4.27	−2.20	−1.44	−1.33	2.77	2.21	2.23	3.80	4.86	4.97
Panama	−5.56	−8.39	−7.79	−3.81	−3.35	−3.47	4.60	4.12	4.15	6.34	7.23	7.17
Peru	−6.75	−7.39	−9.19	−4.66	−5.11	−4.69	5.41	5.12	4.70	7.50	8.24	8.88
Russia	−14.60	−19.13	−27.47	−10.20	−10.13	−8.20	11.05	7.87	8.02	15.46	14.31	14.90
South Africa	−3.61	−5.43	−5.61	−2.49	−1.81	−1.59	2.92	2.07	1.95	4.04	4.31	4.48
Venezuela	−6.85	−8.07	−8.23	−4.74	−3.36	−3.59	5.41	4.84	4.43	7.52	7.58	8.41

Notes:
The table presents VaR estimates for various quantiles and various methods: a normal distribution approximation, the empirical quantile and the implied quantile using the results of extreme value methods (see (4.6)).
All VaRs are expressed as % per week.

Table 4.4 Univariate tail probabilities for various thresholds (% per year)

Weekly return (as %)	−50	−30	−20	−10	10	20	30	50
Composite	1.15	3.15	7.01	27.41	2.72	0.16	0.03	0.00
Argentina	6.52	14.96	28.93	89.30	21.01	2.96	0.94	0.22
Bulgaria	6.77	14.11	25.28	68.50	37.81	4.60	1.34	0.28
Brazil	1.63	4.49	10.04	39.76	8.58	0.63	0.14	0.02
China	0.00	0.01	0.02	0.20	0.21	0.02	0.00	0.00
Ecuador	2.65	8.36	20.79	98.66	72.64	11.91	4.14	1.09
Korea	1.32	2.66	4.64	11.99	6.17	1.55	0.69	0.25
Morocco	1.50	3.93	8.44	31.16	18.43	3.75	1.47	0.46
Mexico	1.40	3.41	6.93	23.23	7.67	0.84	0.23	0.05
Nigeria	3.82	8.83	17.18	53.64	15.24	0.94	0.19	0.02
Philippines	1.54	3.47	6.63	19.99	6.66	1.08	0.37	0.10
Poland	1.75	3.53	6.18	16.07	12.74	3.16	1.40	0.50
Panama	1.29	3.56	7.98	31.67	19.54	2.54	0.77	0.17
Peru	0.90	3.06	8.08	42.49	38.55	6.68	2.40	0.66
Russia	23.43	46.26	79.35	199.66	146.48	24.22	8.45	2.24
South Africa	3.20	6.14	10.30	24.91	10.98	2.87	1.31	0.49
Venezuela	1.58	4.24	9.30	35.64	33.70	5.91	2.13	0.59

Notes:
The table presents univariate tail probabilities for various weekly returns thresholds. The probabilities are expressed as % per year, i.e. they correspond to probabilities inferred from (4.5) multiplied by a factor of 52. Due to this fact, some probabilities can be superior to 100%.

'level' effect, sovereign bonds share a common feature with more 'matured' markets: the asymmetry between both tails of the distribution. For all the countries involved and also for the Composite index, the left tail is larger than the right tail: the risk of a crash is more important than the 'risk' of a boom. In some sense, this point was already visible in Table 4.1, where we reported that for most countries, the minimum return is larger (in absolute value terms) than the maximum return. However as shown by the last two columns of Table 4.2, the difference is significant at the 5% level (one-sided test) in only six cases out of 17: Bulgaria, Brazil, Mexico, Nigeria, Russia and the Composite index.

Table 4.3 reports VaR levels for varying confidence probability using several methods. The first method (denoted by 'Norm') consists in a normal approximation (taking into account the mean and variance of the series), the second ('Emp') uses the empirical quantiles and the third the EVT ('EVT') approximation using formula (4.6). What is clear from Table 4.3 is that the normal approximation yields a very poor tool in fitting the tails. In

Table 4.5 Measures of dependence aggregated by countries

	λ_i for several returns thresholds			Other information	
	−30%	−20%	−10%	Average correlation coefficient	Average conditional probability using bivariate normal approximation(*)
Argentina	0.155	0.157	0.178	0.456	0.005
Bulgaria	0.176	0.192	0.209	0.573	0.006
Brazil	0.249	0.259	0.266	0.609	0.002
China	0.001	0.002	0.006	0.299	0.005
Ecuador	0.201	0.201	0.188	0.499	0.009
Korea	0.174	0.163	0.130	0.456	0.008
Morocco	0.283	0.284	0.276	0.592	0.013
Mexico	0.271	0.271	0.262	0.589	0.006
Nigeria	0.168	0.170	0.180	0.489	0.009
Philippines	0.189	0.183	0.167	0.475	0.002
Poland	0.217	0.204	0.195	0.504	0.009
Panama	0.218	0.216	0.216	0.522	0.010
Peru	0.216	0.218	0.214	0.494	0.006
Russia	0.074	0.082	0.099	0.483	0.005
South Africa	0.174	0.173	0.157	0.363	0.013
Venezuela	0.215	0.208	0.198	0.551	0.009

Note: (*) for a −10% return threshold.

comparison with other methods, the normal approximation overestimates the VaR for moderate probabilities ($p = 0.05$ or $p = 0.95$) but clearly underestimates the VaR for extreme probabilities ($p = 0.01$ or $p = 0.99$). Thus it does not constitute a useful tool for extreme risk management. Concerning the EVT approximation, it does a better job at fitting the tails of the distribution. There is no systematic tendency to underestimate or overestimate the empirical VaR. This does not preclude some differences between the fitted tails and the empirical tails.[11] These differences are mainly observed for the extremal part of the tail ($p = 0.01$), with important differences for Russia and to a lesser extent for Peru. If we except these countries, the absolute differences are less than 7% on average versus more than 25% for the normal approximation. For other probability levels, the absolute differences are less than 6% on average (including all countries) versus between 10% and 25% for the normal approximation.

Table 4.4 shows univariate probabilities based on EVT estimates computed on the basis of expression (4.5). These probabilities are reported as percentage per year (thus they have been multiplied by a factor of 52 since the frequency of data is weekly at the origin). Obviously the probabilities mirror the VaR estimates mentioned above. What is remarkable is that for some countries, these probabilities are enormous, in particular for the left tail. For instance, the 23.43% probability obtained for Russia for a −50% return means that every 4.3 (=1/23.43%) years on average the Russian bonds fell by more than 50% over one week. For comparison, with the normal approximation, such a probability is only of 3.0 10^{e-15}, which means that such an event appears only every 3.3 10^{e14} years. The probabilities allow us also to illustrate further the riskiness of the emerging bond markets relative to more matured markets. For example from the results of Hartmann et al. (2001) we know that the probability of −30% return for the US, which appears as the riskier stock market among the G5 ones, is slightly below 1% per year (note that their sample includes the October 1987 stock market crash). If we compare this result with the column −30% in Table 4.4, we clearly see that we can consider the risk in investing in emerging bonds is for most countries more prominent than the equivalent risk for the stock markets of industrial countries (see for example 3.15% for the Composite index).

By the way, we can wonder about what should be a good measure of risk among the measures offered by EVT, when the notion of risks relate to extreme events and in particular to the risk of facing a major loss. One first candidate would be the tail index α. In broad terms, we can say that the lower α the higher is the extremal risk. Indeed the tail index has been repeatedly used for comparison of risks among various markets and/or assets. However we think that this approach is misleading, at least in cases such as ours. When we look at the tail indexes estimates for the left-hand distribution, we observe that a country like Korea would appear as risky as Russia under such a measure. Now if we consider the thresholds under which the tail indexes are calculated, we can have some doubts that we talk about the same risks. Indeed the volatility of both markets has nothing in common. Obviously this point does not preclude that for certain comparisons the tail index does provide a good characterization of big loss risks (see for instance the fact that China has the largest tail index estimate) but we underline the fact that when individuals are too heterogeneous in terms of volatility one should take care with too literal an interpretation of the results. As shown by expressions (4.5) and (4.6) an obvious way to correct for that point is to concentrate on implied VaRs or implied probabilities since they correct for the level of the threshold which has been used.[12] Moreover with regard to the difficulties in determining the number of ordered statistics and sometimes the sensitivity of tail indices estimates to that number, such implied measures appear much more stable due to that correction.

Figure 4.2 gives some illustrations of the preceding points. In Figure 4.2a we jointly represent the Hill estimate for the left tail and the standard deviation of the returns. One might expect a negative relationship among these two measures. We clearly see that this is not the case with the exception that the location of the countries at both extremes of the spectrum (China and Russia) seems to be consistent. In Figure 4.2b we jointly represent the standard deviation and the VaRs at the 1% probability level. In this case, we have a near linear negative relationship which signifies that both measures give the same message concerning the hierarchy of risks among the group of countries. To a certain extent, this 'perfect' result is quite surprising since as we have stated in the introduction, we might expect the standard deviation to be a noisy measure of big losses risks. Maybe an explanation is that for the assets under study the extreme risks are so important and so frequent that they weight a lot on the standard deviation of the returns. Moreover, the conclusion should be lowered. Indeed due to the presence of Russia, the figure is very extended. For some countries which present similar standard deviation (see for example the countries with a standard deviation around 3%) the VaRs vary from −8.2% to −10.2%. In Figures 4.2c and 4.2d, we jointly represent the VaRs and the third and fourth moments of the distribution respectively. One should exercize great care with these plots since the results from Table 4.2 indicate that these higher moments have chances to be defined (at the 5% level; two-sided test) only for the Composite, China, Morocco, Nigeria, Philippines, Poland, Panama, Peru, Russia, South Africa and Venezuela concerning the third moment and only for China concerning the fourth moment. The plots clearly show that they do not share the same message in terms of hierarchy of risks than the VaRs, even if we might expect the contrary, due to the fact that in some respects the negative skewness and the excess kurtosis can be attributable to the fatness of the left tail of the distribution.

EXTREMAL DEPENDENCIES

In this section, we discuss the results concerning the measures of bivariate risks, that is we discuss the estimates of the conditional probability of a co-crash or a co-boom (see λ in equation 4.2). As we have 16 countries in our sample, we are left with 120 ($= 16 * (16-1)/2$) bivariate conditional probabilities for each returns threshold. To save space, we only report summarized measures.[13] For different returns thresholds, Figure 4.3 presents summary statistics on the estimated conditional probabilities.[14] For example the line entitled 'Max' represents the maximum conditional probabilities obtained for each of the returns thresholds. We see that some

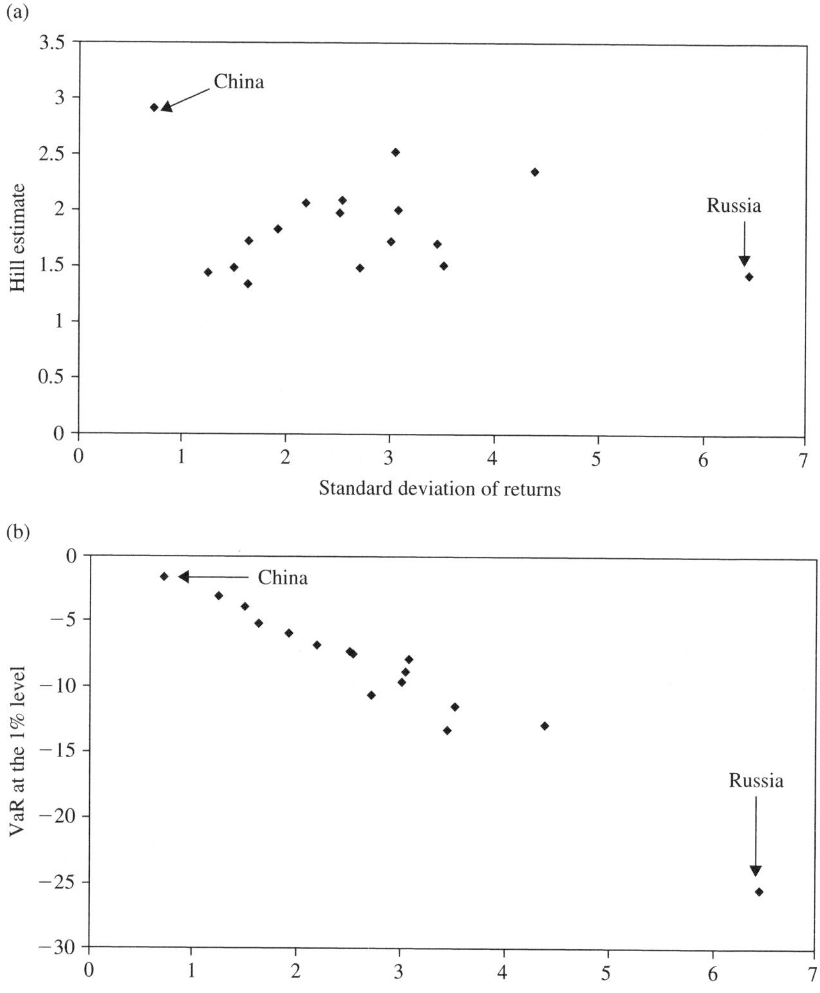

Figure 4.2 Left tail indexes, VaRs at the 1% level and empirical moments of the distribution of returns

conditional probabilities are enormous: given that a −50% crash has occurred in one country, the probability of observing a crash with the same magnitude is over 60% for some other countries. But as shown by the confidence interval (computed on the basis of the first and third quartiles of the estimated bivariate probabilities), these points appear as outliers. Indeed the median conditional probabilities are much lower (slightly less than 20%)

(c)

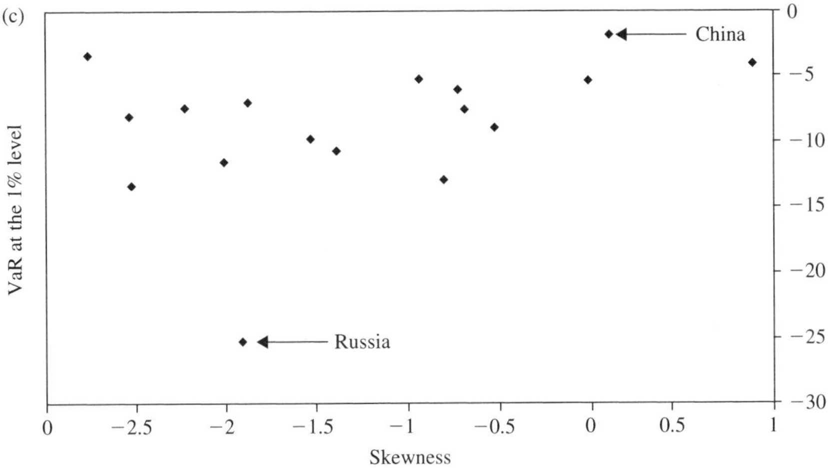

(d)

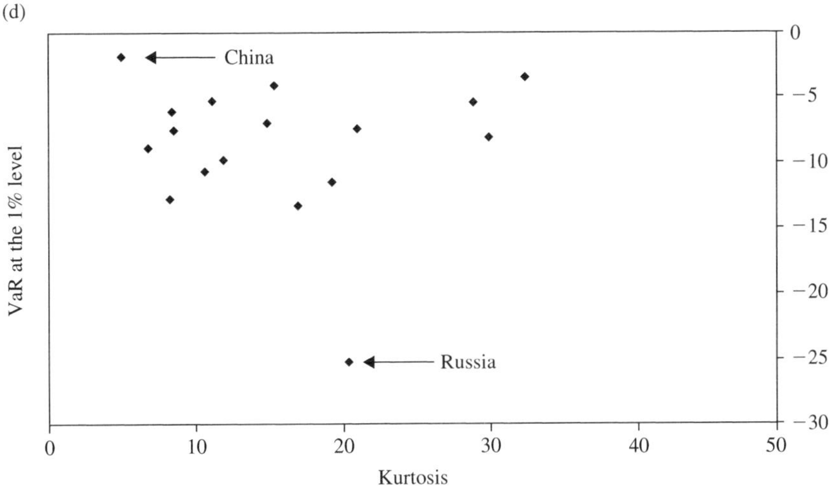

Figure 4.2 (continued)

and they seem comparable to the ones that Hartmann et al. (2001) have reported for the G5 stock markets. All in all, two main results emerge from Figure 4.3. First, whenever the return threshold is considered, conditional probabilities of a co-crash are far more pervasive than conditional probabilities of a co-boom. This result relates to the fact previously mentioned that there is more dispersion in maximum return dates than in minimum returns dates. Second, we observe that while conditional probabilities get

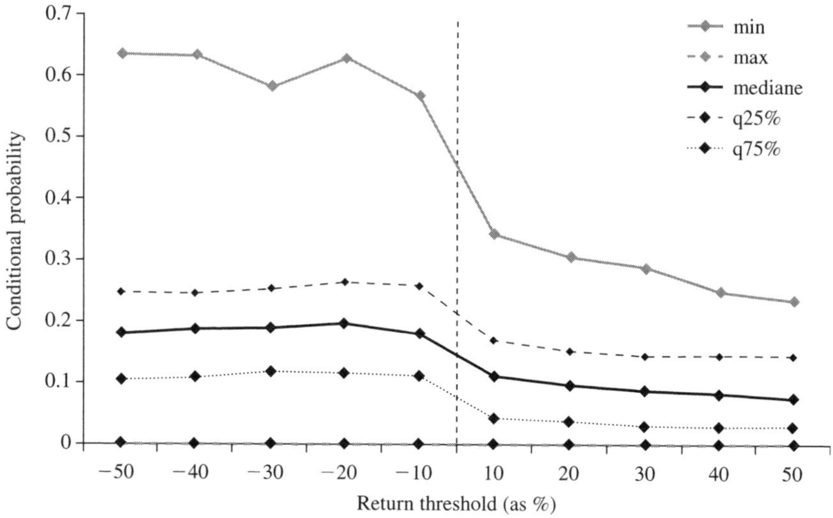

Note: For each return threshold, the figure presents summary statistics concerning the 120 bivariate probabilities.

Figure 4.3 Conditional probabilities of joint extreme variations for various returns levels

lower when we go further in the right tail, they seem stable when we go further in the left tail. This last result opposes that obtained by Longin and Solnik (2001) who have shown that correlation increases when we go further in the left tail of the distribution of G5 stock markets. On the contrary, we agree with their result on the right tail of the distribution.

In Table 4.5 we report results aggregated by country, that is if we denote by λ_{ij} the probability that a crash (or a boom) occurs in country i given that it has also occurred in country j, the table reports $\lambda_i = \Sigma_{j,\, j \neq i} \lambda_{ij} / 15$.[15] These aggregate values serve as measures of 'isolation': the lower λ_i, the less country i is concerned by extreme shocks whatever its origin. Remark that our measure does not tell anything about causality: λ_i can be large because country i is very exposed to shocks in other countries (that is, it is a follower in the crisis) or because country i is a major country whose difficulties put other markets in a turmoil (that is, it is a leader in the crisis). We report these aggregate values for several return thresholds. We see that they are fairly stable across these thresholds. In detail, we see that China appears as the most 'isolated' country. We also see that λ_i is rather small for Russia, despite the shock induced by the Russian crisis. In part this is due to the fact that for other countries, the major part of the shock has been rapidly reversed.

On the opposite part of the spectrum, we see that Brazil and Morocco appear as two of the less isolated countries.[16] Both cases are very different. Brazil is one of the largest issuers and it has the second rank (after China) in terms of GDP. Over the time period, it has known a severe crisis which led it to abandon its (crawling) peg to the US dollar, and spread to other emerging countries. It is thus natural to find an elevated value for $\lambda_{i\cdot}$. Morocco appears as a small country both from an economic point of view (in 1999, its US$ GDP was representing about 4% of Brazil's one) and from the point of view of emerging bond markets (less than 0.1% of the 1999 total debt outstanding for the countries of our sample). Then, the fact that λ_i is large cannot be attributable to its size. Rather it signifies that Morocco acts as a follower: when a shock occurs in one or some emerging countries, the probability that it translates to Morocco is high. This point is also illustrated by column 4 of Table 4.5 where we report the aggregate (average) correlation coefficient for each country: Morocco ranks second in terms of aggregate correlation while Brazil is first.[17] Looking in more detail, one can see that the dates of the four most extreme negative returns of Morocco coincide with the dates of the four most extreme negative returns of the Composite index.

We could infer indirectly from Table 4.5 that the correlation coefficient (which is easier to compute than our measure) would suffice as a dependence measure. Apart from the pitfalls underlined in the first section of this text, we think that this approach would be misleading for at least two reasons. First, while it is globally the case when we average them at the level of a country, it is not warranted that the correlation coefficient and the conditional probability do share the same message at the individual level. On the contrary, Figure 4.4 which jointly reports the 120 correlation coefficients and conditional probabilities (for a −20% return threshold) seems to indicate that there are some important discrepancies. This is typically the case for all the pairs of countries for which the conditional probabilities are near zero while the correlation coefficients range from 0.2 to over 0.5. Second, it is clear that both measures do not answer the same question. While correlation measures dependence for the whole distribution, the conditional probability measures dependence in the tails. Armed with correlation, we could answer the same question using correlation as an input (with mean and standard deviation of individual returns) in a bivariate normal framework. This is what we do in the last column of Table 4.5 for a −10% return threshold. We clearly see that using this framework, we would largely underestimate the probability of a co-crash. Thus we can conclude that while correlation can act as a preliminary tool for studying dependence in the tails of the distribution, one can not rely totally on the results obtained and more work is necessary.

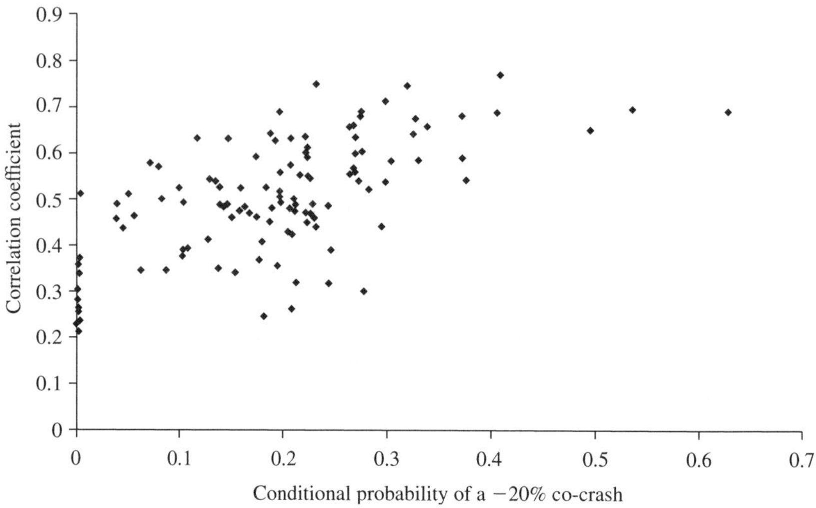

Figure 4.4 *Conditional probability of a –20% return co-crash and correlation coefficient*

EXTENSIONS

In this section, we provide two extensions to the previous results. First, we analyse the sensitivity of the results to sub-sampling. Second, we try to identify economic and financial determinants of the univariate and bivariate measures of risks.

Analysis Over Subperiods

To analyse the dependence of results on the period considered, we have decomposed the sample in three sub-periods with the same length: 6 January 1995 to 2 May 1997, 9 May 1997 to 3 September 1999 and 10 September 1999 to 4 January 2002. The results concerning the univariate probabilities (at the −20% return threshold) are reported in Table 4.6. For most of the countries, the pattern is the following: a sharp increase of the probability of a −20% return threshold from sub-period 1 to sub-period 2 (the average probability has been multiplied by 2.5) and then a sharp decrease of the probability for a crash from sub-period 2 to sub-period 3 (the average probability has reduced by 75%). Notable exceptions to this rule are Peru, for which the riskier period is the first sub-period, and Argentina, for which the last sub-period appears as the riskier one (Argentina defaulted at the end of 2001). Figure 4.5 presents the results for

Table 4.6 Univariate tail probabilities (as % per year) for a –20% return threshold

Period	Whole period (cf. Table 4.4) 06/01/1995–04/01/2002	06/01/1995–02/05/1997	09/05/1997–03/09/1999	10/09/1999–04/01/2002
Composite	7.01	2.82	10.78	0.77
Argentina	28.93	10.76	26.03	61.61
Bulgaria	25.28	28.30	34.22	0.03
Brazil	10.04	6.94	14.92	1.76
China	0.02	0.00	0.00	0.08
Ecuador	20.79	18.84	53.82	4.03
Korea	4.64	0.00	21.45	0.14
Morocco	8.44	7.03	16.62	3.96
Mexico	6.93	2.69	12.81	0.02
Nigeria	17.18	7.81	20.55	12.34
Philippines	6.63	0.93	3.01	4.05
Poland	6.18	0.29	7.06	0.01
Panama	7.98	14.13	14.36	0.01
Peru	8.08	37.85	7.87	13.46
Russia	79.35	48.32	153.14	1.18
South Africa	10.30	0.62	28.06	3.58
Venezuela	9.30	0.77	46.08	3.99

Notes:
The table presents univariate tail probabilities for various subperiods.
The probabilities are expressed as % per year, i.e. they correspond to probabilities inferred from (4.5) multiplied by a factor of 52. Due to this fact, some probabilities can be superior to 100%.

the bivariate conditional probabilities (for a −20% co-crash). We clearly see that they follow the same pattern than the univariate probabilities. The probability of a co-crash was fairly high in the second subperiod before sharply decreasing for most (82.5% of cases) of bivariate probabilities.

These obtained results are not surprising: sub-period 2 covers all major crises of recent years and particularly those which spread to the rest of the world (South-East Asia, Russia, Brazil). Sub-period 3 is characterized by crises which has remained isolated. The most relevant example is Argentina which has defaulted on a large part of its public sovereign debt (which was nearly US$130 billion) at the end of 2001. Surprisingly (given that Argentina was the biggest player at the beginning of 2001), the collapse of Argentina has to date benefited other emerging countries, including countries like Brazil which are economically exposed to the dramatic situation in Argentina. So we might think that the risk of joint crashes has declined over the recent period, due for instance to better discrimination of investors

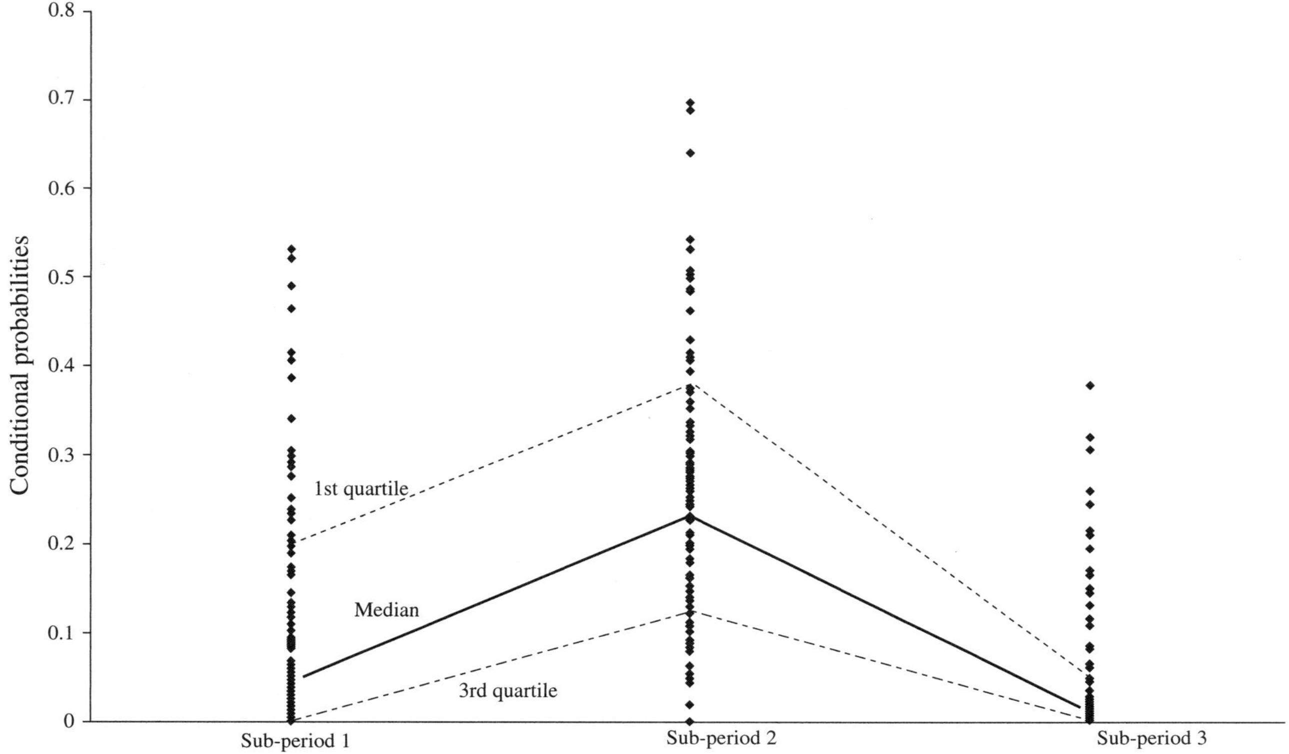

Figure 4.5 *Conditional probability of a –20% return for various sub-periods*

within the fundamental situation of emerging countries. However, this conclusion might be lowered as some non-structural effects might have played. First, the present period is marked by an economic slowdown (contrary to 1998) which implies that speculative (or risky) positions have been gradually closed during the year 2001. Second, contrary to the 1998 crisis, non-dedicated players (crossover funds) have left the market. Third, there was no surprise in the Argentina default since its probability was known to be fairly high for at least one year before it occurred.

Policy Implications

In this subsection we try to identify the determinants of the previous measures of risk, for both the univariate measures and the multivariate ones. Our approach is mainly tentative and should be pursued in further work. There is a large literature trying to identify economic and financial determinants of currency and banking crises (see among many others, Frankel and Rose, 1995; Kaminsky and Reinhart, 1996, Kaminsky et al., 1998, or Berg and Patillo, 1999) where crises are generally defined as qualitative variables (1 if crisis, 0 elsewhere) and macroeconomic variables are favoured. Our approach is comparable to these but at the same time it differs in several dimensions: our measures of risk are less specific and we concentrate on debt crisis, not on currency or banking crises. We also find in the literature some attempts to model the contagion effect (see for instance Glick and Rose, 1999; or Eichengreen et al., 1996). Here we contribute to this kind of analysis by putting into perspective the probability of contagion in emerging bond markets with some economic and financial determinants.

Let us begin with univariate risks. Table 4.7 presents the relationship between the (absolute value of) VaRs at the 1% probability level and some a priori determinants. In each case we report the correlation coefficient and the R^2 obtained from a regression of the VaRs of each country on a constant and the involved variable for each country. Since China appears as a particular country (see above), we consider results for all the set of countries and excluding China. As VaRs are expressed in absolute terms, the sign of the correlation should be interpreted in the following way: if the correlation is positive (respectively negative), the higher the value of the variable, the riskier (less risky) is the sovereign bond market of the country. The first six columns concern ratios which act as proxies to the sustainability, the importance of the debt or its composition. Four of these measures are correlated with the risks of a crash with the correct sign of the correlation (here, positive). In practice, only the two first variables can be considered as satisfactory determinants of risks, and unsurprisingly both are often taken

Table 4.7 *Economic and financial determinants of individual risks*

	Ratios						GDP in US$	Openness degree	Exchange rate regime
	Gov. bond debt to GDP	Gov. bond debt to total exports	Gov. bond debt to total bond debt	Gov. bond debt to total gov. debt	Short term gov. debt to GDP	Short term gov. debt to total exports			
All countries									
ρ	0.286	0.366	0.247	−0.060	−0.018	0.108	−0.149	−0.095	0.054
R^2	0.082	0.134	0.061	0.004	0.000	0.012	0.022	0.009	0.003
Excluding China									
ρ	0.188	0.306	0.289	−0.164	−0.113	0.057	0.079	−0.153	0.213
R^2	0.035	0.093	0.084	0.027	0.013	0.003	0.006	0.023	0.045

Note: For variable definitions, see the main text.

as measures of the debt sustainability. The three last columns present the impact of other variables on crash risks. Contrary to expectations, the correlation is negative for the size of the economy (proxied by GDP level in billion US dollars) or the openness degree. This means that the bigger the economy and the more open it is, the less it is exposed to a bond crisis. However this effect appears minor (see R^2 statistics) and fragile (for the first one) as it depends on the inclusion of China which is a big country in economic terms and whose debt market appears as the less risky one among the emerging countries considered here. The last column reports the impact of the exchange rate regime. This variable is a indicator variable taking values from 1 to 4, depending upon the degree of 'administration' of the exchange rate with 1 for purely floating exchange rate regimes to 4 for purely fixed exchange rate regimes (against the US dollar or a basket of currencies).[18] The positive correlation obtained for the whole panel of countries is thus interpreted as evidence that the more administrated the currency of the country, the more vulnerable the bond market. This is in line with expectations but we note that the effect seems small. In fact this smallness of the effect is again due to a 'China-effect' as shown by the bottom line of the panel. If we exclude China, for which exchange rates are fixed and the bond market appears quite safe, we see that the exchange rate regime is an important determinant of the vulnerability of the sovereign bond market.

The results for the probabilities of a joint co-crash (defined as the probability of a −20% return in both countries) are reported in Table 4.8. Again, these are differentiated by the inclusion or exclusion of China in the panel of countries. The first column analyses the relationship between the probabilities of a co-crash and the share of bilateral trade between both the countries involved relatively to their total trade. Clearly, the trade channel does not appear as an important factor in the probability of a co-crash.[19] The second column analyses the impact of the sizes of the economies involved. The idea behind this is that if one of (or both) the countries involved are important in economic terms, the probability of a co-crash should be important since the countries involved should not be perceived as isolated. Contrary to this expectation, the correlation is strongly negative. Again, it is a China-effect and if we exclude this country, the correlation is less negative but it is near zero such that the explanatory power of this variable is almost nil. The last columns summarize the impact of similarity measures. The idea behind this is that the closer involved the countries are, the higher is the probability of a co-crash. Three such variables appear as important factors. First, we see clearly see the regional nature of co-crashes. This resembles to what have been observed for currency crises (see for instance Glick and Rose, 1999) and challenges the previous results

Table 4.8 Economic and financial determinants of joint risks (cross-country co-crash)

	Sum of shares of bilateral trade in total trade	Sum of GDP	Measures of similarities			
			Same region	Both exchange-rate regimes are mainly fixed	Debt/GDP	Degree of openness
All countries						
ρ	−0.076	−0.397	0.204	−0.167	0.155	−0.169
R^2	0.000	0.158	0.042	0.028	0.024	0.029
Excluding China						
ρ	−0.016	−0.025	0.187	0.068	0.091	−0.150
R^2	0.000	0.001	0.035	0.005	0.008	0.023

Note: For variable definitions, see the main text.

concerning the impact of bilateral trade. Second, we also see the effect of similarities in indebtness: other things being equal, if both countries are largely indebted (relatively to the size of their economy), the probability that they are both affected by a simultaneous crash is higher. Third, we analyse the effect of the exchange rate regime. For this purpose, we have constructed an indicator variable which takes value 1 if both exchange rate regimes are mainly fixed (that is the univariate indicator of exchange rate regime is equal to or above 3; see above) and 0 elsewhere. We see that once we exclude China from the sample we have a positive correlation, which means that, other things being equal, the probability of a co-crash is more elevated when both countries have mainly fixed exchange rate regimes rather than the contrary. Note however that this effect is smaller than that for other measures of similarities.

CONCLUDING REMARKS

In this chapter, we have tried to characterize the risks of investing in emerging sovereign bond markets, both from a univariate (one country) point of view and a multivariate (portfolio of bonds) point of view. For this purpose, we relied on recent advances in EVT. These methods present several advantages over traditional techniques. Notably, they are more robust, and contrary to correlation or standard deviation they are tailored to the main object of interest (risks of extreme losses). This does not preclude some potential pitfalls, such as the fact that little is known about how to deal with dependent observations or the difficult choices of the thresholds employed in computations,[20] but undoubtedly EVT constitutes a promising field for risk management, which will become even truer once multivariate applications and techniques stabilize (probably following the development of finance-oriented research on copulas).

Among the numerous results that this chapter entails, we would like to underline a few. First, we have illustrated that emerging sovereign bond markets constitute a heterogeneous asset class in terms of univariate and joint risks. This means that representations of risk–return profiles such as in Figure 4.1 are too general to base decisions on. Second, while most emerging sovereign bond markets appear riskier than industrial stock markets, we have shown that both share a fundamental asymmetry between extreme risks on the negative side (crashes) and extreme risks on the positive side (boom). Moreover we have documented that this feature, which has been widely documented from an univariate point of view, translates to the multivariate one, confirming the results of Longin and Solnik (2001) on equity markets of industrial countries. Third, we have illustrated the fact that the risks associated with holding emerging bonds have largely fluctuated over time. In particular, since the end of 1999, the risk of contagion and also individual risks have largely reduced for most countries. Fourth, from a methodological point of view, we have repetitively shown that while measures drawn from the standard normal-gaussian framework (standard deviation and correlation) can serve as a preliminary tool for analysing extreme risks, the hierarchies of risks they imply are not strictly equivalent to the ones implied by EVT methods and they offer very unsatisfactory estimates of the importance of these risks. Fifth and finally, we have offered a preliminary analysis of the economic and financial factors behind crises in emerging bond markets. We have shown that the main determinants of the probability of a co-crash are geographical proximity, similarity in financial situations (notably in terms of sustainability of debt) and similarity in exchange rate regimes.

Future directions for research are various. For example, a more in-depth comparison of the characteristics of risks in emerging markets and in industrial countries would be interesting. One could also try to investigate better the implications of the results for international asset allocation, for example extending the result of Susmel (2001) in a multivariate framework. Finally, one could also try to fully model the dynamics of emerging markets sovereign bonds with copulas, in the way described by Patton (2001) or Rockinger and Jondeau (2001).

NOTES

* A more detailed version of this chapter has been presented in the conference Towards Regional Currency Areas in Santiago de Chile, 26–27 March 2002. We would like to thank the participants.

1. Note that the text of Koedijk et al. (1990) was written before the EMS crises of the early 1990s.
2. See moreover Susmel (2001) for a basic analysis of extreme value properties of emerging stock markets but a fine analysis of their implications in terms of international asset allocation.
3. We assume that the threshold is the same only to simplify notations.
4. All along this section, EVT and associated methods are presented such that we concentrate on the right tail of the distribution, that such that the extreme returns are the largest positive returns. Again, this is only for matters of simplification and the expressions directly apply to the left tail of the distribution, that is, the smallest negative returns, as $-\min(-X_1, -X_2, \ldots, -X_n) = \max(-X_1, -X_2, \ldots, -X_n)$.
5. The expression (4.2) follows directly from expression (4.1′) using the standard definition of conditional probability from which we know that $Pr\{X > s,\ Y > s\} >= Pr\{X > s\} + Pr\{Y > s\} - Pr\{X > s \text{ or } Y > s\}$.
6. Much more detail can be found in the book by Embrechts et al. (1997).
7. See Embrechts et al. (2000) for a nice graphical interpretation of the STDF.
8. See however Bouyé et al. (2000) for a large presentation of possible applications of copulas in finance.
9. The number of observations are increased due to the fact that in general $\cos\theta > p_1$ and $\sin\theta > p_2$.

10. See for similar arguments, Hartmann et al. (2001).
11. One might wonder why we compare fitted tails using EVT with empirical tails and could say that if the empirical tail seems to act as a benchmark it might be enough to calculate it. This approach would be misleading as when we go further in the tail, we have less and less data (for example with $n = 366$, we are unable to compute – except if we extrapolate – quantiles for $p = 0.001$ or $p = 0.999$). As stated before, it is one of the major interests of EVT techniques to allow us to compute quantiles for any probability level.
12. This result should not be interpreted as a emphasis of VaR as a risk measure in general. See for example, Artzner et al. (1997) on the limitations of VaR as a risk measure. Here our purpose is to underline that among measures offered by EVT tools, one should prefer implied VaRs rather than tail indexes.
13. The details of the 120 bivariate probabilities are available upon request from the authors.
14. For each return threshold and each pair of countries, we have chosen k to be equal to 37 (near 10% of the total observations). This choice appeared appropriate on the basis of a graphical analysis of the stability of the STDF. Note that the final results appear rather insensitive to this choice.
15. Due to the definition of λ in (4.1′), we have $\lambda_{ij} = \lambda_{ji}$.
16. Another important country in this perspective is Mexico whose case lies between those of Brazil and Morocco.
17. When we analyse the dates associated with the most extreme returns, we also see that the four most extreme negative returns of Morocco coincide with the dates of the four most extreme negative returns of the Composite index.
18. For the 16 countries, the exchange rate regime indicator variable breaks down as follows: 1 for Mexico and South Africa; 2 for Brazil, South Korea, the Philippines, Poland, Peru and Russia; 3 for Bulgaria, Ecuador, Morocco, Nigeria and Venezuela; and 4 for Argentina, China and Panama. Note that the exchange rate regime is evaluated along the whole sample period (1995–2001).
19. As stated before, our approach here is mainly tentative. We cannot exclude that other trade-related measures of dependence (see Glick and Rose, 1999) could lower or reverse our results.
20. See Diebold et al. (2000) for a comprehensive discussion of the dangers in the use of EVT.

REFERENCES

Artzner, P., F. Delbaen, J. Eber and D. Heath (1997), 'Thinking coherently', *Risk Magazine*, **10**, 68–71.

Berg, A. and C. Pattillo (1999), 'Predicting currency crises', *Journal of International Money and Finance*, **4**, 561–86.

Bouyé, E., V. Durrleman, A. Nikeghbali, G. Riboulet and T. Roncalli (2000), 'Copulas for finance – a reading guide and some applications', Working paper, GRO, Crédit Lyonnais; available with other related papers at the URL http://gro.creditlyonnais.fr.

Boyer, B., M. Gibson and M. Loretan (1997), 'Pitfalls in tests for changes in correlation', *International Finance Discussion Paper*, 597, Board of Governors of the Federal Reserve System.

Diebold, F., T. Schuermann and J. Stroughair (2000), 'Pitfalls and opportunities in the use of extreme value theory in risk management', *Journal of Risk Finance*, **1**, 30–36.

Eichengreen, B., A. Rose and C. Wyplosz (1996), 'Contagious currency crises: first tests', *Scandinavian Journal of Economics*, **98**, 463–84.

Embrechts, P., L. de Haan and X. Huang (2000), 'Modelling multivariate extremes', in P. Embrechts (ed.), *Extremes and Integrated Risk Management*, London: RISK Books, pp. 59–67.
Embrechts, P., C. Klüppelberg and T. Mikosch (1997), *Modelling Extremal Events*, Berlin: Springer-Verlag.
Embrechts, P., A. McNeil and D. Straumann (1999), 'Correlation: pitfalls and alternatives', *Risk Magazine*, May, 69–71.
Frankel, J. and A. Rose (1995), 'Currency crashes in emerging markets: an empirical treatment', *Journal of International Economics*, **41**, 351–66.
Glick, R. and A. Rose (1999), 'Contagion and trade', *Journal of International Money and Finance*, **4**, 603–17.
de Haan, L., D. Jansen, K. Koedijk and C. de Vries (1994), 'Safety first portfolio selection, extreme value theory and long run asset runs', in J. Galambos (ed.), *Proceedings from a Conference on Extreme Value Theory*, Dordrecht: Kluwer Press, pp. 471–87.
Hartmann, P., S. Straetmans and C. de Vries (2001), 'Asset market linkages in crisis periods', CEPR Discussion Paper, 2916, August (also available as a ECB Working Paper).
Hill, B. (1975), 'A simple general approach to inference about the tail of a distribution', *Annals of Statistics*, **3**, 1163–73.
Huang, X. (1992), 'Statistics of bivariate extreme values', Tinbergen Institute Research series, PhD Thesis 22, Erasmus University Rotterdam.
Jansen, D. and C. de Vries (1991), 'On the frequency of large stock returns: putting booms and bursts into perspective', *Review of Economics and Statistics*, **73**, 19–24.
Jondeau, E. and M. Rockinger (1999), 'The tail behaviour of stock returns: emerging versus mature markets', Banque de France, Working Paper No. 66.
Kaminsky, G., S. Lizondo and C. Reinhard (1998), 'Leading indicators of currency crises', *IMF Staff Papers*, 45, pp. 1–48.
Kaminsky, G. and C. Reinhard (1996), 'The twin crises: the causes of banking and balance-of-payments problems', *International Finance Discussion Paper*, 544, Board of Governors of the Federal Reserve System.
Kiesel, R., W. Perraudin and A. Taylor (2000), 'An extreme analysis of VaRs for emerging market benchmark bonds', working paper, Birbeck College.
Koedijk, K., M. Schafgans and C. de Vries (1990), 'The tail index of exchange rate returns', *Journal of International Economics*, **29**, 93–108.
Longin, F. (1996), 'The asymptotic distribution of extreme stock markets returns', *Journal of Business*, **69**, 383–408.
Longin, F. and B. Solnik (2001), 'Extreme correlation of international equity markets', *Journal of Finance*, **56**, 649–76.
Lux, T. (2001), 'The limiting extremal behaviour of speculative returns: an analysis of intra-daily data from the Frankfurt Stock Exchange', *Applied Financial Economics*, **11**, 299–315.
Mandelbrot, B. (1963), 'The variation of certain speculative prices', *Journal of Business*, **36**, 394–419.
Patton, A. (2001), 'Modelling time-varying exchange rate dependence using the conditional copula', University of California at San Diego, working paper 01-09.
Poon, S-H., M. Rockinger and J. Tawn (2001), 'New extreme-value dependence measures and finance applications', Lancaster University, preprint.
Rockinger, M. and E. Jondeau (2001), 'Conditional dependency of financial series: an application of copulas', Cahier de Recherche du Groupe HEC, 723/2001.

Starica, C. (1999), 'Multivariate extremes for models with constant conditional correlations', *Journal of Empirical Finance*, **6**, 515–33.
Straetmans, S. (1998), 'Extreme financial returns and their comovements', Tinbergen Institute Research series, PhD Thesis 181, Erasmus University Rotterdam.
Susmel, R. (2001), 'Extreme observations and diversification in Latin American emerging equity markets', *Journal of International Money and Finance*, **7**, 971–86.

PART II

Exchange rate regimes and regional currency areas in emerging countries

5. Financial vulnerability and exchange rate regimes in Latin American and Asian emerging countries: towards new criteria?

André Cartapanis and Vincent Dropsy

INTRODUCTION

Many countries in Latin America and East Asia liberalized their financial markets in the early 1990s and suffered severe currency crises later in that decade. As a result of these violent speculative attacks, most of these emerging nations appeared to have *de jure* selected 'corner solutions' (free floats, hard pegs) as their official exchange rate regime. Fischer (2001) presents initial evidence of a trend towards this bipolar view 'for countries open to international capital flows'. However Masson (2001) concludes that intermediate regimes 'will continue to constitute a sizable fraction of actual exchange rate regimes'. Indeed a closer investigation reveals that many developing countries have *de facto* implemented 'intermediate solutions' (managed floats, target zones, bands, crawling pegs) as their actual exchange rate regime. In this context, there are three types of issues when analysing the choice of an exchange rate regime and its sustainability.

First, this type of study should not be based solely on official (*de jure*) classification of exchange rate arrangements, but also on actual (*de facto*) exchange rate regimes to obtain sensible results. Levy Yeyati and Sturzenegger (2001) produce a *de facto* exchange rate regime classification in five categories (1 = inconclusive; 2 = pure float; 3 = dirty float; 4 = dirty float/crawling peg; 5 = peg) based on the volatilities of exchange rates, exchange rate changes and international reserves. They not only conclude that it is significantly different from the *de jure* exchange rate regime classification provided by the IMF, but also uncover evidence that the durability of a peg, rather than its rigidity, matters in terms of economic performance. Poirson (2001) creates an index of *de facto* exchange rate flexibility based on the ratio of exchange rate absolute percentage changes to absolute variations in international reserves normalized by the monetary base, and finds that the choice of an exchange rate regime is based not only on traditional economic criteria, but also on political factors. In this chapter we use Poirson's index of nominal exchange rate flexibility, but also derive an index of real exchange rate flexibility to improve the determination and analysis of *de facto* exchange rate regimes.

Second, the factors behind the choice of an exchange rate regime should not be limited to the traditional criteria of optimum currency area (OCA) theory. Indeed the liberalization of emerging financial markets in the early 1990s has produced new vulnerabilities amongst developing nations and new risks of exchange rate regime collapse. Currency crises now occur not only as a result of macroeconomic disequilibria (first generation crises of the 1980s), but also as a result of self-fulfilling expectations and contagion effects coupled with financial fragilities (second and third generation crises of the 1990s). In addition to traditional OCA criteria, the choice of an exchange rate regime should include new macro-financial variables, such as the degree of financial liberalization and the vulnerability to external financial shocks (Domaì and Martinez Peria, 2003; Wagner, 2000). For example Poirson (2001) finds that the significant determinants of a choice of exchange rate regime include capital mobility, product diversification, adequacy of reserves, external financial vulnerability, political uncertainty, government temptation to inflate, dollarization and exposure to exchange rate risk. Her results also indicate that traditional OCA criteria, such as economic size and inflation, are significant, but others, such as trade openness, dominant trading partner and economic development level, are not. In our empirical section, we use a set of new macro-financial factors (for example external indebtness, exposure to speculative contagion, ratio of foreign direct to portfolio investment, volatility of capital flows, recent currency crises) which could play a crucial role in the credibility of exchange rate policies of emerging countries.

Third, the issue of transition and convergence from an old to a new exchange rate regime is particularly important for emerging economies since it is likely to take place via an intermediate and less sustainable regime (Hochreiter et al., 2002). This is obviously a more significant issue for a convergence towards a currency area than a float. In particular, discussions about a possible Latin American or Asian currency area have surfaced, following the major currency crises recently experienced by emerging economies in these regions (Berg et al., 2002). For example, Eichengreen and Bayoumi (1999) raise the question of an OCA for Asia, and Williamson (1999) argues in favour of a basket peg. Although these proposals were apparently made before the Asian crises, they are even more relevant today, as argued by Bénassy-Quéré and Cœuré (2000). Indeed the Chiang Mai Initiative, presented at the January 2001 Asia and Europe Finance Ministers' Meeting, suggests that ASEAN countries could adopt an intermediate exchange rate regime (for example a target zone), in preparation for the creation of a permanent regional currency area in the future (Cœuré, 2002). The transitory regime would enable these countries to gain credibility before taking the final step towards a monetary union. In any case it is clear that an analysis of exchange rate regimes should take into account their dynamics. It should be noted that Poirson's results only apply to a static choice (based on a cross-section of nations in 1998) and not to a dynamic selection (for example exit strategies). In this study we use panel data over 25 years and more than 100 countries to analyse the dynamics of *de facto* exchange rate regimes.

In the second section, we re-examine the criteria for choosing an exchange rate regime, while stressing the need to take into account new factors of financial vulnerability. In the third section, we review the list of traditional OCA criteria and propose new (macro-financial) determinants of *de facto* exchange rate regimes. We also construct and use an index of real exchange rate flexibility to measure the degree of real exchange rate targeting (for example crawling peg or target zone), in addition to the index of nominal exchange rate flexibility created by Poirson. In the fourth section, we present an empirical study of the dynamics of *de facto* exchange rate regimes, based on panel data covering more than 100 countries over the post-Bretton Woods era. One major benefit of this dynamic analysis (via an error correction model) is that the long-run determinants of exchange rate regimes can be indirectly estimated, along with the speed of convergence towards these regimes.

EXCHANGE RATE REGIMES AND FINANCIAL VULNERABILITY

A New Debate on the Choice of an Exchange Rate Regime

The arguments in the long-standing debate about fixed vs. flexible exchange rates have not radically changed since the demise of the Bretton Woods system in 1973, or despite discussions of possible reforms (IMF, 1984): these arguments still focus on the optimal conditions for macroeconomic adjustments in an open economy and on the limits of economic policies in these conditions. The benefits of fixed rates include less uncertainty, in the form of lower exchange risk, and thus smaller risk premiums, cheaper access to international capital markets, lower interest rates (spreads over LIBOR), as well as lower likelihood to monetize budget deficits, and so on. On the other hand, the costs of fixed rates consist of weaker credibility (except in the case of currency boards), higher risks of currency crises and subsequent sharp recessions, strong dependence of monetary policy on the anchor country, greater vulnerability to external shocks as well as to internal real shocks, and potential exchange rate overvaluations leading to deterioration of trade balances and unemployment rates. Vice versa, the benefits of flexible rates involve the neutralization of the impact of external or real shocks through exchange rate changes, and the absorption of the effects of higher inflation on external competitiveness. The costs of flexible rates include the risk of imported inflation, the reduction of trade or financial transfers due to higher exchange rate volatility, the possibility of regional competitive devaluations, the absence of incentives for adjustment policies or structural reforms.

However, new theoretical arguments have appeared in recent discussions (Frankel, 2003). In a political economy framework, some authors (Edwards, 1996; Poirson, 2001; Méon and Rizzo, 2002) compare the political costs of macroeconomic adjustments in various exchange rate regimes. Calvo and Reinhart (2002) focus on the 'fear of floating', that is the counterproductive effects of floating exchange rates on foreign currency denominated external indebtness. Other authors (Mundell, 1961, 2000; Honkapohja and Pikkarainen, 1994; Rizzo, 1998; Ricci, 1997) rely on optimum currency area theory to find rational justifications for membership in a currency area (and thus for pegged exchange rates to major trading partners).

Yet the new debate on the choice of an exchange rate regime first appeared and developed as a result of empirical developments in emerging economies (that is currency crises in the 1990s) rather than theoretical arguments (Rogoff et al., 2003). On the one hand, econometric studies (Rizzo, 1998; Berger et al., 2000; Poirson, 2001; Juhn and Mauro, 2002) have integrated numerous explanatory variables in models based on previously mentioned theories to estimate the determinants of exchange rate regimes. On the other hand, the direction of empirical studies has been unavoidably affected by the multiplication of currency crises, first in Europe in 1992–93 and later amongst emerging countries, for example Mexico in 1994–95, Thailand and its Asian neighbours in 1997–98, Russia in 1998, Brazil in 1999, Turkey in 2001 and recently Argentina in 2002. In every case, speculative attacks on these nations' currencies have put an end to exchange rate regimes (based on fixed rates, crawling pegs or target zones), but the traditional 'first-generation' models, that focused on recurrent disequilibria or macroeconomic shocks, were unable to explain these currency crises. Self-fulfilling expectations and multiple equilibria were invoked as a potential cause of exchange rate crises in 'second-generation' models, but these models remain difficult to test empirically. Recent research appears to indicate that microeconomic weaknesses in the banking and financial systems are the most probable sources of these currency crises, renamed 'inter-generational' crises (Flood and Marion, 1999), 'balance sheet' crises (Dornbusch, 2001), 'third-generation' or 'twin' crises (Pesenti and Tille, 2000; Krugman, 2001; Cartapanis, 2004).

In these conditions, the debate on exchange rate regimes had no choice but to focus on financial liberalization and the explosive evolution of capital flows towards emerging countries in South-East Asia and Latin America, as well as on the consequent vulnerability of pegs and target zones. Indeed all exchange rate regimes, *de jure* or *de facto*, are related not only to normative factors such as the preferences of policy-makers (Jadresic et al., 2001), but also to positive factors such as their macroeconomic (un)sustainability. It is no surprise that empirical studies have rediscovered the implications of Mundell's 'impossible trinity': only 'corner solutions', that is pure floats or hard pegs (currency board or dollarization), would be sustainable in this context of high capital mobility; vice versa, intermediate regimes would be intrinsically weak (Fischer, 2001). However the latter view is not shared by all. Some authors contend that intermediate regimes can be not only sustainable, but also beneficial for emerging economies, despite their financial weaknesses (Bénassy-Quéré and Cœuré, 2002; Masson, 2001). On the other hand, Frankel (1999) considers that 'no single currency regime is right for all countries or at all times'.

Consequently, understanding the choice of an exchange rate regime and evaluating its sustainability in a world of high capital mobility requires new macro-financial criteria.

On the Need for New Macro-financial Criteria

Econometric studies related to the choice of an exchange rate regime typically use logit models (due to the multinomial nature of the dependent variable) on cross-sectional or panel data and usually include explanatory variables that are often (but not always) related to various theories. For example Poirson (2001) selects her indicators from three sources: optimum currency area theory, political economy, and 'fear of floating' models. Bénassy-Quéré and Cœuré (2002) and Méon and Rizzo (2002) combine political factors and structural variables while taking into account the macroeconomic volatility. Juhn and Mauro (2002) use four types of determinants: optimum currency area criteria, indicators of capital flows, macroeconomic variables, and historical or institutional factors.

More generally, variables related to international capital movements, financial liberalization, foreign currency-denominated external debt, or other factors of financial vulnerability are often ignored in studies about exchange rate regimes. This is surprising since these factors have played an important role in currency crises, and thus in changes of regimes in the 1990s. Furthermore if the credibility of a peg or a target zone depends on some of these factors of financial vulnerability, then policy-makers should rationally take them into account when selecting an exchange rate regime. This rationale should apply as much in periods of stability, when a long-term development strategy or macroeconomic adjustment policy (including the choice of an exchange rate regime and capital account liberalization procedures, according to the 'sequencing' model) is defined, as in periods of currency crises, when exit strategies need to be quickly delineated. However it appears that the contradictory nature of the two objectives of stable exchange rates and financial liberalization were ignored in the early 1990s (Eichengreen, 1998; Wyplosz, 2001; Edwards, 2001).

Nevertheless some macro-financial criteria have been integrated in recent empirical analyses on exchange rate regimes: degree of *de facto* openness to capital movements, inclusion in the list of emerging stock markets (Juhn and Mauro, 2002); index of capital controls (Edwards, 1996; Frieden et al., 2000; Bénassy-Quéré and Cœuré, 2002; Poirson, 2001; Juhn and Mauro, 2002); ratio of foreign currency deposits to M2, ratio of bank debt in own currency to total bank debt, ratio of international debt securities issued in own currency to total issued, index of openness to international capital flows (Poirson, 2001); external debt (Rizzo, 1998; Berger et al., 2000).

Unfortunately econometric test results do not appear to be stable or robust. The stock of external debt is significant and positively related to floating in Berger et al. (2000), but not in Rizzo (1998). The index of capital controls increases the probability of intermediate regimes in Bénassy-Quéré and Cœuré (2002), but it raises the probability of floating in Frieden et al. (2000), and diminishes it in Poirson (2001). The degree of international capital mobility and the exposure to exchange risk are both positively correlated with *de facto* flexibility in Poirson (2001). However the variables that relate to *de facto* liberalization of international capital movements or capital controls are in general not significant or robust across samples or countries in Juhn and Mauro (2002).

Beyond the lack of robustness of these relationships or the lack of reliability of the proxies, there is another complementary point to be made about explanatory variables. Relative to the wealth of indicators of vulnerability used in the literature on currency crises (warning signals), the list of macro-financial determinants of exchange rate regimes seem far from exhaustive. For example Kaminsky et al. (1998) found more than 100 warning indicators, covering various aspects of the vulnerability to speculative attacks (and thus potentially characteristic of changes of exchange rate regimes from fixed to floating): stock and structure of external financial commitments, indicators of domestic banking weakness, institutional or political factors related to supervision and financial liberalization, and structure of external debt repayments. To which we could add the exposure to speculative contagion (Cartapanis et al., 2002). In these conditions it is important to take into account new macro-financial criteria that could have an effect on the choice of *de facto* exchange rate regimes (in particular among emerging countries in Asia and Latin America) and consequently on the vulnerability of intermediate exchange rate regimes to financial shocks, whether they are domestic or external.

METHODOLOGY

Before presenting the various macro-financial variables that could potentially explain *de facto* exchange rate regimes, we need to define indicators of the actual flexibility of these regimes. The first methodological step in this study is therefore to construct two indexes, which could characterize the flexibility of nominal or real exchange rates:

1. The first index of nominal exchange rate flexibility (FLN), proposed by Poirson (2001), approaches zero when the nominal exchange rate is pegged to a key currency and/or when international reserves are volatile due to foreign exchange intervention on the part of the central bank to defend a parity. Vice versa, the index will take large values when the nominal exchange rate is volatile and/or when international reserves are stable due to the lack of foreign exchange intervention in a floating exchange rate regime.
2. The second index of real exchange rate flexibility (FLR) is close to zero when the central bank targets the real exchange rate (as in a crawling peg, when the nominal exchange rate is pegged to the inflation differential with a key currency) and/or when international reserves are volatile due to foreign exchange intervention on the part of the central bank to defend a sliding parity. Vice versa, the index will take large values when there is no such targeting or foreign exchange intervention (as in a floating exchange rate regime).

The two exchange rate flexibility indexes are defined in annual terms (based on a summation over monthly data) as follows:

$$FLN^i = \Sigma_{k=0 \text{ to } 11} (|NX^i_{t-k} - NX^i_{t-1-k}|) / NX^i_{t-1-k} / (\Sigma_{k=0 \text{ to } 11} (|IR_{t-k} - IR_{t-1-k}|) / MB_{t-1-k}) \quad (5.1)$$

and

$$FLN^i = \Sigma_{k=0 \text{ to } 11} (|RX^i_{t-k} - RX^i_{t-1-k}|) / RX^i_{t-1-k} / (\Sigma_{k=0 \text{ to } 11} (|IR_{t-k} - IR_{t-1-k}|) / MB_{t-1-k}) \quad (5.2)$$

where NX^i = nominal exchange rate relative to the anchor currency i (where an increase in the nominal exchange rate corresponds to an appreciation of the local currency).
$RX^i = NX^i * P/P^i$ = real exchange rate relative to the key currency i.
P = consumer price index of the country
P^i =consumer price index of the anchor country
IR = international reserves
MB = monetary base

Initially, we selected three anchor currencies, the US dollar, the euro (proxied by the Deutschemark, arguably the core currency of the EMS before 1999), and the Japanese yen, given their importance in the international monetary system. In addition, we use the trade weights (exports to the US, to the 'EU 6' founders of the European Community [Belgium, France, Germany, Italy, Luxembourg, Netherlands], and to Japan) of each country studied to build effective exchange rates and flexibility indexes, both in nominal and in real terms. As a result we obtained a total of eight indexes of exchange rate flexibility (nominal and real vs. four anchors). However preliminary investigation revealed that as well as the euro, also the yen was not used as an anchor currency in Latin American and Asian emerging countries. As a result we only present the empirical results for the (four) indexes of nominal vs. real, and dollar-based vs. effective exchange rate flexibility.

The second step in this study is to select indicators for the new macro-financial criteria of *de facto* exchange rate regimes. The financial liberalization that has occurred in many developing countries has produced some expected benefits, but it has also generated some unexpected risks, as demonstrated by the Tequila and Asian crises among others. As argued above, it is reasonable to assume that traditional OCA criteria are not sufficient any more to explain the choices of exchange rate regimes. After rapidly reviewing these OCA criteria and the proxies we use in the econometric study, we will introduce selected indicators of macro-financial vulnerability, whose effects will be estimated in the empirical section.

Our traditional OCA explanatory variables include:

- Inflation differential (with the anchor country or basket). A fixed exchange rate requires similar rates of inflation in the pegging and anchoring countries to be sustainable. Otherwise, persistent or high inflation differentials would cause the local currency to appreciate in real terms, the current account balance to deteriorate, and international reserves to decrease until a speculative attack forces the government to devalue its currency. In a static model we would expect the inflation differential to be positively correlated with the nominal exchange rate flexibility index, but negatively with the real exchange rate flexibility index (higher inflation also means a stronger need for a crawling peg). However in a dynamic model it is not clear if higher inflation will cause the government to float (higher nominal or real exchange rate flexibility index) or to peg (for example exchange rate-based stabilization plan and lower nominal exchange rate flexibility) or to crawl (for example monetary-based stabilization plan and lower real exchange rate flexibility).
- Growth symmetry (with the anchor country or basket). Asymmetric shocks (for example Germany's reunification) can create tensions between the economic (for example monetary) policies of the two nations, and ultimately lead to unsustainable inflation or interest differentials. This concept is proxied by the correlation (over a ten-year period) of real GDP growth between the local and anchor countries. As a result we expect a negative relationship between this growth symmetry variable and the index of exchange rate flexibility (less symmetric shocks means more floating).
- Trade geo-concentration (with the anchor country or basket). The benefits of a fixed exchange rate increase with trade integration with the anchor country. As a result we expect the share of exports to that trade partner in total exports (proxy for trade geo-concentration) to be negatively correlated with its exchange rate flexibility index.
- Trade openness. A greater dependence on foreign trade is a similar argument for pegging a currency, to avoid the costs of exchange rate volatility. We expect our proxy, the sum of exports and imports of goods and services over GDP, to be also negatively correlated with the index of exchange rate flexibility.
- Relative economic size. A small economy is more likely to depend on large foreign markets and to peg its exchange rate for similar reasons. Since our proxy is the ratio of the local country's GDP to the anchor

country's GDP (both calculated in PPP-adjusted US dollars to avoid disruptive effects of currency volatility), it is expected to be positively correlated with the exchange rate flexibility index.

- Trade sectoral structure. A country strongly dependent on trade in primary products would avoid pegging its currency to allow the exchange rate to adjust in order to become less vulnerable to terms of trade fluctuations. Our proxy for such trade sectoral structure is the country's share of agricultural, food, fuel and ores in total exports. It is therefore expected to be positively correlated with the exchange rate flexibility index.

Our new macro-financial vulnerability factors include:

- Financial openness. International capital mobility has an effect on the choice of fiscal and monetary policies, as demonstrated 40 years ago by Mundell and Fleming, but also on the selection of an exchange rate regime, as suggested by the events of the 1990s following the financial liberalization in emerging countries. More specifically, the recent currency crises imply that capital account liberalization promotes floating. As a proxy for financial openness, we use the ratio of gross capital flows to GDP. We expect our proxy to be positively correlated with its exchange rate flexibility index.
- Financial depth. A more mature domestic financial system tends to make fixed exchange rates less necessary, since it can better weather the effects of currency fluctuations. Our proxy for financial depth, the ratio of liquid liabilities (M3) to GDP, is therefore expected to be positively correlated with the exchange rate flexibility index.
- External financing structure. Given that portfolio investment is the more volatile part of international capital flows, the structure of external financing matters for the choice of exchange rate regimes. A higher ratio of foreign direct investment to total capital inflows will ensure less vulnerability to capital movements and less 'fear of floating'. As a result, we expect our proxy to be positively correlated with its exchange rate flexibility index.
- External financing needs. The current account balance as a ratio of GDP is an indicator external financial needs and vulnerability to foreign investors' mood swings. It is also a crucial factor in deciding whether to peg (and risk a currency crisis if the current account deficit becomes unsustainably large) or to float (and relax this external constraint). Larger deficits should thus promote floating. As a result, the current account balance/GDP ratio is expected to be negatively correlated with the exchange rate flexibility index.

- External financing sustainability. Excessive external indebtness is a threat to the sustainability of a fixed exchange rate regime, since large interest payments can reduce the amount of international reserves to the point of speculative attacks. Our proxy, the ratio of external debt service to exports, is therefore expected to be positively correlated with the exchange rate flexibility index.
- External financing maturity. The shorter the maturity of external indebtness, the more vulnerable a country is to a liquidity crisis in case of exchange rate fluctuations. As a result, the ratio of short-term to total external debt is expected to be negatively correlated with the exchange rate flexibility index.
- External financial vulnerability. The number of months that international reserves can cover imports is a good indicator of potential resistance to speculative attacks, and should be negatively correlated with the exchange rate flexibility index.
- Vulnerability to oil shocks. The volatility of terms of trade is an important macro-financial risk to many developing countries, since export revenues are an important part of their GDP. In particular, oil shocks can affect both oil exporters and oil importers, but of course in opposite ways. Our proxy takes that into account since it is the product of real oil prices by the difference between the ratio of oil exports to total exports and the ratio of oil imports to total imports. For example, oil price increases will yield a rise in our proxy for oil exporters (and an improvement of their trade balances) and a decline in our proxy for oil importers (and a deterioration of their trade balances). As a result we expect this proxy to be negatively correlated with the exchange rate flexibility index, similarly to the current account balance.
- Currency overvaluation. Despite its theoretical and empirical weaknesses, the concept of purchasing power parity is still regarded as a simple benchmark for currency overvaluation. Our proxy is the real exchange rate, or equivalently the ratio of the nominal exchange rate to the PPP exchange rate (obtained from the World Bank). Since currency overvaluation can rarely be sustained for long, we expect our proxy to be positively correlated with the exchange rate flexibility index.

The third step in this study is to choose an econometric methodology that can address the issues of transition and convergence from an old currency regime to a new currency regime and therefore take into account the dynamics of these exchange rate regimes. Error correction models offer a great advantage over other econometric techniques based on panel data. They enable the long-run determinants of exchange rate regimes to be indirectly estimated, along with the speed of convergence towards these regimes as well as the short-term dynamics stemming from past fluctuations in all variables. For example, consider the following error correction model:

$$Y_t - Y_{t-1} = c + a\,(Y_{t-1} - bX_{t-1}) + d_1\,(Y_{t-1} - Y_{t-2}) \\ + e_1\,(X_{t-1} - X_{t-2}) + \ldots + u_t$$

From this equation, we can estimate the coefficient b of the cointegrating relationship $Y_{t-1} = bX_{t-1}$. Simultaneously, we obtain the estimate of the coefficient a of mean reversion (convergence to long-run equilibrium), from which we can derive the half-life of deviations from the long-run equilibrium given by the cointegrating relationship. The short-term dynamics are captured by the estimates of the coefficient $d1$, $e1$, . . . Furthermore, panel cointegration tests present technical and interpretative difficulties, which error correction models do not have.

EMPIRICAL RESULTS

Before presenting the estimation results of our panel error correction model for about 100 countries over a post-Bretton Woods annual sample (1975–99), we show in Table 5.1 a sample of the various exchange rate regimes for the major countries in South-East Asia and Latin America. After a long period of pegged and heavily managed floating rates, the 1997 Asian crisis appears to have caused most affected nations to switch to *de jure* floats (except for Malaysia); however recent studies (for example Hernández and Montiel, 2003) have demonstrated that the *de facto* exchange rate regimes could still be considered more dirty than clean floats. The 1994–95 Mexican crisis, the 1999 Brazilian crisis and the 2002 Argentine crisis have also given the impression that *de jure* exchange rate regimes in Latin America were trending towards more flexible rates.

To obtain a more reliable picture of the evolution of exchange rate regimes, we present in Table 5.2 the nominal exchange rate flexibility index relative to the US dollar, for the same currencies. We also included the US, Europe (Germany) and Japan as benchmarks for flexibility. From its height of the Asian crisis in 1998, this index has been decreasing among Asian countries (except for Indonesia), and this evidence seems to confirm that floating rates are still managed, though perhaps not as much as previously. The experience of Latin American currencies is more heterogeneous, and the evidence mixed. Preliminary investigation indicated that the euro and the yen were not anchor currencies for any of the countries studied, contrary to the US dollar. We also present in Table 5.3 the real exchange rate flexibility index relative to the American currency. A low real flexibility index can be interpreted as evidence in favour of real exchange rate targeting, such as a crawling peg or a target zone, as long as the targeted depreciation rate is close to the inflation differential between the country and its anchor. Of course if this inflation differential is zero, then real and nominal exchange rate targeting are identical. The data show that official crawling pegs are often characterized by higher values for the real index than for the nominal index: this suggests that inflation is often more volatile than the targeted depreciation rates, and that real exchange rate targeting is not widely used as exchange rate policy.

Empirical results for the error correction models are presented in Table 5.4 for OCA and macro-financial criteria of exchange rate regimes. The first important observation is that the mean reversion coefficient (lagged flexibility) is always significant (in all four regressions), suggesting evidence of cointegration (panel cointegration tests have not been performed due to methodological issues) between the lagged variables in the error correction model. The value of this coefficient varies between −0.23 and −0.37, representing a half-life (of the deviations from equilibrium) of approximately two to three years. (Perhaps not surprisingly, this is similar to the half-life of exchange rate deviations from equilibrium such as purchasing power parity). Convergence towards the equilibrium exchange rate regime is therefore rather slow, but significant.

Focusing now on the first OCA criterion, we can observe that the inflation differential is always negatively related to the exchange rate flexibility index (and significant when the exchange rate is bilateral relative to the dollar rather than effective), whether it is nominal or real. This suggests that higher domestic inflation tends to push the local government to adopt either a fixed peg (exchange rate-based stabilization) or a crawling peg (monetary-based stabilization), but we cannot differentiate between the two hypotheses. We should note that the error correction model does not suffer from the problem of endogeneity (higher inflation causes pegs, or pegs cause less inflation?) since all the explanatory variables are lagged. On the contrary it allows for this type of dynamic effect, which cannot be captured from cointegration alone. The second OCA variable, related to the symmetry of business cycles or shocks, is negatively correlated with the US flexibility index, as expected, since asymmetric shocks tend to create some tensions on fixed exchange rates. The third OCA criterion, dealing with the geographical distribution of trade, is also negatively related to the flexibility index. For example discussions of potential currency areas often involve strong trading partners. The fourth OCA variable is the trade openness index and its coefficient is negative, as theory predicts, and especially significant for the

Table 5.1 Exchange rate regimes

	1975	1980	1985	1990	1995	1996	1997	1998	1999
China	MF	MF	MF	Deval.	PG($)	PG($)	PG($)	PG($)	PG($)
Hong Kong	FL	FL	CB($)	CB($)	CB($)	CB($)	CB($)	CB($)	CB($)
India	MF	MF	MF	MF	MF	MF	MF	MF	MF
Indonesia	PG($)	PG($)	CR($)	CR($)	CR($)	CR($)	Deval.	FL	FL
Korea	PG($)	MF	MF	MF	MF	MF	Deval.	FL	FL
Malaysia	MF	MF	MF	MF	MF	MF	Deval.	FL	PG
Philippines	PG($)	PG($)	MF	MF	MF	PG($)	Deval.	FL	FL
Singapore	MF	MF	MF	MF	MF	MF	Deval.	FL	FL
Taiwan	MF	MF	MF	MF	MF	MF	Deval.	FL	FL
Thailand	PG($	PG($)	PG(B)	PG($)	PG($)	PG($)	Deval.	FL	FL
Argentina	Deval.	CR($)	CR+PG($)	Deval.	CB($)	CB($)	CB($)	CB($)	CB($)
Bolivia	PG($)	PG($)	Deval.	CR($)	CR($)	CR($)	CR($)	CR($)	CR($)
Brazil	CR($)	CR($)	CR($)	Deval.	MF	MF	MF	MF	Deval.
Chile	CR($)	PG($)	CR($)	CR($)	CR(B)	CR(B)	CR(B)	CR(B)	CR(B)
Colombia	CR($)	CR($)	CR($)	CR($)	CR($)	CR($)	CR($)	CR($)	CR($)
Ecuador	PG($)	PG($)	PG($)	CR($)	CR($)	CR($)	CR($)	CR($)	MF
Mexico	PG($)	PG($)	Deval.	CR($)	MF	MF	MF	MF	MF

Peru	Deval.	CR($)	Deval.	FL	FL	FL	FL	FL	FL
Uruguay	CR($)	CR($)	CR($)	CR($)	CR($)	CR($)	CR($)	CR($)	CR($)
Venezuela	PG($)	PG($)	PG($)	FL	Deval.	Deval.	CR($)	CR($)	CR($)
United States	FL	FL	FL	FL	FL	FL	FL	FL	FL
Europe (Germany)	FL	FL	FL	FL	FL	FL	FL	FL	FL
Japan	FL	FL	FL	FL	FL	FL	FL	FL	FL

Notes:
CB = currency board.
CR = crawling peg.
FL = (free) float.
MF = managed float.
PG = fixed peg.
($)= US dollar.
(B) = basket.
Deval. = devaluation.

Table 5.2 Nominal exchange rate flexibility index (vs. US$)

	1975	1980	1985	1990	1995	1996	1997	1998	1999
China	#N/A	#N/A	#N/A	1.71	0.22	0.06	0.03	0.01	0.02
Hong Kong	#N/A	#N/A	#N/A	#N/A	0.02	0.01	0.01	0.01	0.02
India	2.11	0.99	2.79	1.16	1.53	1.87	0.69	1.07	0.35
Indonesia	0.00	0.03	0.62	0.20	0.40	0.27	2.50	5.23	5.80
Korea	0.15	0.97	0.51	0.45	0.46	0.62	1.15	1.57	0.94
Malaysia	#N/A	#N/A	#N/A	#N/A	0.52	0.26	1.64	1.67	0.00
Philippines	#N/A	#N/A	0.39	0.58	0.62	0.04	1.03	1.67	0.54
Singapore	0.85	0.63	0.57	0.37	0.43	0.29	0.70	0.77	0.56
Taiwan	#N/A	#N/A	#N/A	#N/A	#N/A	#N/A	#N/A	#N/A	#N/A
Thailand	0.00	0.04	0.61	0.20	0.20	0.20	1.03	3.43	1.41
South East Asia*	**0.62**	**0.53**	**0.92**	**0.67**	**0.49**	**0.40**	**0.98**	**1.71**	**1.07**
Argentina	23.70	0.55	6.05	7.13	0.01	0.00	0.00	0.00	0.00
Bolivia	0.00	0.00	13.07	0.76	0.25	0.41	0.19	0.25	0.30
Brazil	#N/A	#N/A	#N/A	27.64	0.64	0.68	0.48	0.27	3.36
Chile	#N/A	0.00	3.28	1.00	1.87	0.54	0.71	0.76	0.98
Colombia	#N/A	#N/A	#N/A	1.17	0.34	0.63	2.35	0.81	1.54
Ecuador	0.00	0.00	1.95	0.48	0.88	0.60	0.35	0.86	3.58
Mexico	0.00	0.56	3.83	0.20	0.61	0.49	0.29	0.81	1.98

Peru	0.26	0.64	2.80	2.80	0.48	0.35	0.23	0.76	0.73
Uruguay	2.34	0.44	7.69	6.96	1.98	2.50	1.26	0.58	1.04
Venezuela	0.00	0.00	0.00	0.31	1.25	1.34	0.24	0.36	0.41
Latin America*	**3.76**	**0.27**	**4.83**	**4.85**	**0.83**	**0.75**	**0.61**	**0.55**	**1.39**
United States	0.00	0.00	0.00	0.00	0.00	0.00	0.00	0.00	0.00
Europe (Germany)	1.83	1.79	2.15	3.48	5.79	2.89	5.11	1.88	#N/A
Japan	1.36	2.98	5.02	5.13	2.84	2.00	4.73	4.93	2.07
World	0.90	0.65	2.11	1.55	1.08	0.77	1.11	0.93	0.86

Note: * Regional average based on available observations.

Table 5.3 Real exchange rate flexibility index (vs. US$)

	1975	1980	1985	1990	1995	1996	1997	1998	1999
China	#N/A	#N/A	#N/A	2.82	1.47	1.46	1.63	2.65	3.58
Hong Kong	#N/A	#N/A	#N/A	#N/A	0.17	0.18	0.07	0.19	0.48
India	3.05	1.38	3.52	1.67	2.25	2.11	0.80	1.69	1.16
Indonesia	0.16	0.19	0.97	0.30	0.35	0.46	2.36	5.62	5.58
Korea	0.70	0.80	0.55	0.41	0.54	0.63	1.09	1.54	0.83
Malaysia	#N/A	#N/A	#N/A	#N/A	0.52	0.35	1.63	1.72	0.15
Philippines	#N/A	#N/A	0.56	0.74	0.62	0.26	1.05	1.68	0.63
Singapore	0.94	0.66	0.60	0.33	0.46	0.46	0.71	0.77	0.57
Taiwan	#N/A	#N/A	#N/A	#N/A	#N/A	#N/A	#N/A	#N/A	#N/A
Thailand	0.27	0.42	0.54	0.30	0.22	0.28	0.96	3.42	1.55
South East Asia*	**1.02**	**0.69**	**1.13**	**0.94**	**0.73**	**0.69**	**1.14**	**2.14**	**1.62**
Argentina	20.41	0.77	1.22	12.30	0.12	0.16	0.10	0.10	0.20
Bolivia	0.26	0.85	20.57	0.73	0.33	0.66	0.49	0.24	0.32
Brazil	#N/A	#N/A	#N/A	9.15	0.57	0.48	0.34	0.27	3.33
Chile	#N/A	0.86	4.35	1.21	1.74	0.50	0.85	0.67	1.01
Colombia	#N/A	#N/A	#N/A	0.31	0.33	0.68	1.79	0.90	1.58
Ecuador	0.74	0.24	2.94	0.24	0.52	0.39	0.17	0.53	2.95
Mexico	0.43	3.55	1.80	0.18	0.61	0.81	0.43	0.87	2.24

Peru	0.52	0.30	0.93	0.82	0.41	0.33	0.36	0.64	0.75
Uruguay	1.90	0.46	4.66	2.65	0.76	0.95	0.30	0.35	1.04
Venezuela	0.08	0.15	0.32	0.33	2.51	1.65	0.90	0.33	0.23
Latin America*	**3.48**	**0.90**	**4.60**	**2.79**	**0.79**	**0.66**	**0.57**	**0.49**	**1.37**
United States	0.00	0.00	0.00	0.00	0.00	0.00	0.00	0.00	0.00
Europe (Germany)	1.97	1.96	2.05	3.39	5.61	3.01	4.96	1.83	#N/A
Japan	1.69	2.95	4.93	5.26	2.79	2.20	4.71	5.17	1.93
World	1.26	0.99	3.09	1.87	1.24	1.06	1.52	2.11	1.26

Note: *Regional average based on available observations.

Table 5.4 Traditional and new criteria for exchange rate regimes

Dependent variable:	vs. US$		Effective	
Exchange rate flexibility	Nominal	Real	Nominal	Real
Constant	0.93	1.60	1.62	1.42
(t-statistics)	(1.41)	**(2.10)**	**(2.40)**	**(2.01)**
Exchange rate flexibility (−1)	−0.35	−0.37	−0.27	−0.23
(t-statistics)	**(4.58)**	**(3.71)**	**(2.14)**	**(2.39)**
Inflation differential (−1)	−0.005	−0.002	−0.001	−0.001
(t-statistics)	**(2.43)**	**(2.61)**	(0.60)	(1.25)
Growth symmetry (−1)	−0.30	−0.28	−0.04	−0.05
(t-statistics)	**(2.05)**	(1.70)	(0.24)	(0.31)
Trade geo-concentration (−1)	−0.27	−0.86	−0.98	−0.70
(t-statistics)	(1.02)	**(3.04)**	(1.67)	(1.15)
Trade openness index (−1)	−0.15	−0.77	−1.26	−1.17
(t-statistics)	(0.60)	**(2.43)**	**(3.82)**	**(3.81)**
GDP differential (−1)	1.17	2.27	0.64	0.91
(t-statistics)	(1.04)	(1.39)	(0.58)	(0.85)
Trade sectoral structure (−1)	0.01	0.53	0.35	0.52
(t-statistics)	(0.06)	**(2.16)**	(1.35)	(1.90)
Financial openness (Capital flows/GDP) (−1) (t-statistics)	−0.218 (1.38)	−0.49 **(2.31)**	−0.17 (0.92)	−0.25 (1.23)
Financial depth (M3/GDP) (−1)	0.23	1.44	2.06	2.03
(t-statistics)	(0.62)	**(2.95)**	**(4.15)**	**(4.39)**
External financing structure (FDI/Capital flows) (−1) (t-statistics)	−0.11 (0.39)	0.33 (0.84)	0.26 (0.58)	0.39 (1.02)
External financing needs (CAP/GDP) (−1) (t-statistics)	−2.22 (1.80)	−2.47 (1.61)	−3.54 **(2.29)**	−3.84 **(2.24)**
External financial sustainability (XD service/Exports) (−1) (t-statistics)	1.29 **(2.67)**	0.25 (0.45)	−0.34 (0.55)	−0.70 (1.20)
External financial maturity (Short-term XD/Total XD) (−1) (t-statistics)	−0.39 (0.74)	−0.82 (1.30)	−0.87 (1.49)	−0.84 (1.25)

Table 5.4 (continued)

Dependent variable:	vs. US$		Effective	
Exchange rate flexibility	Nominal	Real	Nominal	Real
External financial vulnerability (Internat. reserves/imports) (−1) (t-statistics)	−0.01 (0.15)	−0.09 **(2.62)**	−0.06 (1.37)	−0.07 (1.81)
Vulnerability to oil shocks (−1) (t-statistics)	−0.001 (1.26)	0.000 (0.42)	0.001 (0.86)	0.001 (0.42)
Currency overvaluation (% PPP) (−1) (t-statistics)	1.41 (1.74)	2.15 **(2.14)**	1.27 **(2.06)**	1.41 (1.52)
AR(1) (t-statistics)	−0.23 **(2.38)**	−0.29 **(2.33)**	−0.48 **(2.70)**	−0.47 **(3.40)**
R2	31.3%	34.1%	40.7%	38.1%
Adjusted R2	29.7%	32.6%	39.3%	36.6%
Durbin-Watson	2.01	2.09	2.00	1.99

effective exchange rate flexibility index. Open economies tend to limit fluctuations in their nominal or real exchange rates to avoid disruptions or volatility in their international trade patterns, especially with their most important trading partners. The fifth OCA criterion relates to the economic size of the nation, and is positively correlated with the currency regime flexibility, but not significant. As expected, relatively large countries tend to let their currency float. The sixth OCA variable deals with the level of development and reliance on exports of primary goods (agriculture, food, fuel and ore): its coefficient is positive, indicating that more industrialized or service-oriented nations also tend to let their currency float, but not always significantly.

Although OCA theory is confirmed by the previous results, we argued that macro-financial criteria for choosing an optimal exchange rate regime should be also considered. In the second part of Table 5.4, we present our empirical results concerning these new factors. Preliminary research showed that the coefficient of determination R^2 (adjusted for the number of explanatory variables) increased on average from 25 per cent to 33 per cent when these macro-financial criteria were included in the model. In particular, financial depth significantly affects the choice of exchange rate regimes (except for a peg to the dollar): nations with developed financial markets tend to select floats, as their economies are more robust to weather currency fluctuations. On the other hand, financial openness (or international capital mobility) calls for more fixity in the currency regime, albeit to a less significant extent. The external financing structure (and hence the volatility of foreign investment) does not appear to be a significant factor overall. External financing needs are negatively related to flexibility (although only significantly for effective exchange rates), confirming that large current account deficits tend to lead to the demise of fixed rates in favour of more flexible regimes. Rising external debt services have the same effect, when significant. Surprisingly, the shorter the maturity of external indebtness, the more likely a future peg: one would argue that a country becomes more vulnerable to financial shocks when it relies more on short-term debt, as Mexico did in 1994. This logic is confirmed by the negative coefficient of the ratio of international reserves to imports, a proxy for external financial vulnerability. Most exchange rate regimes however do not seem to be significantly affected by their countries' vulnerability to oil shocks. Finally, currency overvaluation relative to purchasing power parity significantly raises the likelihood of future floating, as expected.

CONCLUSIONS

The objective of this chapter was to highlight the need for new 'macro-financial' criteria when selecting an exchange rate regime in an emerging country. First, we distinguished between the official (*de jure*) classification of exchange rate arrangements and the actual (*de facto*) exchange rate regimes. In practical terms, we constructed several indexes of exchange rate flexibility, based on either nominal exchange rates (to identify fixed rates or hard pegs) or real exchange rates (to measure the degree of real exchange rate targeting, for example in crawling pegs or target zones), in bilateral form (relative to the US dollar, since the euro and yen did not appear to play any role as anchor currencies) or effective form (relative to a basket of these trade-weighted currencies). Second, we argued that the determinants of an exchange rate regime should not be limited to the traditional criteria of optimum currency area (OCA) theory, but should also be extended to include new macro-financial variables, such as the degree of financial liberalization and the vulnerability to external financial shocks. Third, we estimated the significance of these criteria as well as the speed of convergence of an exchange rate regime to its newly defined optimum. In particular, we use a panel error correction model to simultaneously analyse the long-run relationships and the short-term dynamics of exchange rate regimes.

Our empirical results confirm that optimum currency area criteria are useful, but they also show that new macro-financial criteria for selecting optimal exchange rate regimes are needed in a more liberalized international financial environment. Another interesting conclusion relates to the slow but significant convergence of currency regimes toward their long-term equilibrium.

REFERENCES

Bénassy-Quéré, Agnès and Benoît Cœuré (2000), 'Big and small currencies: the regional connection', CEPII Documents de Travail, 2000-10.

Bénassy-Quéré, Agnès and Benoît Cœuré (2002), 'The survival of intermediate exchange rate regimes', presented at the conference on Regional Currency Areas, Santiago de Chile, March.

Berg, Andrew, Eduardo Borensztein and Paolo Mauro (2002), 'An evaluation of monetary regime options for Latin America', *North American Journal of Economics and Finance*, **13** (3), 213–35.

Berger, Helge, Jan-Egbert Sturm and Jakob de Haan (2000), 'An empirical investigation into exchange rate regime choice and exchange rate volatility', CESifo Working Paper, 283, March.

Calvo, Guillermo and Carmen Reinhart (2002), 'Fear of floating', *Quarterly Journal of Economics*, **117**, 379–408.

Cartapanis, André (2004), 'Le déclenchement des crises de change: qu'avons-nous appris depuis dix ans?', *Economie Internationale*, **97**, 5–48.

Cartapanis, André, Vincent Dropsy and Sophie Mametz (2002), 'The Asian currency crises: vulnerability, contagion or unsustainability?', *Review of International Economics*, **10**, 79–91.

Cœuré, Benoît (2002), 'The narrow road to the single Asian currency: lessons from optimal currency theory and from the euro', Joint Australia–Japan Project on Financial Arrangements for East Asia, October.

Domaì, Ilker and Maria Soledad Martinez Peria (2003), 'Banking crises and exchange rate regimes: is there a link?', *Journal of International Economics*, **61** (1), 41–72.

Dornbusch, Rudi (2001), 'A primer on emerging market crises', NBER Working Paper Series, 8326.

Edwards, Sebastian (1996), 'The determinants of the choice between fixed and flexible exchange rate regimes', NBER Working Paper Series, 5756.

Edwards, Sebastian (2001), 'Exchange rate regimes, capital flows and crisis prevention', NBER Working Paper Series, 8529.

Eichengreen, Barry (1998), 'Exchange rate stability and financial stability', *Open Economies Review*, **9** (S1), 569–607.

Eichengreen, Barry and Tamim Bayoumi (1999), 'Is Asia an optimum currency area? Can it become one?', in Stefan Collignon, Jean Pisani-Ferry and Young-Cheung Park (eds), *Exchange Rate Policies in Asian Emerging Countries*, London: Routledge.

Fischer, Stanley (2001), 'Exchange rate regimes: is the bipolar view correct?', *Journal of Economic Perspectives*, **15** (2), 3–24.

Flood, Robert and Nancy Marion (1999), 'Perspectives on the recent currency crisis literature', *International Journal of Finance and Economics*, **4**, 1–26.

Frankel, Jeffrey (1999), 'No single currency regime is right for all countries or at all times', *Essays in International Finance*, Princeton, 215.

Frankel, Jeffrey (2003), 'Experience of and lessons from exchange rate regimes in emerging economies', NBER Working Paper, 10032, October.

Frieden, Jeffry, Piero Ghezzi and Ernesto Stein (2000), 'Politics and exchange rates: a cross-country approach to Latin America', Inter-American Development Bank, Research Network Working Paper, R-421.

Hernández, Leonardo and Peter Montiel (2003), 'Post-crisis exchange rate policy in five Asian countries: filling in the hollow middle?', *Journal of the Japanese and International Economies*, **17** (3), 336–69.

Hochreiter, Eduard, Klaus Schmidt-Hebbel and Georg Winckler (2002), 'Monetary union: European lessons, Latin American prospects', *The North American Journal of Economics and Finance*, **13** (3), 297–321.

Honkapohja, Seppo and Pentti Pikkarainen (1994), 'Country characteristics and the choice of the exchange rate regime: are mini-skirts followed by maxis?', in J. Akerholm and A. Giovannini (eds), *Exchange Rate Policies in the Nordic Countries*, London: CEPR.

International Monetary Fund (1984), 'The exchange rate system: lessons of the past and options for the future', *IMF Occasional Paper*, 30, Washington, DC, July.

Jadresic, Esteban, Paul Masson and Paolo Mauro (2001), 'Exchange rate regimes of developing countries: global context and individual choices', *Journal of the Japanese and International Economies*, **15** (1), 68–101.

Juhn, Grace and Paolo Mauro (2002), 'Long-run determinants of exchange rate regimes: a simple sensitivity analysis', presented at the conference on 'Regional Currency Areas', Santiago de Chile.

Kaminsky, Gabriela, Saul Lizondo and Carmen Reinhart (1998), 'Leading indicators of currency crises', *IMF Staff Papers*, **45** (1), 1–48.

Krugman, Paul (2001), 'Crises: the next generation?', presented at the Razin Conference, Tel Aviv.

Larrain, Felipe and Andrés Velasco (2001), 'Exchange rate policy in emerging market economies: the case for floating', *Essays in International Economics*, Princeton, 224.

Levy Yeyati, Eduardo and Federico Sturzenegger (2001), 'Exchange rate regimes and economic performance', *IMF Staff Papers*, **47** (Special Issue), 62–98.

Masson, Paul (2001), 'Exchange rate regime transitions', *Journal of Development Economics*, **64**, 571–86.

Méon, Pierre-Guillaume and Jean-Marc Rizzo (2002), 'The viability of fixed exchange rate commitments: does politics matter? A theoretical and empirical investigation', *Open Economies Review*, **13**, 111–32.

Mundell, Robert (1961), 'A theory of optimum currency areas', *American Economic Review*, **51** (4), 657–65.

Mundell, Robert (2000), 'Global money, currency areas and economic development', presented at the World Bank's conference on Development Economics in Europe, Washington, DC.

Pesenti, Paolo and Cédric Tille (2000), 'The economics of currency crises and contagion: an introduction', *Federal Reserve Bank of New York's Economic Policy Review,* September.

Poirson, Hélène (2001), 'How do countries choose their exchange rate regime?', IMF Working Paper, 01/46.

Ricci, Luca Antonio (1997), 'A model of an optimum currency area', IMF Working Paper, 97/76.

Rizzo, Jean-Marc (1998), 'The economic determinants of the choice of an exchange rate regime: a probit analysis', *Economics Letters*, **59** (3), 283–7.

Rogoff, Kenneth, Aasim Husain, Ashoka Mody, Robin Brooks and Nienke Oomes (2003), 'Evaluation and performance of exchange rate regimes', IMF Working Paper, 03/243.

Wagner, Helmut (2000), 'Which exchange rate regimes in an era of high capital mobility?', *North American Journal of Economics and Finance*, **11** (2), 191–203.

Williamson, John (1999), 'The case for a common basket peg for East Asian currencies', in Stefan Collignon, Jean Pisani-Ferry and Young-Cheung Park (eds), *Exchange Rate Policies in Asian Emerging Countries*, London: Routledge.

Wyplosz, Charles (2001), 'How risky is financial globalization in the developing countries?', presented at the Graduate Institute of International Studies, Geneva and CEPR, London, January.

6. The dollar, the euro and exchange rate regimes in Latin America[1]

Luis Miotti, Dominique Plihon and Carlos Quenan

The creation of the euro on 1 January 1999 was one of the major economic events of the end of the twentieth century. Completing a lengthy process of economic integration, the emergence of the European Monetary Union is likely to produce significant transformations in international monetary and financial relationships. This view is based on the economic weight of the euro zone, close to the weight of the United States, and on the desire of the monetary authorities not to restrain the internationalization process of the new European currency.

However monetary history shows that the process of birth and decline of international currencies is very slow and subject to important inertia. This inertia is particularly important for the functions of medium of exchange and store of value. The first years of existence of the euro confirm this view. They also seem to give some credit to the analyses, proposed before the creation of the euro, which mentioned the possibility of an important role of the euro with respect to financial operations. These approaches also stressed the idea that the evolution of the international monetary system is related to the choice that will be made with respect to endebtment and investment currencies. In this respect the significant growth of international bond issues in euros during recent years is a very important fact. Latin America actively participated in the growth of the international euro bond market. This led us to study the long-term implications of this process of intensification of the financial relationships between Europe and Latin America, with a particular view to the question of exchange rate regimes.

As a matter of fact, we explore one aspect which has not been much looked upon in recent studies on the euro and Latin America: that is, the link between the emergence of the euro and the function of unit of account. This function is not limited to the denomination of international trade; it also deals with the use of international currencies as anchors for monetary policy. The euro already plays the role of an anchor (alone or in baskets) for about

50 countries. This concerns first African countries, but also a great number of Eastern Europe countries, some of which are candidates for future admission to the euro zone. One may foresee the existence of a duopole less and less asymmetrical with respect to international currencies, with an increasing proportion of developing country currencies pegged on the euro and/or the dollar. One interesting question is whether the euro is likely to be used for pegging local currencies in countries that are already strongly dollarized.

The chapter starts with a survey of recent debates on possible evolutions of the international monetary system in the medium to long run as a result of the creation of the euro. The central part of our study deals with a theoretical and empirical analysis of the determinants of *de facto* monetary pegging, as opposed to *de jure* exchange rate regimes published by the IMF. We present an econometrical analysis of the determinants of *de facto* exchange rate regimes of 93 countries. We put a specific emphasis on the case of Latin American countries on this matter.

THE EURO AND THE IMS: THEORETICAL AND EMPIRICAL ASPECTS

The appearance of the euro on the international scene marks the beginning of a new era in international monetary and financial relations. The deepening process of integration that began in the 1950s and the creation of the euro represent decisive steps in the long road toward a truly common European market. At the same time, given the economic weight of Euroland and the will demonstrated by the European authorities, the advent of the euro opens up the possibility of instituting a new international currency capable of competing with the dollar. The scenario that seems most plausible, that is an increasing but gradual bipolarization of the IMS, is very likely to give rise to greater exchange rate volatility unless the US and European authorities implement a strengthened monetary cooperation, which does not for the moment seem to be on the horizon.

Theoretical Framework

The impact of the creation of the euro on international monetary relations will depend largely on the degree of internationalization of the European monetary unit. It is useful therefore to begin by distinguishing between the different private and public uses of currencies at an international level, and then present the conditions required to achieve the internationalization of a currency as they are formulated and analysed in the economic literature. This will make it possible to use these analytical tools to evaluate

Table 6.1 International uses of a currency

Function	Private use	Public use
Medium of exchange	Means of payment/ vehicle currency	Intervention currency
Unit of account	Price-setting/ invoicing currency	Reference currency (anchor)
Store of value	Investment and financing currency	Reserve currency

Source: Krugman (1991).

the extent to which the euro is likely to become an internationally used currency.

A typology of the international use of currencies

On the basis of the typology proposed by Krugman (1991) and following the presentation made by Bénassy-Quéré et al. (1998), we can distinguish six types of international uses of a currency as a function of a twofold criterion: (1), the three traditional functions of currencies, and (2) the private and public use of currencies on an international scale (Table 6.1).

An international currency is used by non-residents as a medium of exchange in trade transactions and capital movements. Private agents use an international currency as a vehicle, that is as an intermediary between two second-ranking currencies. Thus transactions between Brazil and Thailand are broken up into two separate moments: *real*/dollar and dollar/baht. In turn, monetary authorities also use international currencies as a medium of payment in their interventions in foreign exchange markets.

Secondly, an international currency is used as a unit of account by private agents to invoice their trade or financial international transactions. This function is different from that of a medium of payment in the sense that one transaction can be denominated in one currency and then paid in another (the distinction between invoicing currency and medium of payment). Monetary authorities also make use of the unit-of-account function in implementing their exchange policies when they decide to anchor their currencies to an international reference currency. This has to do with exchange system issues.

As a store of value, an international currency is used by private agents with the aim of preserving the value of their assets. They place their assets in different international currency denominations as part of their strategies

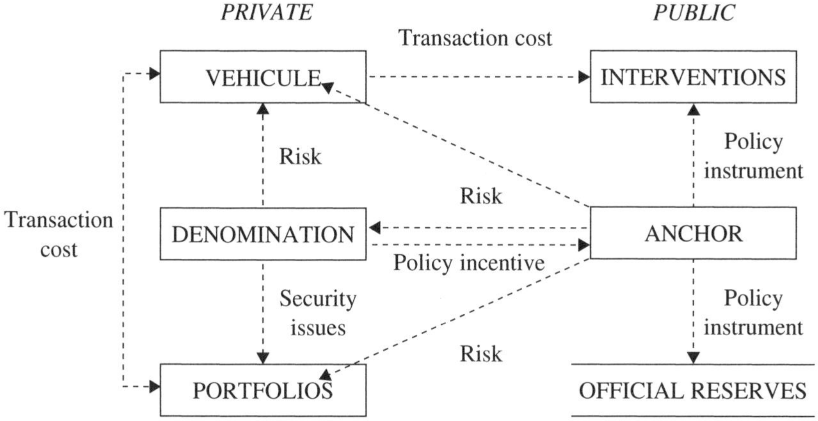

Source: Bénassy-Quéré et al. (1998).

Figure 6.1 Main synergies between international monetary functions

to optimize their risk–yield ratio. In turn, monetary authorities manage the composition of their international reserves as a function both of their objective of optimizing their risk–yield ratio and of the nature of their interventions in the foreign exchange market.

These different international uses of currencies are separable but interdependent. Schematically, the interaction between these different uses can move along various channels (see Figure 6.1). For example, the decision adopted by the monetary authorities to give priority to certain currencies in the composition of international reserves (store-of-value function) can be conditioned in part by the choice of an anchoring mechanism with regard to these currencies (unit-of-account function).

Another channel has to do with transaction costs. If a currency is used as a vehicle currency, transaction costs are low and the monetary authorities will tend to use it in their interventions, while private investors will try to procure assets denominated in that currency.

The degree of use of an international currency by a country can be very different depending on the above-mentioned functions: thus the dollar may be chosen as the anchor currency by monetary authorities due to the overwhelming weight of the US financial markets, even though the trade transactions of that same country may be denominated in other currencies. Likewise it is possible to consider these functions hierarchically, that is the international medium of payment function is frequently considered to be the most important (Bourguinat, 1985).

Conditions for the internationalization of a currency
According to Bourguinat (1987), two criteria should be taken into account:

- Stability – predictability of the currency.
- Acceptability – liquidity: in order to be international, a currency must be universally accepted; it should be a 'vehicle' currency, in the sense that it is used by other countries in transactions that do not involve a direct relationship with the issuing country.

Tavlas (1991) proposes two complementary criteria:

- The country issuing the international currency should have a major weight in international trade, thus reinforcing the use of this currency by the other countries.
- The country issuing the international currency should have free, broad and deep financial markets, thus guaranteeing the liquidity of the currency and making it possible for the currency to play a store-of-value role for private and public participants.

These conditions are necessary but not sufficient to explain the reasons why international operators tend to favour one currency as a key currency. Some authors emphasize the role of transaction costs, economy of scale phenomena, positive externalities (Kenen, 1992) and network effects (Aglietta and Deusy-Fournier, 1994). These approaches make it possible to demonstrate the existence of self-reinforcing and inertial processes in the international use of currencies. From this point of view, the progress of the euro as an international currency should be gradual. In other words, the dollar should maintain its supremacy for a long while yet.

The International Weight of the Euro Zone: Overview

The weight of the euro zone relative to the American and the Japanese economies is one of the first empirical criteria to consider for the future role of the European currency in the international monetary system. If we compare the relative weights of the United States and the euro zone in the world economy, we can see that the euro zone has a greater weight in terms of population. At the same time, the weights of the euro zone and the United States are similar in terms of international trade, as shown in Table 6.2.

On the other hand, if we adopt GDP and stock exchange capitalization as criteria, the weight of the US is greater. These basic statistical data can lead us to consider that the euro has a strong potential to increase its share as an internationally used currency in the world economy.

Table 6.2 *Weight of the United States and the euro zone in the world economy*

	Population	GDP	Stock market capitalization		External openness
	(1)	(2)	(2)	% GDP	(3)
Euro Zone	302.80	5875.60	3709.80	56.80	19.00
United States	273.70	8590.10	11596.50	121.50	14.80
Japan	126.80	4223.20	2263.40	48.20	9.90

Notes:
(1) Millions of inhabitants (2000).
(2) Billions of dollars (2001).
(3) Exports/GDP in % (2000).

Source: World Bank, Eurostat, OECD.

Another relevant factor to be considered is the position of the European authorities with regard to the internationalization of the euro. Knowing that history and economic theory show that progress in the international use of a currency has to be gradual, the European officials are not actively seeking to promote the internationalization of the euro. Unlike Japan however, which has also resisted internationalizing the use of the yen (because the Japanese consider that it might disrupt the behaviour of their monetary policy), the European authorities do not oppose a growing internationalization of the euro. Their position is that the zones strategy in terms of monetary policy is sufficiently strong to face the implications of an increasing internationalization of the eurocurrency (Duisenberg, 2000). Their position is therefore 'neutral', and this in fact favours an increasing international use of the euro.

The Euro in the International Scene

A second empirical aspect of the international role of the euro is the strength of the European currency with respect to the dollar. Contrary to the predictions of a majority of specialists, the euro weakened substantially during its initial stages, and lost almost 30 per cent of its value in the first few years of its existence. Three main groups of factors have been suggested to explain this.

First of all, economic factors. A gap has developed between the US economy, which has been experiencing an exceptionally prosperous phase, and the euro zone, whose growth cycle began later and has been less strong.

One of the consequences of this situation is an interest rate differential that favours the dollar.

Secondly, financial factors, of a more structural nature. Although the US is a major net importer of capital, the euro zone has been experiencing net outflows of long-term capital (portfolio investment and direct foreign investment) that far exceed their current account surpluses since 1994. The US has a growing current account deficit (over 4 per cent of GDP), with a favourable basic balance thanks to massive capital inflows. In turn, the euro zone has a current account surplus (around 0.5 per cent of GDP) together with an unfavourable basic balance due to this significant outflow of capital. The deepening European integration and the creation of the euro have contributed in part to this situation. European companies have been pressed to increase their critical size, which has led to mergers and acquisitions in the US market (which is also the epicentre of the new economy). Moreover European companies have begun to participate increasingly in the movement to achieve geographic diversification of their security portfolios: between 1998 and 2000 the volume of net purchases of foreign stock doubled.

Thirdly, institutional factors. The implementation of the EMU has not clarified the situation in terms of economic governance of the euro zone. Uncertainty still reigns on many levels, and from the viewpoint of foreign investors, the European Central Bank's policy is far from clear. This latter factor will probably be long-lasting; the strengthening of the European monetary authority entails a slow learning process.

Nevertheless the initial nominal depreciation of the euro arose from the fact that the dollar was undervalued at the time the eurocurrency was created. In effect, most of the studies conducted on the basis of a fundamental equilibrium exchange rate (developed by Williamson, 1983), indicate that on the date the euro was introduced it was overvalued *vis-à-vis* the dollar by an estimated 7 per cent to 10 per cent (Borowski and Couharde, 1999; Teïletche, 2001).

The definition of an equilibrium exchange rate is complex however: the short term is dominated by the cycle, the medium term by the savings behaviour of the issuing zones, and the long term reflects the external positions of the two currency zones (Artus, 1999), as well as the difference in their potential growth rates.

This last point is crucial: a medium- and long-term source of uncertainty has to do with the ability of the European economy to draw nearer to the potential growth rate of the US economy. A major portion of the studies on this subject show that the long-term trend in the growth rate of the euro zone is between 2.5 per cent and 3 per cent, while that of the United States is close to 4 per cent. Even though the higher internal savings rate and the usually positive current account balance of the euro zone tend to weaken the dollar, a persistent differential in terms of potential growth works against the strengthening of the euro in the long term.

Another factor of uncertainty in the medium term arises from the behaviour of savings and investment in Europe. As we have seen, the euro zone is characterized by a current account surplus, which is a reflection of surplus savings. This surplus is a result of the existence of substantial private savings, which are higher than the public deficits. This European configuration is just the opposite to that of the United States, which is characterized by a shortfall in savings in spite of its fiscal surplus.

One can foresee that the overall saving rate in the euro zone will continue to be high for two main reasons. First, the reduction of fiscal deficits is an objective of the countries of the zone. Second, it is expected that households will increase their savings efforts for demographic reasons (ageing population and pension funding). From this point of view, the development of financial markets linked to the creation of the euro should stimulate the accumulation of these financial savings.

The appreciation of the euro since mid-2002 is partly linked to the high level of savings in Europe relative to the low level of savings in the United States, as illustrated by the structural current account deficit. However European savings may be insufficient if the companies of the zone increase their investment in Europe in order to reduce their relative lag with respect to the US (in particular in the new technologies). If this takes place the euro zone might even experience a major current account deficit (Artus, 2001), which could contribute to weakening the eurocurrency.

The International Role of the Euro: Three Scenarios

Although they are different issues, the movement of the euro exchange rate and the perspectives for the euro's role in the international sphere are not unconnected. If the euro depreciates permanently and there is skepticism concerning its parity, this could discourage its use and might affect its acceptance among the key IMS currencies.

In any event, many authors expect a rise of the euro as an international currency. A majority of these studies emphasize that the financial role of the euro (that is to say, as a borrowing and lending currency) will develop much more rapidly than its international trade function (that is as an invoicing currency). This is confirmed by the two first years of the euro's life, in particular with regard to its role as a borrowing currency, which has developed significantly. This is a distinctive characteristic of the present internationalization of the euro that will be analysed later on.

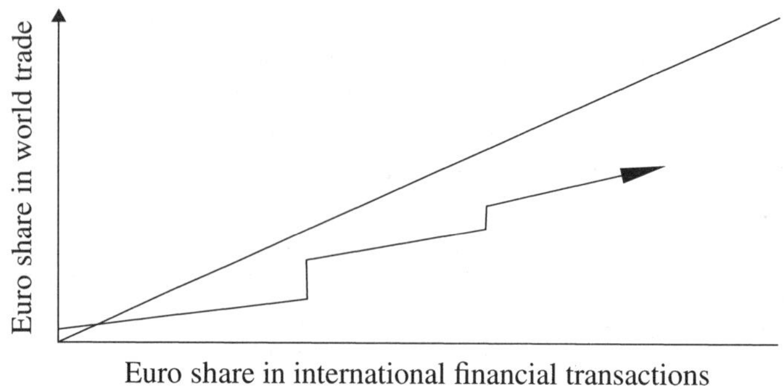

Source: de Boissieu (2000).

Figure 6.2 Theoretical path of the internationalization of the euro

On the other hand, some authors indicate that the progress of the 'trade' euro might occur in 'steps', with qualitative leaps, that should quicken the internationalization of the eurocurrency (de Boissieu, 2000) (Figure 6.2). The same authors however also argue that an excessive delay in the development of the trade function of the euro could work against the establishment of its financial role: a 'complete' international currency should not be subject to excessive or too protracted a divergence between its financial and trade roles.

With regard to the evolution of the IMS in the medium to long term, it is possible to distinguish at least three scenarios. The first is an IMS that will long continue to be dominated by the dollar, which implies that the initial progress observed in terms of the financial function of the euro will be followed by backsliding and that the eurocurrency will fail to win definitive acceptance in that role. Second is the exact opposite scenario: the financial function of the euro becomes firmer and its trade role develops at a faster than expected rate. This would lead to an increasingly symmetrical dollar–euro duopoly. The last and seemingly most plausible scenario, taking into account the first steps of the euro in the international arena and the teachings of economic theory, is a duopoly that gradually decreases in asymmetry. A slow but growing bipolarization of the IMS however also entails the development of the euro's role as an anchor currency in the exchange systems of other countries.

Within the framework of this most likely scenario, it seems clear that the volatility of the dollar–euro exchange rate is unlikely to decrease. On the contrary, as suggested by theoreticians on the role of leadership (such as Kindleberger), asymmetry and the existence of a clearly hegemonic currency are conditions that favour stability. Historic experience shows that the coexistence of two dominant currencies (as occurred with the pound and the dollar in the 1930s) can be a destabilizing element and lead to unfavourable effects in third countries.

Let us analyse the hypothetical reaction of the euro–dollar exchange rate to a trade shock that affects the Euroland–dollar bilateral current account under three possible scenarios for anchoring the currencies of third countries to the key currencies of the system: (1) general flotation where no currency is anchored to the dollar or the euro; (2) a hegemonic system in which all currencies except the euro are anchored to the dollar; and (3) a bipolar system in which both the US and the euro zone conduct half their trade with the countries of their respective monetary blocs. We see that the hegemonic system, although less stable than the general flotation system, is in turn much less volatile than a bipolar IMS (Benassy-Quéré and Coeuré, 2000).

Thus the current situation, set between the hegemonic and bipolar systems (that is an IMS in harmony with the increasingly bipolar but asymmetrical medium- to long-term scenario we see as most likely) entails high volatility between the two main international currencies.

Prior to examining the first steps of the internationalization of the euro in greater depth, it is useful to indicate that within the framework of a growing bipolarization of the IMS, we can foresee two possible configurations regarding the volatility of the euro–dollar parity. On the one hand, a 'pessimistic' configuration of 'competition' between the dollar and the euro, in which the US and European monetary authorities continue to give priority to their domestic objectives and are uncooperative toward each other, which would accentuate the instability of the bilateral parity. On the other hand, an optimistic configuration of strengthened monetary cooperation: the US and European authorities consider that international monetary stability is a public commodity and agree to intervene and monitor the evolution of their exchange rates, and to progress toward coordinating their macroeconomic policies. In this configuration, the volatility of the euro–dollar exchange rate would decline.

The former configuration appears to be most likely. While the IMS is in its current intermediate situation, it is difficult to imagine the US being willing to give lower priority to its domestic objectives. On the other hand, the deficiencies in the institutional architecture of the EMU, including the absence of a unified political authority, makes it difficult to think that Europe could defend a coherent macroeconomic policy on an international scale. In any event it is clear that the European monetary authorities do not have an explicit objective on the subject of the exchange rate and seem to be increasingly inclined to practice a policy of 'benign neglect' as long as

Table 6.3 Volatility of the euro–dollar parity (annual and quarterly averages based on daily data)

	Volatility	Five-month moving average	Trend (Hodrick-Prescott Filter)
1998	5.20	5.23	5.84
1999	6.47	6.61	7.04
2000	9.99	9.50	8.78
Q1 2001	10.89	10.43	9.90

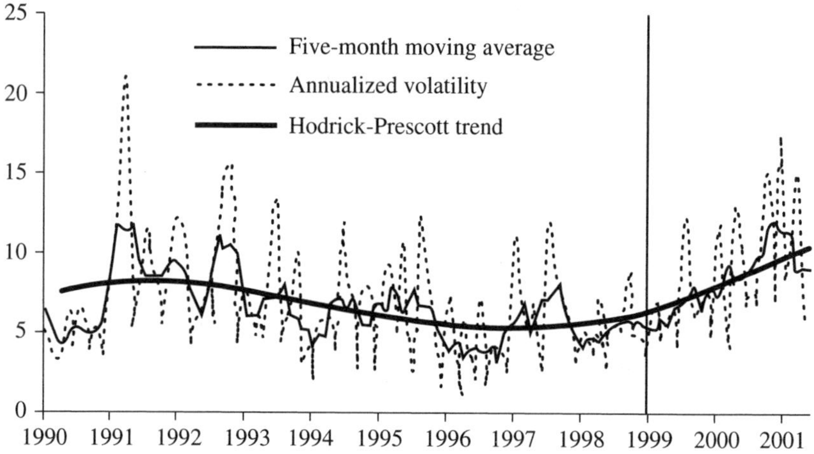

Figure 6.3 Annualized volatility of euro–dollar parity (on the basis of daily data)

the degree of external openness of the euro zone is less than that of their member countries considered individually.

Empirical analysis (see Box 6.1) confirms these hypotheses. As shown in Table 6.3 and Figure 6.3, the euro–dollar exchange rate has become more volatile since the introduction of the eurocurrency.

EMERGENCE OF THE EURO AND THE UNIT-OF-ACCOUNT FUNCTION: IMPLICATIONS FOR LATIN AMERICA

The increased volatility of exchange rates has put forward the question of the unit-of-account function of international currencies. As a result, studies

BOX 6.1 METHOD FOR CALCULATING THE ANNUALIZED VOLATILITY

The data used are taken from the spot quotations in the New York market at their closing price. We have used the exchange rate of the German mark between 1 January 1971 and 31 December 1998 and the exchange rate of the euro between 1 January 1999 and 11 May 2001. As of the introduction of the euro on 1 January 1999, this currency was converted to German marks using the conversion rate established for the member countries of the monetary union.

Annualized volatility was calculated using the following formula:

$$\sigma = \sqrt{\frac{n\sum_{i=1}^{n} x_i^2 - \left(\sum_{i=1}^{n} x_i\right)^2}{n(n-1)}}$$

Where: x_i = daily quotation; i = day; n = number of monthly quotations; σ is multiplied by 100 in accordance with financial standards.

On the basis of the volatility data calculated as shown above, a five-month moving average was calculated using the Hodrick–Prescott method[2] in order to eliminate the strong fluctuations in the volatility and its trend.

on the creation of the euro and its prospect as an international currency have largely focused on its functions as a medium of payment, financing and borrowing. Recently the management of international reserves and the potential role of the euro as a reserve currency have also begun to be studied; most importantly, Eichengreen and Mathieson, 2000. Conversely, the unit-of-account function is often neglected, probably because currency price-setting in international trade is particularly subject to inertia resulting from the existence of grid externalities. Another factor that is usually put forward to explain this is that invoicing currencies appear to derive their use from their other functions (Bénassy-Quéré and Cœuré, 2000).

As previously mentioned, the unit-of-account function not only has to do with price-setting in international trade, it also concerns the use of international currencies as reference (anchor) currencies, which is one of the crucial functions in the internationalization process. In the short term, it will be very difficult for the euro to compete with the dollar as a worldwide anchor currency, given that decisions in this sphere are linked to the type of integration – in both trade (geographic pattern of trade flows) and financing (borrowing currencies, FDI sources and so on) – as well as to trade practices (as previously mentioned, most commodities trade is conducted in dollars). In particular the existence of strong inertia in trade and financial practices hinders a more rapid development of the euro as an international currency. In any event the use of the euro as an anchor currency of third countries can be expected to increase in the medium and long term.

In this chapter, we will: (1) address the issue of the *de facto* determination of currency anchors, as against the officially-stated anchors, that is those published by the IMF (in its *Annual Report on Exchange Arrangements and Exchange Restrictions*); (2) study the real and financial determinants of the options adopted by developing countries in terms of *de facto* anchoring on the basis of an econometric analysis conducted for 93 economies; (3) build a typology of the analysed countries; and (4) explore ways in which the euro could be adopted as an anchor currency across Latin America.

De Facto Anchoring Arrangements: Methodology

Following the approach proposed by Bénassy-Quéré and Cœuré (2000), an estimate is made of *de facto* exchange arrangements through the use of econometric equations based on the generalized moments method (see Appendix 1). The implicit anchors of 111 currencies have been estimated on the basis of weekly data both before and after the financial crises of the emerging countries (1997–98).

The results show that the proportion of currencies with *de facto* anchoring to the dollar is much higher (50 per cent) than could be surmised from the official data published by the IMF (see Tables 6.4 and 6.5). This phenomenon has continued after the Asian crisis, suggesting that at least in the short term, the current system has not changed as substantially as is usually suggested (that is, decline in peg to a reference currency and generalization of pure floats). Therefore, pure floats are much less frequent *de facto* (4 per cent) than *de jure* (30 per cent).

These results converge in part with those obtained by Levy Yeyati and Sturzenegger (1999b), who observed numerous *de facto* anchors. In addition there does not appear to have been a decline in the so-called intermediate arrangements (one of the characteristics of which is an anchor to a basket of currencies).

In sum, according to the approach adopted in this study, the international monetary system does not seem to be evolving toward a general use of floats. Moreover, Bénassy-Quéré and Cœuré (2000) note that the IMS is still a long way from a configuration of different currency blocks of comparable size.

Table 6.4 Official exchange arrangements and their evolution (% of all IMF member country currencies, in December of each year)

Exchange arrangements	1983	1988	1994	1999
Number of currencies	*146*	*152*	*181*	*187*
Fixed anchor to one currency (including currency boards)	35.6	38.3	26.0	30.0
Dollar	23.3	25.7	13.8	15.0
Franc, mark, euro	8.9	9.2	8.3	12.3
Other	3.4	3.4	3.9	2.7
Fixed anchor to a basket of currencies	27.4	25.7	13.3	9.6
SDR	8.9	5.3	1.7	3.2
Ecu	0.7	0.7	0.6	0.0
Other	17.8	19.7	11.0	6.4
Limited flexibility	11.0	7.2	7.2	5.9
European exchange mechanism	4.8	4.6	5.0	1.1
Other	6.2	2.6	2.2	4.8
Limited float	19.9	17.8	19.9	23.0
Free float	6.1	11.2	33.7	31.6
TOTAL	100.0	100.0	100.0	100.0

Source: IMF, *Annual Report on Exchange Arrangements and Exchange Restrictions*, various numbers.

Financial and Trade Determinants of *De Facto* Anchors

On the basis of the results presented in the previous section, we will now focus on the real and financial determinants of the *de facto* anchoring arrangements adopted by the 93 countries considered. Table 6.6 shows the correlations between the anchoring coefficients and the trade, financial and geographic variables.[3]

This table shows, mainly, that the anchoring coefficients are correlated with the trade and financial variables. The use of the euro as a *de facto* anchor currency correlates significantly with the use of the euro as a borrowing currency (0.197) and with the geographic pattern of trade (0.458), that is those cases in which Europe is predominant as a client and supplier of the countries considered. It is not surprising therefore to find that the countries of Europe (Central, Eastern and Southern), as well as the African countries of the franc zone, have a strong correlation with the use of the euro as a *de facto* anchor currency (either as the sole currency or as the dominant currency in anchor baskets).

Table 6.5 De facto *exchange arrangements (% of all currencies analysed)*

	April 1995–June 1997 (prior to the Asian crisis)	October 1998–December 1999 (after the Asian crisis)
Number of currencies	*107.0*	*107.0*
Unit anchor to one currency	61.8	59.8
Dollar	50.6	49.5
Euro	10.3	10.3
Yen	0.9	0.0
Partial anchor to one currency	13.0	9.3
Dollar	12.1	6.5
Euro	0.9	1.9
Yen	0.0	0.9
Anchor to a basket of currencies	20.5	27.1
Dollar/euro	12.1	14.0
Dollar/yen	5.6	2.8
Euro/yen	1.9	2.8
Euro/dollar/yen	0.9	7.5
Free float	4.7	3.7
TOTAL	100.0	100.0

Note: The 14 African countries of the franc zone are treated as a single country.

Source: Bénassy-Quéré and Coeuré (2000).

Table 6.6 Trade, debt and de facto *anchoring arrangements*
Correlation table

	Dollar	Euro	Yen	Dolbin	Eurobin	Yenbin
Dollar	1.000	−0.969	−0.612	0.911	−0.937	−0.589
Euro	−0.969	1.000	0.396	−0.859	0.884	0.393
Yen	−0.612	0.396	1.000	−0.634	0.649	0.927
Dolbin	0.911	−0.859	−0.634	1.000	−0.865	−0.602
Eurobin	−0.937	0.884	0.649	−0.865	1.000	0.652
Yenbin	−0.589	0.393	0.927	−0.602	0.652	1.000
Debt structure by currency						
In Dollars	0.019	−0.044	0.069	−0.032	−0.021	0.096
In Euros	**−0.272**	**0.197**	**0.378**	**−0.356**	**0.292**	**0.350**
In Yens	**0.205**	**−0.144**	**−0.292**	**0.213**	**−0.142**	**−0.251**

Table 6.6 (continued)

	Dollar	Euro	Yen	Dolbin	Eurobin	Yenbin
Degree of dollarization of the economies						
Dollarized	0.089	−0.016	**−0.276**	**0.166**	**−0.154**	**−0.206**
Oil exports						
Oil-exporting	**0.140**	**−0.129**	−0.104	**0.144**	**−0.202**	**−0.155**
Foreign trade structure						
With United States	**0.355**	**−0.352**	**−0.195**	**0.370**	**−0.371**	**−0.198**
With Japan	**0.251**	**−0.240**	**−0.164**	**0.226**	**−0.222**	**−0.178**
With Europe	**−0.451**	**−0.458**	**0.211**	**−0.465**	**0.439**	**0.159**

Geography and anchoring arrangements
Correlations table

	Dollar	Euro	Yen	Dolbin	Eurobin	Yenbin
Geographic distances						
kmUS	0.017	−0.019	−0.005	−0.032	0.020	−0.043
kmJapan	−0.089	0.017	**0.274**	**−0.143**	0.092	**0.241**
kmEurope	**0.446**	**−0.468**	**−0.162**	**0.454**	**−0.415**	**−0.174**
Geographic areas						
LATIN AMERICA	**0.341**	**−0.331**	**−0.208**	**0.398**	**−0.360**	**−0.179**
CENTRAL	**0.202**	**−0.199**	**−0.112**	**0.276**	**−0.195**	−0.032
SOUTH	**0.245**	**−0.234**	**−0.162**	**0.240**	**−0.278**	**−0.210**
ASIA	**0.312**	**−0.284**	**−0.252**	**0.299**	**−0.287**	**−0.261**
MIDDLE EAST	**0.153**	**−0.132**	**−0.146**	**0.139**	**−0.161**	**−0.122**
EUROPE	**−0.358**	**0.456**	−0.127	**−0.209**	**0.273**	−0.087
AFRICA	**−0.364**	**0.253**	**0.539**	**−0.506**	**0.424**	**0.481**
AFRICA-CFA	**−0.532**	**0.365**	**0.805**	**−0.668**	**0.578**	**0.765**
AFRICA-NCFA	0.047	−0.029	−0.085	0.001	−0.017	**−0.118**

Notes:
Figures in boldface indicate statistically significant correlations.
CFA: CFA franc zone.
CNFA: other African countries.

Sources: Trade: DOTS-IMF (2000), Debt: World Bank (WDI 2000), Dollarization: IMF 174 (1998), Exchange arrangements: Bénassy-Quéré (2000).

To complete the analysis, we conducted an econometric probability study (Table 6.7).

The econometric estimates suggest that the likelihood of using the dollar

Table 6.7 Probability of using an international currency

	Dollar			Euro			Yen		
	Coef.	Z-Stat	Proba.	Coef.	Z-Stat	Proba.	Coef.	Z-Stat	Proba.
Constant	1.40	1.22	0.222	−0.32	−0.36	0.716	−0.66	−0.57	0.568
Direction of trade									
With Japan	**0.27**	2.30	**0.022**	**−0.19**	−2.64	**0.008**	−0.03	−0.35	0.724
With Europe	**−0.04**	−3.04	**0.002**	**0.03**	2.20	**0.028**	**−0.03**	−2.11	**0.035**
With USA	**0.04**	2.12	**0.034**	**−0.04**	−2.52	**0.012**	**−0.09**	−3.59	**0.000**
Debt composition by currency									
In dollars	0.00	0.034	0.973	−0.01	−0.44	0.660	0.06	2.42	**0.015**
In euros	**−0.10**	−3.441	**0.001**	**0.06**	2.70	**0.007**	**0.16**	3.57	**0.000**
In Yen	**0.12**	3.501	**0.001**	**−0.06**	−2.33	**0.020**	**−0.90**	−3.75	**0.000**
Other determinants									
Oil-exporting	**1.82**	2.79	**0.005**	**−1.26**	−2.15	**0.032**	**−1.78**	−2.07	**0.039**
Dollarized	0.21	0.43	0.666	−0.19	−0.46	0.645	**−1.70**	−2.43	**0.015**

Restr. log likelihood	−19.55	−25.44	−13.66
Probability (LR stat)	0.00	0.00	0.00
Obs with Dep = 0	27.00	58.00	68.00
Obs with Dep = 1	63.00	31.00	18.00
Included observations	90.00	89.00	86.00
McFadden R-squared	0.64	0.56	0.69
% Correct	92.1%	83.9%	72.2%

Notes:
Figures in bold indicate variables with a significance level at least 90%.
Owing to problems of multicollinearity between the trade variables and those that represent geographic distances, the latter have not been included in the econometric estimate.

as an anchor currency increases when the United States is a major trading partner of the country in question. Symmetrically, the likelihood declines when the main partner is Europe.

As regards to the predominance of a currency for borrowing purposes, when a country is indebted mainly in dollars, the likelihood of using the US currency as an anchor is not significant. This is explained by that fact that all the countries of the sample are mainly indebted in dollars. In addition, the likelihood of anchoring a currency to the dollar declines significantly when a major part of the external debt of the country considered is denominated in euros. On the other hand, oil-exporting countries have a strong likelihood of anchoring their currencies to the dollar because the international oil trade is conducted in dollars.

For the yen, the results of the econometric equations concerned with the likelihood of anchoring a currency to the Japanese currency are poor. Thus being a major trading partner of Japan does not increase the likelihood of using the yen as an anchor currency. Moreover the likelihood of using the yen as an anchor decreases significantly when the foreign debt of a country is denominated in that currency. Lastly, as would be expected, in the oil-exporting countries and those that are noted for a high degree of dollarization in their economies, the likelihood of anchoring their currencies to the yen is slight. Several factors serve to explain these econometric results. One is the crisis that has affected Japan since 1990. Another is the strong nominal and real short-term fluctuations experienced by the yen in recent years. Uncertainty regarding the Japanese economy and the volatility of the yen increases transaction costs and exchange rate risks. Yet another factor is the absence of political will – not to mention the hostility – of the Japanese authorities with regard to developing the yen as an international currency.

For the euro, the likelihood that a country will use it as an anchor currency decreases when the trade of a country is conducted mainly with Japan or the United States, and increases if it is conducted with the euro zone countries, again assuming these countries are major trading partners. Likewise the results of the exercise confirm that the likelihood of using the euro as an anchor increases when a major part of the external debt of the country considered is denominated in euros. On the other hand, and inverting the equation that analyses the use of the dollar as an anchor, the likelihood of anchoring a national currency to the euro declines significantly for oil-exporting countries.

A Typology of Countries

The factors considered up to now can be analysed more deeply in order to identify the positioning of the countries of the sample. To achieve this, a

Table 6.8 Inherent values and correlations between main variables and factors (for the first four significative axes)

Inherent values	1	2	3	4
Value	2.40	2.05	1.19	1.02
% variability	26.63	22.75	13.23	11.35
% aggregate	26.63	49.37	62.60	73.95
	factor 1	factor 2	factor 3	factor 4
Trade with USA	**0.75**	−0.09	0.00	**0.45**
Trade with Japan	0.01	**0.70**	−0.03	**−0.35**
Trade with Europe	**−0.72**	**−0.26**	−0.03	**−0.28**
Debt in dollars	**0.61**	**−0.36**	**−0.22**	**−0.39**
Debt in yen	0.06	**0.66**	−0.13	**0.38**
Debt in euros	**−0.60**	**−0.26**	**0.30**	**0.52**
Distance from USA	**−0.40**	**0.65**	**0.42**	−0.15
Distance from Japan	0.12	**−0.55**	**0.71**	−0.14
Distance from Europe	**0.64**	**0.36**	**0.59**	−0.08

factor analysis of the main components is conducted (see Appendix 2), making it possible to group the countries with homogenous trade, financial and geographical features. We begin by showing how we organized the information (Table 6.8).

The four main axes represent 74 per cent of the aggregate variability. In other words, approximately three-quarters of the total information contained in the variables can be summarized in these four main axes. Figure 6.4 makes it possible to identify the opposition between the variables that are more strongly linked to the dollar with regard to those that are more related to the euro.

Figure 6.5 presents the projection of the countries in the factor space defined by the two main axes, which summarize approximately 50 per cent of the total information contained in the variables used. Predictably, a great majority of the Latin American countries are situated in the south-eastern region of the factor space dominated by trade with the United States and indebtedness mainly denominated in dollars.

From the country coordinates in the factor space defined by the main four axes, we can identify five different groups (Table 6.9).

A second econometric exercise, taking into account the coordinates of the countries on the factor plane (which summarize the information provided by the variables used to calculate the factor axes) confirms that the fact of exporting oil increases the likelihood of anchoring the national currency to the dollar and significantly decreases the likelihood of anchoring

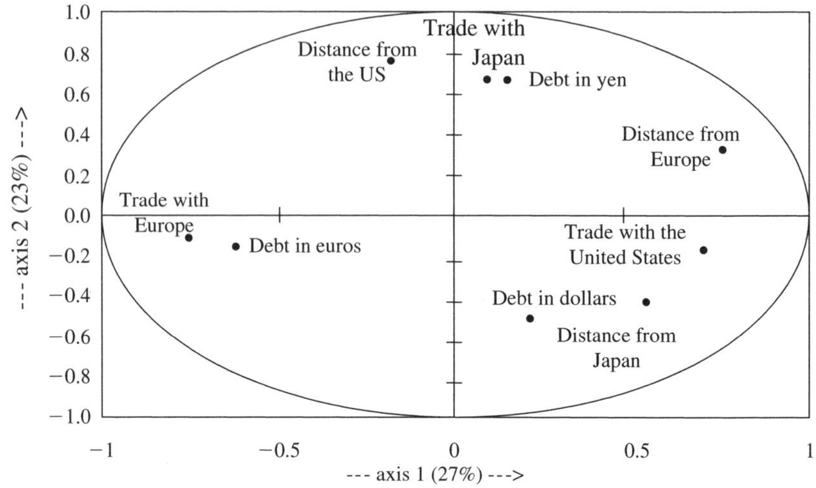

Figure 6.4 Circle of correlations: axes 1 and 2 (50%)

it to the euro. In turn, a high degree of dollarization of the economy strongly increases the likelihood of anchoring the national currency to the dollar and appreciably decreases the likelihood of anchoring it to the euro (Table 6.10).

Even more importantly, a final econometric exercise relating the groups of countries and the *de facto* anchoring currencies shows that groups 3 and 4 have a statistically significant relationship with the dollar. At the same time, groups 1 and 2 appear to be areas that anchor to a basket (dollar–euro in group 1, euro–yen in group 2), whereas group 5 is characterized by a statistically significant relationship with the euro. The Latin American and Caribbean countries, included mostly in group 4, are unequivocally part of the dollar zone (Table 6.11).

Implications for Latin America

In spite of their apparent obviousness, the results obtained are not devoid of interest. Our evidence confirms the logical assumption that the pre-eminence of the dollar as an anchor currency is favoured by inertial factors. In addition the degree of dollarization of the economies considered, as well as the intensity of the financial and trade relations with the United States, are factors that reinforce the role of the dollar as an anchor currency. Thus virtually none of the Latin American countries breaks away from the dollar zone. Our analysis shows that the often-mentioned rifts between Mexico

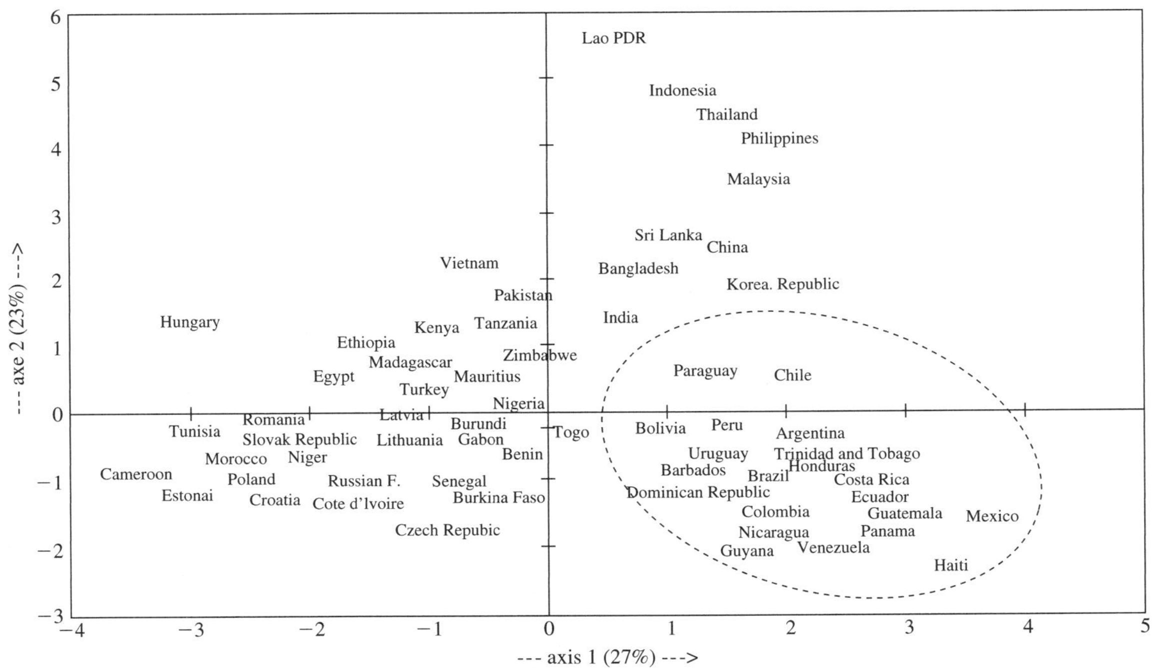

Note: To make the above figure readable, only 60 countries out of the 93 countries of our total sample are pictured on this figure. Our estimates derived from the factor analysis are based on the whole sample.

Figure 6.5 Projection of countries in the factor space defined by axes 1 and 2 (50%)

Table 6.9 *Typology of countries on the basis of PCFA results (Classification of observations/Number of countries)*

Group 1 15	Group 2 26	Group 3 16	Group 4 22	Group 5 14
Bulgaria	Benin	Bangladesh	Argentina	Cameroon
Croatia	Burkina Faso	Cambodia	Barbados	Congo, Rep.
Czech Rep.	Burundi	China	Bolivia	Cote d'Ivoire
Dominica	Central African Rep.	India	Brazil	Egypt, Arab Rep.
Equatorial Guinea	Chad	Indonesia	Chile	Estonia
Grenada	Comoros	Jordan	Colombia	Gabon
Kazakhstan	Djibouti	Korea, Rep.	Costa Rica	Hungary
Latvia	Ethiopia	Lao PDR	Dominican Rep.	Mali
Lebanon	Gambia, The	Malaysia	Ecuador	Morocco
Lithuania	Ghana	Mongolia	El Salvador	Niger
Poland	Guinea-Bissau	Nepal	Guatemala	Nigeria
Romania	Iran, Islamic Rep.	Pakistan	Guyana	Russian Federation
Slovak Republic	Kenya	Philippines	Haiti	Tunisia
Syrian Arab Rep.	Madagascar	Sri Lanka	Honduras	Turkey
Ukraine	Malawi	Thailand	Jamaica	
	Mauritania	Vietnam	Mexico	
	Mauritius		Nicaragua	
	Mozambique		Panama	
	Paraguay		Peru	
	Senegal		Trinidad and Tobago	
	Seychelles		Uruguay	
	Sierra Leone		Venezuela	
	Tanzania			
	Togo			
	Zambia			
	Zimbabwe			

and the countries of Central America, on the one hand, and the countries of South America, on the other, have little basis in fact.

However the use of the euro as the sole anchor currency is clearly confined to countries whose trade and financial relations with the European Monetary Union are very close (group 5 of our typology, made up mainly of African and Central/East European countries). As shown by Boone and Maurel (1999) for example, for these countries the euro represents a more 'natural' regional anchor currency than the dollar. In particular the countries of Central and Eastern Europe and those of North Africa, which conduct a sizeable portion of their trade with the euro zone, display activity cycles that coincide quite closely with those of Europe, as well as specialization structures that are relatively similar to those of Western Europe.

Our study also indicates however that the euro participates, in numerous cases (groups 1 and 2 of our typology), in *de facto* anchoring baskets. This point is important: in a medium- to long-term perspective, the euro's potential for increasing its share in the anchor baskets cannot be disregarded. Indeed another result of this study is that the likelihood of anchoring a national currency to the dollar decreases strongly when the share of debts denominated in euros increases.

Since 1997 there has been an increase in the euro-denominated bonds as a share of total issues by Latin American countries. Table 6.12 shows that for a group of selected countries – the largest economies of the region – the use of the euro as a borrowing currency is increasing rapidly. More precisely, the euro's share of government securities issue has reached very high levels in the case of Argentina, Brazil, Colombia and Venezuela.

On the other hand, as was noted in the second part of this chapter, the international component of private sector bonds in euros has grown substantially. It is not unlikely therefore that Latin American firms may tend progressively toward debt issues denominated in euros. The growing penetration of the European banks in Latin America, the sustained increase of European banking loans to Latin American countries and the boom of foreign investment of European origin in the region could intensify this trend.

Thus in the medium to long term the Latin American countries that participate more actively in the process of development of the single European currency as a borrowing currency might consider the use of the euro as a component of anchor currency baskets. Obviously the dollar would continue to have a pre-eminent position in these currency baskets, given its entrenchment in Latin America.

This hypothesis is consistent with the analyses in the theoretical and applied literature on the choice of anchor currencies. According to Bénassy-Quéré and Lahrèche-Révil (1999) for instance, the relatively diver-

Table 6.10 Probability of using an international currency (probit equations on the factor coordinates)

	Dollar			Euro			Yen		
	Coef.	Z-Stat	Proba.	Coef.	Z-Stat	Proba.	Coef.	Z-stat	Proba.
Constant	**1.35**	2.82	**0.005**	−0.45	−1.48	0.139	**−1.28**	−3.04	**0.002**
Direction of trade									
Axis 1	**1.45**	3.65	**0.000**	**−1.02**	−4.50	**0.000**	**−0.26**	−2.13	**0.034**
Axis 2	**2.27**	3.38	**0.001**	**−1.35**	−3.35	**0.001**	**−1.26**	−3.30	**0.001**
Axis 3							**0.83**	2.79	**0.005**
Other determinants									
Oil-exporting	**1.56**	1.87	**0.061**	**−1.67**	−2.41	**0.016**	−0.75	−1.38	0.168
Dollarized	**1.83**	2.74	**0.006**	**−0.99**	−2.12	**0.034**	−0.36	−0.86	0.391
Restr. log likelihood		−54.10			−57.68			−49.16	
Probability (LR stat)		0.00			0.00			0.00	

Obs with Dep=0	27.00	57.00	70.00
Obs with Dep=1	63.00	31.00	21.00
Included observations	90.00	88.00	91.00
McFadden R-squared	0.70	0.60	0.38
% Correct	95.3%	81.3%	57.1%

Note: Figures in bold indicate variables with a significance of at least 90%.

Table 6.11 Geographic groups and international currencies (probit equations on the basis of the typology)

	Dollar			Euro			Yen		
	Coef.	Z-Stat	Proba.	Coef.	Z-Stat	Proba.	Coef.	Z-stat	Proba.
Constant	**−1.16**	−2.77	**0.006**	−0.85	−1.84	0.065	**−0.71**	−1.42	**0.156**
Groups resulting from the typology									
Group 1	**1.23**	2.75	**0.006**	**0.87**	1.80	**0.071**	**0.52**	1.01	**0.315**
Group 2	Reference			**2.56**	4.40	**0.000**	**1.34**	2.18	**0.030**
Group 3	**9.56**	22.74	**0.000**	Reference			**0.08**	0.14	**0.889**
Group 4	**9.62**	22.89	**0.000**	**−0.48**	−0.75	**0.454**	**−7.28**	−14.89	**0.000**
Group 5	**0.61**	0.98	**0.329**	**1.56**	2.70	**0.007**	Reference		
Other determinants									
Oil-exporting	**0.47**	1.11	**0.269**	**−0.39**	−1.10	**0.271**	−0.33	−0.91	0.364
Dollarized	**1.07**	2.07	**0.039**	**−1.51**	−2.68	**0.007**	−1.08	−2.46	0.014
Restr. log likelihood		43.56			37.86			24.05	
Probability (LR stat)		0.00			0.00			0.00	
Obs with Dep=0		28.00			59.00			70.00	
Obs with Dep=1		65.00			34.00			23.00	
Included observations		93.00			93.00			93.00	
McFadden R-squared		0.38			0.31			0.23	
% Correct		87.7%			82.4%			21.7%	

Notes: Figures in bold indicate variables with a significance of at least 90%.

Table 6.12 Change in share of euro-denominated issues in selected countries (%)

	Argentina	Brazil	Chile	Colombia	Mexico	Venezuela
Private-sector bond issues						
1993	0.0	0.0	0.0	0.0	1.0	0.0
1994	0.0	12.9	0.0	0.0	0.0	0.0
1995	21.0	6.5	0.0	0.0	0.0	0.0
1996	7.5	2.2	0.0	0.0	0.0	0.0
1997	8.6	3.9	0.0	0.0	0.0	0.0
1998	5.8	3.6	0.0	0.0	5.4	0.0
1999	29.2	4.5	18.5	0.0	0.0	0.0
2000	20.9	16.8	0.0	0.0	40.1	0.0
Government bond issues						
1993	28.2	0.0	0.0	0.0	4.5	14.4
1994	22.4	0.0	0.0	0.0	0.0	0.0
1995	37.8	34.7	0.0	21.1	12.8	48.8
1996	47.2	30.5	0.0	11.0	18.7	68.6
1997	28.4	29.1	0.0	0.0	33.1	0.0
1998	57.0	32.5	0.0	16.0	16.1	26.0
1999	56.1	58.3	0.0	0.0	13.9	54.3
2000	51.7	25.3	0.0	36.1	19.9	68.5
Total bond issues (private-sector + government)						
1993	10.7	0.0	0.0	0.0	2.3	13.8
1994	9.9	11.5	0.0	0.0	0.0	0.0
1995	33.3	15.7	0.0	8.8	11.1	48.8
1996	39.2	13.6	0.0	9.7	15.7	68.6
1997	22.8	16.6	0.0	0.0	22.5	0.0
1998	44.3	17.7	0.0	16.0	11.9	26.0
1999	52.9	43.2	12.7	0.0	8.3	54.3
2000	47.7	24.4	0.0	36.1	23.7	68.5

Sources: CDC IXIS, Department of Economic and Financial Analysis, Country-Risk and Emerging-Markets Unit, Bondware.

sified geographic patterns of the foreign trade of some of the large Latin American countries (except Mexico) could justify the adoption of a basket including the euro. These authors even suggest the hypothesis that countries of the region might create regional monetary unions linked to a basket of currencies including the euro. On the strength of our findings, we might add that a key factor to increase the possibility of adopting baskets including the euro is the intensification of financial relations between Europe and Latin America.

Undoubtedly anchoring to a single currency – in this case the dollar – represents a very attractive alternative in Latin America. With regard to the prospect of regional monetary unions, the unilateral decision to link the national currency to the dollar is an easy solution that involves fewer demands in terms of regional coordination and cooperation. In addition, full participation in the dollar zone may increase foreign investment attracted by exchange rate risk diversification (Bénassy-Quéré, et al., 1999). Still more importantly, a policy of anchoring to a single key currency can easily be tested by the market. Transparency thus contributes to rapidly reinforce the credibility of the countries that adopt this type of policy (Frankel et al., 1999). In turn, in Latin America, where the degree of dollarization is in fact high and the question of credibility is crucial to many countries, the issue of the dollar's role goes beyond the discussion of a dollar peg. The debate conducted openly since 1999 is increasingly focused on the advantages and disadvantages of total dollarization; that is to say, the replacement – in principle, irreversible – of the national currencies by the dollar, as has recently occurred in Ecuador and El Salvador.

As long as credibility in Latin America is associated with establishing a close relationship with the dollar (in the form of *de jure* anchoring or floating arrangements involving *de facto* anchoring) and, in some way, to the Federal Reserve, the possibility of adopting baskets including the euro will be limited. There are two arguments however that can serve to temper this statement:

1. As indicated by Levy Yeyati and Sturzenegger (1999c), with the launching of the euro the European Central Bank could – if its policy is successful – offer a new alternative in the medium or long term to countries in search of credibility. Although both the Federal Reserve and the ECB are obviously extremely wary of any proposal to share the management of monetary policy with third countries, these authors argue that they might be less reluctant to enter some type of exchange agreement with certain Latin American countries. The so-called European Monetary System bis (EMS bis), an exchange agreement that links the European Union with other European countries that are applying for membership, represents an interesting antecedent – although of course it is intrinsically inapplicable to other countries or regions.
2. The previously mentioned factors conducive to adoption of anchor baskets could be strengthened by the medium- to long-term international scenario that is favoured in this study. An increasingly bipolar but asymmetrical IMS presupposes high volatility between the two main international currencies. In this context, anchoring exclusively to the dollar could prove fatal for countries that have major trade and

financial relations with the euro zone. Conversely, anchoring to a basket that includes the euro would be decisive in reducing vulnerability – and, hence increase credibility – to abrupt exchange rate swings among the main reference currencies.

CONCLUDING REMARKS

The internationalization of the euro is in its initial stages and it is therefore difficult to draw any definitive conclusions regarding its scope and its implications for Latin America. Indeed as indicated at the beginning of this study, the emergence of an internationally used currency is slow and subject to inertial forces. Nonetheless several fairly robust conclusions can be inferred from the results of our analysis.

First, with regard to the development of the IMS, if one takes into account the initial experience of the euro on the international scene and the teachings of economic theory, the most plausible medium- to long-term scenario seems to be development of an asymmetrical duopoly. This means the euro will come to share the dollar's role as a financial currency, while the US currency will continue to prevail in trade transactions.[4] Even though one can argue with this hypothesis, it seems credible that the dollar will maintain its dominant position for a considerable time, during which there will be a gradually increasing bipolarization of the IMS. In a context of scant international monetary cooperation, this scenario presupposes high volatility between the two main international currencies, which will be a powerful destabilizing factor for third countries.

Secondly, the first years of the euro's existence confirm that its growing use in financial operations – which now far outweigh transactions in goods and services – will represent a decisive vector (although insufficient in the long term) in its internationalization. In turn, the effects of the expansion of the euro bond markets on the capital markets of the issuing zone are not neutral. Together with other factors, the growth of the bond market will tend to increase the pressure to widen and deepen the euro financial market and make it more liquid. This should favour the development of better terms for payback period, refinancing, coverage and arbitrage conditions for both European and third-country participants.

Third, the study of the channels for generalizing the use of the different key currencies as anchor currencies shows that the likelihood of anchoring a national currency to the dollar decreases when the share of a country's external debt denominated in euros increases. If the Latin American countries continue to increase their borrowing in euros and this translates into a greater diversification of their international reserves, some of them might consider the possibility of using the eurocurrency in anchor baskets, especially in those cases where the euro zone is a major trading partner. Nevertheless the dollar will continue to have a preponderant role in those baskets, given the entrenchment of the US currency in Latin America. On the other hand, the medium- to long-term consequences of exchange arrangements will have to be included in the international scenario that is beginning to take shape since the creation of the euro. The previously mentioned factors tending to enhance the possibility of adopting anchor baskets (at least in the case of some Latin American countries) would be further supported by the medium- to long-term scenario we regard as more likely: an increasingly bipolar but asymmetrical IMS presupposes high volatility between the two main international currencies. In this context, *de facto* and *de jure* anchoring focused exclusively on the dollar, which in theory offers substantial gains in terms of credibility, could turn out to be fatal for countries that maintain close trade and financial relations with the euro zone.

APPENDIX I: METHOD OF CALCULATION OF *DE FACTO* ARRANGEMENTS AND THEIR RESULTS

The most frequently used method to identify a *de facto* arrangement consists in estimating an equation that explains the exchange rate variations of each currency by means of the exchange rate fluctuations of the major reference currencies (dollar, yen, mark, euro, and so on):

$$\dot{e}_{ikt} = a_0 + a_{1\dot{e}\$kt} + a_2\dot{e}_{Ekt} + a_3\dot{e}_{Ykt} + u_t$$

where, $\dot{e}_{ikt}$ = designates the exchange rate variation of currency i in relation to currency k between t and $t-1$. \$, E and Y designate the dollar, the euro and the yen, respectively.

The constant a_0 is positive if i is depreciated (or devalued) regularly to compensate for a positive inflation differential (case of real anchors or crawling pegs). Coefficients a_j are interpreted as the weight of each reference currency in the implicit basket of country i.

The cases that can arise are: $a_{ij} = 1$, which represents unit anchoring in relation to one currency (a single significant coefficient, equal to the unit); $0 < a_{ij} < 1$, which represents anchoring to a basket of currencies (at least two significant coefficients, where the sum is equal to the unit); $a_{ij} = 0$ for $\forall_j$, which represents a free float (no coefficient is different from zero).

As the direct estimate of the equation poses the problem of defining the numeraire k (a currency that fluctuates independently from the major explanatory currencies), Bénassy-Quéré and Coeuré use:

$$\alpha_i' X_{it} = \beta_i + u_{it}$$

where, $X_{it} = (\dot{e}_{i\$t}, \dot{e}_{iEt}, \dot{e}_{iYt})$, α_i represents the weighting vector and β_i is a scalar.

The equation is estimated as a condition of orthogonality using the generalized-moment method, with the restriction:

$$\sum_{ji=1}^{3} \alpha_{ij} = 1$$

The estimate was made for 111 currencies, on the basis of weekly exchange rates and covering two periods: April 1995 to June 1997 (prior to the Asian crisis) and October 1998 to December 1999 (after the crisis). The euro was identified with the ecu prior to January 1999. Of the 111 countries used by Bénassy-Quéré and Cœuré, the following 93 were selected for this study.

Argentina	Cote d'Ivoire	Guyana	Mexico	South Korea
Bangladesh	Croatia	Haiti	Mongolia	Sri Lanka
Barbados	Czech	Honduras	Morocco	Syria
Benin	Republic	Hungary	Mozambique	Tanzania
Bolivia	Djibouti	India	Nepal	Thailand
Brazil	Dominica	Indonesia	Nicaragua	The Gambia
Bulgaria	Dominican	Iran	Niger	Togo
Burkina Faso	Rep.	Jamaica	Nigeria	Trinidad and
Burundi	Ecuador	Jordan	Pakistan	Tobago
Cambodia	Egypt	Kazakhstan	Panama	Tunisia
Cameroon	El Salvador	Kenya	Paraguay	Turkey
Central	Equatorial	Laos	Peru	Ukraine
African	Guinea	Latvia	Philippines	Uruguay
Rep.	Estonia	Lebanon	Poland	Venezuela
Chad	Ethiopia	Lithuania	Romania	Vietnam
Chile	Gabon	Madagascar	Russian	Zambia
China	Ghana	Malawi	Federation	Zimbabwe
Colombia	Grenada	Malaysia	Senegal	
Comoros	Guatemala	Mali	Seychelles	
Congo	Guinea-	Mauritania	Sierra Leone	
Costa Rica	Bissau	Mauritius	Slovakia	

APPENDIX II: PRINCIPAL COMPONENT FACTOR ANALYSIS (PCFA)

Principal component factor analysis makes it possible to represent numerous relations between variables in a small number of factors. The observations (or individuals) can be represented (projected) on a plane defined by the factor axes.

This quantitative method adjusts better to the analysis of a group of heterogeneous variables, that is, expressed in units that are *a priori* different. Standardizing each variable eliminates the arbitrariness resulting from the use of different measuring scales, which is expressed in a non-comparable dispersion. Thus, each variable has a variance that is equal to 1. For *J* variables, the total variance (that measures the overall dispersion of the individuals resulting from all variables) is equal to *J*.

Geometrically, the variables are represented by points situated on a sphere. The angle between two variables illustrates the correlation between them (Bravais-Pearson's linear correlation coefficient): this is the cosine of the angle. The correlation is more strongly positive when the angle is acute and more strongly negative when the angle is obtuse. The correlation is nill when the two variables form a right angle.

The PCFA provides an orderly group of axes and corresponding eigenvalues. Eigenvalue n° α is the variance of the factor corresponding to axis α. The sum of the eigenvalues is always equal to the total variance. If the original variables all have a variance that is equal to 1 (by construction), the first factors will have a variance that is notably greater than 1: each of them embodies the disparity of observations attributable to a group of variables. As of a certain range, the factors associate with eigenvalues that are lower than 1. Thus, these last factors express less disparity between individuals than any of the original variables; this leads us to consider that the information they provide in terms of disparity between individuals is residual, and therefore allows us to eliminate them from the result-interpretation process.

The factor coordinates of individuals (projections on the factor axes) can be used as new (compound) variables in econometric equations. These variables, that summarize the information contained in the original group of variables, present orthogonality as a fundamental characteristic, that is they eliminate all risk of multicollinearity.

NOTES

1. This chapter draws upon a study sponsored by ECLAC on 'The euro and financial relations between Latin America and Europe: medium- and long-term implications' (Miotti, 2002; Escaith and Quenan, 2003).
2. This is a smoothing method that is widely used among macroeconomists to obtain a smooth estimate of the long-term trend component of a series. The method was first used in a working paper (circulated in the early 1980s and published in 1997) by Hodrick and Prescott to analyse post-war US business cycles.
3. The anchoring coefficients are taken from Bénassy-Quéré and Cœuré (2000). The follow-

ing binary variables were associated with those variables: Dolbin= 1 if the coefficient is equal to or higher than 0.5, 0 if it is lower; Eurobin = 1 if the coefficient is equal to or higher than 0.3, 0 if it is lower; Yenbin = 1 if the coefficient is equal to or higher than 0.1, 0 if it is lower. The 'oil-exporting' binary variable is assigned to countries whose oil sales represent over 10 per cent of their total exports. The 'dollarized' binary variable is attributed to countries where the dollar share in M3 is high, following IMF typology. Geographical distances are measured in kilometres (km) between ports or capitals.

4. An asymmetrical duopoly of rivalry between the dollar and the euro that has both economic and political implications (Cohen, 2000). Also, as certain recent studies suggest (Artus, 2001), the internationalization – and thus its strengthening – assume the euro – and therefore of its strength – assumes a substantial increase in the euro zone's potential for economic expansion. The latter essentially depends on the zone's demography and capital stock, which implies widening it to include young and undercapitalized countries.

REFERENCES

Aglietta, M., C. Baulant and V. Coudert (1997), 'Pourquoi l'euro sera fort, une approche par le taux de change d'équilibre', Working Paper, Banque de France, Paris.

Aglietta, M. and M. Deusy-Fournier (1994), 'Internationalisation des monnaies et organisation du système monétaire', *Economie Internationale*, **59**, Paris.

Alesina, A. and R. Barro (2000), 'Currency Unions', *Working Paper 7927*, NBER, September.

Artus, P. (1999), 'Dollar/euro/yen: rôles respectifs, parités d'équilibre', *Etude*, 99-13, CDC, Paris, September.

Artus, P. (2000a), 'L'euro, seconde monnaie de réserve internationale et le dollar, seule monnaie de transaction', *Document de travail*, 2000-39, CDC, Paris, May.

Artus, P. (2000b), 'Le rôle international de l'euro ne va pas en grandissant', *Flash*, 2000-191, CDC, Paris, October.

Artus, P. (2001), 'Pour sauver l'euro, il faut une zone monétaire plus large', *Flash*, 201-136, CDC, Paris, July.

Bénassy-Quéré, A. and B. Coeuré (2000), 'Big and small currencies: the regional connection', *Document de travail*, 2000-10, CEPII, Paris.

Bénassy, A., Fontagné, L. and A. Lahrèche-Révil (1999), 'Exchange-rate strategies in the competition for attracting FDI', *CEPII Working Paper*, 99-16, CEPII, Paris.

Bénassy-Quéré, A. and A. Lahrèche-Révil (1998), 'Pegging the CEEC's currencies to the euro', *Document de travail*, 98-04, CEPII, Paris.

Bénassy-Quéré, A. and A. Lahrèche-Révil (1999), 'L'Euro comme monnaie de référence à l'est et au sud de l'Union européenne', *Revue Economique*, 50-2, Paris.

Bénassy-Quéré, A. and B. Mojon (1998), 'EMU and transatlantic exchange rate stability', *Document de travail*, 98-02, CEPII, Paris.

Bénassy-Quéré, A., B. Mojon and A-D. Schor (1998), 'The international role of the euro', *Document de travail*, 98-03, CEPII, Paris.

Bergstein, Fred (1997), 'The impact of the euro on exchange rates and international policy co-operation', in P.R. Masson T.H. Krueger and B.G. Turtelboom (eds), *EMU and the International Monetary System*, Washington, DC: IMF.

Boone, L. and M. Maurel (1999), 'L'ancrage de l'Europe centrale et orientale à l'Union européenne', *Revue Economique*, **50** (6), November.

Borowski, D. and C. Couharde (1998), 'Parité euro/dollar et ajustements macro-économiques: que révèle une analyse en termes de taux de change d'équilibre?', *Revue d'Economie Financière*, 49, Paris.

Bourguinat, Henri (1985), 'La concurrence des monnaies véhiculaires: vers le polycentrisme monétaire?' in *Croissance, échange et monnaie en économie internationale*, Mélanges en l'honneur de J. Weiller, Paris: Economica.

Bourguinat, Henri (1987), *Les vertiges de la finance internationale*, Paris: Economica.

Boyer, R. (1998), 'An essay on the political and institutional deficits of the euro', Working Paper, CEPREMAP, Paris, August.

Cohen, B. (2000), 'EMU and the Developing Countries', Working Paper 177, UN World Institute for Development Economics Research (ONU/WIDER), March.

Créel, J. and H. Sterdyniak (1998), 'A propos de la volatilité de l'euro', *Revue de l'OFCE*, Paris, April.

De Boissieu, Ch. (2000), 'L'euro et le rééquilibrage du système monétaire et financier international', in *Rapport Moral sur l'Argent dans le Monde 2000*, Paris, December.

Dornbusch, R. (1999), 'The euro: implications for Latin America', Massachusetts Institute of Technology, Working Paper prepared for the World Bank. March.

Duisenberg, W. (2000), 'The International role of the euro', speech, www.ecb.int, November.

Ecu Institute (1995), 'International currency competition and the future role of the single European currency, final report of the working group 'European Monetary Union – International Monetary System', London: Kluwer Law International.

Eichengreen, B. (1998), 'The euro as a reserve currency', *Journal of the Japanese and International Economies*, **12**.

Eichengreen, B. and D.J. Mathieson (2000), 'The currency composition of foreign exchange reserves: retrospect and prospects', IMF Working Paper, WP/00/131, Washington, DC.

Escaith, H. and C. Quenan (eds) (2003), 'Emergencia del Euro y sus implicaciones para América Latina y el Caribe', *Serie Macroeconomia del desarollo*, 20, Economic Development Division, ECLAC, January

European Central Bank (BCE) (1999), 'Le rôle international de l'euro', *Bulletin Mensuel*, Frankfurt, August.

Frankel, J.A., S. Scumeckler and L. Serven (1999), 'Verifiability: a rationale for the failure of intermediate exchange rate regimes', Working Paper.

Garcia Herrero, A. and G. Glockler (2000), 'Unilateral Dollarisation versus Regional Monetary Union: Options for Latin America', working paper prepared for a strategic seminar at CERI, Paris, November.

Giambiagi, F. (1999), 'Mercosul: Por que a unificaçao monetaria faz sentido a longo prazo?', *Ensaios BNDES*, Rio de Janeiro, December.

Heymann, D. (1999), 'Interdependencias y políticas macroeconómicas: reflexiones sobre el Mercosur', in J. Campbell (ed.), *Mercosur entre la realidad y la utopia*, Buenos Aires: CEI-Grupo Editor Latinoamericano.

Kenen, P. (1992), 'Exchange rates and the international monetary system', *Recherches Economiques de Louvain*, **59**, (1–2).

Krugman, Paul (1991), 'The international role of the dollar: theory and prospects', in P. Krugman, *Currency and Crises*, Cambridge, MA: MIT Press.

Levy Yeyati, E. and F. Sturzenegger (1999a), 'The euro and Latin America: is EMU a blueprint for Mercosur?', working paper, Universidad Torcuato Di Tella, Buenos Aires.

Levy Yeyati, E. and F. Sturzenegger (1999b), 'Classifying exchange rate regimes: deeds vs words', working paper, Universidad Torcuato Di Tella, Buenos Aires.

Levy Yeyati, E. and F. Sturzenegger (1999c), 'The Euro and Latin America: Implications of the euro for Latin America's financial and banking systems', working paper, Universidad Torcuato Di Tella, Buenos Aires.

McCauley, R. (1997), 'The euro and the dollar', *Essays in International Finance*, 205, Princeton University, November.

Miotti, L., C. Quenan and D. Plihon (2002), 'The euro and financial relations between Latin America and Europe: medium- and long-term implications', *Series Macroeconomia del desarrollo*, **13**, Economic Development Division, ECLAC, March.

Portes, R. and H. Rey (1998), 'The emergence of the euro as an international currency', *Economic Policy*, **5**.

Tavlas, Garv (1991), 'On the international use of currencies: the case of the Deutsche Mark', Princeton University, *Essays on International Finance*, 181, March.

Teïletche, J. (2001), 'La parité euro/dollar durant les décennies 80 et 90: peut-on trouver une spécification raisonnable et à quel horizon?', *Etude CDC*, Paris.

Williamson, J. (1983), 'The exchange rate systems', *Institute for International Economics*.

Zahler, R. (1999), 'The euro and its effect on the economy and the integration of Latin America and the Caribbean', presentation at the Annual Meeting of the Board of Governors, IDB, Paris, March.

7. Big and small currencies: the regional connection

Agnès Bénassy-Quéré and Benoît Cœuré

INTRODUCTION

It is now widely recognized that the liberalization of capital flows casts doubts on the sustainability of the so-called 'intermediate' or 'middle-of-the road' exchange rate regimes, that is of those regimes lying in between free floating, and hard pegs (currency boards, full dollarization or currency unions). This new consensus follows the currency crises experienced in Europe and in a number of emerging countries throughout the 1990s. This is the 'two-corner approach' to the choice of exchange rate regimes (see for instance Eichengreen, 1994; Fisher, 2001).

Indeed a number of policy moves have followed this approach. A number of countries have rejected intermediate regimes in favour of one or the other of the 'corner' solutions. The European exchange rate mechanism gave way to the euro; full dollarization was undertaken in Ecuador; and various countries such as Brazil, Russia and some Asian countries moved to free floats.

Reality is mixed however. The breakdown of the Argentine currency board at the end of 2001 has shown that hard pegs can be vulnerable too. At the other range of the spectrum, a series of empirical studies have shown that most countries with officially floating exchange rates do in fact intervene on foreign exchange markets to stabilize their currencies.

In this chapter, we argue that the two-corner approach omits a crucial dimension of exchange rate regimes: the regional dimension. Hard pegs can fail when they are not consistent with other regimes in the region, as was the case in Argentina. Stabilizing the exchange rate against the dollar is the simplest way to coordinate exchange rate policies within a region. Lastly, the survival of intermediate regimes depends crucially on regional monetary cooperation.

The next section describes the recent evolution of the international monetary system. Then the regional dimension is introduced, before examining. how to implement regional cooperation or coordination.

RECENT EVOLUTION OF THE INTERNATIONAL MONETARY SYSTEM (IMS)

During the 1990s, the IMS was hit by three major shocks. The first was the expansion of international capital flows at a much higher speed than the development of trade, the arrival of powerful players, such as hedge funds, whose balance sheets may exceed those of central banks, and as a consequence the greater autonomy of the 'bottom' of the balance of payments (foreign direct investment, portfolio investment) from the 'top' of the balance (trade in goods and services). The second shock, which partly resulted from the first one, was the financial crises in emerging economies (1994 in Mexico, 1997 in Asia, 1998–99 in Brazil and Russia, 2001 in Turkey and Argentina), and the floating of many currencies previously pegged to the US dollar. The third was the creation of the euro, which is now a key currency of the IMS.

Focusing on the second shock, we investigate this force by comparing the evolution of exchange rate regimes before and after the crises.

Official Exchange Rate Regimes

A comprehensive view of exchange rate regimes is provided by the International Monetary Fund (IMF), which classifies member countries according to the degree of flexibility of their currency. According to the IMF, since the 1970s the share of developing countries with a fixed exchange rate has declined steadily (from 90 per cent in 1975 to 45 per cent in 1997), whereas the share of flexible exchange rates has risen (from 10 per cent in 1975 to 55 per cent in 1997). Figure 7.1 extends this diagnosis to all member countries over 1983–99.[1] It also shows that most switches occurred in the late 1980s to early 1990s. The relative share of both groups of regimes have stabilized since then, despite EMU (which mechanically reduced the proportion of limited flexibility regimes) and financial crises in emerging countries (which reduced the share of fixed pegs, see *infra*).

However this diagnosis is insufficient. First, these two groups mix exchange rate regimes which are quite different. Second, the anchor currencies are not identified. Table 7.1 provides some more detail on the scissor-like evolution illustrated in Figure 7.1. It confirms the striking extension of free floating regimes at the expense mainly of pegs on baskets of foreign currencies.[2] Fixed pegs on single currencies have survived better, due to the longevity of the French franc zone and of regional arrangements around the South African rand and the Indian rupee, together with the creation of several currency boards in the 1990s. However the share of

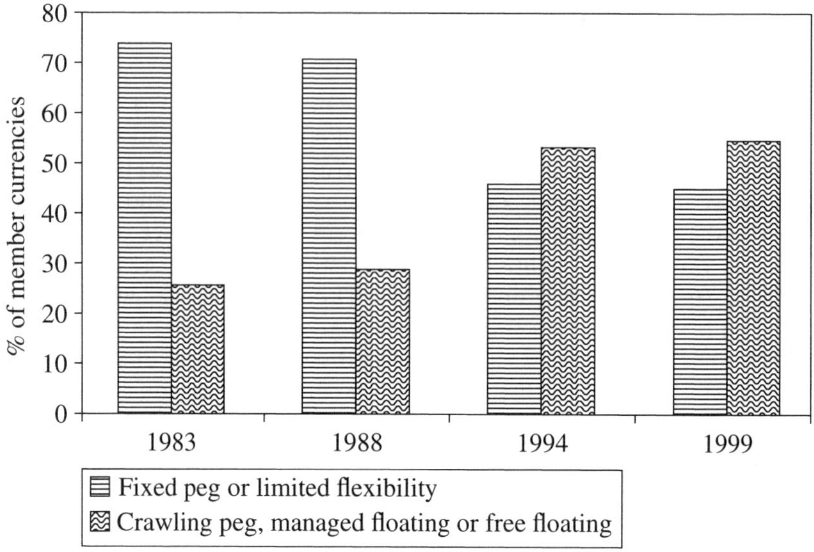

Source: IMF, *Annual Report on Exchange Arrangements and Exchange Restrictions*, various issues.

Figure 7.1 Share of fixed and flexible regimes among IMF member countries (end of year)

crawling pegs and managed floating regimes has resisted too, and it actually rose between 1994 and 1999.

The scissors effect evidenced in Figure 7.1 can best be described as a substitution of free and managed floating regimes to pegs on the US dollar and on currency baskets. No evolution towards a multipolar system is apparent.

De Facto Exchange Rate Regimes

It is now widely acknowledged that official exchange rate regimes only partially reflect the actual behaviour of monetary authorities. Several methods are used to identify *de facto* regimes.

Corrected official regimes

Since 1999, exchange rate regimes published by the IMF have been corrected to account for actual practice, on the basis of the evolution of nominal exchange rates and of official reserves. Corrected regimes have been retropolated back to 1990 to allow for comparisons (Bubula and Ötker-Robe, 2002). The results, as summarized in Figure 7.2, tend to

Table 7.1 Share of various regimes among IMF member countries (end of year)

Exchange rate regimes	1983	1988	1994	1999
Fixed pegs on single, currencies, incl. currency boards	**35.6**	**38.2**	**26.0**	**29.9**
US dollar	23.3	25.7	13.8	15.0
FF, DM, euro	8.9	9.2	8.3	12.3
Others	3.4	3.3	3.9	2.7
Fixed pegs on baskets	**27.4**	**25.7**	**13.3**	**9.6**
SDR	8.9	5.3	1.7	3.2
ECU	0.7	0.7	0.6	–
Other baskets	17.8	19.7	11.0	6.4
Limited flexibility	**11.0**	**7.2**	**7.2**	**5.9**
European exchange-rate mechanism	4.8	4.6	5.0	1.1
Other arrangements with bands	6.2	2.6	2.2	4.8
Crawling pegs, managed floats	**19.9**	**17.8**	**19.9**	**23.0**
TOTAL	100.0	100.0	100.0	100.0
Number of currencies	146	152	181	187

Source: IMF, *Annual Report on Exchange Arrangements and Exchange Restrictions*, various issues.

confirm the rising share of flexible regimes (free floats and managed floats). In addition, the distinction between hard pegs (monetary unions, full dollarization and currency boards) and soft pegs (fixed but adjustable pegs, with or without target zones, crawling pegs) show the growing importance of the extremes at the expense of intermediate regimes.

Estimated regimes

Other studies have focused on the evolution of exchange rates and official reserves. Levy Yeyati and Sturzenegger (2000) have run a cluster analysis based on the observed volatility of nominal exchange rates and of official reserves. They found that the proportion of free floats has remained fairly stable over the 1990s, as have the shares of fixed exchange rate regimes and managed floats.

In Bénassy-Quéré and Coeuré (2004), we have proposed a method based on the stability of nominal exchange rates. We test the existence of a stable relationship between each currency *i* and the US dollar, the euro and the yen. The test is implemented for 139 currencies with daily, weekly and monthly data over two periods: from January 1994 to June 1997 (between the Mexican

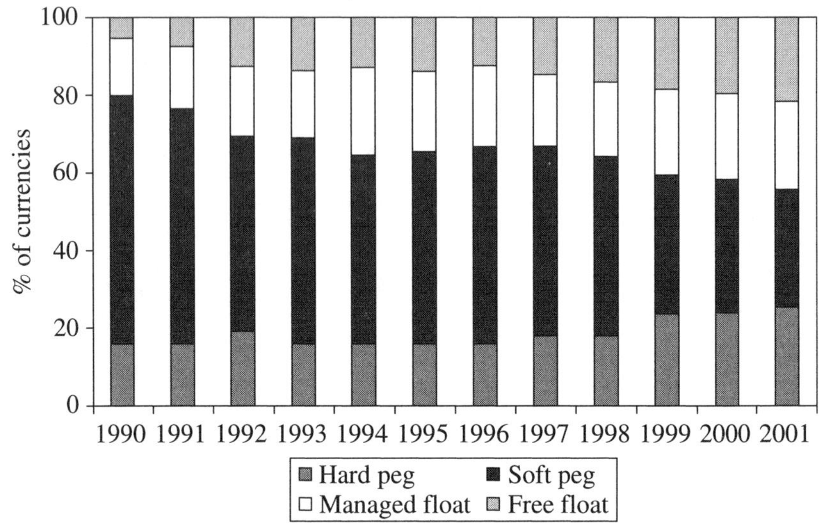

Source: Bubula and Ötker-Robe (2002).

Figure 7.2 The hollowing out of intermediate exchange rate regimes

crisis and the Asian crisis), and from January 1999 to April 2004 (after the Asian, Brazilian and Russian crises). One advantage of this method is that it allows us to identify anchor currencies. The results are summarized in Table 7.2. Strikingly, no massive shift towards free floats is observed. However comparing *de facto* and *de jure* regime on a country-by-country basis shows that intermediate regimes, defined as fixed regimes which are not classified as hard pegs by the IMF, tend to decline to the benefit of hard pegs. We find the same result when using Levy Yeyati and Sturzenegger data. We also find that the US dollar remains the major anchor: the IMS has not yet moved towards a multipolar system.

Table 7.2 De facto *exchange rate regimes*

	Number of currencies	Free floats	Fixed regimes	of which:			
				USD	EUR	JPY	basket
Pre-crises	84	6%	94%	50%	18%	0%	26%
Post-crises	138	7%	93%	62%	14%	0%	17%

Source: Bénassy-Quéré and Coeuré (2004), weekly data.

MAPPING EXCHANGE RATE REGIMES

A Two-Dimension Approach: Flexibility and Commitment

The IMF classification is based on two criteria: the degree of flexibility, and the existence or not of a commitment by monetary authorities. In Figure 7.3, we position exchange rate regimes along two dimensions: flexibility and policy commitment. Since the two criteria are obviously correlated, exchange rate regimes are aligned along diagonals, with corner solutions at the two extremes.

The two-corner approach can be rephrased as follows: only South-West and North-East corners are sustainable when capital mobility is high.

The Missing Regional Dimension

When monetary authorities do not commit to a fixed exchange rate, the anchor can only be domestic: credibility is 'earned', not 'borrowed' (Braga de Macedo et al., 2001). This is why some emerging countries have adopted inflation targeting when moving to flexible exchange rates. A prerequisite for such strategies is strong institutions: economically literate bureaucrats and politicians, an independent central bank, reliable statistics, and so on. In the absence of such a framework, that is when credibility cannot be built from the inside, full dollarization is usually thought as the only option.

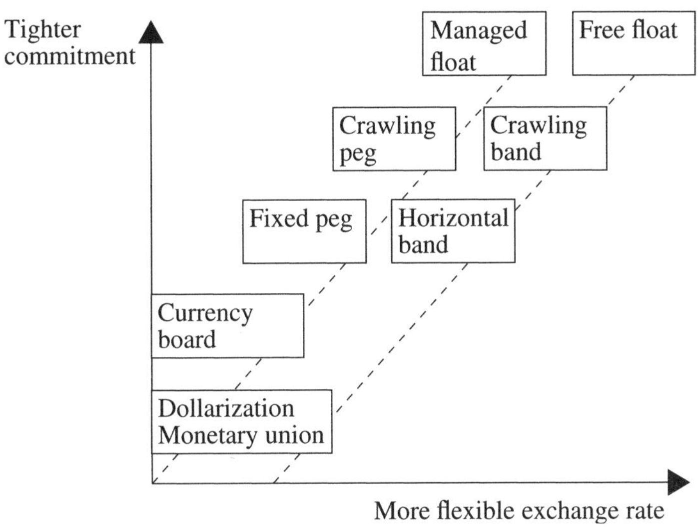

Figure 7.3 The two dimensions of exchange rate regimes

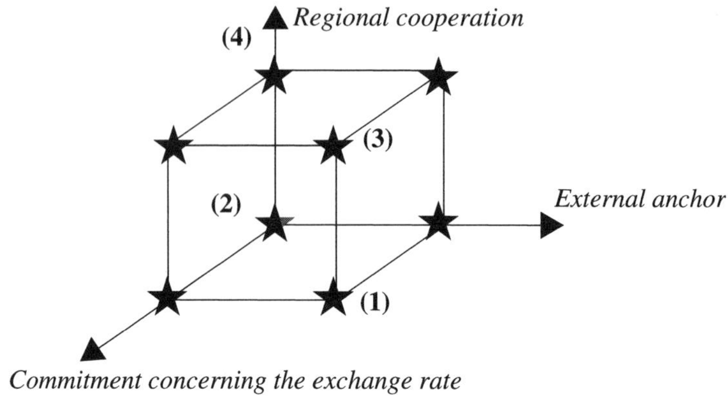

Figure 7.4 The three dimensions of exchange rate regimes

In this line of reasoning, dollarization is considered the same way as monetary union, which is a multilateral, regional arrangement. This neglects a crucial dimension. A supranational central bank, which is by construction less dependent on political developments in any national component of the union, may prove more credible than a national central bank. Indeed the European Central Bank is more credible than most national central banks ever were.

Adding the regional dimension, we identify eight 'corners', of which four only are serious options (Figure 7.4). This can be contrasted with the two possible corners of Figure 7.3.

The two traditional corner solutions are (1) the currency board or full dollarization, and (2) the free float. When regional cooperation is added, the equivalent of the currency board/dollarization solution is the monetary union (3), and free floating now involves coordinating economic policies regionally (4). There are few examples of the latter regime however, perhaps because fixed exchange rates work as leading forces of policy coordination. Although not on the regional basis, the aim of G7 coordination resembles corner (4). It is likely that such coordination could be made easier in a regional framework.

The Regional Corners

European monetary unification has inspired a number of studies looking at the pros and cons of forming monetary unions elsewhere in the world (for example in East Asia, in South America, in the Middle East, in West Africa).[3] It is hard to find a region outside Europe displaying the optimum currency areas criteria (indeed most studies, following Bayoumi and Eichengreen's,

(1993) seminal analysis, already find the euro zone not to be an optimum currency area). In particular such analyses stress the large intra-regional differences in income per capita or in product specialization (especially as far as commodities are concerned), and the lack of intra-regional trade and investment. The heterogeneity of the East Asian region as compared with Europe is illustrated in Figures 7.5 and 7.6 taken from Cœuré (2004). Leaving Luxembourg aside, GDP per capita is less heterogeneous in the EU25 than in East Asia. Of course this feature is even more striking when considering the EU15 group or the euro zone (EU12) group. Consistently, GDP growth is less heterogeneous in the EU15 than in East Asia.

However monetary union may concern only a sub-group of countries (for instance Singapore and Malaysia, or South Korea and Japan; see Yuen, 2000). More importantly, full monetary union is a long-term project[4] which deserves a dynamic treatment; that is it is necessary to extrapolate the growing regionalization of trade and the endogeneity of some optimum currency area criteria (see Frankel and Rose, 1998).

Even though monetary union can only constitute a long-run focal point for most regions, such perspective changes the terms of the choice of an exchange rate regime even in the short run. Firstly, the unilateral two-corner solutions may not be advisable if the long-run goal is a monetary union. On the one hand, it is well known that a free float is conducive to non-cooperative strategies which are suboptimal in case of common shocks. On the other hand, whereas dollarization is irreversible, currency boards are not and they lack an exit strategy, as exemplified by the Argentinian crisis. Hence they are suited only when dollarization or a monetary union with the anchor currency is expected in the near future, as is the case for some CEECs.

Secondly, the perspective of a monetary union in the long run can make intermediate regimes more robust in the meantime, provided that these regimes are properly defined and managed in a regional framework. This point is studied in more detail in the next section.

REACHING THE CORNERS

We have found from the previous section that the two-corner solutions may not be optimal in a dynamic perspective, once the regional dimension is taken into account. We now turn to the transition towards regional corners.

Common Pegs

The main objective of a regional monetary arrangement is to provide relatively stable exchange rates within the region, and an institutional

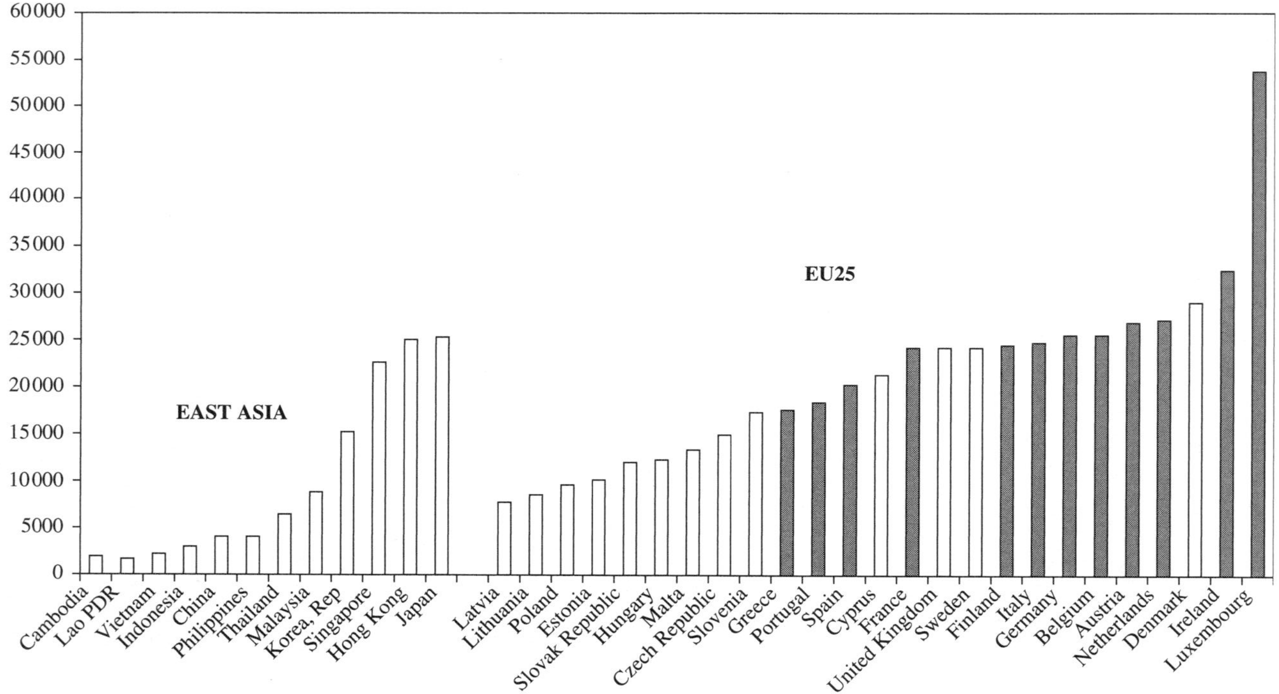

Source: World Bank, *World Development Indicators 2003.*

Figure 7.5 GDP per capita in purchasing power standard, Asia and Europe, year 2001 (in US dollars)

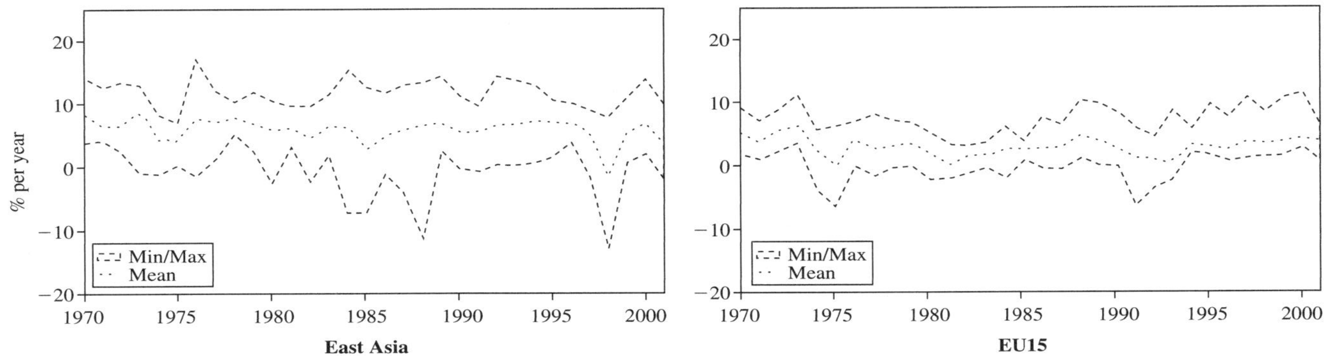

Source: World Bank, *World Development Indicators 2003.*

Figure 7.6 Heterogeneity of yearly growth rates, Asia and Europe

framework for exchange rate realignments. It has been argued above that in the short run, this can be achieved through the use of external anchors.

In a highly integrated region, the selection of a specific foreign anchor is of secondary importance. The most important thing is the mere existence of such a common anchor. In this vein, Williamson (1999) shows that a common basket peg for nine Asian countries would yield similar stability of effective exchange rates as would tailor-made baskets for each of the nine countries. However adopting a common currency as a common peg is not optimal when the anchor country fails to be the prominent partner outside the region, as evidenced by the Asian crisis: the appreciation of the US dollar from 1995 to 1997 is often cited as one of the causes of the 1997 crisis (Ito et al., 1998). Finally, choosing a foreign anchor constrains monetary policy. Hence there should not be too much asymmetry in business cycles with the anchor country, and optimum currency criteria should be taken into account.

From the literature on the choice of an anchor currency, it can be concluded that the euro is *a priori* a more straightforward anchor than the US dollar. Indeed CEECs and Northern African countries are good candidates for a euro peg since they carry out most of their trade with the euro zone; they also display business cycles and (for some of them) specialization patterns which are rather close to those of the euro zone (Boone and Maurel, 1999; Bénassy-Quéré and Lahrèche-Révil, 1999). In contrast, Asian and Latin American countries should peg their currencies to dollar/euro/yen baskets rather than to the sole US dollar, given the balanced distribution of their foreign trade (Williamson, 1999; Bénassy-Quéré, 1999; Ogawa and Ito, 2000).[5] It can be argued however that this reasoning underestimates the importance of trade invoicing and debt denomination, both of which point to dollar pegs (Calvo and Reinhart, 2002).

Hence, using a common peg could be achieved without regional cooperation around the euro zone, whereas the lack of regional cooperation constitutes a major impediment in Asia or in South America. Even though a common basket can be defined relatively easily, its use would necessitate a high degree of political commitment (see Bayoumi et al., 2000; and the next section). In the absence of regional cooperation, the dollar can be used as a second-best option (Bénassy-Quéré, 1999; Ito et al., 2000). Consider a situation where each country chooses its exchange rate policy, taking the policy of its neighbours as given. Theoretically this gives birth to multiple equilibria (regional pegs on the yen, on the euro, on the dollar, on a basket, and so on). In practice, history, politics and the initial patterns of trade and debt denomination (the so-called 'original sin') have led most countries to focus on the US dollar.

As a conclusion, a soft peg on a single currency (contrasting with a peg on a common basket) remains an attractive system due to its low requirement in terms of cooperation. In addition this type of peg is more easily verifiable by market participants, which grants it more credibility (Frankel et al., 1999).

The tendency for countries that have been hit by crises to come back to *de facto* pegs on the dollar can be understood in this context. The use of the euro as a currency anchor has so far been limited by the inertia of the international monetary system. However in regions like Asia or South America, pegs on the dollar are less advisable than regional cooperation which could be organized around common baskets of foreign currencies. We study below how such cooperation could be organized.

Institutions for Regional Integration

Classical analyses of monetary regionalism, from the early work of Cooper (1975) to Canzoneri and Henderson (1991), highlighted the superiority of cooperation (that is joint optimization of a common loss function) over coordination (that is the selection of a specific Nash equilibrium). Coordination only rests on information sharing, whereas cooperation rests on a commitment not to accommodate only domestic shocks.

It can be strongly argued that in order to be credible and to avoid renegotiation, such commitments have to be backed by binding agreements such as treaties or supranational bodies. One step further, some have argued that the essence of money is political and that monetary relations reflect permanent bargaining and, ultimately, the hierarchy of power between sovereign states (Cohen, 2000). At any rate, the political economy dimension is key to understanding the dynamics of monetary integration.

From coordination to cooperation

The degree of formalization and constraint of regional agreements can be adjusted according to the desired degree of coordination. Networks of personal relationships among monetary officials and bureaucrats, discussion forums convened on a regular basis, are first steps of cooperation and their usefulness should not be understated. However in order to be operational, such coordination needs parallel steps to be made in terms of economic integration: tariff cuts, development of a regional financial market allowing the countries to avoid the 'original sin' which consists in having the debt invoiced in foreign currencies. The irreversibility of economic integration then works in favour of stronger cooperation, as evidenced by the European case.

Until 1 January 1999, the European exchange rate mechanism probably constituted the most ambitious example of regional monetary cooperation because it included all forms of coordination and cooperation, from the least formal to the most formal: information sharing and the building of a common doctrine in the framework of various committees, formal swap agreements, existence of federal institutions (such as the European Commission and the European Monetary Institute) endorsing the role of technical assistance and of policy impulse.

History matters: the monetary issue in Asia

The weight of historical factors is evident in the case of Europe, where the process of economic and then monetary integration is rooted in century-old political debates. As early as in the mid-nineteenth century, the French writer and politician Victor Hugo advocated a political union in Europe. After the Second World War, the so-called 'founding fathers of Europe' had the ultimate goal to ensure war between France and Germany never happened again.

Asia provides a different example of a cooperation process which is obviously neither planned nor comprehensive, but where instruments have nevertheless been developed over years (see Ito, 2001).

As early as in 1957 (the very year the Treaty of Rome was agreed in Europe), technical discussions were initiated among central banks from Asia and the Pacific region, the number of which has now reached 20 (SEANZA).[6] Meetings of South-East Asian central banks (SEACEN) have been organized since 1966 and were complemented in 1991 by a twice-yearly forum for technical discussion among 11 countries (EMEAP)[7] and then, after the Mexican crisis, by a network of currency swap agreements between central banks. Informal forums for macroeconomic discussion also exist: a short-lived 'Asian G6' was launched in 1996 a few months before the financial crisis, and meetings of APEC[8] or ASEAN[9] finance ministers now take place on a regular basis. ASEAN countries have also met since 1999 together with the three regional powers, the People's Republic of China, the Republic of Korea and Japan, in the so-called ASEAN+3 framework.

The Chang Mai initiative launched in May 2000 was the first practical achievement of this ASEAN+3 group in the monetary field. It consists in a network of bilateral swap agreements amongst the central banks of the group. The next step could be a regional monetary arrangement. Bayoumi et al. (2000) underline the needs for a strong political commitment, which they see as a remote perspective. It seems however that such ideas have increasingly been tested by Asian politicians. Hong Kong Finance Secretary Donald Tsang suggested in October 1999 to create a common currency for Hong Kong and Singapore with a five- or six-year horizon. In addition several Asian heads of state, among which are counted the Malaysian prime minister Mahatir and the Philippines president Estrada, have favoured at times a common currency in Asia. In the latter case the main rationale does not seem to be economic but rather political. Building on the European example, monetary union is seen as a catalyst to regional political cooperation.

Political impediments are more frequently quoted than economic pros and cons to explain why such projects are envisaged only for the very long run.[10] In particular, as pointed out by Eichengreen (1997), a prerequisite is the settlement of long-lasting political conflicts, some of which are inherited from the Second World War (notably between Japan, Korea and China), and others are due to ethnic or religious patterns – for a discussion of the pro and cons of an Asian Monetary Union, see Henning (2002) and Coeuré (2004).

We conclude from this discussion that the commitment to an intermediate regime has to be stronger than in the past, along two lines.

First, give some guarantees of short-term robustness, which can either be domestic (foreign exchange reserves, flexibility in exchange rate management so as to limit the likelihood of macroeconomic misalignments, control of short-term inflows, surveillance of the financial system) or external (regional or international assistance in case of a speculative crisis).

Second, indicate clearly that the chosen exchange rate regime fits into an overall economic and political strategy, covering trade, the financial sector and fiscal policies, among others.

With these two prerequisites, regional monetary cooperation is feasible, and it helps participating countries escape from the choice between dollarization and free floating. Full-fledged regional currencies are unlikely to emerge in the short and even in the medium term. In the meantime, regional monetary cooperation will have to take the form of common pegs on baskets of extra-regional currencies. The impact of such arrangements on the stability of the global system can then be questioned.

Vertical Integration of the International Monetary System

The impact of exchange rate fluctuations between key currencies on the sustainability of 'small' currency regimes has been discussed extensively. In particular, the appreciation of the US dollar against the yen from 1995 to 1997 is generally viewed as one major cause of the Asian crisis. The reverse impact of 'small' currency regimes on the stability of key currencies is less frequently evoked.[11] Two views can be contrasted.

The first view is that of Kindleberger (1973), according to whom the Great Depression was due to the lack of economic leadership at that time, after the weakening of the United Kingdom and before the rise of the

United States. For Kindleberger, the existence of a dominant power is stabilizing since the corresponding country can impose some cooperation on its partner while supporting most of its costs:

> In these circumstances, the international economic and monetary system needs a leadership, a country which is prepared, consciously or unconsciously, under some system of rules that it has internalised, to set standards of conduct for other countries; and to seek to get others to follow them, to take on an undue share of the burdens of the system, and in particular to take on its support in adversity by accepting its redundant commodities, maintaining a flow of investment capital and discounting its paper. Britain performed this role in the century to 1913; the United States in the period after the Second World War to, say, the Interest Equalisation Tax in 1963. (Kindleberger, 1973, p. 28).

According to Kindleberger, amongst the tasks of the leader, one is to implement a system of relatively stable exchange rates.

The second view is that of the 'volatility transfer' (Fratianni and Von Hagen, 1990). The idea is that the exchange rate is an adjustment variable: fixing it transfers the burden of the adjustment to other variables, especially on other exchange rates. Considering the balance-of-payments equilibrium, Collignon (1999) shows that even the fundamental equilibrium exchange rate (FEER) is more volatile when some exchange rates are fixed, because remaining exchange rate fluctuations are less able to bring the current account back to balance.[12]

Hence the building of monetary blocks around the US dollar, the euro and possibly the yen could have a destabilizing impact on euro–dollar and yen–dollar exchange rates. This reinforces the importance, for third countries, of the currency anchor(s). In this context regional monetary cooperation could protect the participating countries from destabilizing effects of key currency fluctuations (intra-regional exchange rates would remain stable). The volatility of key currencies would then be supported by the United States, the euro zone and Japan, which can more easily hedge due to more developed financial markets.

On the whole, there is no incompatibility between the two views: the building of currency blocks could raise inter-block instability, but the cost of this volatility would be mainly borne by leading countries.

CONCLUSION

We have argued that a practical way to escape the 'two-corner' debate is to recognize the regional dimension of exchange rate regime choice: the 'good' regime for a given economy will depend both on its own characteristics and on the choices made by regional partners. Recent monetary history provides a number of illustrations of this reasoning. Regional monetary cooperation can constitute an alternative to suboptimal behaviour of emerging countries to focus their economic policy on controlling their bilateral exchange rate to the US dollar. One option is of course monetary union, which however can only constitute a long-run target. Another more easily implementable option consists in stabilizing national currencies against a common basket of foreign currencies and discussing exchange rate in a regional multilateral framework. Regional monetary cooperation is also a way for emerging market economies to protect themselves against the destabilizing impact of the fluctuations of key currencies. Major economies should therefore continue to cushion the instability of the international monetary system while encouraging the building of regional currency blocks, before new 'big', possibly regional, currencies can emerge.

NOTES

1. The IMF's system of classification changed in 1999. The data in Figure 7.1 and in Table 7.1 refer to the old classification. See below for the new classification.
2. The retreat of limited flexibility regimes is essentially attributable to the merger of 11 currencies into the euro.
3. See, for instance, Anthony and Hughes Hallett (2000), Eichengreen (1997), Masson and Pattillo (2001), Sadeh (1997).
4. There were 30 years between the first monetary union project (the Werner plan) and the introduction of the euro.
5. In addition, Jadresic et al. (1999) underline that a common peg on a single foreign currency (the dollar) raises the vulnerability of each country to the crises in other countries, this effect being weaker with a common basket.
6. SEANZA stands for South-East Asia, New Zealand and Australia.
7. Executive meeting of East Asia and Pacific central banks: Hong Kong, Malaysia, Indonesia and Thailand, later joined by Japan, Singapore and the Philippines.
8. APEC is made up of 11 Asian economies (Japan, Korea, the Philippines, Indonesia, Malaysia, Brunei, Singapore, Thailand, PR China, Taiwan and Hong Kong), three Pacific economies (Australia, New Zealand and Papua New Guinea) and four American economies (Canada, Mexico, Chile and the US).
9. ASEAN is made of ten economies: Brunei, Cambodia, Indonesia, Laos, Malaysia, Myanmar, the Philippines, Singapore, Thailand and Vietnam.
10. Bergsten (2000) is more optimistic concerning the timetable, viewing the building of regional institutions as the 'new Asian challenge'.
11. The pros and cons of exchange rate stability are well reviewed by Honohan and Lane (1999). They do not apply in the same way for industrial countries and for emerging countries. Hence one should be concerned by the potential transfer of volatility from one group of currencies to another.
12. The FEER is defined as the exchange rate that is consistent with external and internal equilibrium (see Williamson, 1983). More volatility of the FEER would not necessarily transfer into higher short-run volatility. This possibility is left for further research.

REFERENCES

Anthony, M.L. and A. Hughes Hallett (2000), 'Is the case for economic and monetary union in the Caribbean realistic?', *World Economy*, **23**, 119–44.

Bayoumi, T. and B. Eichengreen (1993), 'Shocking aspects of EMU', in F. Torres and F. Giavazzi (eds), *Adjustment and Growth in the European Monetary Union*, Cambridge: Cambridge University Press.

Bayoumi, T. and B. Eichengreen (1999), 'Is Asia an optimum currency area? Can it become one?' in S. Collignon and J. Pisani-Ferry (eds), *Exchange Rate Policies in Asian Emerging Countries*, London: Routledge.

Bayoumi, T., B. Eichengreen and P. Mauro (2000), 'On regional monetary arrangement for ASEAN', CEPR discussion paper 2411.

Bénassy-Quéré, A. (1999), 'Optimal pegs for East-Asian currencies', *Journal of the Japanese and International Economies*, **13**, March.

Bénassy-Quéré, A. and B. Coeuré (2000), 'Big and small currencies: the regional connection', CEPII working paper 2000-09.

Bénassy-Quéré A. and B. Coeuré (2004), 'On the identification of de facto currency pegs', *Journal of the Japanese and International Economies*, forthcoming.

Bénassy-Quéré A. and A. Lahrèche-Révil (1999), 'L'euro comme monnaie de référence à l'est et au sud de l'Union européenne', *Revue Economique*, **50** (2), 1185–1202.

Bergsten, F. (2000), 'The new Asian challenge', Institute for International Economics working paper 00-04.

Boone, L. and M. Maurel (1999), 'L'ancrage de l'Europe centrale et orientale à l'Union européenne', *Revue Economique*, **50** (2), 1123–38.

Braga de Macedo, J., D. Cohen, and H. Reisen (eds) (2001), 'Don't fix, don't float', OECD Development Centre.

Bubula, A. and I. Ötker-Robe (2002), 'The evolution of exchange rate regimes since 1990: evidence from de facto policies', IMF working paper 02/155.

Calvo, G. and C. Reinhart (2002), 'Fear of floating', *Quarterly Journal of Economics*, **117** (2), 379–408.

Canzoneri, M. and D. Henderson (1991), *Monetary Policy in Interdependent Economies: A Game-theoretic Approach*, Cambridge, MA: MIT Press.

Coeuré, B. (2004), 'The narrow road to the single Asian currency', in G. de Brouwer (ed.), *Monetary Cooperation in East-Asia.*

Cœuré, B. and J. Pisani-Ferry (2000) 'The euro, the yen and the dollar: the case against benign neglect', in A. Swoboda and P. Kenen (eds), *Key Issues in the Reform of the International Monetary and Financial System*, International Monetary Fund.

Cohen, B. (2000), 'Money and power in world politics', in T. Lawton, J. Rosenau and A. Verdun (eds), *Strange Power*, Ashgate Publishing.

Collignon, S. (1999), 'Bloc floating and exchange rate volatility : the causes and consequences of currency blocs', in S. Collignon and J. Pisani-Ferry (eds), *Exchange Rate Policies in Asian Emerging Countries*, London: Routledge.

Cooper, R. (1975), 'Prolegomena to the choice of an international monetary system', in R. Cooper, *The International Monetary System: Essays in World Economics*, reprint 1987.

Eichengreen, B. (1994), *International Monetary Arrangements for the 21st Century*, Washington, DC: The Brookings Institution.

Eichengreen, B. (1997), 'Is there a monetary union in Asia's future ?', *Brookings Review*, Spring.
Eichengreen, B. and T. Bayoumi (1999), 'Is Asia an optimum currency area? Can it become one? Regional, global and historical perspectives on Asian monetary relations', in S. Collignon and J. Pisani-Ferry (eds), *Exchange Rate Policies in Asian Emerging Countries*, London: Routledge.
Fischer, S. (2001), 'Exchange rate regimes: is the bipolar view correct?', *Journal of Economic Perspectives*, **15** (2), 3–24.
Frankel, J.A., E. Fajnzylber, S. Schmukler and L. Servén (1999), 'Verifying exchange rate regimes', *Journal of Development Economics*, **66** (2), 351–86.
Frankel, J. and A. Rose (1998), 'The endogeneity of optimum currency area criteria', *Economic Journal*, **108**, 1009–24.
Fratianni, M. and J. von Hagen (1990), 'The European monetary system ten years after', *Carnegie-Rochester Conference Series on Public Policy*, **32**, 173–241.
Henning, R. (2002), *East-Asian Financial Cooperation*, Institute for International Economics, Washington, DC.
Honohan, P. and P.R. Lane (1999), 'Pegging to the dollar and the euro', Trinity College Dublin Economic Papers 996.
Ito, T. (2001), 'Regional surveillance mechanisms in East Asia', report of the study group on Strengthening Financial Cooperation and Surveillance, Kobe Research Project, February.
Ito, T., E. Ogawa and Y. Sasaki (1998), 'How did the dollar peg fail in Asia?', NBER working paper 6729.
Ito, T., E. Ogawa and Y. Sasaki (2000), 'On the desirability of a regional basket currency arrangement', NBER working paper 8002.
Jadresic, E., P. Masson and P. Mauro (1999), 'Exchange rate regimes of developing countries: global context and individual choices', ADBI-CEPII-KIEP International Conference on Exchange Rate Regimes in Emerging Market Economies, Tokyo, 17–18 December, available at www.cepii.fr.
Kindleberger, Ch.P. (1973), *The World in Depression, 1929–1939*, London: Allen Lane, Penguin Books.
Levy Yeyati, E. and F. Sturzenegger (2000), 'Classifying exchange rate regimes: deeds vs words', mimeo, Universidad Torcuato di Tella, forthcoming in *European Economic Review.*
Masson, P. and C. Pattillo (2001), 'Monetary union in West Africa (ECOWAS): is it desirable and how could it be achieved?', IMF occasional paper 204.
Ogawa, E. and T. Ito (2000), 'On the desirability of a regional basket currency arrangement', NBER working paper 8002.
Sadeh, T. (1997), 'The economic desirability of Middle-Eastern monetary cooperation', *World Economy*, **20** (6), September, 809–28.
Williamson, J. (1983), *The Exchange Rate System*, Institute for International Economics.
Williamson, J. (1999), 'The case for a common basket peg for East Asian currencies', in S. Collignon and J. Pisani-Ferry (eds), *Exchange Rate Policies in Asian Emerging Countries*, London: Routledge.
Yuen, H. (2000), 'Is Asia an optimum currency area? 'Shocking' aspects of output fluctuations in East Asia', unpublished manuscript, National University of Singapore.

8. Regional integration and the issue of choosing an appropriate exchange rate regime in Latin America

Hubert Escaith, Christian Ghymers and Rogerio Studart*

INTRODUCTION

In the 1990s significant changes in macroeconomic policies and structural reforms in Latin America and the Caribbean (here after referred to as LAC) led to a convergence in macroeconomic policies, objectives and instruments, as well as a clear increase in the interdependencies of these national economies on both the trade and the financial fronts. In addition, as a result of financial globalization, economic events in one country produce direct impacts on financial spreads in the whole region.

Despite this increased convergence of policy orientation and interdependency, macroeconomic policies are still uncoordinated and continue to be made in close-knit national circles without considering any spillovers at all. In particular there is a disturbing picture concerning national choices of exchange rate regime, characterized by two clear trends: (1) a general increase in the flexibility of exchange rates, that is a larger number of countries adopting floating schemes or widening the existing range for fluctuations; and (2) a significant polarization towards the corners of the range of possible systems: either pure floats or dollarization and currency boards.

This chapter contends first that, due to external financial shocks and to the difficulties of sustaining coherent macroeconomic policies in the region, exchange rate regimes in Latin America tend also to be highly vulnerable; and that the adoption of 'corner solutions' does not solve these problems, but also tends to create even further macroeconomic imbalances and vulnerability. Second, we claim that even though Latin American economies do not comply with the optimal currency areas, moving towards a monetary union (by slowly enhancing coordination of macroeconomic policies) could offer both an intermediate and a more coherent option for LAC exchange rate regimes, and the missing link for a concrete institution-building process on which macroeconomic sustainability could be founded.

In order to deal with these issues the chapter is organized into five sections, including this introduction. In the following section we briefly review the literature on optimal choices of exchange rate regimes (ERR hereafter) and optimal currency areas (OCAs). The third section analyses the processes of commercial and financial integration within LAC economies in order to assess how these economies meet the OCA criteria and the degree of interdependencies among them. The fourth section builds on the previous two to claim that even though LAC economies do not meet the OCA criteria, there is a strong case for aiming at regional monetary arrangements, based on the incentives such a process can have on building the institutions and the coordination required for long-term stability in the region. The final section summarizes our findings and presents our final remarks.

LESSONS FROM THE DEBATE ON THE OPTIMAL CHOICE OF EXCHANGE-RATE REGIMES

The succession of financial and exchange rate crises in the second half of the 1990s has led to a polarization of the ERR debate between what have come to be known as 'corner solutions'. More recently however these corner solutions have shown themselves to be not so much 'solutions' as 'problems' for emerging economies and their regional partners, and the discussion is now entering into a new phase. In this section we explore what can be learned from this debate and how it can be applied to the analysis of monetary arrangements in Latin America nowadays.

The Early Debate on ERR and OCA

In the early literature on ERRs, the debate was centred on the most appropriate ERR for single economies. Exchange rates were seen as the natural instrument to mitigate the effect of external shocks on output and employment by changing relative prices (elasticity approach) under the well-known Marshall–Lerner conditions.

This approach was complemented in the 1950s by greater macroeconomic insight into the direct relationship between internal absorption and the exchange rate, which ultimately led to a monetary approach that was more focused on demand for monetary balances.[1] This approach was particularly relevant to LAC countries in the 1980s. Indeed in countries with a recent history of high inflation, the exchange rate debate was complicated by the elusive nature of demand for (fiat) money. By its very definition, fiat money relies on the credibility of national authorities, which is another dimension of people's confidence in a currency. Confidence is a fuzzy concept, itself based on past experience and present expectations. It entails building a social contract between policy-makers and policy takers that ultimately has to be analysed in terms of political economy.

The literature on optimum currency areas (OCAs), in turn, is an outgrowth of the macroeconomics of the 1960s, but interest in it was stimulated by the discussions that took place prior to the establishment of the European Monetary Union. In the Mundell–Fleming (MF) model, then, the ERR determined the degree of freedom availability for the use of monetary policy as a response to external (real) shocks.

A currency area is defined as one where a fixed exchange rate is assumed among all participants, while a flexible ERR is maintained with the rest of the world. As in any other pegged rate regime, the cost is defined as the loss of policy autonomy. The benefits are supposedly related to the reduction of transaction costs, disappearance of exchange rate uncertainty for regional trade, and the elimination of the adjustment costs of exchange rate misalignments.

Following Mundell's (1961)[2] definition, the usefulness or sustainability of an OCA is often determined in terms of labour mobility, economic size and openness, similarity of production structure and the incidence (or asymmetry) of economic shocks. Deep trade interrelationships, symmetric exposure to external shocks and synchronization of business cycles increase the expected net benefits of adopting a common currency and a common monetary policy. Indeed shocks affecting all the countries in a similar fashion, at the same point in their business cycle, do not call for a change in exchange rates. Labour market flexibility and mobility reduce the real adjustment costs when shocks and cycles are not perfectly symmetric, while the existence of fiscal compensation schemes opens up the possibility of transfers between losers and winners.

Despite their theoretical interest, the practical usefulness of OCA criteria for decision-making purpose is limited (McCallum, 1999). Moreover a more recent trend in the literature centres on two empirical questions that may be useful in reassessing the relevance of the above-mentioned OCA criteria. The first one examines the actual cost for a country of losing the ability to use the exchange rate as a policy instrument. When an economy suffers a nominal shock, adjusting parities is not always an adequate instrument, and a regime with a fixed exchange rate will do better in terms of welfare (see Parrado and Velasco, 2002). Indeed the exchange rate is potentially useful as an instrument in situations that are simultaneously country-specific, real and temporary. The probability of such situations is becoming smaller as trade integration reduces the significance of national borders and as stability-oriented policies curtail policy-induced shocks. Furthermore, contemporary advocates of monetary unions think that modern-day trade and financial interrelationships make full exchange rate flexibility a non-viable option (Buti and Sapir, 1998).

The second 'revisionist' trend in the OCA literature analyses the exogenous nature of the OCA criteria. As Frankel and Rose (1996) indicate, these criteria cannot be considered independently – at least in the European context that they reviewed. Regional trade integration increases business cycle correlation and promotes new institutional initiatives that will set up a positive feedback loop for intra-regional trade itself. In the words of the authors, 'cyclic correlation is endogenous with respect to trade integration, while integration is also affected by policy'.

This revision is important because it shows that even though economies may not *ex ante* comply with the OCA criteria, the process of monetary integration itself may lead to the convergence of cyclical behaviour, further complementary trade integration and other structural features that *ex post* do justify monetary integration. This is a particularly important result for Latin America, given that even though LAC economies do not overall comply with OCA criteria (as will be shown below), there are other reasons that may justify coordination and convergence of policies that may ultimately lead to a monetary union. These reasons are our next topic.

Political Economy and Financial Considerations on Monetary Unions

The political economy dimension of the debate on OCAs refers to the fact that economies are managed in a way that does not correspond to an optimal textbook situation. In such a second-best world, some important macroeconomic gains could be generated insofar as the formation of a monetary union with explicit fiscal rules entails a systemic improvement in the policy-making process (Ghymers, 1999). The European example of macroeconomic convergence in the economic and monetary union (EMU) process and its mutual surveillance arrangements illustrates how the macroeconomic policy regime may move towards more credibility, transparency and stability.

The macroeconomic cost of losing monetary policy tools and imposing binding budgetary rules must be compared to the significantly higher gains brought by the ensuing monetary stability and budgetary consolidation, which in future may warrant a more flexible monetary policy and the use of fiscal policies to cushion economic shocks. Indeed the maintenance of a common budgetary discipline creates a safety margin that allows automatic stabilizers to freely and symmetrically fulfil their anti-cyclical role.

With the financial globalization, turbulent international flows of capital increase the importance of credibility in front of regional contagion and herding pressures. This means that financial interdependency goes beyond financial integration *stricto sensu*: currency areas have to be analysed in a larger context than the traditional OCA criteria, taking account of credibility aspects and possible regional arrangements.

In particular, as a result of financial globalization, economic or development policies in one country will have direct impacts upon financial spreads and exchange rates in the entire geographical area as well as upon the business climate. This clear symptom of the emergence of a subregional reality, on top of increasing trade relationships during the 1990s, means that national macroeconomic stability should be treated as a regional public good.

Thus the comparison should not be made with the unrealistic textbook case that ignores the weight of vested interests and of past budgetary mistakes and the consequent rising debts and fiscal disequilibria. For these 'real economies', the acceptance of binding rules as a condition for joining a monetary union brings important advantages (in terms of stability and credibility) even if the traditional OCA criteria are not met as is the current case in Latin America – as shown in the next section. Before that, we find it appropriate to discuss some of the problems of the alternative choices for Latin America put forth by the conventional wisdom.

The Conventional Wisdom of Advocating Corner Solutions for Latin America

The succession of financial and exchange rate crises in the second half of the 1990s has led to a polarization of the ERR debate between what have come to be known as 'corner solutions'. Although the corner solutions rely upon reasonable arguments, existing analyses of the institutional and structural conditions required for either extreme option to be sustainable in developing countries are remarkable for their shallowness. In particular, problems arise on four basic points.

Firstly, is there any reason to believe that a country deemed to be lacking in credibility in its monetary policy owing to political or institutional factors should be automatically credible and able, with dollarization or hardened fixed rate, to control its fiscal and financial policies? On the contrary, as monetary policy is more technical, it should be easier to reform and to control than fiscal policy, which is socially and politically more complex and involves more social groups and political actors. The

European Union example with the Maastricht criteria and the Stability and Growth Pact shows that in a monetary union, fiscal policy clearly has to compensate with an additional discipline for the loss of the other national macroeconomic instrument.

Why was such a discipline suddenly expected to spontaneously develop in countries whose institutional weakness was such that it excluded the use of monetary policy? The example of Africa with the CFA area (a peg against the French franc whose full and unlimited convertibility is warranted by the French Treasury) had already demonstrated the danger that the acquired credibility could be used for postponing fiscal adjustment and other structural reforms, increasing external debt and 'consuming' FDI resources (Ghymers, 1994). Therefore advocating dollarization for reasons of political economy (the difficulty of maintaining a credible monetary policy) seems very myopic, as the prerequisites for sustainable dollarization include fiscal and financial reforms that are even more radical than implementing a credible autonomous monetary policy.

Conversely, for most emerging economies, the ability to implement the required credible fiscal and financial policies greatly reduces the case for tying the hand of the monetary authorities. Thus the dollarization argument proves to be a conceptual *non sequitur* (Escaith, 1999). Empirically there is no evidence at the international level that dollarized countries have had more prudent fiscal policies than non-dollarized nations, or have had smaller current account deficits. (Edwards, 2001). Considering that their average growth rates were also significantly lower, this corner solution seems to lead to increased macroeconomic fragility rather than strength.

Secondly, how could a full opening of the capital account or/and a pure float have been recommended so uniformly to recently emerging economies? How could it have been assumed that despite huge inflows of foreign capital – that amount to a very high proportion of GDP and M2 in the emerging economies – and herd behaviour, the markets would be able to assess properly the balance of risk? Why were all intermediary options of capital control so dogmatically excluded despite existing success stories such as the Chilean or Colombian case?

Thirdly, why has a regional approach been generally excluded from the debate? Calls for regional or hemispheric free trade and integration agreements were not matched by similar initiatives in the macroeconomic area. There was no systematic and operational regional or subregional scheme that tried to deal with the regional or subregional spillovers, despite the effective measures for regional integration that were implemented during the past decade in the context of a general opening in market access. Almost nothing was organized on the macro-financial side at the regional level. The case for balanced anchors (such as a basket of international currencies) were generally neglected, while not only the structure of trade, but also the currency composition of financial liabilities have now to be taken into account when analysing currency anchoring strategies (Miotti et al., 2002).

Fourthly, why does the recent move of many LAC countries to inflation targeting not consider regional commitments as a superior solution to national ones? Indeed inflation targeting and its application in developing countries is a possible and superior regime at least in the case of high- and middle-income developing countries, when the financial system is sufficiently developed and there is no fiscal dominance (Loayza and Soto, 2002). In particular, a crucial point is that monetary authorities should be able to resist political pressures to stimulate the economy in the short term. When this condition is imperfectly fulfilled, the peer pressure implied by a regional arrangement may fill the credibility gap.

Moreover regional macroeconomic coordination might – as it does for trade integration – reinforce the endogeneity nature of the credibility-building process. When the national macroeconomic and institutional settings are not too unstable, inflation targeting can be used domestically to overcome credibility problems because they increase accountability of national monetary policy and targets, and mimic optimal performance incentive contracts (Agenor, 2002). In suboptimal national contexts, explicit and regionally enforced contracts should be more effective: a flexible exchange rate regime, managed nationally within a regional agreement and including agreed inflation targets, could be used with greater profit and better results to overcome the problems caused by reputation and national political economy factors.

In the next section we analyse some of the empirical aspects relating to exchange rate, trade and financial integration in LAC in the 1990s.

RECENT TRENDS IN COMMERCIAL AND FINANCIAL INTEGRATION IN LATIN AMERICA AND THE OCA CRITERIA

Do Latin American economies comply with the OCA criteria? If not, what are the advantages of proposing a common monetary arrangement? The answers to these questions depend in part upon (1) their exposure to shocks, either real or financial, and (2) the 'political economy' potential advantages that may emerge from such an arrangement. In this section we analyse the first set of economic issues, and in the following section we analyse the second set. The first aspect to be analysed is trade integration.

Commercial Integration

One of the central factors in macroeconomic policy coordination and OCA is the degree of trade interrelationship between potential partner countries throughout the trade sector. This is traditionally analysed in terms of trade interrelationship and symmetry of external shocks.

Intraregional trade

Since the recovery from the 1982 debt crisis, trade with other LAC countries, particularly within integration subregions (the Andean Community, CARICOM, Central American Common Market, Mercosur), increased faster than trade with other countries, at least up to 1997. This rapid growth is particularly significant if one considers that external trade has grown much more rapidly than domestic product (see Table 8.1).

Economic transactions with other LAC countries, and especially within subregional integration schemes, have thus been taking an increasingly important role in the national economies (see Figure 8.1). This is especially important because intraregional trade is based on manufactured products, allowing national economies to diversify their export base (see Benavente, 2001).

This trend has two important (and potentially conflicting) consequences for the purposes of the present chapter. First, it increases the transmission of shocks through trade, in the traditional OCA perspective, and thus is a factor of greater interdependence between countries. Second, it increases the potential for conflict between national exchange rate policies, as these exports consist of consumer and intermediary products that are sensitive

Table 8.1 Trends in trade and domestic product, 1991–2002

Latin America and the Caribbean (LAC)	Average annual growth rate 1991–2002 a/
1. Total supply	3.3%
Of which:	
– GDP	2.5%
– Imports of goods and services	8.0%
2. Exports of goods and services	7.3%
Of which:	
– Exports to other LAC countries	9.2%

Note: Constant 1995 prices.

Source: ECLAC, Preliminary Overview of the Economies of Latin America and the Caribbean, 2002.

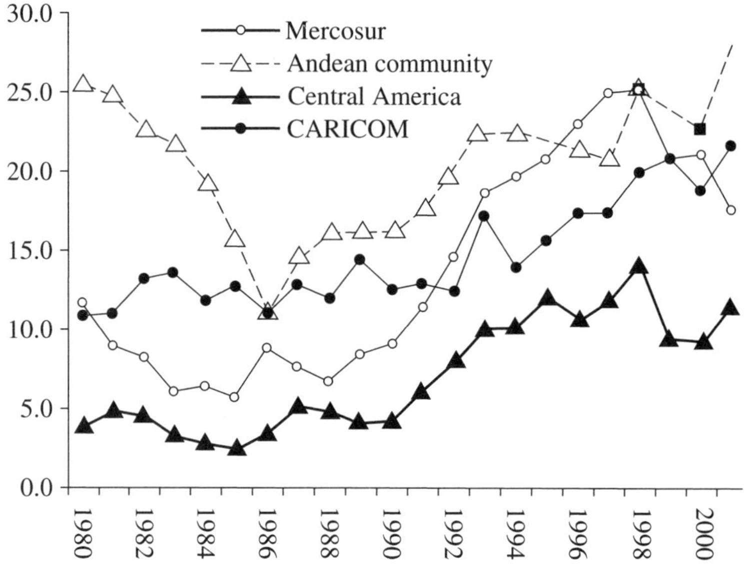

Source: Based on ECLAC data.

Figure 8.1 Intraregional trade in relation to total exports (%), 1980–2001

to relative prices. Thus devaluation by one of the regional trading partners could have a strong impact on regional trade flows, triggering regional tensions (as occurred in Mercosur after devaluation in Brazil) or competitive devaluations (as in Europe in the late 1970s). Obviously these cross-effects are directly relevant to both the choice of national ERR and the potential gains for regional coordination.

Terms of trade

In small open developing economies, terms of trade fluctuations are a major source of instability. Structural characteristics make export prices very volatile (because of the high proportion of commodities) and there is little capacity for substituting imports internally (because of their higher technological content), even when their relative prices increase. Non-transitory shifts in relative prices (deteriorating terms of trade) are apparently very damaging for national income, but short-term fluctuations are perhaps more detrimental, as they increase systemic uncertainty and diminish the capacity for sound decision-making. The latter are also more relevant when it comes to macroeconomic policy coordination.

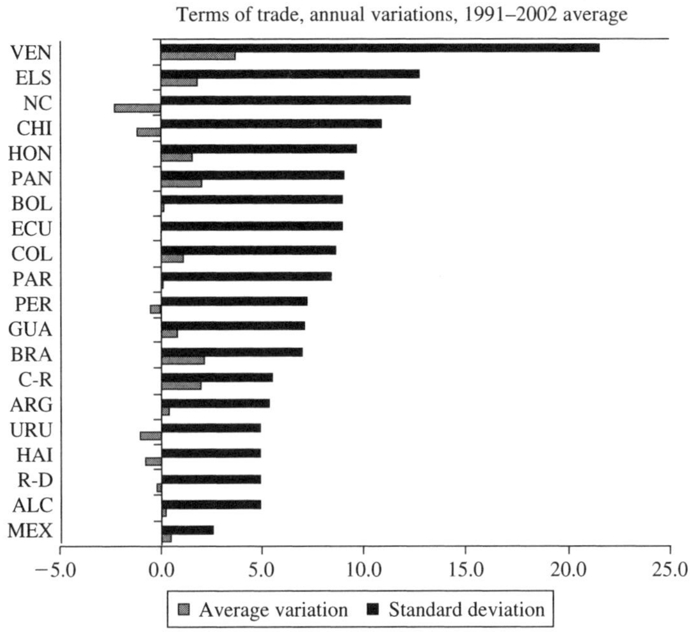

Source: Based on ECLAC data.

Figure 8.2a Terms of trade, 1991–2002a: annual variations

As shown in Figure 8.2a, the situation of each country has been quite different over the 1991–2002 period in terms of trends[3] or of volatility. As an annual average over the 1991–2002 period, negative and positive shifts were reasonably well distributed. In contrast, volatility is very different from country to country, with standard deviations ranging from a low 2.8 in Mexico, which has the advantage of a diversified export structure, to as high as 22.4 in Venezuela, a mono-exporter of oil.

Looking at the correlation between countries, one notes that most countries in the region share a common positive interdependence, while a small group evidences diverging behaviour. This is best seen from Figure 8.2b that shows the clustering of LAC countries according to a breakdown of the principal components of their terms of trade variations. On the first two axes, that explain jointly 65 per cent of total variance, one may note a first cluster of countries in the North-West quadrant, composed of Ecuador, Venezuela, Argentina and Mexico. These are oil-producing countries. Panama is isolated because of its specificity as a processing and transit zone.

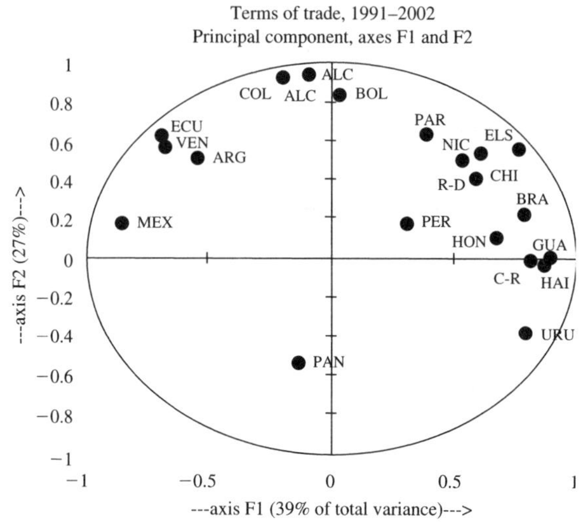

Source: Based on ECLAC data.

Figure 8.2b Terms of trade, 1991–2001b: correlations circle on axes 1 and 2 (65% of total variance)

Except for Colombia and Bolivia, and to a lesser extent Peru, all other LAC countries are clustered into a compact group on the West part of the graph. This cluster includes all countries in the Central American Common Market and almost all countries from Mercosur, with the exception of Argentina. This means that the countries from these two integration areas share the same (short-term) trends for terms-of-trade variations, which is an important basis for coordinating a regional response to common external shocks. The situation of the Andean countries is more diversified from this point of view, because of their respective specializations in oil exports (Ecuador and Venezuela, but also Colombia) or in other minerals (Bolivia and Peru).

Effective exchange rates

Exposure to common terms-of-trade shocks and stronger intraregional trade should lead to greater covariation of effective real exchange rates (ERERs). Obviously, when regional partners account for a significant share of external trade, variations in neighbouring countries' exchange rates (or internal prices) will greatly affect the overall trade competitiveness of each country. This merely quantitative and mechanical effect is compounded by the potentially greater price elasticity of intraregional trade. Because intraregional trade in Latin America is more intensive in manufactured goods, demand is potentially more sensitive to changes in relative prices than the goods exported to the rest of world (especially in South America, where exports to the rest of the world are mainly primary products).

In the graphs shown in Figure 8.3, for each subregion (Mercosur, Andean countries and Mesoamerica) the evolution of the real exchange rate for each country is shown in relation to (1) its regional (Latin American) partners, and (2) the United States economy. The latter has two very distinct impacts on LAC economies. The first is on trade competitiveness with the rest of the world, either for exports to the United States economy or for those commodities priced internationally in United States dollars (for example oil or minerals). The second is mainly financial, as most of the external debt and part of the domestic debt is denominated in, or indexed to, the United States dollar. In several countries with a recent history of hyperinflation, even non-tradable goods and services may be indexed to the dollar to some degree.

Figures 8.3a and 8.3b show a sharp contrast between Argentina and Brazil on the one hand, and the other southern cone countries on the other. The evolution of the regional exchange rates for Argentina and Brazil is symmetric: an increase in one means a decrease in the other, and by the end of 2001 – before its devaluation – the Argentine peso was significantly overvalued with respect to the Brazilian real. This resulted in a strong advantage for Brazilian products in relation to Argentine products in bilateral trade.

Other Mercosur and associated countries (Paraguay, Uruguay and Chile) did not show such a trend and their regional competitiveness remained basically stable over the 1992–2001 period. Nevertheless after 1997 and because of the effects of the Asian and Russian crises, all currencies registered a real devaluation with respect to the United States dollar (albeit due to a favourable inflation differential in the Argentine case).

Although the pattern is less obvious in the Andean case (see Figures 8.3c and 8.3d), real exchange rate dynamics in that subregion are also dominated by two countries, Colombia and Venezuela, which show symmetric variations. The Ecuador case is due to internal factors, and the changes in its regional competitiveness closely follow the evolution of the bilateral real parity with the United States dollar. Within the Central American subregion (Figure 8.3e), Costa Rica and Guatemala show a common trend of gaining exchange rate competitiveness in relation to El Salvador and Honduras in the post-1998 period. Nevertheless the latter group did not lose too much of its regional competitive advantage thanks to the steady revaluation of the Mexican peso after 1996.

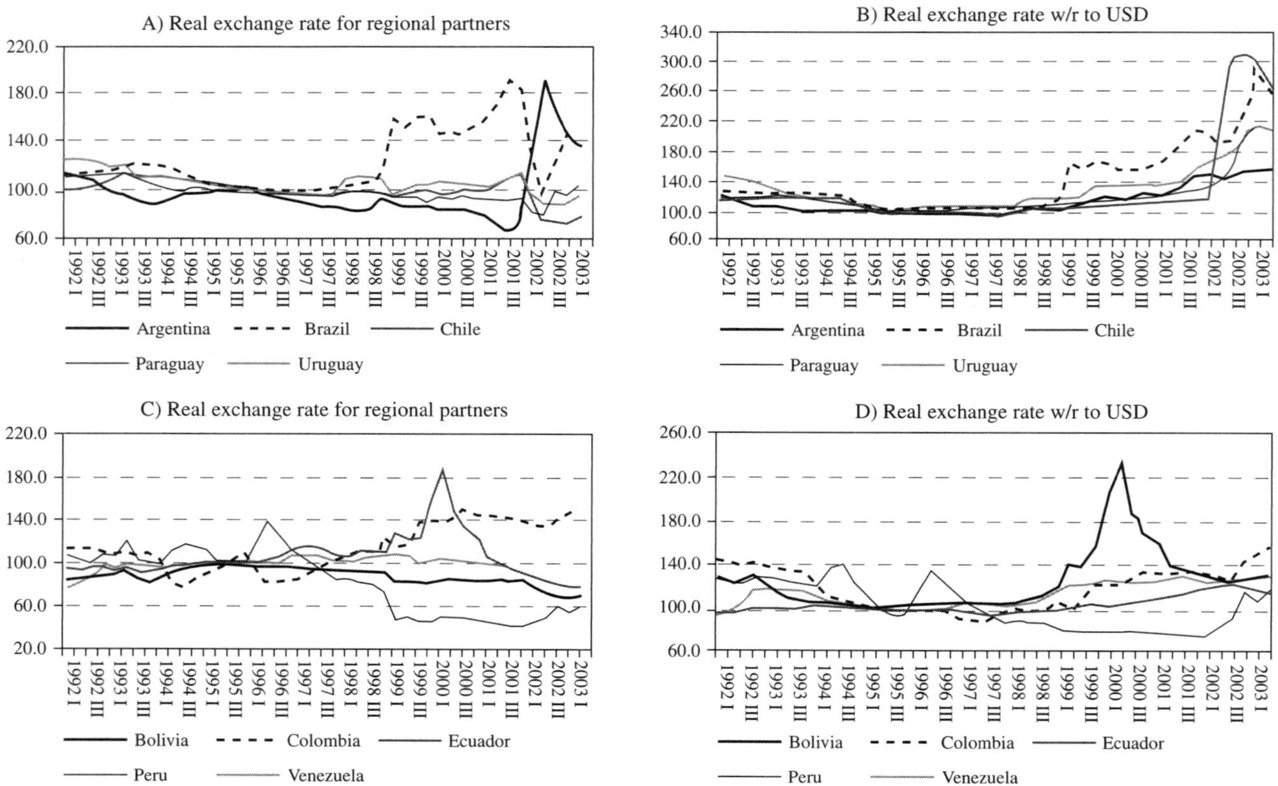
A) Real exchange rate for regional partners
220.0
180.0
140.0
100.0
60.0
1992 I
1992 III
1993 I
1993 III
1994 I
1994 III
1995 I
1995 III
1996 I
1996 III
1997 I
1997 III
1998 I
1998 III
1999 I
1999 III
2000 I
2000 III
2001 I
2001 III
2002 I
2002 III
2003 I
Argentina
Brazil
Chile
Paraguay
Uruguay
B) Real exchange rate w/r to USD
340.0
300.0
260.0
220.0
180.0
140.0
100.0
60.0
Argentina
Brazil
Chile
Paraguay
Uruguay
C) Real exchange rate for regional partners
220.0
180.0
140.0
100.0
60.0
20.0
Bolivia
Colombia
Ecuador
Peru
Venezuela
D) Real exchange rate w/r to USD
260.0
220.0
180.0
140.0
100.0
60.0
Bolivia
Colombia
Ecuador
Peru
Venezuela

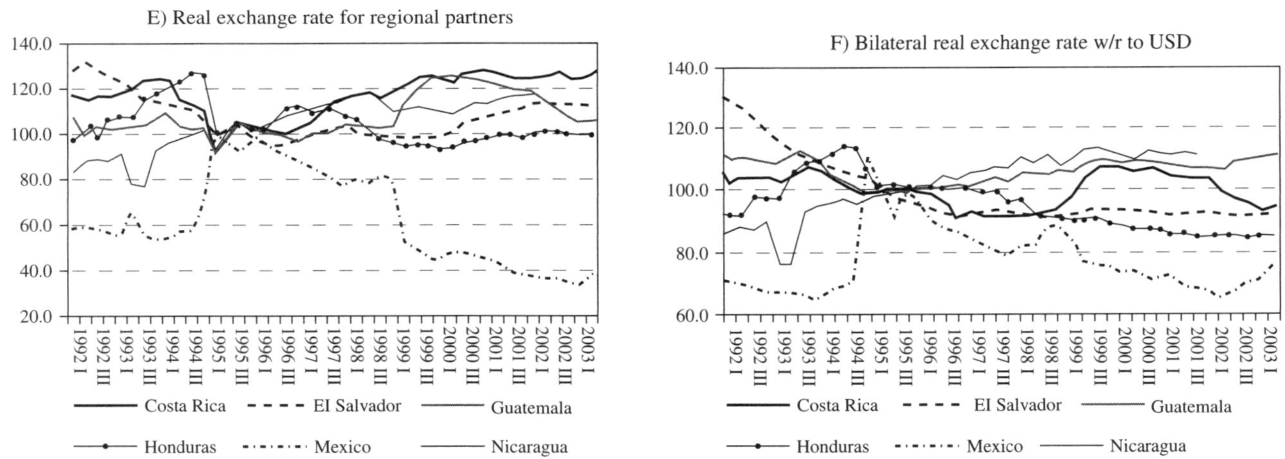

Source: Based on ECLAC and IMF data.

Figure 8.3 Effective real exchange rates

Thus in the medium term and for at least half of the countries considered, the primary evidence indicates that there is a strong interrelation of the relative evolution of regional effective real exchange rates. This relationship among ERERs may be more closely assessed for a shorter time frame by looking at the inter-country correlation coefficients obtained for quarterly variations. Correlation coefficients between LAC exchange rates were calculated for the quarterly variations of four categories of real exchange rate: bilateral with the United States economy, effective with regional trading partners, effective with non-regional trading partners (except for the United States) and the effective exchange rate for all trading partners. Trading partners are weighted by their exports to the reporting country.

The correlation coefficients obtained for the ERER with regional partners are the most interesting in the present case, as they reflect the intensity of the shocks passed from one LAC country to the others through the exchange rates. But part of the interaction analysed through the behaviour of regional ERERs may be due to a third, external, factor to which all countries in the region react simultaneously (an external shock of large magnitude, such as the Asian and Russian crises of 1997–98, for example). To filter out this noise, the correlation coefficients obtained for real exchange rates with the US dollar were subtracted from the results obtained with the regional ERER. An index was constructed using the sum of the absolute values of the results obtained for each country, normalized by the total across countries (see Figure 8.4). On purpose, the index does not include the most recent 2002–2003 period after the Argentinean devaluation, because the strong overshooting of the nominal exchange rate created too much noise and biased the calculation.

As expected, the larger LAC countries (Argentina, Brazil and Mexico) are those showing greater interaction with the rest of the LAC region. Yet irrespective of their size, Mercosur countries have a larger regional ERER index than other LAC countries (except for Guatemala and Venezuela), at least up to the massive Argentinean devaluation of January 2002 that distorted – at least temporarily – the situation.

When shifting the analysis to the ERER with non-regional trading partners, it is striking that (1) most elements of the correlation matrix are positive, and (2) many have a high value, in contrast with the regional ERER and the bilateral US dollar tables. It appears that most LAC countries share a common trend with respect to non-US dollar monies (basically European currencies and the yen in our sample). This is easily explained considering that *de facto* or *de jure* these economies belong to the dollar area, and thus tend to share the same exchange rate fluctuations with other international currencies.

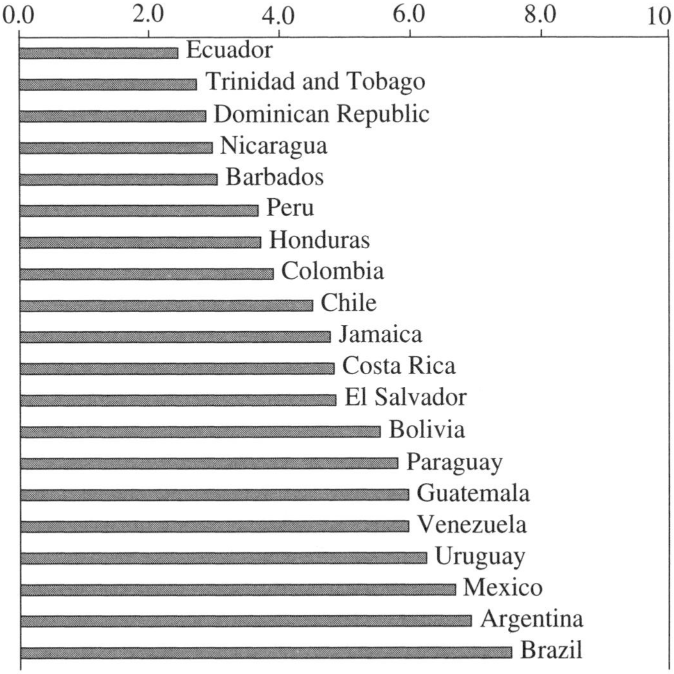

Figure 8.4 Regional exchange rate integration index

Internal Economic Cycles

In the previous sections we looked at the transmission of shocks via terms-of-trade or exchange rate channels. In view of the high external vulnerability of the region, these shocks would be expected to have an impact on short-term growth dynamics. In the present section, we will look into the coincidence of the 'real cycles' within the region.[4]

Two sets of indicators are used, one being the quarter-to-quarter GDP growth rate, and the other the size of the output gap, calculated by reference to a medium-term tendency obtained by smoothing real GDP time series, using the standard Hodrick-Prescott filter.

Tendencies for GDP annual growth using the filtered series capture the medium-term trends observed during the 1990s. Figure 8.5 shows two different dynamics at the beginning of the present decade. The low-growth subset was composed of South American countries severely hit by the 1997–99 crisis that affected many emerging economies. Mexico, Caribbean and Central American countries were able to escape this crisis thanks to

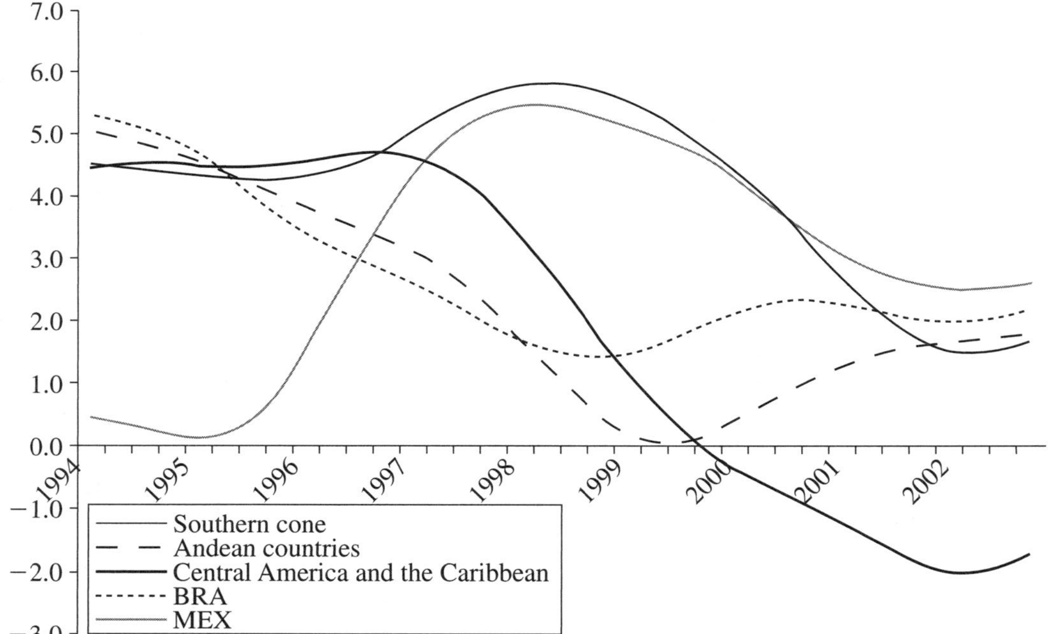

Source: Based on ECLAC data.

Figure 8.5 Potential GDP, 1994–2002

Table 8.2 Quarterly GDP variations: inter-country correlation coefficients 1993–2002

	Correlation within each subregion			Correlation within LAC region
	Average correlation within:			Average
	Mercosur	Andean countries	Mesoamerica*	All countries
Period averages:				
Total 1993–2002	0.15	0.14	0.06	0.11
1993–1997	−0.01	0.07	−0.08	0.05
1998–2002	0.31	0.20	0.19	0.16

Note: *Mexico, Central America and Dominican Republic.

Source: Based on ECLAC data.

their closer links to the booming United States economy and lesser dependence on exports based on primary products. When the USA, together with other industrialized economies, eventually entered recession in the second semester of 2001, this difference vanished.

This is nevertheless a loose interrelation: there is little correlation of the quarterly GDP across the region as a whole. A very interesting pattern emerges however when looking at the situation within each of the subregions. Not only is the correlation higher when calculated within each subregion, but it is also increasing over time (see Table 8.2).

This indicates that during the 1990s, LAC countries tended to cluster around common subregional patterns. This is quite an interesting feature considering that the correlation of business cycles across countries is an argument in favour of macroeconomic policy coordination and optimum currency areas.[5]

However this somehow higher correlation in growth rates does not translate into a coincidence of the real cycles within subregions, as evidenced when considering the very low and insignificant correlation coefficients obtained for output gaps. Indeed countries within subregions do not pass simultaneously through peaks and dips, which makes it more difficult to reach a common agreement on the timing of short-term macroeconomic policy.

Financial Flows and Financial Interdependency

In the terms of the analysis so far, financial interdependency has to do with the fact that international investors hold larger LAC stocks of financial assets, issued domestically and in the international financial markets. Given that the portfolio allocations of such investors are highly determined by their expectations concerning the whole portfolio, often changes in their mood generates shifts of flows to developing economies and to their markets. This implies a high correlation between domestic asset prices and country risks as determined by the spreads of sovereign debt instruments, but also of asset prices domestically issued

In Latin America, this interdependency is clearly seen by the effect that national financial crises have on the overall spreads charged on sovereign bonds issued by the whole region. This is indicated by Figure 8.6 which presents the spreads on sovereign LAC bonds in relation to US Treasury bonds (weighted by their maturities). The first striking feature that comes out from the analysis of this graph is the high correlation of such indexes among countries with substantially different fundamental. The second is that at times of crisis, these correlations tend to increase substantially (such as occurred in the 1994 Tequila crisis, the 1998 Russian crisis, the 1999 Brazilian crisis and the 2001–2002 Argentinean crisis).

As regards domestic financial assets, one good indicator of financial interdependency is the correlation between changes in stock market indexes in economies with considerably different market fundamentals. That this correlation is significant can be evidenced by Figure 8.7.

The stock indexes from Argentina, Brazil, Peru, Venezuela and Colombia do present similar trends as those of the spreads presented in Figure 8.7: not only do they move very closely together, but their correlation tends to increase at periods of external crises. Another interesting aspect is that from the 1998 Russian crisis not only does the correlation seem to have increased significantly, but also there has been a convergence of the average LAC index and the average Asian indexes – two regions that are known to have completely different macro- and microeconomic fundamentals (remember that stock indexes should in principle reflect the fundamentals of the listed companies they represent).

Thus what these figures indicate is that the financial interdependency among countries in the region in the beginning of the 1990s is quite significant, and tends to increase rapidly in periods of crisis.

Another facet of the financial interdependency has to do with the volatility of financial capital flows and their impacts on key macroeconomic variables in the region. Here we must consider two interrelated aspects of the problem: first, that in economies with underdeveloped financial assets markets, such surges of financial flows can generate self-fulfilling bubbles that tend to artificially maintain the attractiveness of such assets for foreign investors; second, that such surges in economies with little capacity to absorb them – such as in economies with low investment ratios and growth

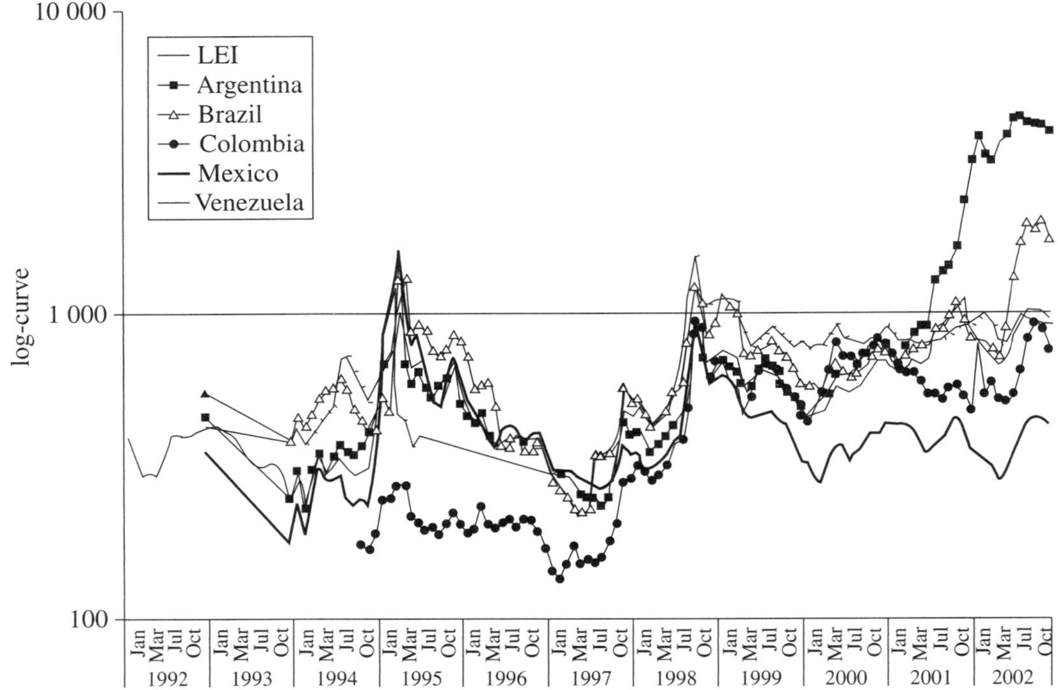

Source: Based on data from JP Morgan.

Figure 8.6 Premiums on government bonds: LAC average (LEI) and selected LAC countries

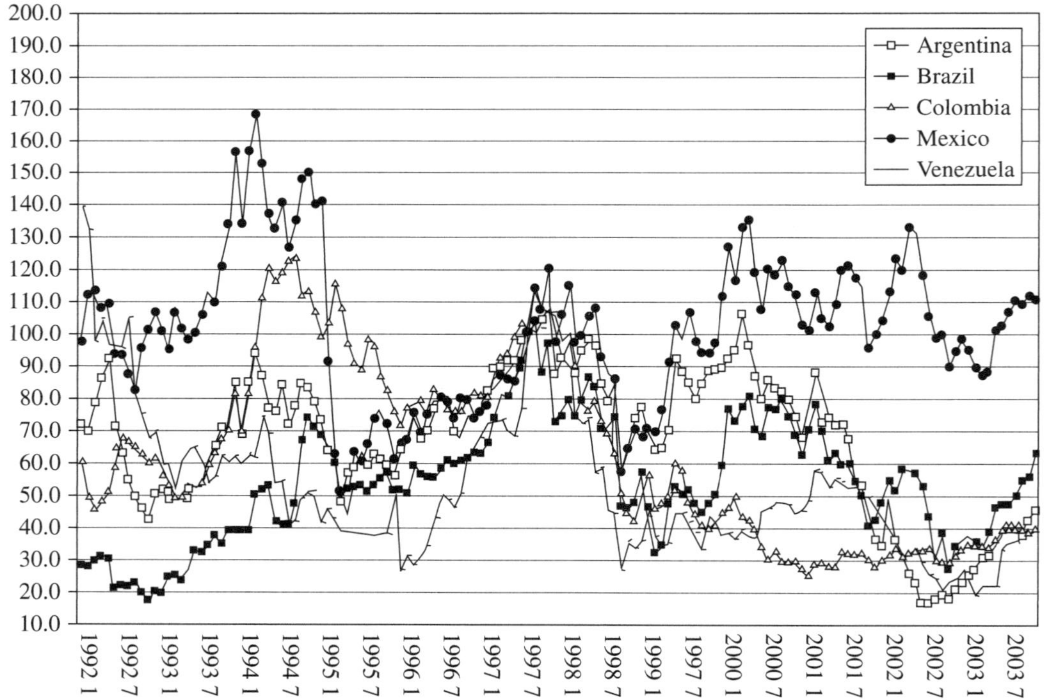

Source: Based on ECLAC data.

Figure 8.7 Compared stock market indexes in selected Latin American economies and Asia (June 1997 = 100)

ratios – can be highly destabilizing, as they affect key macroeconomic variables such as exchange rates and domestic interest rates.

If we cross these data with the increase of the dependency of financial flows to the financing of the balance of payments of these economies, we begin to have a wider picture of how these factors interacted in creating the boom–bust performance of the economies in the region.

Figure 8.8 clearly shows us two trends in the period. In the first period, from 1990 to 1994, the growth of private capital inflows increases rapidly – leading to a deterioration of the current account which has to do with the exchange rate revaluation and loss of competitiveness that followed this process. Despite the growth of exports (including intra-regional trade, as seen above), the growth of imports was higher, leading to then increasing deterioration of current accounts until 1998.

The reduction of flows to the region in 1998 led to the structural adjustments that in general provoked a reversal in the trend of net exports – as exports increased much more rapidly than imports. Nevertheless the accumulation of external debt related to the capital surges of the early 1990s led to an increasing demand for finance of interest payments and debt amortization. Therefore the dependency on future capital inflows, and therefore the financial interdependency between these economies' is likely to remain strong in the near future.

Such increasing dependency has led to lesser discretionarity of domestic policy-makers in affecting key macro financial variables – including exchange rates and interest rates. It is true that another important change has been observed in the structure of the flows: there has been a decline in portfolio investments from 1998 onwards; the role of FDI as a residual source of external financing has increased. It is also true that such flows are more stable than portfolio flows. Nevertheless the high levels of external debt determine that domestic policy-makers avoid abrupt changes in the overall return of foreign investment – by consistently avoiding continued real exchange rate devaluations and/or declines in dollar-deflated returns on domestic assets.

In sum, these stylized features of the trends in commercial and financial integration of the region make LAC a very particular case in the debate of optimal ERRs. Building on such stylized facts we can briefly review the current debate before going to an analysis of the possible solutions for the challenges faced by the region in choosing an appropriate ERR. Financial interdependency has to do with the fact that international investors hold increasing stocks of LAC financial assets, issued domestically and in the international financial markets. Given that the portfolio allocation of such investors are highly determined by their expectations concerning the whole portfolio, often changes in their mood generate shifts of flows to developing

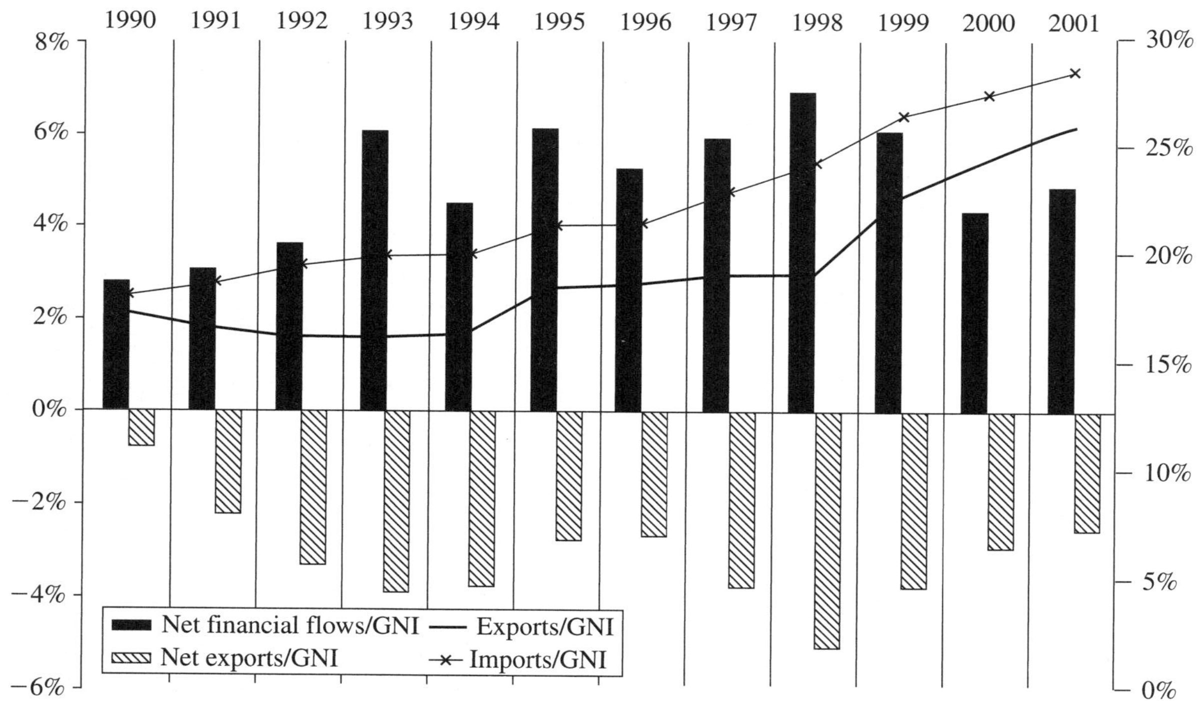

Sources: Based on ECLAC and IMF data.

Figure 8.8 Capital flows, exports of goods and services and net exports (% of Gross National Income)

economies and their markets. This implies a high correlation between domestic asset prices and country risks as determined by the spread of sovereign debt instruments.

INSTITUTIONS, COORDINATION AND ERR

The previous sections showed the need to extend the debate on the optimum ERR to the institutional aspects and to the regional dimension. The thesis we sustain here is that linking the two through the gradual development of coordination among subregional partners offers a concrete solution both to exchange rate regime (EER) issue and to the institutional caveats or weaknesses in Latin America.

Considering the criticisms of corner solutions, importing some aspects of the European experience and giving due weight to political economy arguments, leads us to argue that there is a clear case for regional cooperation in the macroeconomic field in LAC, especially for EER. More specifically, in a situation where macroeconomic stability is a regional public good, but is difficult to achieve through cooperation in view of the well-known 'prisoner's dilemma' (Ghymers, 2001; Paunovic, 2001), an appropriate macroeconomic mutual monitoring scheme designed for the regional or subregional level is a superior systemic solution for the LAC compared to dollarization or independent free-floating. The main argument in favour is that it might offer an opportunity to compensate for the lack of credibility and anchoring of national exchange rates and policies, without tying blindly the policy-makers' hands but by creating mutual checks and balances. By triggering the institutional-building process that is necessary for any sustainable EER for the LAC, it would contribute decisively to the progress of regional integration and the triggering of a higher sustainable growth path.

The Case for Regional Coordination

The regional option is not a panacea and should not be abused. No initiative is guaranteed success by virtue of being regional. However in the macroeconomic field, there are clear spillovers to deal with whilst the regional option is not actually used. Economists should therefore be more aware of the powerful regional dynamics and political economy that were behind the convergence process in the EU. We consider that LAC could find in the as yet unexplored regional (that is geographical subregional) dimension the missing tool to compensate for most of their intrinsic lack of monetary and fiscal credibility and to resolve the apparently impossible equation of the optimum EER for LAC.

In order to be able to deliver both credibility and flexibility at the national level, a regional arrangement must essentially include a strong and transparent scheme for mutual monitoring of national monetary, exchange rate and fiscal policies, backed by appropriate incentives and sanctions. Such a scheme implies a full respect of the subsidiarity principle, not just with regard to state sovereignty, but also with respect to constitutionally autonomous public bodies such as central banks and auditors' courts. There are thus some institutional requirements. We argue that this is a realistic option for LAC since it does not require any big changes, but a progressive self-validating practice building upon what is already in place in the different subregional groups of nations (Mercosur, CAN, CACM, CARICOM).

Under the condition of being transparent, technically consistent and institutionally resilient, a macroeconomic cooperation at the subregional level could have much more credibility than purely national rules such as 'fiscal responsibility laws' or a 'monetary independence law', or dollarization options (such as currency boards), while also offering the advantages of flexible exchange rates.

By imposing an institutional discipline from outside – a supranational subregional set of transparent monetary and fiscal objective rules – a subregional macroeconomic monitoring activates the same principle of tying politicians' hands as dollarization does, with some advantages and disadvantages.

The advantages are as follows:

1. All macroeconomic policies are covered and not just the monetary creation process.
2. There is no obligation to import an inappropriate US monetary policy stance. With dollarization, the radical abandonment of monetary policy undermines the higher credibility that it supposedly has owing to its irreversibility or the high cost of abandoning it insofar as it exposes the economy to a pro-cyclical or unbalanced policy mix.
3. The combined effect of the two previous advantages is to provide the group and each of its member states with the additional flexibility of being able to tailor adequate rules and policy stances to each country-specific situation or any cyclical position.
4. It reduces the room for discretionary policies, but without being obliged to opt for a rigid peg. On the other hand, it preserves the much needed flexibility of the exchange rates but reduces the possibility of non-cooperative policies at the subregional level.
5. The most significant advantage is the explicit and more complete integration dynamics that could be triggered by choosing more realistic partners for regional integration. A subregional arrangement provides

the required opportunity for internalizing the spillover effects of national policies and designing a common coherent policy answer to the challenges of globalization. Except for some specific geographical cases, choosing the USA as an integration partner does not, on purely economic grounds, guarantee such an integration dynamics.[6]

This combination of advantages means that it would be possible to keep the same gains as those of dollarization without paying for its rigidity and exogenous nature, combined with the same flexibility gains as in floating without the same degree of risk of instability and overshooting.

However, the main weaknesses or disadvantages are as follows:

1. The absence of a pre-existing anchor (such as the mark in Europe) inside the subregions and the lack of consensus on a clear set of macroeconomic rules.
2. The absence of credibility or a positive reputation for the subregional dimension.
3. The two previous disadvantages are amplified by the complexity of a macroeconomic monitoring scheme for public opinions, in a situation where private sector expectations, public policy transparency and visibility are key factors in building up and maintaining economic stabilization.

A Concrete Proposal for Regional Coordination in LAC

Taking into account the above advantages and weaknesses, the solution requires a specifically organized consensus-building machinery, transparency and simplicity in the rule-setting process and their enforcement. Contrary to the *a priori* view, this does not imply revolutionary changes or big institutional transformations, but rather introducing a radically cheap, new method for creating the required checks and balances, countervailing powers and open public debates.

This step, as we shall see, involves only a very minor institutional change with the creation by subregions of small independent technical assessment bodies as complements to the existing committees or groups in each subregion. All these subregions already have the technical and institutional basis for collegially monitoring the national policies: Mercosur and CAN created in June 2000 (GMM)[7] and June 2001 (GTP)[8] respectively the technical groups of policy-makers in charge of convergence and coordination of policies, while they also provide the regional decision-making level through their respective ministerial councils and joint meetings with the governors of central banks. The Central American states also have their regional decision-making level with the Council of Ministers of Economic Integration, which includes the governors of their central banks.[9]

The basic idea is to strengthen and guarantee national policy credibility by completing the existing subregional level with a new, independent tool able to focus public attention upon, and to spur technical monitoring and collegial assessment of, national exchange rates and macroeconomic policies. For macroeconomic policies, the existing deficit of credibility and transparency implies a radical, fresh approach which gives priority to open professional debate, independent assessment and to local origin and sensitivity. This corresponds to the same basic idea as the proposal of Eichengreen et al. (1999) for creating Independent National Fiscal Councils, but with two significant improvements: first making them regional and not only national, and second giving them more scope by extending the formula to the monitoring of monetary and exchange rate policies.

Specifically, this means the need for the creation of a two-tier subregional system, in order to improve credibility by triggering a positive dynamics of open debates able to create market and public opinion rewards or sanctions for the national policies:

1. At the official level: national policy-makers meeting as a collegial policy group for the subregion concerned, first the preparatory and advisory group of official 'technicians' that is the 'Group of Official Macroeconomic Monitoring' (GOMM) which consists of the macroeconomists from the national policy authorities, that is generally the top technical officials of national finance ministries and central banks. Second, the decision-making body or the minister level, for taking decisions on technicians' proposals or advises
2. At the technical countervailing power level: a subregional technical 'Group of Autonomous Macroeconomists' (GAM), consisting of a few independent and recognized macroeconomists in charge of permanent regional monitoring of exchange rates and national macroeconomic policies.

The independent GAM would have the technical responsibility of proposing the specific subregional methods, criteria and targets, and producing regular assessment reports on the exchange rate and macroeconomic development of the subregion, its national components, and policy measures. It would submit all of its output first to the official GOMM. The latter would debate the proposals and assessments and prepare, in the presence of the GAM, recommendations for the decision-making body (the CMCB, 'Council of Ministers and Central Bankers'), which would issue a policy recommendation report.

In order to ensure a fair balance of power, the GAM would have the warranted option of issuing as an annex its own recommendations and comments on the Council's recommendations, and of organizing public hearings with the media and the international macroeconomic and financial community.

In such an institutional framework, the interplay between the official macroeconomists and the independent ones allows for spontaneous checks and balances and an automatic, credible surveillance. This regional method is expected to generate a higher level of credibility, flexibility and stability in the decision-making process than would be achieved by remaining alone with any of the corner solutions.

Our proposal is to use this two-tier regional system of mutual surveillance to (1) progressively design and implement a ruled-based subregional scheme for macroeconomic convergence, and (2) monitor and assess exchange rate development. Concretely, this means that each regional macroeconomic monitoring scheme would have two closely inter-linked basic components: the Regional Monitoring Arrangement (RMA), which establishes progressively the supranational rules and criteria according to the development, and the results of the Regional Monetary System (RMS), by which a monetary cooperation is launched.

The dynamics of the monitoring process relies upon the learning-by-doing which would accumulate as a result from the implementation of the RMS. This system would merely be the common framework in which exchange rates of each participating country are monitored, discussed and agreed upon at the subregional level, according to the general regional principle of 'mutual concern' for exchange rate credibility and stability. This process of consensus-building on each exchange rate is managed first at the GOMM level with the technical support of the GAM. Second, at the end of this first technical step, if the GOMM could reach a common view on sustainable exchange rate targets, the CMCB would ideally announce recommended bands for exchange rates that were compatible with the stated and expected national policies. This concept of recommended bands does not imply a system of fixed bilateral parities or compulsory limits, since it is also applicable to floating rates. Initially these bands would be broad and non-binding. In the future, RMS could be easily transformed into a Subregional Exchange Rate Mechanism (SERM), if needed and once a sufficient degree of convergence and consensus among the members had been achieved through the establishment of the RMA and its rules and sanctions. In the meantime, the RMS would be a way to inform market agents about policy intentions and to contribute to shaping their expectations. The arrangement would work simply by triggering formal consultations when the limits of the consensual broad bands were being approached. These compulsory consultations would facilitate the design of the rules and procedures of surveillance scheme (the RMA). The consultations would work by consensus, thus giving a veto to each member, even to a single national central bank, trying to mobilize a range of concrete common instruments. These instruments cover a broad range from merely issuing an ad hoc joint communiqué to launching convergence criteria and compulsory rules of the games with rewards or sanctions. They also cover ad hoc cooperative actions, such as deciding on joint interventions in favour of specific currencies or announcing new consensual bands, or implementing coordinated policy adjustment for supporting the achievement of the bands.

After a training test-period, the system should have the potential for designing a common system for orientation of exchange rates by anchoring market expectations through precise criteria and formal procedures, providing transparent information on the respective policy stances behind the bands and the required adjustment path. Progressively, the option of trying a real or a nominal fixed parity grid would be discussed if the participating members were able to achieve an effective degree of consensus and cohesion shown by respecting the common criteria and rules established by the RMA.

Institutions for Regional Integration

There is no a priori argument against the implementation of the above proposal in LAC. Nevertheless their bad record of cooperation should be understood.

Our diagnostic is that many obstacles to regional integration come from the wrong perception of an opposition of interests between national powers and the regional one. This misconception relies upon the fact that the regional integration is generally associated with an old-fashioned centralist view of governance where the supranational level dominates the national one, confusing it with a federal power taking over the local state sovereignty. This tends to fuel nationalistic sensibilities.

Our proposal is to develop a regional cooperative approach based upon the subsidiarity principle, that is an international cooperation that is motivated by the self-interest of national administrations. One cannot ask these administrations to sacrifice their own national goals for the sake of their neighbours or the community, but one could channel the driving force of their legitimate self-interest to protect them from the mistakes of their neighbours in order to create sound competition for applying and ensuring respect for some shared rules in the regional game. As the proposal is based upon a progressive building of mutual confidence and associated gains, it does not require either intense previous negotiation or any formal commitment, but merely needs to be launched as a progressive self-validating process which fully preserves national sovereignty. It is thus more realistic and politically acceptable than other formulas.

It is also in their own direct interest to benefit from the higher level of credibility that their own policies will receive owing to the mere existence of an effective collegial system of rules and scrutiny. This is subsidiarity, and means a combination of cooperation and competition among autonomous national administrations, which prohibits undue centralization but which leads to cooperation for the sake of the significant advantages accruing to these individual administrations.

In sum, an efficient regional tool should not become a reproduction at a higher level of the interventionist–centralist state, but should rather be limited to a collegial way of creating in LAC the checks and balances that are very much needed in order to ensure more accountability to their public opinion and financial markets. The reactions of public opinions and those markets provide the incentives and sanctions for the policy-makers, able to internalize their spillovers. The result is a win–win game both for the different national actors as well as for the different countries and the whole region.

The 'globalization threat' feeds the political economy of regional cooperation. Through a combination of cooperation and competition among autonomous partners, the right regional tool should meet the needs of national administrations while protecting them against the possible mistakes of both their neighbours and themselves. A workable scheme is one which works in the self-interest of the participants, providing the right set of incentives for respecting the agreed rules and monitoring their application by their neighbours, resulting in the win–win game. As explained above, this game corresponds merely to the application of the subsidiarity principle.

In this spirit, there is a possibility of reaching a consensus among national administrations for developing common rules and criteria, and deciding to enforce them at the appropriate subregional level, that is in a joint, collegial monitoring among peers and under the scrutiny of economists and markets. Such a transparent method would become a powerful catalyst for reforms and an appropriate level for institutional capacity building. Most of the urgent reforms that each economy needs could be designed, stimulated and monitored using this regional cooperative method, allowing for economies of scale, credible accountability and genuine regional harmonization, triggering endogenous motivation and winning social support in a context of reluctant public opinions. In particular, the exchange rate and macroeconomic stability issue could more easily and safely become a common subregional matter, contributing both to democratic participation and to shaping regional identity. Of course, as mentioned first, this dynamic supposes a no-centralist, no-bureaucratic regionalism (strict subsidiarity and transparency) and a permanent opt-out option to prevent any free-riding or moral hazard situation.

CONCLUDING REMARKS

Since 1990 most LAC countries have achieved a greater degree of convergence in terms of results and instruments used for their macroeconomic policies, despite differences in exchange rate regimes. Reforms implemented during the 1990s also contributed to a greater convergence in the institutional frameworks. Yet the observations collected on trade and real cycles for LAC countries during the 1990s show that despite greater trade integration and convergence of their macroeconomic policies, the whole region still does not fit all of the traditional OCA criteria. At the subregional level, the picture looks more promising, as several facts point to a deeper interrelation and symmetry on both external and GDP criteria.

However we state in this chapter that two other interrelated dimensions have to be added to the analysis of optimality of monetary unions in the LAC context. First, the political economy aspect, that joining a monetary union or an exchange rate mechanism could improve the policy-making process. Important macroeconomic gains could result from a new ERR insofar as the economy alone was not well managed and insofar as this new ERR would bring the required discipline for changing such a suboptimality. Second, the development of financial markets is induced by globalization, which has increased the importance of political economy factors.

Behind the discussion on optimal ERR lies the need of LAC policymakers to achieve external and internal equilibrium, and thus create an appropriate macroeconomic climate for sustained growth and development. Due to the increased commercial integration and financial interdependency, and to the new environment of international finance, achieving these equilibria simultaneously requires something more than a nationally determined ERR, giving an explicit weight to the regional dimension.

In particular, the choice of corner solutions is seen as short-sighted, and unsound as they try to avoid problems rather than solve them. They cannot obviate the need for deeper reforms in order to establish credible macroeconomic stability and sustainability. On the contrary, corner solutions create the dangerous illusion of easier solutions, exposing the authorities to the fatal temptation of buying time and postponing more profound changes. They do not in fact constitute solutions for at least two sets of reasons. First, most LAC countries do not form an OCA with the United States economy. Therefore our analysis does not see the so-called dollarization (or the currency board option) as a standard, ideal solution for LAC. Nevertheless we are aware of the political economy argument and the other important links between LAC countries created by financial globalization and which might imply some revision of the traditional OCA doctrine. Second, for these reasons, we do not consider either a pure floating among all the LAC and the Caribbean economies, would be a priori a realistic alternative solution. Indeed, such an option would require more independent central banks, more transparent and resilient institutions and policy-making than presently seems to be the case. Furthermore even pure national (uncoordinated) floating would be suboptimal when considering the regional context, where economic interaction has been on the rise during the 1990s.

In our view, the ERR should be one that truly supports and is supported by the achievement and sustainability of sound, balanced domestic (and particularly monetary and fiscal) policies. Therefore the poor record of most LAC countries in these fields points to the need for institution-building with regard to macroeconomic decision-making. The solution thus lies in not tying the hands of domestic monetary policy-makers, but in creating a set of strong checks and balances at the regional level, which rationally reduces the discretionary dimension of both fiscal and monetary policies in order to avoid circumstantial problems that might affect the long-term goal of good fiscal and monetary management. In our view, such a set can be better achieved by binding national policy-making to a greater goal of regional monetary integration, as described above, under a sequenced proposal for ERR within a subregional currency area.

NOTES

* The views expressed herein are those of the authors and do not necessarily reflect those of the Organizations.

1. See Claassen (1997) for a comprehensive review and Polac (2001) for a more detailed discussion on the genesis of the monetary approach.
2. McKinnon (1963) and Kenen (1969) were also important benchmarks for the literature on OCA.
3. The term 'trends' is used here in the sense of tendency, and does not refer to what statisticians may understand by deterministic trends (for example in contrast to random movements).
4. Real cycle understood as GDP fluctuations around an observed trend.
5. Albeit not a necessary one if one takes into consideration the endogeneity of these OCA criteria, as we mentioned in the introduction.
6. This scheme does not close the door to extra-regional alliances (for example with the North American economies or Europe), on the contrary it could make the negotiations easier.

7. In Mercosur, GMM is the Group for Macroeconomic Monitoring, and is composed of the top officials from ministries of finance and economy, together with their peers from the national central banks.
8. In the CAN, GTP is the Permanent Technical Group of top officials from the same kind of origins, plus the macroeconomists peers from the General Secretariat of the CA, in charge of preparing the meetings of the Consejo Asesor (Council of Ministers of Finance and Economy, plus the governors of central banks).
9. However, at the technical level, they still need a joint group for gathering central bankers with their peers from the ministries of finance and economy.

REFERENCES

Agenor, P.R. (2002), 'Monetary policy under flexible exchange rates: an introduction to inflation targeting', in N. Loayza and R. Soto (eds), *Inflation Targeting: Design, Performance, Challenges*, Series on Central Banking, Analysis and Economic Policies, Central Bank of Chile.

Bank for International Settlements (1986), 'Recent innovations in international banking', April (mimeo).

Benavente, José Miguel (2001), 'Exportaciones de manufacturas de América Latina: desarme unilateral o integración regional?', Serie Macroeconomía del desarrollo 3, Santiago: CEPAL.

Bloomestein, H.J. (1995), 'Structural Changes in Financial Markets: Overview of Trends and Prospects', in OECD, pp. 9–47.

Buti, Marco and André Sapir (eds) (1998), *Economic Policy in EMU: A Study by the European Commission Services*, Oxford: Clarendon Press.

CEPAL (2001), Estudio Económico de América Latina y el Caribe, 2000–2001.

Claassen, Emil-Maria (1997), *Global Monetary Economics*, New York: Oxford University Press.

Corbo, Vittorio (2000), 'Monetary policy in Latin America in the 90s', Central Bank of Chile Working Papers 78.

Edwards, Sebastian (2001), 'Dollarization and economic performance: an empirical investigation', NBER Working Paper 8274, Washington, DC, May.

Eichengreen, B., R. Haussmann and J. Von Hagen (1999), 'Reforming fiscal institutions in Latin America: the case for a national fiscal council', mimeo, IDB, Washington, DC.

Escaith, Hubert (1999), 'América Latina e Dolarização', *Network* **8** (3), July/August/September, Centro de Estudos das Américas Rio de Janeiro.

Feeney, P.W. (1994), *Securitization: Redefining the Bank*, Hohn R. Presley (ed.), The Money and Banking Series, New York: St. Martin's Press.

Frankel, Jeffrey and Andrew K. Rose (1996), 'The endogeneity of the optimum currency area criteria', NBER Working Papers 5700, August.

Franklin, R.E. (1993), 'Financial markets in transition: or the decline of commercial banking', in Federal Reserve Bank of Kansas, *Changing Capital Markets: Implications for Monetary Policy*, Seminar Proceedings, Jackson Hole, WY, 19–21 August, Kansas: Federal Reserve Bank.

Ghymers, Christian (1994), 'Intégration économique et union monétaire en Afrique de l'Ouest', Revue 'De Pecunia', **6**(2), September, 87–116.

Ghymers, Christian (1999), 'Economic policy coordination in the euro-area: origins, development and challenges with some possible lessons for Latin

America', 11th Regional Seminar on Fiscal Policy in Latin America, ECLAC and Finance Ministry of Brazil, January Brasilia.

Ghymers, Christian (2001), La Problemática de la Coordinación de Políticas Económicas. Serie Macroeconomía del desarrollo, 10, Santiago: CEPAL.

Helleiner, E. (1994), *States and the Reemergence of Global Finance: From Bretton Woods to the 1990*s, Ithaca and London: Cornell University Press.

Kenen, Peter B. (1969), 'Theory of optimum currency areas: an eclectic view', in Robert A. Mundell and Alexander K. Swoboda (eds), *Monetary Problems of the International Economy*, Chicago, IL: University of Chicago Press.

Kregel, J. (1999), 'Capital flows, global banking and financial crises in the post-Bretton Woods era as a guide to the 21st century's financial crises', paper prepared for the Seminario Evaluación y Perspectivas de la Economía Mundial: La Crisis del Sudeste Asiático organized by the Instituto de Investigaciones Económicas y la Facultad de Economía, UNAM, Mexico City, 8–9 June.

Loayza, N. and R. Soto (2002), 'Inflation targeting: an overview', in N. Loayza and R. Soto (eds), *Inflation Targeting: Design, Performance, Challenges*, Series on Central Banking, Analysis and Economic Policies, Central Bank of Chile.

McCallum, Bennett (1999), 'Theoretical issues pertaining to monetary unions', NBER Working Paper 7393, October.

McKinnon, Ronald I. (1963), 'Optimum currency areas', *American Economic Review*, **53**, 717–25.

Miotti, Luis, Dominique Plihon and Carlos Quenan (2002), *Euro and the Financial Relations Between Latin America and Europe: Medium-and Long-term Implications*, Serie Macroeconomía del desarrollo, 13, Santiago: CEPAL.

Mundell, Robert (1961), 'The theory of optimum currency areas', *American Economic Review*, **51** (4), 509–17.

Parrado, Eric and Andrés Velasco (2002), 'Alternative monetary rules in the open economy: a welfare-based approach', in N. Loayza and R. Soto (eds), *Inflation Targeting: Design, Performance, Challenges*, Series on Central Banking, Analysis and Economic Policies, Central Bank of Chile.

Paunovic, Igor (2001), 'Regional macroeconomic coordination in Latin America: selected political economy and institutional aspects', mimeo, CEPAL, REDIMA Working Papers (electronic files in http://www.eclac.cl:8080/~redima), October.

Polac, Jacques (2001), 'The two monetary approaches to the balance of payments', IMF Working Paper WP/01/00.

Studart, Rogerio (2002), 'Financial integration, instability and macroeconomic performance in the 1990s: some possible perverse links', CEPAL (mimeo).

Studart, Rogério and Jennifer Hermann (1999), 'Sistemas financeiros no Mercosul: desenvolvimento recente e perspectivas de integração', final report of a research funded by CEPAL-Brasilia (mimeo).

9. Is a monetary union in CARICOM desirable?

Olivier Manioc and Jean-Gabriel Montauban

INTRODUCTION

At present, four monetary unions are active in the world. Apart from the European experience, they concern developing countries in Africa, where two monetary unions operate, and in the Caribbean region. These monetary initiatives were not the result of ambitious political steps, as in Europe, but arose from a will to limit the cost of independence, to take advantage of monetary assistance from former colonial powers, and to ensure the economic viability of these new countries.

These arrangements have indirectly contributed to perpetuate the monetary community created by the former colonial powers. The unions did not permit those countries to get over the economic rivalries, sometimes numerous, and did not promote the market integration of their member countries; the common currency is only a veil masking the difficulties developing countries have to undergo. Their strong external dependence and the weak relations established between these economies are often considered as major hindrances. They have given rise to doubts concerning the efficiency of such monetary arrangements between developing countries.

Despite all these uncertainties, the idea of forming a monetary union in CARICOM has been suggested.[1] As soon as CARICOM was created, the member countries acknowledged that monetary stability was essential for the good working of the common market.[2] This necessity gave birth to the establishment of a compensation procedure aimed at favouring the use of currencies of member countries. Unfortunately this attempt failed. Nevertheless the different heads of governments, conscious that the development of the common market was subordinated to the establishment of a strong monetary cooperation between member states, asked their central bankers to study whether the creation of a monetary union could be possible between CARICOM states. This report, made in March 1992, explains the steps necessary to form a monetary union in 2000. This new stage in the economic cooperation is far from the crowning success of CARICOM.

It appears as a way to boost a process that some are not afraid to qualify as dead. The relevance of this project is also questioned; indeed all CARICOM countries, involved in the dollar zone, and most of their currencies are closely related to the US dollar. Moreover, the advantages of the creation of a single currency seem limited.

The aim of this chapter is to evaluate the opportunity for a monetary unification between CARICOM states. We will link up our ideas around three main areas. The first will describe CARICOM and the potential advantages of a monetary union. Emphasis will be placed on the actual trade policies in these states. It is widely accepted that the adoption of a single currency would favour trade, allowing an optimum assignment of the factors of production, and would increase welfare. Considering all these a priori, we will look at trade potentials between these countries, comparing their degree of economic specialization. Finally, we will undertake some econometrics tests which will allow us to examine the efficiency of a monetary union between CARICOM states.

A MONETARY UNION FOR CARICOM: WHY AND HOW?

Criticisms against CARICOM are particularly severe, as gains from economic integration are quite limited. The lack of a formal space to surround the necessary monetary cooperation is an obvious illustration. The adoption of a single currency could boost the economic integration by creating a public common good which will only be sustainable if there is a convergence of national interest.

The Mitigated Results of CARICOM

More than 30 years after the Chaguaramas treaty was signed instituting CARICOM, the economic results are modest, even pathetic according to some comments (Celimene and Watson, 1991). This reality increases the risks of dislocation of this group.

The failures of trade

CARICOM encountered difficulties like most economic organizations between southern countries during the 1980s (Boxill, 1993). These institutions, whose aim is to promote economic cooperation, faced the decline of worldwide trade and a paradoxical non-cooperative behaviour of their member states. This latter was expressed through the fierceness of commercial rivalries, the dissensions about foreign policy and an obvious predisposition to break off concluded agreements. Several reasons could explain these facts: the existence of trade barriers, and the difficulty abolishing them; commercial conflicts between nations, which were created or worsened by economic crisis; and an evident lack of political goodwill. CARICOM did not succeed in unifying the differing national interests of its member states.[3] As evidence, no intergovernmental meeting was organized during the 1970s up to the 1982 meeting.

Out of the different integration movements between the southern countries, CARICOM has the worst performances regarding intra-zone trade. For example commerce inside CARICOM rose by 8 per cent per year between 1980 and 1987 compared to 14 per cent for the commerce between countries of the Latin American Integration Movement (which includes the ten South American countries and Mexico), 22 per cent for the countries of the Central American Common Market, CACM (whose members states are Costa Rica, El Salvador, Guatemala, Honduras and Nicaragua) and 50 per cent for the economies of the Association of South East Asian Nations. These modest results reveal the strong competitive relations which exist between CARICOM member states.

The failures of industrial cooperation

Concerning industrial cooperation, CARICOM does not seem to have reached its objectives of 1973. Although tax harmonization between member countries and free circulation of factors of production were inscribed in the Chaguaramas treaty, they never became reality. Economic initiatives were never clearly extended, or their materialization was incomplete.

For instance in the early 1980s the creation of two large-scale aluminium production units was planned. The first plant was to be set up in Trinidad and Tobago and was to be owned by the governments of Jamaica, Guyana and Trinidad and Tobago (respectively at 33 per cent, 33 per cent and 34 per cent). The bauxite was to be supplied by Jamaica and Guyana whereas the natural gas was to be brought by Trinidad and Tobago. The second plant was to be established in Guyana, powered by hydroelectric energy and owned by Guyana (52 per cent), Jamaica (24 per cent) and Trinidad and Tobago (24 per cent). Both projects failed because of the unilateral decision of Jamaica to trade bauxite for oil with Venezuela.

The failures of the common commercial policy

Within the common market, quantitative or tariff restrictions could not have been defined in a uniform way. This is also the case for the Common External Tariff (CET) which contrary to its name has never been common to all countries. The CET was supposed to be implemented from 1985, but since the early 1990s, there are four customs tariffs: one for the more developed countries named MDCs (Barbados, Guyana, Jamaica, Trinidad), one for the OECS countries, one for Montserrat and one just for Belize.[4]

The failures of monetary cooperation

In order to promote trade development between CARICOM countries, a monetary compensation system, the CARICOM Multilateral Clearing Facility (CMCF) was instituted between member countries.

This system, which was bilateral at first, became multilateral in 1977. The bilateral system was limited because it forced each state to hold an account for each of its trade partners, which had to be balanced at the end of the credit period.

The CMCF was supposed to favour the use of currencies internal to CARICOM for the settlement of transactions and was intended to promote monetary cooperation and banking relations between member states. Each currency of CARICOM was valued in US dollars and each member state could use a credit line whose limits were clearly defined (Table 9.1). At the end of the credit period, the debit balance of a country had to be credited in US dollars to the countries with a credit balance. Trust was such that the initial credit period of three months was extended to six months, and the overall limit which was fixed at US$40 million was extended to US$100 million between 1977 and 1982. The ambient optimism brought the idea that the increase of regional trade with inflows of currencies coming from third countries would insure the system's liquid assets.

Table 9.1 Exchange rate and credit line in millions of US$

	Exchange rate per US$	Credit line June 1977	Credit line February 1978	Credit line June 1980	Credit line March 1982
Barbados	2	5.5	11	14	10
Belize	2	5	10	12	8
Guyana	2.55	8.5	19	25	29.5
Jamaica	0.91	9.5	18	23	27.5
Trinidad and T.	2.4	6	6	6	2
West Indies States Association	2.7	5.5	16	20	23
Total		40	80	100	100

Source: Freckleton and Lalta (1993).

Table 9.2 Situation in April 1983 in millions of US$

	Debit balance	Credit balance
Barbados	–	65.1
Belize	–	0.7
Guyana	98.6	–
Jamaica	2.3	–
Trinidad and Tobago	–	25.2
West Indies State Association	–	9.9
	100.9	100.9

Source: Freckleton and Lalta (1993).

Thanks to benevolence of Barbados and Trinidad and Tobago, the CMCF worked. Unfortunately in the early 1980s the external positions of Barbados and Trinidad and Tobago began to deteriorate. The inability of Guyana to settle its debts and the impossibility of Barbados granting new terms of payment caused the CMCF to end (Table 9.2).

A Particular Monetary Organization

The reflections concerning monetary union in CARICOM show the sub-optimality of the situation. The monetary division is detrimental to CARICOM countries because they have to adopt the US dollar as an invoicing device and they are also subjected to strong financial restraints which limit the exports of US dollars. The idea of a single currency, when the economic integration has hardly started, is different from the one that led to European unification. It leads to the question of the efficiency of a monetary unification before or after an achieved economic integration. On this, the theoretical debate is open. In the economists' view, economic cooperation should occur only after a series of satisfactory conditions are met: it is the crowning theory. In the monetarists' view, the implementation of a monetary process could be the driving force behind the economic integration between Caribbean states (Pisany-Ferry, 1994).

The diversity of the exchange regimes

The countries of CARICOM can be classified in several families according to the characteristics of their exchange rate policy – fixed or flexible – and according to the currency to which their national currency is attached. Three categories can be distinguished. First, the OECS countries whose currency is the East Caribbean Dollar (EC$). This currency is strictly attached to the US$ at the rate US$1 to EC$2.7. Second, the currencies of the Bahamas, Barbados and Belize which are also strictly attached to the US$, at the rate of US$1 to one unit of the national currency for the Bahamas, and US$1 against two units of national currency for Barbados and Belize. Lastly, the currencies of Haiti, Guyana, Trinidad and Tobago, Jamaica and Surinam which freely fluctuate on the exchange markets. However it is important to note that none of the countries of CARICOM has adopted the US dollar as an official currency.

The advantages of a single currency

According to the literature about monetary unification, the disappearance of exchange dealings and risk of exchange should ease trade relations. Therefore the economies should also benefit from the 'home bias', as agents increase trade with operators sharing the same currency. For the profits of the unification to be significant, the exchange rate fluctuations between moneys of CARICOM have to be important, but only five countries float their currency – all the other currencies are linked with the US dollar.

Losing monetary independence is described as the major drawback. Nevertheless for the disappearance of monetary autonomy to be a problem, the interest in having it available has to be manifest. But the authorities of the countries choosing the fixed rate of exchange are not quite free to manage independent monetary policies. The authorities can use the monetary instrument for conjectural political purposes only by means of quantitative measures restricting the liquid assets in circulation in the economy.

Is CARICOM an optimum monetary zone?

Traditional theories on optimum monetary areas have emphasized that the degree of mobility of the factors of production and the characteristics of international trade are important ingredients to determine whether a zone is an optimum monetary area.

For Mundell (1961), the pioneer of such analysis, the main factor is the degree of input mobility, especially of the labour force. When two countries produce different goods, any transfer of demand from one country to the other will lead to changes in these economies. An increase in unemployment and a trade deficit will characterize the country which produces the good for which demand has contracted. In a Keynesian world where prices and exchange rates are fixed, migration of workers from the country in crisis towards the expanding one is the only way to adjust both economies. In the Caribbean area the territorial discontinuity is a natural hindrance to such mechanism and the lack of political will to liberalize the movements of CARICOM nationals is obvious. According to this contribution, the geographic and administrative hindrances to migration alter the ability for CARICOM countries to support fixed exchange rates.[5]

According to MacKinnon (1963), the more an economy is open, the greater its interest in choosing fixed exchange rates in order to avoid fluctuations in the relative prices between traded goods and non-traded goods. Moreover the internal aim of price stability cannot be reached if a significant fraction of the locally consumed goods is imported and subject to large price swings because of the variation in exchange rates. On this point, all CARICOM countries are characterized by a very important degree of opening.[6] If the small countries of CARICOM have chosen fixed exchanges, the larger ones have adopted regimes of floating exchange rates. In these cases, fixed exchange rates are defined according to the US dollar. Indeed for a majority of the countries the United States is the main trading partner. Fixed exchange rates with the first trading partner is therefore widely established as MacKinnon suggested.

According to Kenen (1969), the more specialized a country is, the bigger its interest in a floating currency scheme. If world demand decreases, those countries must be able to adjust their exchange rates to boost external demand for their export products, if this demand is related to price level. Despite this rule of decision, main specialized developing countries choose fixed exchange rates because they believe that fixing the exchange rate has no real effect on their competitiveness. According to Semedo (1998), this choice has insured the full transmission of the export benefits of price fluctuations observed in world markets of basic products.

THE TRADING FLOWS BETWEEN CARICOM COUNTRIES

Recent analyses about optimum monetary zones have suggested that the countries whose bilateral exchange rates are fixed should not encounter asymmetric shocks. Indeed if a country is hit by a specific shock of supply or demand and it cannot use an accommodating monetary policy or an active trade policy, its needs in terms of stabilization policy will strongly differ from those of the other members of the monetary zone. Mundell had mainly considered this second hypothesis based upon asymmetric shocks.

At the same way, a consensus was established that monetary unification reinforces economic relationships between states. But from two competing analyses emerge two opposite conclusions about the impact of this intensification of trade relationships upon economic convergence. The first conforms with the conclusions of the European Commission Report (1990) about monetary unification in Europe; it upholds the idea that the convergence of economies goes together with the reinforcement of trade. The second analysis is shared between Eichengreen (1990) and Krugman (1993), and upholds that trade integration increases the risks for a specific shock to occur. This analysis is often called the Eichengreen–Kenen–Krugman view. This controversy will be the starting point of the second part of this chapter. During this part, focusing on the characteristics of trade inside CARICOM and the specialization of the member states, we will try to see the impact of a potential intensification of trade between states of CARICOM on the economic structures. Can we expect a reinforcement of the economic correlation or should we be afraid of an increase in the number of asymmetric shocks?

The European Commission against Eichengreen–Krugman

In its preparatory report for the adoption of a single currency, the European Commission has insisted on the advantages of monetary unification. It favours the development of trade inside Europe by suppressing exchange rate risks. The specific demand shocks, emphasized by Mundell, would disappear as the commerce inside Europe is widely an intrabranch trade. As argued by De Grauwe (1999): 'This commerce is based on scale economy and on the defects of competitiveness caused by the differentiation of the products.' So as the European countries trade similar goods, this closeness of productive structures reduces the probability of specific demand or supply shocks.

For Eichengreen–Krugman, the reinforcement of trade will lead to an increased specialization of the economies; this movement would be guided by the exploitation of scale economies allowed by the large European market. The relocation of production units and their integration in given geographical spaces will, by nature, favour the appearance of asymmetric shocks. This analysis is closely related to Kenen's which argued that only diversified economies could accept fixed exchange rates. There are two major objections to this argument. First of all, the movement of geographical integration can take place in border zones such that if an industry is hit by a specific shock, it will concern more than one country. Secondly, the authors seemed to have insisted on supply shocks which considering the increasing specialization are destined to be less correlated between countries (Frankel and Rose, 1996). But a priori a demand-specific shock can spread to its neighbours through the propensity to import, despite the increased specialization of the economies. The recession experienced by a country reduces its import capacity and limits the exports of its partners.

Concerning the CARICOM countries, it seems that the increased specialization at an individual level has been one of the main objectives of the countries that signed the Chaguaramas treaty. Then, according to Jainarain (1976), the individual specialization was to be the basis of a collective diversification: 'The larger market should also increase competition and efficiency through increased specialization in individual partner [each member state], while stimulating the diversification of production in the region as a whole. Finally, integration should improve the international bargaining position of the partners *vis-à-vis* third countries.' The territorial discontinuity does not allow much room for a geographic concentration in the frontiers of the member states. Only the continuation of industrial integration could have prevented the specialization from reinforcing the appearance of a specific supply shock. But as we have said before, very few experiences of industrial cooperation have been implemented successfully.

At this stage, it is particularly difficult to decide which one of the two analyses best fits the CARICOM members. Only the study of commerce inside CARICOM and of the levels of states' specialization will allow us to be more precise in our conclusions about the possible impact of a trade reinforcement.

The Weight and the Evolution of Commerce Inside CARICOM

The intensity of trade is often the argument for increased integration and for the abolishment of hindrances to free circulation of goods and people; economic operators' needs guide political choices. It is the opposite situation in the Caribbean where the trade movements are rather too small and weak to inspire integration dynamics.

The intensity of the trading flows is often taken as an indicator of the complementary degree between economies. Thus the analysis of the commerce inside CARICOM would particularly reveal the difficulties of creating sustained relationships between those states.

The evolution of commerce inside CARICOM between 1968 and 1996

The contribution of intra-CARICOM trade to the overall trade of CARICOM countries has clearly increased since the 1960s: it grew from 5 per cent to 13 per cent in 1996. Nevertheless this increase is still modest considering what was announced initially, and the willingness to reinforce trade between those countries (Table 9.3).

Three main sub-periods can be identified. Between 1968 and 1981, a strong increase in trade between Caribbean countries is observed. Thanks to CARIFTA agreements (CARIbbean Free Trade Association), commerce increased on average by more than 20 per cent a year between 1973 and 1980. The average yearly growth rate reached its highest point at 27 per cent between 1971 and 1976 and came back to 11 per cent a year between 1977

Table 9.3 Contribution of intra-CARICOM trade to overall trade of CARICOM countries

Years	%
1968	5
1980	8.9
1985	11.1
1990	10.5
1996	13

Source: CARICOM.

and 1981. Massive direct investments, thanks to the strategy of import substitution and of industrialization at invitation, have favoured the trade of manufactured goods. But from 1977, Jamaica and Guyana faced large deficits in their balance of payments and limited their imports from CARICOM by establishing quotas. Under the pressure of the International Monetary Fund, their currencies were devalued. Two official exchange rates were defined for the Jamaican dollar. The former exchange rate was reserved for the government's operations, for bauxite export and for basic products and drugs imports. A new devalued exchange rate was installed for the import of basic consumer goods called 'non-fundamental' and the export of goods coming from favoured sectors (Célimène and Watson, 1991). These measures of structural adjustment have increased the divisions and made the economic integration of CARICOM states more delicate.

Between 1981 and 1986, a strong decrease in the volume of trade can be noted. The average yearly downturn was 11.8 per cent. Trading inside CARICOM contracted during the 1980s particularly because of the difficulties linked to the debt of some countries, the decrease of import ability of Trinidad and Tobago due to the fall in the oil price, and the collapse of the multilateral compensations system. The forced import restrictions have been harsher for commerce inside CARICOM as they concern consumer goods, which can be locally produced. Exports outside CARICOM concern mainly capital goods where exchange cannot be limited without altering the capacity of production of the economy concerned.

Between 1987 and 1996, the revival of the commerce inside CARICOM was obvious. It progressed on average by 4.5 per cent a year with an increase of 10 per cent between 1990 and 1995. It was led by the economic renewal in the early 1990s.

The evolution of commerce inside CARICOM intensifies the trends of the total commerce of the member states. Indeed, in a period of trade

Table 9.4 The average yearly growth rate of the commerce inside CARICOM and of the total commerce

Period	Trade inside CARICOM (%)	Total trade of the member states (%)
1981–96	1.9	0.1
1981–86	−11.8	−10.3
1987–96	4.5	3.1

Source: CARICOM.

expansion, commerce inside the zone increases more than total commerce, and in a period of trade contraction commerce inside the zone decreases more than the gross volume of trade (Table 9.4).

The commerce inside CARICOM per countries

The contribution of the commerce inside CARICOM varies from one country to another (Table 9.5).

Trinidad and Tobago is the only country whose trade with the other members is increasing: it went from 5.8 per cent to 15 per cent between 1980 and 1995. The other countries encountered wide fluctuations during that period. Generally speaking, the contributions of commerce inside CARICOM in 1980 are quite similar to 1995.

Table 9.5 Contribution of commerce inside CARICOM to the total commerce of the member states (%)

Country	1980	1985	1990	1995
Antigua and Barbuda	37.4	N.A.	N.A.	N.A.
Barbados	20.1	17.5	19.1	21.1
Belize	3.2	2.6	6.3	4.3
Dominica	32.7	29.4	22.5	31.2
Grenada	27.8	25.9	24.2	27.7
Guyana	18.8	22.8	9.4	N.A.
Jamaica	6.6	5.0	5.2	5.8
Montserrat	59.6	27.6	17.8	N.A.
Saint Kitts and Nevis	19.9	22.5	14.1	16.5
Saint Lucia	24.6	19.3	17.7	20.6
Saint Vincent	32.1	37.3	25.9	35.9
Surinam	–	–	–	7.3
Trinidad and Tobago	5.8	9.1	10.3	15.0

Source: CARICOM.

Table 9.6 Contribution of the three groups to commerce inside CARICOM in 1996

	(%)
Group 1	7.4
Group 2	67.5
Group 3	25.1

Source: CARICOM.

Three groups can be distinguished. First, countries in which commerce inside the zone reaches a higher level than 30 per cent; Saint Vincent and Dominica (group 1). Second, countries in which commerce inside the zone is bounded between 15 per cent and 30 per cent; Barbados, Grenada, Saint Lucia, Saint Kitts and Nevis, Trinidad and Tobago (group 2). And third, countries in which commerce inside the zone reaches a lower level than 15 per cent; Belize, Jamaica, Surinam (group 3).

These three groups contribute unequally to commerce inside CARICOM (Table 9.6).

Larger countries (Jamaica, Trinidad and Tobago, Suriname) are the ones for whom intra-CARICOM trade is the least important.

Apart from the limited contribution of commerce inside the zone, the sparseness of the bilateral export and import matrices is a second element confirming the relative weakness of the trade relationships between the member states. The number of bilateral relationships less than EC$ 30 000 for exports and imports is stable between 1980 and 1995. But it represents almost 15 per cent of the potential trade flows between CARICOM states.[7] Montserrat and Belize are typical cases. Montserrat is the country which exports the least within CARICOM, while Belize has few trade contacts with either imports or exports (Table 9.7).

Specialization and Trade inside CARICOM

The nature of trade inside CARICOM

The crude oil exports from Trinidad and Tobago constitute the main item of commerce inside CARICOM. The strong decrease in trade observed in 1990 is linked to the decrease in crude oil price and to oil purchases by Guyana outside CARICOM (Venezuela). The trading of manufactured products (products 6 to 8) increased at a yearly growth rate of 45 per cent between 1970 and 1981. The increase of products 5 and 6 is noteworthy between 1980 and 1995 (Tables 9.8).

Table 9.7 Trading flows inside CARICOM inferior to EC$30 000

Number of export flows	1980	1985	1990	1995
8			Montserrat	
7		Belize		
6		Montserrat		Montserrat
5	Belize		Belize	Surinam
4	Grenada	Grenada		
3	Montserrat	Saint Kitts and Nevis		Belize Saint Kitts and Nevis
2	Antigua and Barbuda Saint Kitts and Nevis Saint Vincent and Grenadines	Saint Vincent and Grenadines	Grenada	Grenada Saint Vincent and Grendines
1	Dominica Saint Lucia	Antigua and Barbuda Saint Lucia	Guyana Antigua and Barbuda Dominica Saint Kitts and Nevis Saint Vincent and Grenadines	
Total	20	24	20	21

Number of import flows	1980	1985	1990	1995
7	Guyana		Belize	
6	Belize	Belize		
5				Surinam Belize
4				
3		Guyana Jamaica Saint Vincent and Grenadines		Grenada
2	Grenada Montserrat Saint Kitts and Nevis	Montserrat Grenada	Guyana Grenada Montserrat	Jamaica Saint Kitts and Nevis Saint Vincent and Grenadines
1	Saint Vincent and Grenadines	Antigua and Barbuda Saint Lucia Trinidad and Tobago Dominica Saint Kitts and Nevis	Barbados Jamaica Trinidad and Tobago Dominica Saint Kitts and Nevis Saint Lucia Saint Vincent and Grenadines	Dominica Saint Lucia
Total	20	26	20	21

Source: CARICOM.

Table 9.8 Composition of commerce inside CARICOM per SITC (Standard International Trade Classification)

SECTIONS SITC	1980		1985		1990		1995	
	Value	%	Value	%	Value	%	Value	%
0 – Food, living animals	266 234	18.7	219 650	17.8	242 337	17.6	372 501	16.5
1 – Drinks and Tobacco	36 122	2.5	38 645	3.2	90 301	6.6	143 301	6.3
2 – Inedible crude equipments	13 468	0.9	11 843	1	14 770	1.1	8 066	0.4
3 – Fuels, minerals and lubricants	620 217	43.4	623 367	50.7	289 580	21	825 213	36.6
4 – Oil, animal and vegetable fat	12 255	0.9	4 554	0.4	21 754	1.6	18 238	0.8
5 – Chemicals	141 677	9.9	112 200	9.2	208 420	15.1	279 634	12.4
6 – Manufactured items	125 471	8.8	119 672	9.8	293 476	21.3	383 802	17
7 – Transport machines and equipments	66 112	4.6	32 492	2.7	76 450	5.6	88 381	3.9
8 – Various manufactured items	143 965	10.1	58 232	4.8	135 833	9.9	138 360	6.1
9 – Unclassified items and transactions	2 374	0.2	5 171	0.4	3 264	0.2	289	0
All sections (in thousands of EC$)	**1 427 895**	**100**	**1 225 826**	**100**	**1 376 185**	**100**	**2 257 785**	**100**

Source: CARICOM.

Table 9.9 Ventilation of trade inside CARICOM between basic products and manufactured goods (%)

	1980	1985	1990	1995
Manufactured products (sections 6 to 8)	23.5	17.2	36.8	27.0
Base products including crude oil (sections 0 to 4)	66.4	73.3	47.9	60.6
Others (sections 5 and 9)	10.1	9.6	15.4	12.4
Total	100	100	100	100

Source: CARICOM.

Between 1980 and 1995, the share of manufactured goods in CARICOM trade increased irregularly and represented more than one-quarter of overall trade in 1995 (Table 9.9).

The degree of specialization within CARICOM countries

The degree of trade specialization inside CARICOM and of each member state can be estimated using the traditional Herfindhal index, which is defined as the sum of the contribution squares of each export product:

$$H_{i,t} = \sum_{j=1}^{10} \left(\frac{x_{i,j,t}}{\sum_{j=1}^{10} x_{i,j,t}} \right)^2$$

This index is calculated for the country i and for the period t, j points out the SITC category. The stronger the index (near 1), the more specialized the country, the weaker the index (near 1/10), the more the country has a diversified structure of its foreign trade. The inferior value of the Herfindhal index is 1/10 because exports are ventilated on the basis of the SITC with ten posts.

The decrease in the contribution to trade of the crude exports automatically resulted in more diversified exchanges inside CARICOM (Table 9.10).

The same index will be used to evaluate the degree of specialization of the member states of CARICOM. Their export structure will be used to

Table 9.10 Evolution of the Herfindhal index for trade inside CARICOM

	1980	1985	1990	1995
Herfindhal index	0.254	0.311	0.161	0.215
Herfindhal index (excluding section 3)	0.204	0.225	0.187	0.200

Table 9.11 Herfindhal index for the member states of CARICOM in 1996

Countries	Herfindhal index
Barbados	0.180
Intra-CARICOM	0.216
Bahamas	0.248
Trinidad and Tobago	0.326
Jamaica	0.329
Haiti	0.368
Guyana	0.393
Suriname	0.398
Dominica	0.443
Saint Kitts and Nevis	0.454
Montserrat	0.462
Saint Lucia	0.489
Grenada	0.561
Antigua and Barbuda	0.604
Saint Vincent and Grenadines	0.618
Belize	0.636

calculate the Herfindhal index. Barbados has the most diversified structure in CARICOM (Table 9.11).

The seven countries of the OECS are among the eight countries whose structure of foreign trade is the most specialized. Rose and Engel (2000) have shown that the Herfindhal index was systematically higher for the countries sharing the same currency, a proof according to them that monetary unification and polarization of the productive base go together. Nevertheless they do not mention the relations of cause and effect, and do not conclude that monetary unification would lead to an increasing specialization of the productive system. Besides, they suggest that the characteristics of the productive structure would be prior to the monetary unification.

The national export structures confirm the strong specialization of the states. Thus, a single category covers at least 31 per cent of the total export and 79 per cent for the maximum. The national situations are rather different. Almost 80 per cent of the foreign trade of Belize, Saint Vincent and Grenadines and Antigua and Barbuda rests on a single item of export. Lastly, category 0, which includes food and living animals, appears in the first or second position in the hierarchy of export for 13 of the 15 countries of CARICOM[8] (Table 9.12).

Table 9.12 Structure of national export

	Number of SITC categories to cover 75% of exports	SITC categories which cover at least 75% of exports	Corresponding percentage of exports	Contribution of the main export post (%)
Intra-CARICOM trade	4	3-6-0-5	84	36
Barbados	5	0-6-7-3-5	85	31
Bahamas	3	0-7-2	81	37
Jamaica	3	2-0-8	89	50
Trinidad and Tobago	3	3-5-6	86	50
Dominica	2	0-5	94	48
Grenada	2	0-6	84	74
Guyana	2	0-9	77	55
Haiti	2	8-0	76	55
Saint Kitts and Nevis	2	0-7	91	59
Saint Lucia	2	0-8	79	68
Suriname	2	2-0	80	58
Montserrat	2	7-0	94	57
Belize	1	0	79	79
Saint Vincent and Grenadines	1	0	78	78
Antigua and Barbuda	1	7	77	77

As the countries are quite strongly specialized, and intra-CARICOM trade is rather diversified, it seems possible to make the assumption that the current possibility for trade inside CARICOM is widely exploited. It is still true that the economic similarities restrict the exchanges and the weakness of the economic complementarities limit trade between states to a limited part of their production.

The Economic Correlations

According to the international division of labour, the states of CARICOM are quite similar. This closeness reduces the probability of specific demand and supply shocks for a certain number of countries. Nevertheless the productive structures are not strictly identical. Trinidad and Tobago, which is an oil exporter, and Barbados, which is an oil importer, cannot react the same way to a change in crude oil prices on the world market. Even the natural disasters which can cause important supply shocks do not have the same consequences in all the states of CARICOM considering how far they are from each other. In fact it seems important to value the correlation degree of the economies of CARICOM countries.

The study of the correlation coefficients of the growth rates and of the inflation rates puts forward another feature of these states. The correlation degrees of the growth rate of real GDP are quite low, even negative, while the inflation rates are strongly correlated. We should also notice that almost all the correlation coefficients of the inflation rates between the OECS countries are significant at the 1 per cent level (Table 9.13).

However the weakness of the real correlations must not lead to the hasty conclusion that a single currency would not be viable inside CARICOM. Besides, the growth rates were not one of the convergence criterion in the European Union treaty. Moreover, the inflation rates have converged between 1980 and 1996, except for Jamaica. The inflation gap between the most and the least inflationist countries, which was 16.3 in 1980, was only 5.3 in 1996, excluding Jamaica in this latter case. Note that only three countries, Jamaica, Belize and Saint Vincent and Grenadines, do not meet the rule required in the European Union treaty in terms of inflation.[9]

THE ECONOMETRICS IMPLEMENTATION

In this third part, we will introduce the econometric methodology kept to check the nature of the existing relations between economic correlations and trade flows. We will test the hypothesis that the reinforcement of trade between countries increases economic closeness and reduces the probability of asymmetric shocks. The method used follows the work of Frankel and Rose (1996, 1998).[10] It is based upon the following relation:

$$Corr_{ij,t} = a \times \ln Trade_{ij,t} + b + \varepsilon_{ij,t} \qquad (9.1)$$

where $Corr_{ij}$ is a correlation index between economy i and economy j, and $Trade_{ij}$ is an index of trade intensity between country i and country j.

The Variables Used

The correlation indicators used as proxy of the correlation degrees between the economies are based on the growth rates of the real GDP (g) and on the

Table 9.13 Correlation coefficients of real GDP growth and inflation in CARICOM

	Barbados	Guyana	Jamaica	T-Tobago	Belize	A-Barbuda	Dominica	Grenada	St Kitts	St Lucia	St Vincent
Barbados	–	0.18	−0.06	0.57*	0.73**	0.62**	0.81**	0.90**	0.85**	0.79**	0.83**
Guyana	0.06	–	−0.55*	0.29	0.15	0.44	0.01	0.14	−0.06	0.03	−0.06
Jamaica	−0.07	−0.32	–	−0.42	−0.06	−0.27	0.01	−0.09	0.01	0.03	−0.05
T-Tobago	−0.25	0.47	−0.02	–	0.54*	0.48*	0.58*	0.68**	0.58*	0.52*	0.61**
Belize	−0.01	0.06	0.72**	0.01	–	0.77**	0.92**	0.85**	0.89**	0.79**	0.84**
A-Barbuda	0.53*	−0.05	−0.02	−0.55*	0.03	–	0.78**	0.71**	0.64**	0.73**	0.57*
Dominica	0.07	−0.07	0.18	−0.14	0.09	0.26	–	0.87**	0.93**	0.88**	0.86**
Grenada	0.37	−0.18	0.14	−0.21	0.27	0.44	0.29	–	0.92**	0.83**	0.87**
St Kitts	0.50*	0.10	−0.09	−0.03	0.20	0.43	0.38	0.46	–	0.89**	0.92**
St Lucia	0.29	−0.32	−0.07	−0.44	0.13	0.38	0.34	0.35	0.41	–	0.85**
St Vincent	0.02	−0.28	0.11	−0.27	0.26	−0.11	0.56*	0.07	0.26	0.62**	–

Notes:
Above main diagonal, correlation coefficients of growth rate; below main diagonal, correlation coefficients of inflation rates.
* significant at 5% level.
** significant at 1% level.

inflation rates (π). The lack of statistics on labour and industrial production indices forces us to limit our work to these macroeconomics data. Thus the five following correlation indicators will be successively used.

CORR(1) is the opposite of what we call the economic distance between two countries. The stronger the distance, the less important the correlation:

$$CORR(1)_{ij} = -\sqrt{(g_i - g_j)^2 + (\pi_i - \pi_j)^2}$$

CORR(2) and *CORR*(3) are binary variables; the relations in which they are set will be estimated with a probit model:

$$CORR(2)_{ij} = \begin{cases} 1 & \text{if } |g_i - g_j| < 1\% \\ 0 & \text{else} \end{cases}$$

$$CORR(3)_{ij} = \begin{cases} 1 & \text{if } |\pi_i - \pi_j| < 1\% \\ 0 & \text{else} \end{cases}$$

CORR(4) is the opposite of the growth rate differential; the weaker this differential, the stronger the correlation:

$$CORR(4)_{ij} = -|g_i - g_j|$$

CORR(5) is the opposite of the inflation rate differential; the weaker this differential, the stronger the correlation:

$$CORR(5)_{ij} = -|\pi_i - \pi_j|$$

Six indicators of trade intensity will be used. They will be established from the combination of the following variables:

$X_{ij,t}$: Exports from country *i* to country *j* in *t*
$X_{i,t}$: Total exports from country *i* in *t*
$X_{j,t}$: Total exports from country *j* in *t*
$M_{ij,t}$: Imports of country *i* from country *j* in *t*
$M_{i,t}$: Total imports of country *i* in *t*
$M_{j,t}$: Total imports of country *j* in *t*

$$TRADE(1)_{ij,t} = \frac{X_{ij,t}}{X_{i,t} + X_{j,t}}$$

$$TRADE(2)_{ij,t} = \frac{M_{ij,t}}{M_{i,t} + M_{j,t}}$$

$$TRADE(3)_{ij,t} = \frac{X_{ij,t} + M_{ij,t}}{(X_{i,t} + X_{j,t}) + (M_{i,t} + M_{j,t})}$$

$$TRADE(4)_{ij,t} = \frac{X_{ij,t}}{X_{i,t}}$$

$$TRADE(5)_{ij,t} = \frac{X_{ij,t}}{X_{i,t} + M_{j,t}}$$

$$TRADE(6)_{ij,t} = X_{ij,t}$$

Thirty regressions will be implemented using these five indicators of economic correlations (indexed by k) and these six indicators of trade intensities (indexed by l):

$$Corr(k)_{ij,t} = a \times \ln Trade(l)_{ij,t} + b + \varepsilon_{ij,t} \tag{9.2}$$

The Estimation Results

The results in the following table have been obtained from the estimation of the relation (1).[11] Only the coefficients a and their respective *t-student* have been reported in the following table (Table 9.14).

Apart from four coefficients, all of them are positive. Of the 17 coefficients significant at 5 per cent of risk, 15 are positive. Moreover all the negative

Table 9.14 Econometric estimations for parameter a

	CORR(1)	CORR(2)	CORR(3)	CORR(4)	CORR(5)
ln TRADE(1)	0.5545**	0.07488**	0.03426**	0.1922**	0.5202**
	(3.561)	(3.40488)	(3.7707)	(3.34108)	(3.513)
ln TRADE(2)	0. 1463*	0.05061*	0.03192	0.01247	0.2056
	(0.904)	(2.31695)	(1.6351)	(0.21918)	(1.3252)
ln TRADE(3)	0.0765	0.06977**	0.01701	0.08530	0.05887
	(0.472)	(2.87629)	(0.83906)	(1.42732)	(0.3762)
ln TRADE(4)	0.3593*	0.04088	0.02603	0.11705*	0.3520*
	(2.345)	(1.97758)	(1.37259)	(2.1238)	(2.4126)
ln TRADE(5)	0.2865	0.06208**	0.0509**	0.0838	0.3107*
	(1.7997)	(2.28471)	(2.62199)	(1.46371)	(2.0422)
ln TRADE(6)	−0.5749**	0.04099*	−0.01354	−0.0632	−0.5162**
	(−4.7499)	(2.56788)	(−0.94678)	(−1.4777)	(−4.4132)

Notes:
* significant at 5% level.
** significant at 1% level.

values concern the bilateral exchange indicator LTRADE(6). We can thus admit the hypothesis that the *a* parameter is positive. This result is not very surprising and only confirms former results: it transposes to the Caribbean case the conclusions of the European Commission which said that trade intensification led to high economic correlation.

Thus it appears that:

- The economic distance reduces between countries when trade intensifies (column 1).
- The probability that the growth rate differential is inferior to 1 per cent increases with the trade flow (column 2). It is the same with the inflation rate differential (column 3). Nevertheless trade has a more important impact on the probability of the growth rate differentials to be inferior to 1 per cent; the coefficients of column 2 are systematically superior to those in column 3.
- The inflation rate differential is more sensitive to trade intensification than the growth rate differential (columns 4 and 5). The impact of exchanges on the convergence of inflation rates would be stronger than the real growth rates.

The influences of two dummies are also tested: *DUMMYOECS*[12] and *DUMMYFIX*.[13] They are supposed to indicate the impact of pertaining to OECS and the impact of adopting a fixed exchange rate on economic correlations.

The indicative variables are successively introduced in relations following the pattern:

$$Corr(k)_{ij,t} = a \times \ln Trade(l)_{ij,t} + \mu \times DUMMY + b + \varepsilon_{ij,t} \qquad (9.3)$$

They are both significant at the level of 1 per cent in the regressions of *CORR*(1), *CORR*(4) and *CORR*(5).

However, let us not rush to conclude that a single Caribbean currency and its corollary and the reinforcement of trade relationships can remove the probability of asymmetrical shock. Indeed, let us not forget that commerce inside CARICOM holds a marginal place in the overall commerce of the states of the zone. This marginal characteristic and the strong dependence of the countries towards foreign trade partners (the United States of America) or international market conditions (the world market of oil and sugar) can obviously influence the apparently positive relationship between the economic correlations and the intensity of trade flows. In the case of a recession in the USA, the American imports would contract and the Caribbean would witness a fall in exports, which would prevent them from stocking up and would cause them to limit their trade relations with their partners. In order to take into account these potential influences, we will estimate relation (1) using the instrumental variables methods and using the gravity model of international trade.

The Gravity Model

The gravity model explains the basics of international trade with a set of variables representing the attraction and resistance forces to trading between countries.[14] Many assumptions are used when the gravity model is applied to international trade. The transactions between two countries are mapped to the gross domestic product of both the economies considered (Y_i and Y_j), their population size (L_i and L_j) and their development level represented by the gross domestic product per capita (y_i and y_j). The resistance forces are represented by transport costs which can be studied by the distance in kilometres (D_{ij}). Non-economic factors are also considered. For example cultural elements such as language or common history (P_{ij}). The formulations usually considered are the following:

$$X_{ij,t} = \alpha_0 Y_{i,t}^{\alpha_1} Y_{j,t}^{\alpha_2} L_{i,t}^{\alpha_3} L_{j,t}^{\alpha_4} D_{ij}^{\alpha_5} P_{ij,t}^{\alpha_6} e^{u_{ij,t}} \tag{9.4}$$

$$X_{ij,t} = \beta_0 y_{i,t}^{\beta_1} y_{j,t}^{\beta_2} L_{i,t}^{\beta_3} L_{j,t}^{\beta_4} D_{ij}^{\beta_5} P_{ij,t}^{\beta_6} e^{v_{ij,t}} \tag{9.5}$$

$$X_{ij,t} = \delta_0 Y_{i,t}^{\delta_1} Y_{j,t}^{\delta_2} y_{i,t}^{\delta_3} y_{j,t}^{\delta_4} D_{ij}^{\delta_5} P_{ij,t}^{\delta_6} e^{w_{ij,t}} \tag{9.6}$$

The closeness of CARICOM states and the geographic discontinuity of the whole avoids taking into account particular difficulties linked to the non-equivalence between the distance in kilometres and the transport restraints.[15]

The GDPs of the exporting and importing country are supposed to be positively linked to trading between both countries. The gross domestic product of the exporting country (Y_i) shows the productive ability and the aptitudes of the country to take part in international trade. The gross domestic product of the importing country (Y_j) shows the absorption capacity of this economy.

The import and export abilities are not closely linked to the gross domestic products. Indeed of the three countries with the highest gross domestic product in CARICOM, namely Trinidad and Tobago, the Bahamas and Jamaica, only Jamaica is among the more open countries according to the export and import rates per capita.[16] In the same way, the three countries with the lowest gross domestic product, namely Montserrat, Dominica and Saint Kitts, do not have the lowest import and export rate per capita.[17]

The signs of the coefficients related to the population of both countries are ambiguous. The population gives an indication of the size of the country and of the degree of diversification of the economy. But the more an economy is diversified, the less it should participate in international trade because the economy meets the demand of its local population. Assuming this, the population should be negatively linked to international trade. Nevertheless the supply of the wide local market can lead to a certain specialization of the economy, the domestic market allowing it to reach a critical size. The will to exploit the scale economies of supplying foreign markets would be strong: under these conditions, the relation between the population and trade should be positive. The more populated countries of CARICOM, namely Haiti, Jamaica and Trinidad and Tobago, seem to confirm the positive correlation.[18]

The GDP per capita is a proxy of the development degree. The more important the wealth per inhabitant, the more it is expected that the necessary infrastructures are present. The relation would therefore be positive. But the inhabitants can show more sensibility towards the quality of the products proposed, and search for differentiation. It is not certain that CARICOM countries can meet the need of differentiation of the countries when GDP is the highest. As a proof, the three countries whose GDP per capita is the highest, namely the Bahamas, Barbados, and Trinidad and Tobago, do not trade that much in CARICOM.

Distance is a resistance factor to international trade: the higher the distance, the weaker the trade relations should be.[19] The relation to be estimated is:

$$\ln TRADE(l)_{ij,t} = \alpha_0 + \alpha_1 \ln Y_{i,t} + \alpha_2 \ln Y_{j,t} + \alpha_3 \ln y_{i,t} + \alpha_4 \ln y_{j,t} + \alpha_5 \ln D_{ij} + \varepsilon_{ij,t} \quad (9.7)$$

The estimation results of the six relations are reported in Table 9.15.

The coefficient signs are identical for the different trade intensity indicators with two exceptions: the two gross domestic products per capita. Both real gross domestic products are positively correlated to trade indicators, and distance negatively influences bilateral trade flows. There is still an ambiguity for the coefficient signs affected to both gross domestic products per capita. The gross domestic product per capita of the importing country negatively affects trade, confirming the idea that CARICOM products are essentials. They can be replaced by items of higher quality as soon as the purchasing power allows it.

The R^2 are similar to Thoumi's results (1992) who found R^2 between 0.515 and 0.721 in a similar study. But they are inferior to standard gravity

Table 9.15 Econometric estimations for gravity equation

	ln TRADE(1)	ln TRADE(2)	ln TRADE(3)	ln TRADE(4)	ln TRADE(5)	ln TRADE(6)
R^2	0.454	0.499	0.609	0.559	0.484	0.680
α_0	−2.1524	0.6068	0.1496	−0.9458	−0.5440	11.3200**
	(−1.923)	(0.583)	(0.170)	(−0.965)	(−0.507)	(12.293)
α_1	0.6466**	0.3192**	0.562**	0.240**	0.7912**	1.375**
	(19.796)	(10.629)	(22.173)	(8.470)	(25.449)	(50.053)
α_2	0.1273**	0.8426**	0.5637**	0.8189**	0.2147**	0.8058**
	(3.930)	(27.844)	(22.218)	(28.652)	(6.890)	(29.620)
α_3	−0.4673**	0.092	−0.2493**	−0.229**	−0.5801**	−1.036**
	(−4.721)	(1.031)	(−3.216)	(−2.650)	(−6.1327)	(−13.4164)
α_4	0.4123**	−0.832**	−0.2718**	−0.0085	0.1123	0.0191
	(4.215)	(−9.212)	(−3.505)	(−0.1021)	(1.2167)	(0.2403)
α_5	−1.2666**	−1.2844**	−1.386**	−1.3122**	−1.2663**	−1.3318**
	(−29.159)	(−31.549)	(−42.037)	(−34.344)	(−30.2509)	(−36.3046)

Notes:
t-student in parenthesis.
* significant at 5% level.
** significant at 1% level.

Table 9.16 Econometric estimations for method of instrumental variables

	CORR(1)	CORR(2)	CORR(3)	CORR(4)	CORR(5)
ln TRADE(1)	0.83**	0.045	0.005	0.13**	0.85**
	(4.39)	(1.69)	(0.219)	(1.93)	(4.64)
ln TRADE(2)	−0.013*	0.032	−0.054*	0.023	0.023
	(−0.07)	(1.24)	(−2.28)	(0.36)	(0.13)
ln TRADE(3)	0.26	0.039	−0.036	0.06	0.0301
	(1.44)	(1.50)	(−1.55)	(0.93)	(1.68)
ln TRADE(4)	0.289	0.035	−0.025	0.06	0.32
	(1.66)	(1.44)	(−1.11)	(0.988)	(1.90)
ln TRADE(5)	0.295	0.037	−0.032	0.06	0.32
	(1.57)	(1.40)	(−1.33)	(0.94)	(1.79)
ln TRADE(6)	−0.88**	0.011	−0.092**	−0.091	−0.82**
	(−6.77)	(0.59)	(−5.22)	(−1.95)	(−6.51)

Notes:
t-student in parenthesis.
* significant at 5% level.
** significant at 1% level.

models results, generally between 0.65 and 0.85. Thoumi explained this by the weakness of the relations inside CARICOM. Trade inside CARICOM would be insensitive to the evolutions of macroeconomic variables because the main trade partners would be outside the zone. There should be other determinants to the intensity of trade between countries.

The dummy variable *DUMMYOECS* is significant at 1 per cent in all the regressions in which it is introduced. The *DUMMYFIX* variable is significant only twice in the regressions of *LTRADE*(1) and *LTRADE*(5).

The Estimation Results by the Method of Instrumental Variables

The results are far more ambiguous. Only eight coefficients are significant at 5 per cent and the signs are far more fluctuating since eight out of 30 coefficients are negative. Among the coefficients significant at the 1 per cent level, there are positive elements as well as negative ones.

Considering the significance of *DUMMYOECS* and *DUMMYFIX* in the initial equation and in the trade intensities, we will introduce it in the new correlation equation. Considering their strong similarity, the two cannot be introduced efficiently without altering the significance of one of them. The final relation to estimate is the following:

$$Corr(k)_{ij,t} = a \times \ln Trade(l)_{ij,t} + \mu \times DUMMYFIX + b + \varepsilon_{ij,t} \qquad (9.8)$$

Table 9.17 Econometric estimations for method of instrumental variables

		a	μ	b	R^2
CORR(1)	ln TRADE(1)	0.754**	10.003**	−10.26**	0.227
		(4.49)	(22.20)	(−9.32)	
	ln TRADE(2)	0.599**	10.32**	−11.04**	0.224
		(3.63)	(22.55)	(−9.75)	
	ln TRADE(3)	0.684**	10.262**	−10.74**	0.226
		(4.19)	(22.61)	(−10.10)	
	ln TRADE(4)	0.596**	10.20**	−12.03**	0.225
		(3.879)	(22.52)	(−14.57)	
	ln TRADE(5)	0.65**	10.21**	−10.80**	0.225
		(3.92)	(22.54)	(−9.68)	
	ln TRADE(6)	0.25*	10.46**	−17.09**	0.220
		(1.96)	(20.96)	(−15.27)	
CORR(2)	ln TRADE(1)	0.044	0.093	−0.885**	
		(1.65)	(1.27)	(−5.016)	
	ln TRADE(2)	0.038	0.114	−0.909**	
		(1.467)	(1.54)	(−5.012)	
	ln TRADE(3)	0.043	0.109	−0.898**	
		(1.642)	(1.487)	(−5.272)	
	ln TRADE(4)	0.038	0.106	−0.975**	
		(1.56)	(1.451)	(−7.381)	
	ln TRADE(5)	0.0406	0.107	−0.904**	
		(1.525)	(1.453)	(−5.060)	
	ln TRADE(6)	0.027	0.142	−1.39**	
		(1.29)	(1.752)	(−7.56)	
CORR(3)	ln TRADE(1)	−0.001	0.839**	−1.39**	
		(−0.07)	(11.42)	(−8.22)	
	ln TRADE(2)	−0.012	0.833**	−1.47**	
		(−0.51)	(11.236)	(−8.36)	
	ln TRADE(3)	−0.008	0.836**	−1.44**	
		(−0.36)	(11.339)	(−8.87)	
	ln TRADE(4)	−0.004	0.838**	−1.407**	
		(−0.182)	(11.378)	(−10.79)	
	ln TRADE(5)	−0.008	0.837**	−1.441**	
		(−0.33)	(11.36)	(−8.314)	
	ln TRADE(6)	−0.011	0.821**	−1.29**	
		(−0.575)	(10.29)	(−7.37)	
CORR(4)	ln TRADE(1)	0.11	1.82**	−4.97**	0.0600
		(1.77)	(10.40)	(−11.59)	
	ln TRADE(2)	0.13**	1.89**	−4.80**	0.0607
		(2.12)	(10.65)	(−10.91)	

Table 9.17 (continued)

		a	μ	*b*	R^2
	ln TRADE(3)	0.13**	1.87**	−4.85**	0.0608
		(2.15)	(10.62)	(−11.72)	
	ln TRADE(4)	0.11	1.86**	−5.12**	0.0604
		(1.95)	(10.57)	(−15.93)	
	ln TRADE(5)	0.12*	1.86**	−4.88**	0.0604
		(1.97)	(10.58)	(−11.24)	
	ln TRADE(6)	0.13**	2.05**	−6.80**	0.062
		(2.63)	(10.59)	(−15.66)	
CORR(5)	ln TRADE(1)	0.79**	9.56**	−7.21**	0.208
		(4.79)	(21.53)	(−6.65)	
	ln TRADE(2)	0.61**	9.88**	−8.14**	0.204
		(3.78)	(21.90)	(−7.29)	
	ln TRADE(3)	0.70**	9.82**	−7.79**	0.206
		(4.41)	(21.97)	(−7.44)	
	ln TRADE(4)	0.62**	9.77**	−9.10**	0.205
		(4.12)	(21.88)	(−11.19)	
	ln TRADE(5)	0.67**	9.78**	−7.85**	0.205
		(4.12)	(21.89)	(7.14)	
	ln TRADE(6)	0.26*	10.04**	−14.40**	0.200
		(2.10)	(20.39)	(−13.10)	

Notes:
t-student in parenthesis.
* significant at 5% level.
** significant at 1% level.

CONCLUSION

The appearance of a monetary project in the CARICOM countries' agenda shows their willingness to carry on the integration process started in the early 1970s. The adoption of a single currency would be political proof that CARICOM wants to improve cooperation between member states. Unfortunately on the basis of the economic criteria the attempt is almost groundless. Individually taken, the economies are more competitive than complementary. Trade potential among them seems to be already exploited.

Moreover some of these economies have currencies linked to the US dollar in a stable way. For these countries, giving up their monetary power could be done only by favouring a unity stronger than the current one or a unity in which exchange rate towards the dollar is fixed. Considering these evolutions and economic specializations, the needs in terms of conjectural policy are sensibly different and are hardly affected by the trade volume between these countries. It seems delicate at the moment to disagree with opponents to monetary union. Nevertheless such an attempt can finally provide the members states with the currently lacking collective public good. Managing this monetary unity could be the catalyst for integration policy and the cradle of a new public common good.

Monetary unification is a strong political act whereby economic benefits can be important only if the unification is accompanied by measures aiming at increasing the industrial integration and the economic cooperation between member states.

NOTES

1. CARICOM (CARIbbean COMmunity and Common Market) was created on 1 August 1973 according the Chaguaramas treaty signed one month earlier. First member states are Barbados, Guyana, Jamaica and Trinidad and Tobago. OECS countries and Belize joined the community on 1 May 1974. The Bahamas became the thirtieth member state on 4 July 1974, followed by Surinam on 4 July 1995 and Haiti in 1997. OECS (Organization of Eastern Caribbean States) was created in 1983. There are seven member states: Antigua, Dominica, Grenada, Montserrat, St Kitts–Navis–Anguilla, Sainte Lucia and Saint Vincent. These countries share a common currency, the East Caribbean dollar (EC$).
2. Article 43 of the annex of the Chaguaramas treaty: 'the member states, acknowledging that the fixedness of exchange rates among themselves is compulsory for the good working of the common market, agree . . . to examine the ways in order to harmonize their policies in terms of currencies, exchange rates and payments towards the good working of the common market . . . They agree to have all the necessary measures taken by their central bankers or their monetary authorities and to have the notes and coins of each of them exchanged on the other's territory at the official parity without commission, to elaborate the co-operation agreements for other monetary issues such as the implementation of a clearing agreement between the central monetary authorities.'
3. Speaking about the Balkanization of the Caribbean area at the end of the 1960s, Lewis suggested the hugeness of the task (Lewis, 1968).
4. OECS countries are described in note 1.
5. Article 38 of the Chaguaramas treaty argue: 'No arrangements of the present treaty will be interpreted as forcing a member state to give the right to free movement of people on his territory even if they are citizens of other member states.' As a matter of fact, a citizen of the European Union had easier access to a CARICOM country than a CARICOM citizen.
6. The opening degree of CARICOM countries are superior to 90 per cent except Haiti and Saint Lucia.
7. The data about the Bahamas do not appear in Table 9.7. One hundred and thirty-two bilateral import or export relations can be established in 1980, 1985 and 1990. This number increased to 156 since Surinam became a member state in 1995.
8. The non-alcoholic drinks are among the ten first export posts for seven CARICOM countries, sugar is among the first three exports for five of the 15 CARICOM countries.
9. In Europe, to enter the monetary union, national inflation was not to exceed 1.5 per cent the average of the three most virtuous countries.

10. This method is also presented in Frankel (1999) and Rose (1999).
11. 2244 available data of bilateral trade for 12 CARICOM countries between 1980 and 1996 are used.
12. Antigua and Barbuda, Dominica, Grenada, Montserrat, Saint Lucia, Saint Kitts and Nevis and Saint Vincent.
13. The OECS countries to which Barbados and Belize are added.
14. For a survey and some developments concerning the gravity model, see Fontagné et al. (2000).
15. Several types of difficulties can emerge, the goods cannot follow a direct trajectory, natural hindrances can lead to consequent detours.
16. In fact, Jamaica is the third one, Trinidad and Tobago are fifth and the Bahamas are eighth.
17. Classified in an increasing order of their export rate per inhabitant, these countries are fourth, ninth and twelfth. Classified in an increasing order of their import rate per inhabitant, these countries are seventh, tenth and twelfth.
18. Except for Haiti which is an atypical case, Jamaica is second, Trinidad and Tobago are fifth considering their export and import rate per capita.
19. Distances will be calculated apart from the positions in latitude and longitude of the capitals of CARICOM countries. To calculate distances in kilometres, one must know that 1° in latitude on the same meridian or 1° in longitude on the same parallel equals 40.000 km/360°, around 111 km.

REFERENCES

Boxill, Ian (1993), *Ideology and Caribbean Integration*, Consortium Graduate School of Social Sciences, Mona Campus, Jamaica.

Célimène, Fred and Patrick Watson (1991), *Economie Politique Caribéenne*, Paris: Economica.

Eichengreen, Barry (1990), 'Is Europe an optimum currency area?', *CEPR Discussion Paper*, 478.

European Commission Report (1990), 'One market, one money', *European Economy*, **44**, October.

De Grauwe, Paul (1999), *Economie de l'intégration monétaire*, third edn, De Boeck Université.

Fontagné, Lionel, Michael Pajot and Jean-Michel Pasteels (1997), 'Potentiels de commerce entre économies hétérogènes: un petit mode d'emploi des modèles de gravité', *CEPII Working Papers*, unpublished.

Frankel, Jeffrey and Andrew Rose (1998), 'The endogeneity of the optimum currency area criterion', *Economic Journal*, **108** (449), July, 1009–25.

Frankel, Jeffrey and Andrew Rose (1996), 'Economic structure and the decision to adopt a common currency', unpublished.

Frankel, Jeffrey (1999), 'No single currency regime is right for all countries or at all times', *NBER Working Paper*, 7338, September.

Freckleton, Marie and Stanley Lalta (1993), *Caribbean Economic Development: The First Generation*, Kingston: Ian Randle Publishers.

Jainarain, Iserdeo (1976), *Trade and Underdevelopment*, Institute of Development Studies, Guyana.

Kenen, Peter (1969), 'The theory of optimum currency areas: an ecclectic point of view', in R. Mundell and A.K. Swoboda (eds), *Monetary Problems of the International Economy*, Chicago, IL, University of Chicago Press, pp. 41–60.

Krugman, Paul (1993), 'Lessons of Massachusetts for EMU', in F. Giavazzi and F. Torres (eds), *The Transition to Economic and Monetary Union in Europe*, Cambridge: Cambridge University Press, pp. 241–61.
Lewis, Arthur (1968), *The Growth of the Modern West Indies*, London: MacGibbon and Kee.
MacKinnon, R. (1963), 'Optimum currency areas', *American Economic Review*, **53**, 717–25.
Mundell, Robert (1961), 'A theory of optimum currency areas', *American Economic Review*, **51**, 657–64.
Pisany-Ferry, Jean (1994), 'Union monétaire et convergence: qu'avons-nous appris?', *CEPII Working Paper*, 94–14.
Rose, Andrew (1999), 'One money, one market: estimating the effect of common currencies on trade', *NBER Working Paper*, 7432, December.
Rose, Andrew and Charles Engel (2000), 'Currency union and international integration', unpublished.
Semedo, Gervaisio (1998), 'Nouveau regard sur la théorie des zones monétaires optimales', in Gervaisio Semedo and Patrick Villieu, *Mondialistation, intégration économique et croissance: nouvelles approches*, Paris: L'Harmattan, pp. 199–249.
Thoumi, Francisco (1992), 'Trade flows and economic integration among the LDC's of the Caribbean Basin', in Irma Tirado de Alonso, *Trade Issues in the Caribbean*, Miami: Gordon and Breach.

PART III

Regional currency areas and economic policy

10. Exchange rate regimes in the route to EMU

Michel Aglietta, Camille Baulant and Sandra Moatti

INTRODUCTION: DILEMMAS IN THE ROUTE TO EMU

Monetary integration into the euro zone of central European countries, candidates for EC membership, will not be a smooth process. Between 1998 and 2001, most of these countries have moved to more flexible exchange rate regimes. They have done so for good reasons. This chapter shows that preparing for EMU will be a tortuous and lengthy process. A precipitous move to the ERM-2 arrangement would be a cardinal error, which could undermine real convergence.

To shed light on this matter the chapter is organized as follows. The first part depicts the changes made by the main Central European countries in their respective monetary policy after the excesses of high inflation had been tamed. It epitomizes how these changes were made as a reaction to tensions triggered by the opening of the capital account and how a degree of flexibility in the exchange rate was combined with domestic monetary management.

The second part studies the combination of different exchange rate regimes and monetary policy in a simple macroeconomic model. It shows that their interplay depends on imperfections in the domestic financial system of these countries. Because of the destabilizing effect of capital flows, a managed float cum monetary policy dedicated to stabilizing the foreign currency debt looks capable of compromising better between external and domestic imbalances. The third part deals with the possible trade-off between nominal and real convergence in the route to EMU. Special features in the structural adjustment of transition countries are still at work. They plead for keeping exchange rate flexibility in these countries, which introduced it in the wake of strong speculative pressures, instead of jumping into ERM-2 as soon as they become EC members. A conclusion advocates a change in the procedure of admission regarding the criterion of exchange rate stability. Better to ascertain it *ex post* than to go to a probation period with an arrangement ill-suited to the convergence process under full capital mobility.

SHIFTING TO A WIDE VARIETY OF EXCHANGE RATE REGIMES

In the first decade of economic transition, monetary policies in Central European countries relied on fixed exchange rates for building monetary stability and credibility. Commitment to stable exchange rates helped these countries lower inflation to single-digit levels. But as the transition progressed, currency pegs were plagued by real appreciation of domestic currencies and subsequent foreign currency debt that generated financial instability. Pegging the exchange rate may lead market participants to underestimate the degree of foreign exchange risk and encourage excessive capital inflows. In countries where bank supervision is weak, such inflows can fuel a domestic lending boom, leading to the accumulation of bad loans, which may cause financial fragility and increase the susceptibility to a financial crisis.

Inflation stayed put or rebounded. In response, governments of Central European countries decided to depart from exchange rate targeting and look for a more credible nominal anchor for monetary policy. Their exit strategies were made possible by the ongoing institutional development of financial markets and banking systems that enabled the application of indirect instruments of monetary policy. Consequently, central banks in transition economies of Central Europe were searching for appropriate autonomous monetary policies that could underpin their commitment to pursuing price stability. But the range of such policies was rather limited.

Financial market developments undermined money supply control because money demand became very unstable in the late 1990s. Interest rate targeting would have been erroneous as well, because small open transition economies are subject to sizeable changes in capital inflows that induce large, temporary shocks to interest rates. Lately, the most advanced transition countries opted for inflation targeting, that is monetary policies that use a numerical target for inflation, publicly announced, as a nominal anchor and that commit to price stability as their overriding goal.

The Czech Republic was the first to make this choice, in 1998, after the 1997 crisis and the subsequent demise of the currency peg had created the need for a new nominal anchor. In December 1998, the bank announced a policy of inflation targeting. Poland followed in 1999. The shift was more recent in Hungary, which adopted inflation targeting in summer 2001, just after having widened the fluctuation band of the forint from 2.25 per cent to 15 per cent in May and before having abolished the crawling peg in October.

Despite the increasingly widespread adoption of inflation targeting as a framework for monetary policy in the more advanced transition countries, its apparent uniformity tends to hide significant differences in the management of inflation objectives and in the exchange rate. Table 10.1 summarizes these differences. It shows that only Poland has adopted a strict inflation-targeting regime cum pure floating. The other countries implement a flexible inflation targeting coupled with an intermediary exchange rate regime.

Table 10.1 Inflation-targeting regimes: the Czech Republic, Poland and Hungary

	Czech Republic	Poland	Hungary
Type of inflation-targeting regime	Headline CPI inflation targeting (with net inflation as a supporting target); relatively strict prior to 2001	CPI inflation-targeting, strict	CPI and core inflation targeting, flexible with some attention to exchange rate stability
Corresponding exchange rate regime	Managed float	Float	Fixed peg to the euro with ±15% fluctuation bands
Policy inception date	January 1998	January 1999	June 2001
Long-term inflation target	2.0% net inflation with ±1% tolerance band for the end of 2005, prior to EMU accession	CPI inflation of 4.0% for the end of 2003	CPI inflation of 2.0% reached by March 2004, prior to EMU accession
Recent operating targets: a. December 2001 b. December 2002	a. 2–4% net and 4.3–5.8% CPI inflation b. dynamic range descending evenly from 3.0–5.0% CPI and 2–4% net inflation to the long-term target	a. 6–8 % CPI inflation b. 4–6 % CPI inflation	a. 6–8% CPI inflation b. 3.5–5.5% CPI inflation

Source: Orlowski (2001), based on CNB, NBP and NBH data and reports.

There are several reasons why it may be appropriate to attach a greater weight to the exchange rate in transition countries. Relatively thin foreign exchange markets, pronounced shocks and large capital flows may lead to excessive exchange rate volatility, if it freely floats. The exchange rate serves as a focal point for inflation expectations where a track record of monetary stability does not exist. Sharp fluctuations in exchange rates may have an impact on the relative profitability of firms across sectors, leading to financial difficulties in some areas of the economy.

The balance sheets of firms, financial institutions and the government sector may be quite sensitive to exchange rate changes because of the importance of foreign currency borrowing. A large exchange rate change may therefore lead to bankruptcies in the corporate sector, which in turn is likely to reduce the value of bank assets. This effect may be exacerbated by the fact that central banks in some transition countries enjoy relatively limited credibility. An adverse movement in the exchange rate may therefore require a sharp increase in interest rates, which could worsen the financial conditions of firms and banks alike.

Therefore the trade-off between external and internal objectives raises two questions. To what extent has the move to a domestic monetary objective accompanied by a more flexible exchange rate entailed a transfer of volatility from the interest rate to the exchange rate? To what extent has it improved the conduct of monetary policy in achieving a reduction of both interest rate and exchange rate volatility? Table 10.2 provides interesting insights.

The Czech and Slovak republics exhibit a successful transition from an external monetary anchor to an internal one. Since the beginning of 1999, both exchange rate and interest rate volatility have declined substantially. The reduction has occurred without the central bank announcing a reference rate or even implicitly defending one. This achievement should be seen in the context of balance of payments financing. Since the 1997–98 financial turmoil external deficit has been reduced and the origin of financing has shifted from bank credit to direct investment. Such a stable financing has strengthened the balance of payments and allowed monetary policy to become independent of external objectives. Yet since the fall of 2001 their exchange rates have moved in opposite directions: a depreciation for the Slovak and an alarmingly sharp appreciation for the Czech.

The success of Poland is less clear-cut. Looking strictly at the attainment of its inflation objectives, the Bank of Poland largely overshot its target in 1999 and in 2000 before undershooting it in 2001. Such forced disinflation resulted in a strong rise in short-term interest rates – nearly 7 points between the last quarter of 1999 and the end of 2000. This sharp rise has had a disastrous effect on growth and caused a very strong exchange rate appreciation in both nominal and real terms. While the volatility of the zloty has increased markedly since the nominal exchange rate anchor was abandoned, the free currency float and the redirection of monetary policy towards a purely internal goal has not resulted in a noticeable drop in interest rate volatility. Furthermore the rise of the zloty in the first half of 2001 provoked the unholy combination of current account deficit and short-term capital inflows.

Here again this unclear outcome must be seen in the light of the balance of payments. The appreciation of the zloty contributed to deepening the current account deficit, to a point where it was no longer covered by direct investment. Portfolio investment has thus made up a large part of balance-of-payment financing. As a result the movement of the zloty is subject to speculative capital flows. They cause a vicious cycle of currency appreciation/current account deficit/volatile capital inflows, which are potentially devastating.

Hungary has set an inflation targeting regime while keeping an explicit exchange rate objective. Not only is the forint officially tied to the euro by a fixed rate with a 15 per cent fluctuation band, but also within this wide band the Bank of Hungary has pinpointed a tighter band which identifies the rate compatible with its medium-term inflation target. The priority to domestic monetary policy has given rise to a volatility transfer. The falling interest rate volatility is traded against mounting exchange rate volatility around the reference rate. The central bank tries to make compatible its diminishing inflation target and a medium-term exchange rate objective, without fretting over the short-term fluctuations of the currency.

EXCHANGE RATE REGIMES AND CAPITAL MOBILITY

One important objective of monetary policy in transition countries is to counter excessive capital movements. In the first section of the chapter a move toward more flexible exchange rates was detected in the largest CEEC. But the performance of monetary policy dedicated to inflation targeting was contrasted between those countries as far as nominal variables are concerned. The reason for the difference was the pattern of capital flows. Therefore it is insightful to discuss more formally the role of foreign borrowing in the existence and stability of macroeconomic equilibrium.

In the short run markets are imperfect. Exchange rate regimes depend on how many prices are rigid in goods and labour markets, on risk aversion and control in capital markets. In this section four types of monetary policy combined with fitting exchange rate regimes are compared: stabilizing

Table 10.2 Exchange and interest rates volatility under successive exchange rate regimes in the main accession countries

Poland	ZLOTY		Interest rate		Reserves	
	var 1%*	var 2.5%*	var 0.25*	var 0.5*	var 2.5%*	var 5%*
from 27/08/93 to 16/05/95 (crawling peg narrow bands)	94.4%	4.4%	68.9%	53.3%	60.0%	55.0%
from 16/05/95 to 25/02/98 (crawling peg, 7% bands)	54.5%	7.0%	62.9%	35.7%	54.5%	30.3%
from 25/02/98 to 12/04/00: crawling peg bands from 10 to 15%	49.1%	14.5%	68.2%	51.8%	36.0%	20.0%
from 12/04/00 on: floating	78.4%	38.7%	58.6%	39.8%	34.8%	4.3%
all periods	66.5%	16.0%	63.9%	43.1%	45.3%	25.5%

Hungary	FORINT		Interest rate		Reserves	
	var 1%	var 2.5%	var 0.25	var 0.5	var 2.5%	var 5%
up to 13/03/95: peg to a basket with frequent devaluations	46.4%	21.8%			52.0%	88.0%
from 13/03/95 to 01/01/2000: crawling peg to a basket, narrow bands	52.4%	5.6%	61.6%	35.2%	66.7%	40.4%
from 01/01/2000 to 03/05/2001: crawling peg to the euro	1.5%	0.0%	70.6%	32.4%	86.7%	20.0%
from 03/05/2001: (crawling) peg large bands (15%)	63.2%	24.6%	45.6%	22.8%	75.0%	16.7%
all periods	44.8%	10.7%	65.2%	35.3%	71.0%	34.6%

Czech Republic	Czech koruna		Interest rate		Reserves	
	var 1%	var 2.5%	var 0.25	var 0.5	var 2.5%	var 5%
up to February 96: peg with narrow bands	0.0%	0.0%	57.8%	44.8%	87.0%	69.6%
from February 96 to 27/05/97: peg with 7.5% bands	45.5%	7.6%	27.3%	9.1%	59.3%	33.3%
from 27/05/97: managed float	54.2%	16.3%	40.0%	24.2%	41.2%	15.7%
(from 02/04/99)	44.8%	5.5%	17.6%	1.2%	29.7%	13.5%
all periods	38.5%	10.7%	46.3%	30.3%	52.3%	29.9%
Slovak Republic	**Slovak koruna**		**Interest rate**		**Reserves**	
	var 1%	var 2.5%	var 0.25	var 0.5	var 2.5%	var 5%
up to 16/07/1996: peg narrow bands (1.5 to 3%)	2.2%	2.2%	73.8%	56.3%	82.5%	67.5%
from July 96 to 01/10/98: peg with widened bands (5 and 7%)	26.1%	0.0%	87.0%	79.1%	51.4%	24.3%
from 01/10/98: managed float	47.6%	9.5%	46.4%	36.3%	62.5%	29.2%
(from 01/01/2000)	40.5%	7.9%	22.2%	11.9%	60.0%	30.0%
all periods	25.8%	5.1%	62.8%	51.6%	64.0%	40.0%
Germany	**DEM**		**FIBOR 3M**		**Reserves**	
	var 1%	var 2.5%	var 0.25	var 0.5	var 2.5%	var 5%
from January 1993	71.7%	35.0%	14.1%	2.9%	28.0%	9.3%

Note: * Volatility is measured as the probability that monthly variation of the data (exchange rate against reference currency or basket, interest rate, foreign exchange reserves) do not outpass a certain percentage change. For example, var 1% for the exchange rate represents the ratio. Number of monthly variations superior to 1%/number of observations.

domestic prices with flexible exchange rates, stabilizing nominal exchange rates, stabilizing the foreign currency value of external debt, stabilizing real exchange rates.

Structure of the Model

In the model all variables are in logs except interest rates and all equations are log-linear. Dynamics apply to the short run. Therefore production capacities are given.

Equation (10.1) is the accounting of the balance of payments. The net increase in foreign debt expressed in domestic currency is equal to the debt service and to the primary surplus or deficit in the current account. The interest rate paid on foreign debt (f) is the sum of the international interest rate (i^*) and the country risk premium (ρ).

$$\hat{f} = i^* + \rho + f - x \tag{10.1}$$

Equation (10.2) portrays net exports as a function of price competitiveness ($e-p$) and an exogenous parameter standing for non-price competitiveness (z). In transition countries this parameter increases with the industrial specialization in production, which is induced by trade integration.

$$x = \alpha(e - p) + z \tag{10.2}$$

Equation (10.3) is the financial arbitrage between domestic and foreign assets with imperfect capital mobility. The domestic interest rate must make foreign investors willing to hold domestic debt. It implies that this interest rate must include the international interest rate, the expected change in the exchange rate and the risk premium.

$$i = i^* + \hat{e} + \rho \tag{10.3}$$

Equation (10.4) stipulates that the risk premium is proportional to the external debt denominated in foreign currency ($f-e$). The coefficient λ is a measure of imperfection in capital markets. The less capital mobility, the higher the risk premium paid to non-residents to make them accept holding a given level of debt expressed in their own currency. At the other extreme, a zero coefficient depicts perfect capital mobility, the risk premium being zero whatever the level of foreign indebtedness.

$$\rho = \lambda(f - e) \tag{10.4}$$

Equation (10.5) describes real aggregate domestic demand (y). It is decreasing in the domestic interest rate, increasing in price competitiveness, decreasing in nominal prices to capture nominal rigidities, increasing in net government expenditure (g).

$$y = -\beta i + \gamma(e - p) - \delta p + g \tag{10.5}$$

Equation (10.6 or 10.6 bis) determines the adjustment on the goods market whether domestic prices are perfectly or imperfectly flexible. In (10.6) there is an instantaneous price adjustment so that demand is always equal to production capacities. In (10.6 bis) the speed of price adjustment is proportional to excess demand.

$$y = \bar{y} \tag{10.6}$$

Or

$$\hat{p} = \sigma(y - \bar{y}) \tag{10.6 bis}$$

Summing up the description of the model, one can find that there are seven endogenous variables for six equations. It leaves one degree of freedom to define monetary policy. The regimes, which will be compared in the model, are defined in Table (10.3).

The four regimes of exchange rate and compatible monetary policy will be studied with the same method. The stationary equilibrium will be computed first, then the dynamic path and finally the results will be compared.

Macroeconomic Equilibrium and Stability

First case: domestic price stability

$p = 0$ The dynamic is in $\hat{e}$, $\hat{f}$.

$$\hat{f} = i^* + \lambda(f - e) + f - \alpha e - z$$

$$\hat{f} = -(\alpha + \lambda)e + (1 + \lambda)f + i^* - z$$

$$\hat{e} = i - i^* - \lambda f + \lambda e$$

$$= \frac{g - \bar{y}}{\beta} + \frac{\gamma}{\beta}e - i^* - \lambda f + \lambda e$$

$$= (\frac{\gamma}{\beta} + \lambda)e - \lambda f + \frac{g - \bar{y}}{\beta} - i^*$$

Table 10.3 Choice of different exchange rate regimes for CEEC

Choice of exchange rate regime	Flexible exchange rate regime	Fixed exchange rate regime	Intermediary exchange rate regime
Monetary policy aims at:	Stabilizing domestic prices	Stabilizing nominal or real exchange rate	Stabilizing debt in foreign currency
Endogenous variables	Flexible exchange rate Endogenous debt	Variable inflation Endogenous debt	Variable inflation Managed floating
Stability conditions for debt in foreign currency	Debt ratio stable if: 1) High price elasticity 2) High capital market imperfections	Debt ratio stable if: 1) High price elasticity 2) Low capital market imperfections	Debt ratio stable if: High price elasticity
Working of the exchange rate regime	Flexible exchange rate and stability of prices can stabilize foreign debt in commercially integrated countries with an under-developed national financial system	Joining euro will be possible with the progress of financial integration	Monetary policy is used to regulate short-term capital inflow The management of foreign currency debt protects the country of the imperfection of internal finance

The system reduces to the two dynamic equations:

$$\hat{f} = -(\alpha + \lambda)e + (1 + \lambda)f + i^* - z$$

$$\hat{e} = (\frac{\gamma}{\beta} + \lambda)e - \lambda f + \frac{g - \bar{y}}{\beta} - i^*$$

The stationary equilibrium is defined by $\hat{e} = 0$ and $\hat{f} = 0$.

These equations determine the equilibrium values of the exchange rate ($\bar{e}$) and the foreign debt ($\bar{f}$):

$$\bar{e} = \frac{i^* + \lambda z + \frac{(1 + \lambda)}{\beta}(\bar{y} - g)}{(1 - \alpha + \frac{\gamma}{\beta})\lambda + \frac{\gamma}{\beta}}$$

$$\bar{f} = \frac{(\alpha - \frac{\gamma}{\beta})i^* + (\frac{\gamma}{\beta} + \lambda)z + \frac{\alpha + \lambda}{\beta}(\bar{y} - g)}{(1 - \alpha + \frac{\gamma}{\beta})\lambda + \frac{\gamma}{\beta}}$$

The foreign currency value of the debt is:

$$\bar{f} - \bar{e} = \frac{-(1 - \alpha + \frac{\gamma}{\beta})i^* + \frac{\gamma}{\beta}z - \frac{1 - \alpha}{\beta}(\bar{y} - g)}{(1 - \alpha + \frac{\gamma}{\beta})\lambda + \frac{\gamma}{\beta}}$$

It is the higher the stronger non-price competitiveness (↗function of z); the higher the foreign interest rate and the larger the domestic production available to private domestic demand ($\bar{y} - g$), as soon as α (sum of the price elasticity of exports and imports) is above $1 + \gamma/\beta$.

With the equilibrium values ($\bar{f}, \bar{e}$), the two dynamic equations are written in matrix form:

$$\begin{pmatrix} \hat{f} \\ \hat{e} \end{pmatrix} = \begin{bmatrix} 1 + \lambda & -(\alpha + \lambda) \\ -\lambda & (\frac{\gamma}{\beta} + \lambda) \end{bmatrix} \begin{pmatrix} f - \bar{f} \\ e - \bar{e} \end{pmatrix}$$

The matrix trace is above zero: $1 + 2\lambda + \gamma/\beta$

For the path of debt accumulation not to be divergent, it is sufficient that the determinant of the matrix be negative:

$$(1 + \lambda)(\frac{\gamma}{\beta} + \lambda) - \lambda(\alpha + \lambda) < 0$$

$$\text{or } \frac{\gamma}{\beta} + (1 + \frac{\gamma}{\beta})\lambda < a\lambda \text{ for } \lambda > 0$$

The conditions are satisfied if the sum of the price elasticity of foreign trade is high enough: $\alpha \rangle 1 + \gamma/\beta$ and if the degree of capital market imperfection is large enough:

$$\lambda \rangle \frac{\gamma/\beta}{\alpha - 1 - \frac{\gamma}{\beta}} \geq 0.$$

When these conditions are satisfied, the dynamic of the debt is convergent and determined as follows. The characteristic equation from the matrix of the dynamic system has a negative root $v1$, which depends on the matrix coefficients. The path of the foreign debt is thus depicted by the function of time: $f(t) - \bar{f} = (f_0 - \bar{f})\exp(v_1 t)$

The path of the exchange rate is: $e(t) - \bar{e} = A\exp(v_1 t)$

Constant A must be such that the equation of the exchange rate is satisfied while $e(t)$ and $f(t)$ respect the above functions. Let us write the equation for $t = 0$. It gives:

$$v_1 A = -\lambda(f_0 - \bar{f}) + (\frac{\gamma}{\beta} + \lambda)A$$

$$A = \frac{\lambda(f_0 - \bar{f})}{\frac{\gamma}{\beta} + \lambda - v_1}$$

The convergent path toward $(\bar{f}, \bar{e})$, is a saddle path, portrayed by the equation:

$$\frac{e - \bar{e}}{A} = \frac{f - \bar{f}}{f_0 - \bar{f}}$$

or
$$e - \bar{e} = \frac{\lambda}{\frac{\gamma}{\beta} + \lambda - v_1}(f - \bar{f})$$

One can check that the movement of the exchange rate mutes the evolution of the debt valued in foreign currency. When (e, f) is on the saddle path:

$$f - e = \frac{\frac{\gamma}{\beta} - v_1}{\frac{\gamma}{\beta} - v_1 + \lambda} f + \frac{\lambda}{\frac{\gamma}{\beta} + \lambda - v_1} \bar{f} - \bar{e}$$

The coefficient of f is less than 1.

One may conclude from the conditions of convergence in this first case that emerging market countries with an already advanced trade integration, but underdeveloped domestic financial system, benefit from capital controls and a flexible exchange rate regime coupled with a monetary policy dedicated to stabilizing domestic prices in the short run.

Second case: nominal exchange rate stability

This case is defined by $e = 0$. The dynamic is dual from the prior one in $\hat{f}, \hat{p}$.

$$\hat{f} = i^* + (1 + \lambda)f + \alpha p - z$$

$$i = i^* + \lambda f$$

$$\hat{p} = -\sigma\beta\lambda f - \sigma(\gamma+\delta)p + \sigma(g-\bar{y}) - \sigma\beta i^*$$

The stationary solution for $\hat{f} = 0$ and $\hat{p} = 0$ is:

$$\bar{p} = \frac{-(1+\lambda)(\bar{y}-g) + \beta\lambda z - \beta i^*}{(1+\lambda)(\gamma+\delta) - \beta\alpha\lambda}$$

$$\bar{f} = \frac{\alpha(\bar{y}-g) + (\gamma+\delta)z - (\gamma+\delta-\alpha\beta)i^*}{(1+\lambda)(\gamma+\delta) - \alpha\beta\lambda}$$

When the denominator is above zero, that is when:

$$\alpha \langle \frac{\gamma+\delta}{\beta} \text{ whatever } \lambda \geq 0$$

or $\alpha \rangle \dfrac{\gamma+\delta}{\beta}$ and $0 \langle \lambda \langle \dfrac{\gamma+\delta}{\alpha\beta-(\gamma+\delta)}$, which is the interesting economic configuration, meaning:

- price elasticity of foreign trade high enough
- capital market imperfection low enough

the foreign debt is an ↗function of z and $\bar{y} - g$ and a ↘ function of i^*
The matrix system becomes:

$$\begin{pmatrix} \hat{f} \\ \hat{p} \end{pmatrix} = \begin{bmatrix} 1+\lambda & \alpha \\ -\sigma\beta\lambda & -\sigma(\gamma+\delta) \end{bmatrix} \begin{pmatrix} f-\bar{f} \\ p-\bar{p} \end{pmatrix}$$

By the same method one can find the condition for a converging saddle path toward $(\bar{f}, \bar{p})$. The sign of the determinant of the matrix is negative if:

$$\alpha \rangle \frac{\gamma+\delta}{\beta} \text{ and } 0 \langle \lambda \langle \frac{\gamma+\delta}{\alpha\beta-(\gamma+\delta)}$$

The condition is similar to the first case for the goods market, but contrasts markedly for the capital market. If capital market imperfection is low, therefore if the domestic financial system is robust enough, so that the sensitivity of the risk premium to the external debt is reduced substantially, it might be to the advantage of the country to adopt a fixed exchange rate regime to stabilize the foreign debt. Applied to CEEC the formal analysis confirms the intuition that they will not be able to join the euro before their financial systems have been restructured. Any attempt to force a premature participation will be counterproductive.

However the two corner regimes, which make the substance of the first two cases, are stable under partly common and partly opposite conditions. The capital market condition shifts from one regime to another, depending on a threshold which is highly hazardous to estimate. Therefore one might wish to investigate intermediary regimes to find out if they are convergent over a larger set of values of the structural parameters. Two such regimes can be studied in the present framework. The first is the floating regime cum monetary policy stabilizing the currency value of the foreign debt. The second is a regime which aims at stabilizing the real exchange rate.

Third case: stability of the external debt in foreign currency

The foreign currency debt is: $\varphi = f - e$

The objective is: $\varphi = \bar{\varphi}$

Hence the domestic currency value of the debt varies proportionally to the exchange rate: $\hat{f} = \hat{e}$

The risk premium is constant:

$$\rho = \lambda\bar{\varphi}$$

The twin dynamic of the exchange rate and inflation $(\hat{e}, \hat{p})$ is given by the two equations:

$$\hat{e} = (1 - \alpha)e + \alpha p - z + (1 + \lambda)\bar{\varphi} + i^*$$

$$\hat{p} = -\sigma(\alpha\beta + \gamma + \delta)p + \sigma[\gamma + \beta(\alpha - 1)]e$$
$$+ \sigma(g - \bar{y}) + \sigma\beta z - \sigma\beta\bar{\varphi} - 2\sigma p(i^* + \lambda\bar{\varphi})$$

The stationary values are given by: $\hat{p} = \hat{e} = 0$

One can acknowledge that the dynamic does not depend on λ. The prudent policy toward the foreign debt prevents the divergent path which stems from a high-risk premium feeding into the cost of the debt, creating a current account deficit which increases the debt and the risk premium.

$$\begin{pmatrix} \hat{p} \\ \hat{e} \end{pmatrix} = \begin{bmatrix} -\sigma(\alpha\beta + \gamma\delta) & \alpha(\gamma + \beta(\alpha - 1)) \\ \alpha & -(\alpha - 1) \end{bmatrix} \begin{pmatrix} p - \bar{p} \\ e - \bar{e} \end{pmatrix}$$

The characteristic equation drawn from the matrix shows that the roots are real.

The sum of the roots is negative. The determinant of the matrix is:

$$\sigma(\alpha - 1)(\alpha\beta + \gamma + \delta) - \alpha\sigma(\gamma + \beta(\alpha - 1)) = \sigma[(\alpha - 1)\delta - \gamma]$$

The system is always stable. When the sum of the price elasticity is low: $\alpha \langle 1 + \gamma/\delta$, the convergence is a saddle point. When it is high: $\alpha \rangle 1 + \gamma/\delta$, the convergence is global, whatever the trajectory.

The regime which restrains the foreign debt requires a stance of monetary policy in the short run to smooth out capital inflows. It is more robust than the corner regimes if financial safety is to be enhanced. While being formally flexible, the exchange rate is managed as a means to aim at the sustainability of the foreign debt.

Fourth case: real exchange rate stability
It is defined by $e - p = 0$, hence $\hat{e} = \hat{p}$
It ensues: $x = z$

$$\hat{f} = i^* + \lambda(f - e) + f - z = (1 + \lambda)f - \lambda p + i^* - z$$
$$i = i^* + \hat{p} + \lambda(f - p)$$
$$y = -\beta\hat{p} - \beta\lambda(f - p) - \delta p + g - \beta i^*$$
$$\hat{p} = -\beta\sigma\hat{p} - \beta\lambda\sigma(f - p) - \delta\sigma p + \sigma(g - \beta i^*) - \sigma\bar{y}$$
$$\hat{p} = \frac{\sigma}{1 + \beta\sigma}[-\beta\lambda f + (\beta\lambda - \delta)p - (\bar{y} - g) - \beta i^*]$$

The stationary equilibrium $(\bar{f}, \bar{p})$ is given by $\hat{f} = \hat{p} = 0$
The dynamic system is:

$$\begin{pmatrix} \hat{f} \\ \hat{p} \end{pmatrix} = \begin{bmatrix} 1 + \lambda & -\lambda \\ \dfrac{-\beta\lambda\sigma}{1 + \beta\sigma} & \dfrac{\sigma(\beta\lambda - \delta)}{1 + \beta\sigma} \end{bmatrix} \begin{pmatrix} f - \bar{f} \\ p - \bar{p} \end{pmatrix}$$

The sum of the roots is positive:

$$1 + \lambda + \frac{\sigma(\beta\lambda - \delta)}{1 + \beta\sigma} = \frac{1 + \lambda + \beta\sigma + 2\beta\sigma\lambda - \delta}{1 + \beta\sigma} \rangle 0, \forall \lambda \geq 0$$

The determinant is:

$$\frac{\sigma(1 + \lambda)(\beta\lambda - \delta)}{1 + \beta\sigma} - \frac{\beta\sigma\lambda^2}{1 + \beta\sigma} = \frac{\beta\lambda - (1 + \lambda)\delta}{1 + \beta\sigma}$$
$$\langle 0 \text{ if } (\beta - \delta)\lambda - \delta \langle 0$$
$$0 \langle \lambda \langle \frac{\delta}{\beta - \delta}$$

There is a saddle-point equilibrium. This regime is akin to nominal exchange rate stability. Nonetheless the condition on λ is less strict.

From this formal investigation one may draw the following conclusion. A flexible exchange rate regime cum successful monitoring of international capital flows appears to be a robust arrangement to pursue domestic objectives. It remains to be seen if the CEEC, which have contained foreign borrowing, can match nominal and real convergence in the course to EMU.

NOMINAL AND REAL CONVERGENCE: HOW DO THE CANDIDATES STAND?

The potential conflict between nominal and real convergence is not a new issue. It already nurtured a hot debate in the early 1990s between the advocates of a political agreement to create EMU and the proponents of the optimum currency area theory who advised waiting until real conditions were ripe.

In the latter view, real convergence is what matters if the likelihood of asymmetrical shocks is to be eschewed once a country has entered a monetary union. Because the macroeconomic costs of such shock are felt not only by the country involved but also by the union as a whole, the opportunity of participation in the EMU is a matter of common concern. The decision cannot be left to the candidate country alone. Currency unification is perceived as a coronation after real convergence has been achieved. Firmly adopting this view the EC Commission and the ECB have issued strong warnings to the candidates, letting them know that their acceptance into the EC should not lead to an immediate preparation of EMU entry. As real adjustments depend on real exchange rate changes, they can be better engineered by active economic policy including nominal exchange rate changes.

The opposite view can pinpoint the historical precedent of the constitution of EMU itself. The strategy adopted was nominal convergence acted in the achievement of the Maastricht criteria, which were strictly nominal and had no counterpart in real variables. The implicit belief was that the improvement in macroeconomic management, hoped for from the policy objectives set by the respect of the nominal criteria, would lead to higher growth and lower unemployment in all countries. The reward was the advantage of much lower interest rates expected as soon as the financial markets were convinced that participation in EMU had become likely. The stability of the nominal exchange rate in a probation period of two years prior to EMU entry was one of them. Equality of treatment advocates that this procedure should be followed for the CEEC, so it says. The disciplining virtue of nominal convergence calls for an immediate entry into the countdown period to EMU, as soon as candidates are admitted to the EC. Some of the candidate countries are already mimicking the exchange rate policy which would be required in ERM2, or worse are planning even tighter exchange rate rules, completely reversing the move to more flexibility which was so beneficial in the late 1990s. Therefore the attraction of EMU can trigger perverse reactions, more feared by EC institutions than by EC governments which are sensitive to the political benefits of enlargement.

The political arguments tilt toward nominal convergence because an agreed-upon procedure is required for the admission to the EMU. Whatever their economic pertinence, nominal convergence criteria are embodied in indicators and thresholds that can be defined and measured with minimal contest while the whole political mechanism has been ratified. For the CEEC the mechanism is a 'take it or leave it' alternative, unless the council of the EC chiefs of state decides to modify it. On the contrary, real convergence does not give rise to indisputable and easily measurable indicators. Accession countries fear that talking of real convergence issues might be a pretext to postpone their EMU membership indefinitely.

As far as economic arguments are concerned, nominal convergence entails disinflation close to the EC rate, a substantial narrowing of interest rate spreads, a decline in exchange rate volatility to be compatible with ERM2, and fiscal consolidation in both the budget deficit and the public debt. Real convergence implies a narrowing of the gap in GDP per capita, an upward trend of wage and price levels to EU levels, and real exchange rates driven to their long-run equilibrium value. For transition countries the progress in real convergence stems from structural transformations such as openness to world trade, mobility of production factors and elasticity of trade flows.

In the following subsections the progress in real convergence will be assessed, the trade-offs between real and nominal convergence and the consequences for exchange rate arrangements will be highlighted, before reaching a conclusion about the proper attitude toward those countries in their quest to join the EMU.

Progress in Real Convergence

Table 10.4 compounds measures of income per capita in standard purchasing power parity, estimations of equilibrium real exchange rates, and two indicators of real exchange rate discrepancies relative to the equilibrium exchange rate and to PPP.

GDP per capita exhibits huge differences between CEEC, ranging from 32 per cent of the EU level in Latvia to 70 per cent in Slovenia. This measure alone points out how far most of them are from real convergence. Even

Table 10.4 Real exchange rates and GDP per capita in CEEC relative to EU levels for year 2001 (in PPP)

	GDP/capita in PPP (1)	RER in level relative to EU (2)	Equilibrium RER (3)	Balassa over-valuation or under-valuation (2)–(3)/(3)
European Union	100	100	69	46
Spain	83	84	65	29
Greece	71	71	62	21
Portugal	73	75	62	15
Poland	39	56	51	10
Slovenia	70	64	61	4
Latvia	32	48	48	0
Estonia	42	45	52	−14
Lithuania	37	43	50	−15
Hungary	52	47	56	−16
Romania	25	35	45	−22
Czech Republic	59	44	58	−25
Slovak Republic	49	36	55	−34
Bulgaria	31	26	48	−45

Notes:
(1) The level of the real exchange rate for 2001 is calculated by dividing the nominal exchange rate against the dollar by the PPP rate for GDP against the dollar. Then real exchange rates relative to European countries are computed. An index under 100 means an undervaluation of the currency relative to PPP.
(2) The GDP per capita in PPP rates is the GDP per capita in constant prices divided by PPP rates of the base year.
(3) Equilibrium real exchange rate (*RER**) is computed by the regression made by Coudert and Couharde (2002) for 200 countries including developing and industrial countries: *RERi**= 0.31 log[(GDP/head)*i*/(GDP/head)*eu*]+2, 8.

Sources: OECD, *Main Economic Indicators* (July 2002), Eurostat, and authors' calculations.

putting aside the Baltic countries that are very poor and very small, the largest, Poland, has an average level of income at 39 per cent of the EU.

Unsurprisingly low price levels support these low levels of income. Measured in PPP standards the undervaluation of their currency ranges from 36 per cent in Slovenia to 64 per cent in the Slovak Republic. Were the price levels to converge in EMU, the CEEC would be a long way behind. It means that their inflation rate should be consistently higher than the EU average inflation rate for a long time to come, were the nominal exchange rate pegged to the euro. To some extent this real exchange rate adjustment is arising in the EMU and bothering the ECB, since an apparent overshooting of the EMU-wide inflation target may be due to the adjustment of price levels in relatively less-developed countries. This problem for monetary policy will undoubtedly be magnified by a premature admission of the CEEC.

However a crude estimation of the equilibrium real exchange rates using a wide panel of countries gives a different picture. Relative to their level of development the accession countries differ markedly in the degree of undervaluation of their exchange rate. Poland is the only country to have in 2001 an overvaluation ranging from 10 per cent. As regards the same norm, Estonia, Lithuania and Hungary are undervalued by around 15 per cent. In marked contrast, currencies of the Czech and the Slovak republics are respectively 25 and 34 per cent undervalued. This is a second cause for future price increases due to the change in the structure of relative prices (Balassa effect).

However the long-run appreciating trend of the real exchange rate, which can be deduced from the real factors of convergence displayed here above, may be misleading for the conditions which will arise after the accession of the CEEC in EU. Since about 80 per cent of their exports is shipped to the euro zone, price competitiveness against the euro zone is more relevant for the external constraint that these countries might face were they to stabilize their exchange rate immediately after their accession.

Measured by the rise in the real exchange rate in consumer prices against euro consumer prices, the loss of competitiveness for all the countries except Slovenia has been staggering in the five years following April 1997. Poland has lost 30 per cent competitiveness, the Czech Republic 28 per cent, Hungary 24 per cent, the Slovak Republic 22 per cent. These magnitudes have provoked foreign exchange crises in Latin America and Asia. However the CEEC have upgraded their industry structures in opening to competition. The manufacturing sector has been developing, propped up by FDI, which used privatization and joint ventures. Therefore it is hardly surprising that the evolution of price competitiveness measured on producer prices in manufacturing gives a different picture.

These prices have not been collected before 1998. In the three years after the first quarter of 1998 price competitiveness on manufactured goods declined 7 per cent in the Czech Republic and 8 per cent in Poland. But it increased 6 per cent in Hungary, 2 per cent in Slovenia and 1.5 per cent in the Slovak Republic. The gap between the variation measured in consumer prices and the variation in manufacturing prices suggests a substantial Balassa effect, probably aggravated by the conversion of subsidized prices into market prices in the service sector.

The picture of real convergence is mixed. On this basis it illustrates the difficulty of finding an agreement about the opportunity to prepare for an early entry into the EMU or the acknowledgement that these countries are

Table 10.5 Degree of overevaluation of CEEC currencies in 2001 and 2002 (%)

	Misalignment ER/FEER approach in 2001 (1)	Misalignment ER/co integration approach in 2001 (2)	Misalignment/ FEER approach measured at 13/12/02 (3)	Misalignment/ PPP index from benchmark April 2000 13/12/02 (3)
Czech Republic	−2	11	23	19
Hungary	1	2	12	20
Poland	2	15	4	5
Slovenia	1	2	−5	−6

Notes:
(1) Coudert and Couharde (2002), p. 20.
(2) Egert and Lahrèche-Révil (2002), p. 18.
(3) Authors' calculations with data of OECD and CDC, *Risques émergents*, 66, January 2003.

Sources: OECD, *Main Economic Indicators*, Coudert and Couharde (2002), Egert and Lahrèche-Révil (2002), and CDC, *Risques émergents*, 66, January 2003.

still in transition and must delay their application until price adjustments have abated.

In Table 10.5 estimations of the degree of overvaluation or undervaluation of the equilibrium exchange rate performed by different researchers have been gathered to give the most thorough picture so far.

There is some consistency in the estimations of the trend in the equilibrium real exchange rate as opposed to the measure in price level. In 2001, the currencies were not much overvalued according to the FEER methodology. But in 2002, the overvaluation was much greater for the Czech Republic and Hungary. Except Slovenia, the CEEC are overvalued according to relative PPP and are still undervalued according to absolute PPP.

Real and Nominal Convergence

Table 10.6 shows how the candidate countries stand according to the Maastricht criteria except for the stability of the exchange rate. The Czech Republic and Poland appear to have inflation rates close to that of the EMU. The former has also a low level of interest rate, which seems to indicate that the financial markets judge favourably the macroeconomic equilibrium.

Table 10.6 Position of the main Central European countries to the nominal convergence criteria

Convergence criteria	Fiscal deficit*	Public debt	Inflation**
Time of observation	2001	2001	(May 2002)
Criterion	−3	60	2 + 1.5
Poland	−5.6	42.9	3.9
Hungary	−4.3	53.6	7.4
Czech Republic	−5.5	19.4	4.25

Notes:
* % Of GDP. Fiscal Data are not yet comparable among countries.
** Criterion on price stability: the 'average rate of inflation observed over a period of one year before the examination' should 'not exceed by more than 1.5 percentage points that of, at most, the three best performing Member States in terms of price stability'.

It has also a very low public debt despite its present fiscal deficit. On the contrary Poland has high interest rates despite its spectacular disinflation. This configuration reflects the concern of the financial markets about the real economy. A high level of real interest rate coupled with a sharp overvaluation of the exchange rate undermines growth, which has come to a virtual standstill. In contrast Hungary, which has kept the most satisfactory competitiveness until lately with an exchange rate regime aiming at driving the real exchange rate, still has an inflation differential of about 5 per cent with the euro zone and an interest rate which embodies a sustained inflation expectation.

The pieces of evidence reviewed here above suggest that the CEEC have entered a zone of turbulence since 2001. This is a time when macroeconomic management needs the use of interest and exchange rate changes to compromise between conflicting forces. Too much emphasis on nominal convergence will impair the vital growth differential with EU, necessary to keep a high enough investment rate and boost productivity in the manufacturing sector. With the persistence of high capital inflows but a slowdown of FDI caused by the ebbing of the privatization tide, foreign capital might become more volatile. The risk of more instability in exchange rates should not be underestimated. Keeping these foreign conditions in mind and taking into account the structural factors of higher price increases in these countries than in the euro zone, one comes to the conclusion that an inflation target is more appropriate for the time being. This target should be careful not to force too fast a disinflation, as Poland is trying to do, because the cost of further disinflation to get to the average EMU rate will be very high.

If the convergence in overall inflation rates to the EMU average is aimed at, while non-tradable prices increase substantially faster in the CEEC for structural reasons, it can only be achieved with deflation in the tradable goods sector. Sizeable output loss will result and real convergence will be impaired. Besides, forcing early fiscal convergence might be counterproductive while public sector reforms have not been completed. Public investments are badly needed in health care, education and local government, and pension reform. Moreover fiscal policy is an instrument of macroeconomic management which must not be discarded in the short run. Fiscal policy should be kept flexible, as much as monetary policy is tied to a nominal target and its transmission to the real economy is impaired by inefficient financial systems.

CONCLUSION: A CAREFUL POLICY NEEDED

The review of exchange rate developments in Central and Eastern European countries does not warrant a single route to EMU going through ERM2. A wide diversity of exchange rate regimes has been implemented responding to the pressure of foreign capital flows. Managed floating combined with a kind of flexible inflation targeting has been successful in reducing the volatility of both exchange and interest rates. This stance of policy is akin to what the UK and Sweden have chosen. Other countries have adopted currency boards. As much as they have proved able to keep this regime without too much damage for their economy, currency boards should be taken as substitutes to ERM. Yet no country should be encouraged to set a currency board, let alone euroization, as means of fulfilling nominal convergence criteria. EC authorities should accept the diversity of regimes and assess exchange rate stability *ex post* on the basis of their past performance at the time their application is examined.

Despite the political appeal of EMU for all CEEC, that time shall not come too soon. The trade-off between nominal and real convergence is strong for these countries. It requires a flexible use of all macroeconomic management tools available. Domestic prices have a long way to rise to catch up with EC levels. This structural adjustment will put an upward pressure on core inflation for some time. This effect should be discounted if their inflation rate is compared to the inflation threshold, which should be met as a condition for EMU entry. If on the contrary applicant governments are pressured to achieve rigidly the Maastricht formula, the disinflationary policy necessary to erase the remaining differential would be very costly in terms of real convergence.

Beyond the catching-up effect of price levels, an inflation rate higher than the EC rate is part of a higher growth rate compatible with an investment ratio which raises capital intensity and labour productivity. For the last few years investment has been largely financed by FDI attracted by the opportunities of privatization. With less future opportunities for non-debt capital inflows, and household saving still suffering from a lack of financial instruments, the macroeconomic investment saving balance will become more strained. If nominal stability is to be maintained, foreign indebtedness should be continuously kept in check, as shown in the model above. Therefore to keep investment riding high, more domestic saving will have to be generated internally by the corporate sector. A temporary increase in the self-financing of their investment will stem from higher margins, that is from producer prices increasing faster than costs. This requirement is temporary until productivity growth provided by investment reduces production costs and profit margins have converged to an equilibrium level.

Therefore real convergence is a growth path whose conditions of financing intertwine nominal and real variables. Either exchange rate and price stability should be assessed with insight for the acceptance of EMU participation of these countries, or participation should be postponed until the benefits of transitional growth have been reached.

BIBLIOGRAPHY

Aglietta, M., C. Baulant and V. Coudert (1999), 'Compétitivité et régime de change en Europe centrale', *Revue Economique*, **50** (6), November, 1221–36.

Aglietta, M., C. Baulant and S. Moatti (2003), 'Exchange rate management in Central Europe and the debate on exchange rate regimes', *Revue Economique*, **54** (5), September, 963–82.

Amato, J.D. and S. Gerlach (2001), 'Inflation targeting in emerging market and transition economies: Lessons after a Decade', *CEPR Discussion Paper Series*, 3074.

Balassa, B. (1964), 'The purchasing power parity doctrine: a reappraisal', *Journal of Political Economy*, December, 584–96.

Baulant, C. (2001), 'Niveaux de prix relatifs des PECO: apport des taux de PPA de l'enquête 1996', Banque de France DGO-SAMI, C 01-093, May.

Begg, D., B. Eichengreen, L. Halpern, J. Von Hagen and C. Wyplosz (2003), 'Sustainable regimes of capital movements in accession countries', CEPR, Policy Paper, 10, March.

Begg, D., L. Halpern and C. Wyplosz (1999), 'Monetary and exchange rate policies, EMU and Central Europe', *Forum Report of the Economic Policy Initiative*, 5, CEPR.

Benassy-Quere, A. and B. Coeure (2000), 'L'avenir des petites monnaies: solutions régionales contre solutions en coin', *Revue d'Economie Politique*, **110** (3), 346–76.

Bofinger, P. and T. Wollmershaeuser (2000), 'Options for the exchange rate policies of the EU accession countries', *CEPR Discussion Paper*, 2379, February.
Buch, C. and L. Lusinyan (2002), 'Short-term capital, economic transformation and EU accession', Discussion paper 02/02, Economic Centre of the Deutsche Bundesbank, January.
Coats, W. (ed.) (2000), 'Inflation targeting in transition economies: the case of the Czech Republic', IMF and Czech National Bank.
Commission of European Communities (2001), Regular Reports on Progress Towards Accession.
Coricelli, F. and B. Jazbec (2001), 'Real exchange rate dynamics in transition economies', Center for Economic Policy Research, Discussion Papers Series, 2869, July.
Corker, R., C. Beaumont, R. Van Elkan and D. Iakova (2000), 'Exchange rate regimes in selected advanced transition economies: coping with transition, capital inflows and EU accession', *IMF Policy Discussion Paper*, 00/3.
Coudert, V. (1999), 'Comment définir un taux de change d'équilibre pour les pays émergents?', *Economie Internationale*, **77**, 1st Quarter.
Coudert, V. and C. Couharde (2002), 'Exchange rate regimes and sustainable parities for CEECs in the run-up to EMU membership', Document de travail CEPII, 2002-15, December.
Coudert, V. and J.-P. Yanitch (2001), 'Les stratégies des pays d'Europe centrale et orientale candidats à l'Union Européenne', *Revue d'Economie Financière*, Hors Série.
De Broeck, M. and T. Slok (2001), 'Interpreting real exchange rate movements in transition countries', *IMF Working Paper*, 56, May, Washington, DC.
Doyle, P., L. Kuijs and G. Jiang (2001), 'Real convergence to EU income levels: Central Europe from 1990 to the long term', *IMF Working Paper* 01/146, September.
Edwards, S. (1994), 'Real and monetary determinants of real exchange rate behavior: theory and evidence from developing countries', in J. Williamson (ed.), *Estimating Equilibrium Exchange Rates*, Washington, DC: Institute for International Economics, pp. 61–92.
Eichengreen, B., P. Masson, H. Bredenkamp, B. Johnston and J. Hamann (1998), 'Exit strategies: policy options for countries seeking greater exchange flexibility', *IMF Occasional Paper*, 168, August.
Egert, B. and A. Lahreche-Revil (2002), 'Estimating the fundamental equilibrium exchange rate of Central and Eastern European Countries: the EU enlargement prospect', Colloque GDR Lyon, 4–5 June.
Frait, J. and L. Komarek (2001), 'Real exchange rate trend in transition countries', Warwick Economic Research Papers, 596, July.
Freytag, A. (2002), 'Accession to EMU and exchange rate policies in central Europe; decision under institutional constraints', Working Paper, 6, Institute for Economic Policy, University of Cologne, January.
Grafe, C. and C. Wyplosz (1997), 'The real exchange rate in transition economies', *CEPR Discussion Paper*, 1773, December.
Halpern, L. and C. Wyplosz (1996), 'Equilibrium exchange rates in transition economies', *IMF Working Paper*, 125.
Halpern, L. and C. Wyplosz (2001), 'Economic transformation and real exchange rates in the 2000s: the Balassa–Samuelson connection', *Economic Survey of Europe*, UNECE 2001/1, Chapter 6, pp. 227–39.

Kopits, G. (1999), 'Implications of EMU for exchange rate policy in Central and Eastern Europe', *IMF Working Paper*, 99/9.
Masson, P. (1999), 'Monetary and exchange rate policy of transition economies of Central and Eastern Europe after the launch of EMU', *IMF Policy Discussion Paper*, PDP/99/5.
Morales, R.A. (2001), 'Czech koruna and polish zloty: spot and currency option volatility patterns', *IMF Working Paper*, WP/01/120, August.
Nielsen, E. (2002), 'Managing Central European currencies', *Global Economic Papers*, 73, Goldman Sachs Economic Research.
Orlowski, L.T. (2001), 'Monetary convergence of the EU candidates of the euro: a theoretical framework and policy implications', ZEI Working Paper, 25, September.
Siklos, P.L. (2001), 'Is Hungary ready for inflation targeting?', National Bank of Hungary and Wilfrid Laurier University, Canada, September.
Szapary, G. (2000), 'Maastricht and the choice of exchange rate regime in transition countries during the run-up to EMU', National Bank of Hungary, Working Paper, 7, October.
Thygesen, N. (2002), 'The path to the euro for enlargement countries', Economic and Monetary Affairs Committee, European Parliament, 2nd Quarter.
WIIW (2001), 'Countries in transition, 2001', *Handbook of Statistics*, Vienna Institute for International Economic Studies.
Williamson, J. (2000), 'Exchange rate regimes for emerging markets: reviving the intermediate option', Institute for International Economics, September.
Wyplosz, C. (2002), 'The path to the euro for enlargement countries', Committee for Economic and Monetary Affairs, European Parliament, 2nd Quarter.

11. Can the free-rider behaviour of small countries offset the profligacy spending bias of large countries in the euro zone?

Patrick Artus

INTRODUCTION

Manifestly, there is significant tax competition from countries with lower per capita income or from small countries in the euro zone, particularly since the late 1990s.

The tax burden is markedly lower in some countries (we take in Figure 11.1 the examples of Spain and Portugal) than in France and Germany. Other countries (Ireland) have steadily lowered their tax burden. Divergences are notably impressive with respect to mandatory welfare contributions (Figure 11.2). They are made possible by the fact that different choices are made about public finances, the role of the state and social welfare. In the countries with a low tax burden, government expenditure is also weak (Figure 11.3). The gap with respect to total government expenditure in 2003 between France and Ireland stood at 17 per cent of GDP. Regarding spending on transfer payments (excluding government investment, Figure 11.4), it stood at 19 per cent of GDP.

This policy of cutting the tax burden therefore naturally entails the cost of reducing the amount of government expenditure that can be financed. Clearly, it allows these countries to attract business via foreign direct investment (Figure 11.5), and it is consequently higher in Spain and Portugal than in France and Germany (excluding exceptional operations), far higher in Ireland. This has allowed Spain and Ireland (but not Portugal since 2000) to post more robust growth than France and Germany (Figure 11.6a and b) as well as markedly faster growth in employment (Figure 11.7).

It is also well known that growth gaps due to the attractiveness of these countries with a low tax burden are amplified by real yield spreads. The countries with a low tax burden and more robust growth have higher inflation

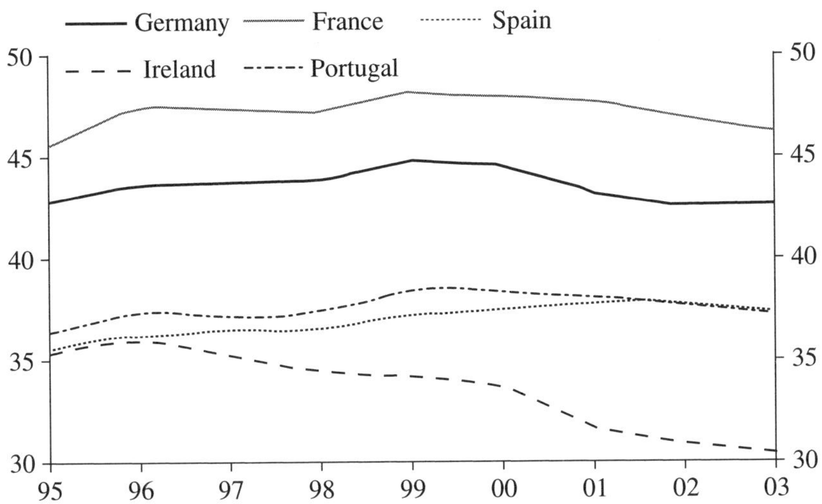

Source: OECD.

Figure 11.1 Taxation rate (as % of GDP)

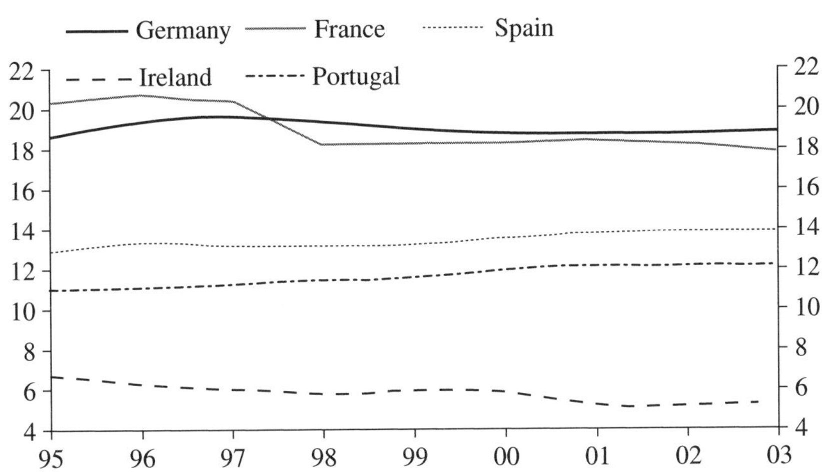

Source: OECD.

Figure 11.2 Welfare contribution rate (as % of GDP)

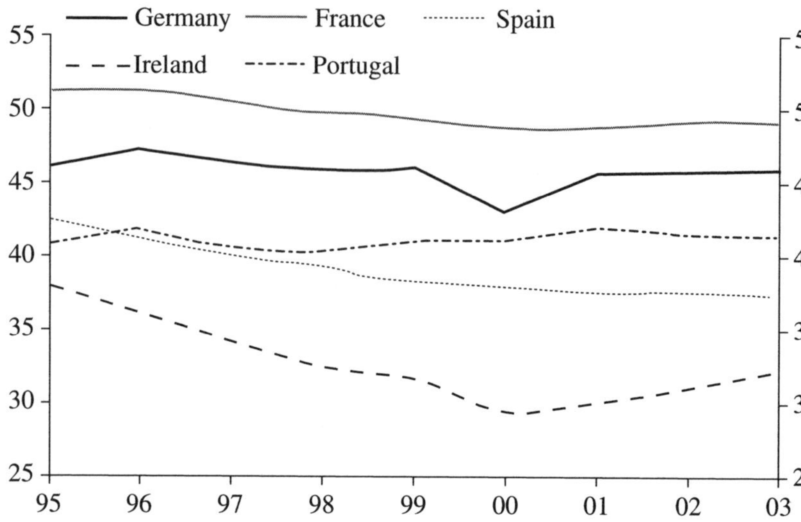

Source: OECD.

Figure 11.3 Government expenditure (as % of GDP)

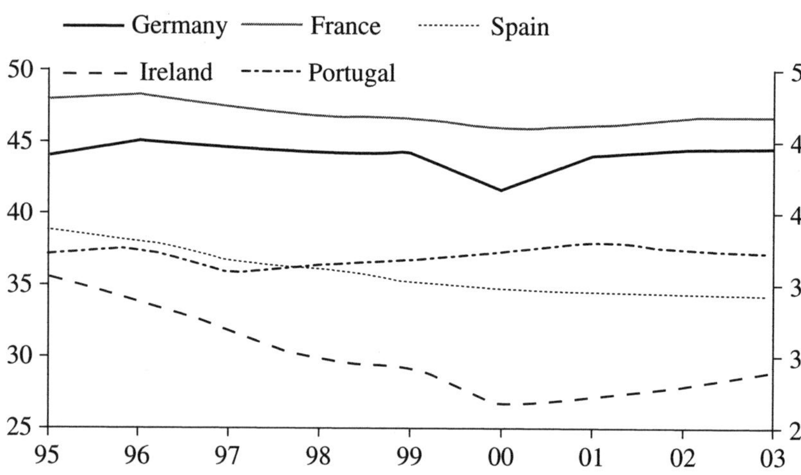

Source: OECD.

Figure 11.4 Government expenditure ex government investment (as % of GDP)

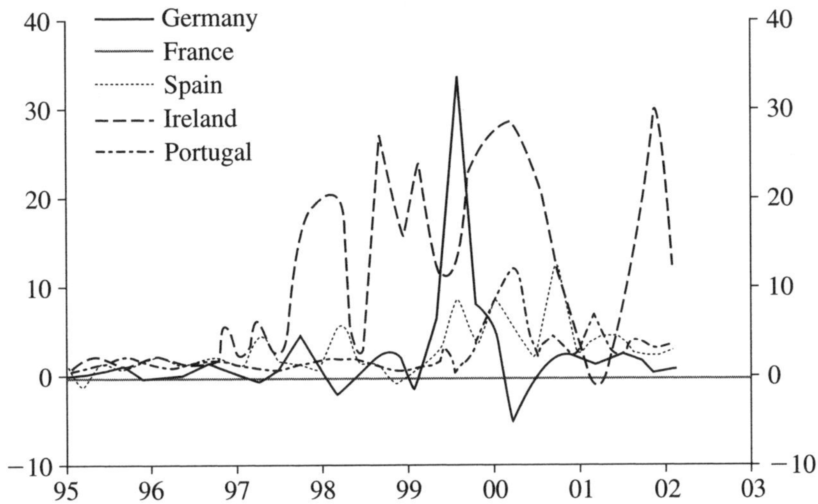

Source: Datastream.

Figure 11.5 Net direct investment inflows (as % of GDP)

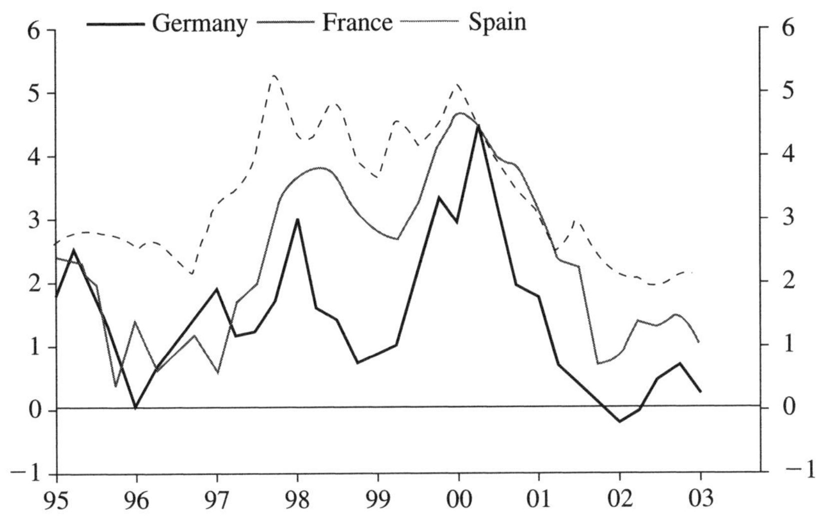

Source: Datastream.

Figure 11.6a Real GDP growth (as %)

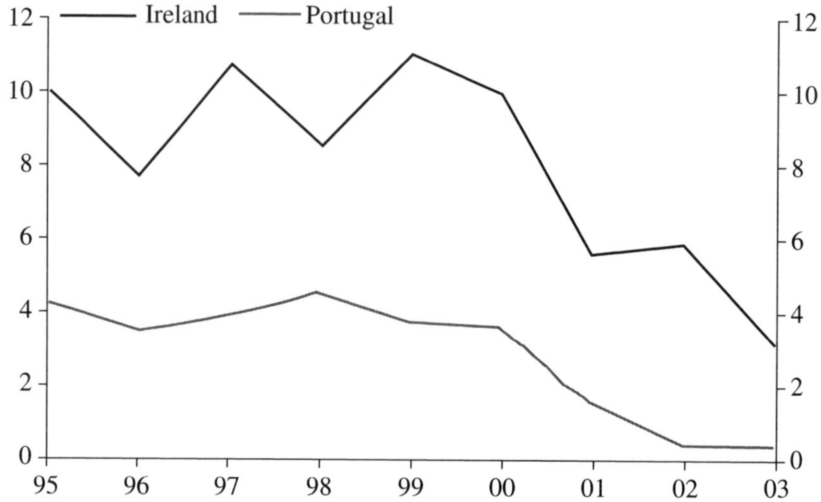

Source: OECD.

Figure 11.6b Real GDP growth (as %)

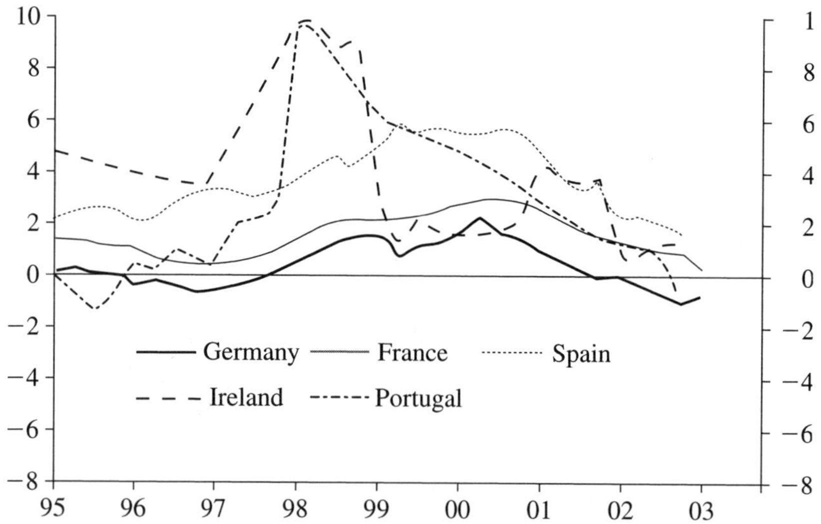

Source: Datastream.

Figure 11.7 Total employment (as %)

rates than countries with a heavy tax burden (Figure 11.8). Consequently in a currency area with single nominal interest rates, they benefit from lower real interest rates (Figure 11.9). In turn this also helps stimulate investment and growth.

We can therefore see that such a configuration describes the euro zone's situation well:

- Some countries have a smaller preference than others for government expenditure, and choose to pursue tax competition (that is reduce their tax burden to attract business); as a result they enjoy more growth and incur less government expenditure than the others.
- With euro zone inflation controlled by the ECB, these countries post higher than average inflation, and therefore benefit from low real interest rates (and even negative rates).

We can take two approaches regarding this situation:

- Say that it would be preferable to have coordination of taxation (Artus, 1997–98; Newell and Symons, 1987; Razin and Sadka, 1991; Sinn, 1990), to prevent the hijacking of business to small countries that practice tax competition. Clearly, coordination would reduce the well-being of these countries, and would increase that of large countries with a major preference for government expenditure.
- Argue that the problem stems precisely from the excessively high preference for government expenditure in certain large countries, which exceeds what is socially optimal. Tax competition would then force these countries to reduce their government expenditure, and this would be a desirable outcome (Artus, 2001; Beetsma and Bovenberg, 1998).

The purpose of this chapter is to ascertain whether effectively tax competition can be the way to prevent the spending bias of large EMU countries or if it is a serious drawback of currency areas in which the size of countries is very different.

To study this question, we have built a theoretical two-country model in which the size of the countries is unequal and they are members of a currency area in which the central bank's target is price stability.

The small country has an incentive, at non-cooperative equilibrium, to implement an aggressive taxation policy, since it generates capital transfers it benefits from and that are large relative to its production via a size effect.

The large country has a behaviour bias that leads it to favour an increase in government expenditure, and therefore in the tax burden required to finance it, at the expense of supporting employment.

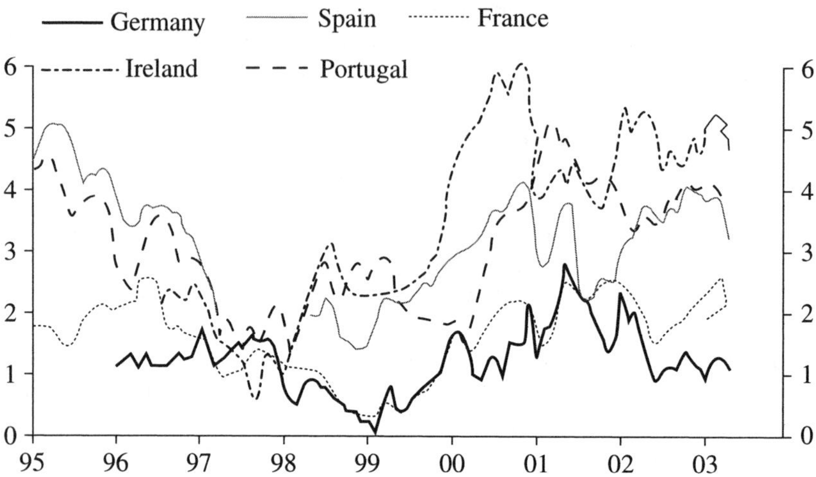

Source: Datastream.

Figure 11.8 Harmonized CPI (Y/Y as %)

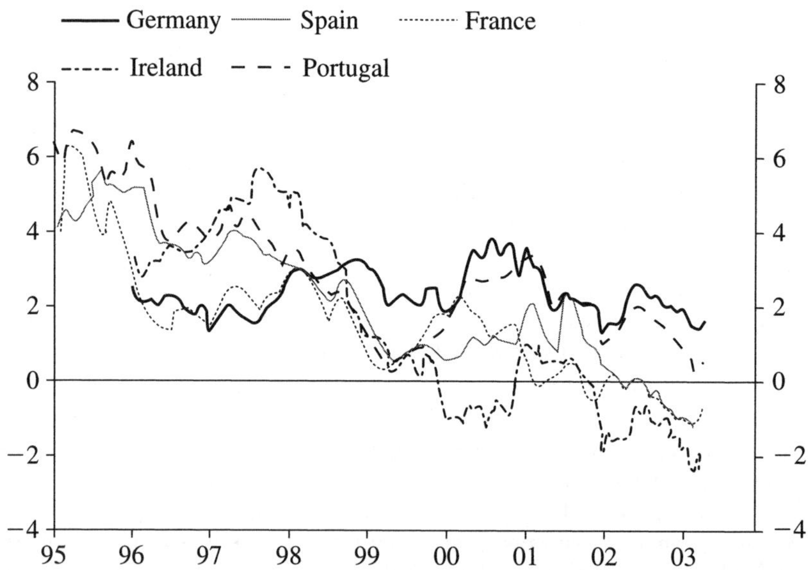

Source: Datastream.

Figure 11.9 Real 3-month interest rate

We will seek to establish in what cases tax competition reduces this behaviour bias of the large country. We will compare tax competition with two types of coordination of taxation:

- a type of coordination where the weight of each country corresponds to its size;
- symmetrical coordination where the countries are given the same weight within the currency area's collective target.

OUR MODEL

We consider a currency area with two countries, a small country (with a relative size $\delta < 1$ in relation to the large country), and a large country (we denote its variables with *).

Economic developments are described as follows. For a small country:

Production (demand):

$$y = -\alpha r + \beta z \tag{11.1}$$

y is the production logarithm, r the currency area's single interest rate, and z the logarithm of the supply of goods. If the supply of goods increases, via various mechanisms (decline in prices, appearance of new products, faster productivity gains therefore faster wage rises, and so on) demand for goods is increased. We suppose that $\beta < 1$.

Supply of goods:

$$z = -\gamma t + \lambda(t^* - t) \tag{11.2}$$

z is the logarithm of the supply of goods, t the tax burden in the small country, t^* the tax burden in the large country.

The first term ($-\gamma t$) represents the direct negative effect of the tax burden on supply (rise in pay costs, decline in profitability). The second term represents the capital relocations from the large country into the small country that occur if the tax burden is high in the large country ($t^* > t$).

Inflation:

It varies simply in line with excess demand for goods:

$$p = \theta(y - z) \tag{11.3}$$

Government expenditure:

We have:

$$G = tY$$

where G stands for the level of government expenditure, and Y the level of production, hence:

$$g = \ell n(t) + y \tag{11.4}$$

where g is the logarithm of government expenditure.

In the large country, the equations that determine the economic equilibrium are similar:

$$\begin{cases} y^* = -\alpha r + \beta z^* \\ z^* = -\gamma t^* + \delta\lambda(t - t^*) \\ p^* = \theta(y^* - z^*) \\ g^* = \ell n(t^*) + y^* \end{cases} \tag{11.5}$$

The only difference between the small country and the large country is the term of capital transfer (and therefore of supply of goods) linked to the gap between taxation rates. The coefficient of this term is multiplied $\delta < 1$, the relative size of the small country, in the equation corresponding to the large country. At an absolute level, this transfer is similar in the two countries (it is a transfer of production capacity from one country to the next); relative to the level of the supply of goods, it is therefore lower in the large country (from the factor δ that gives the relative size of the two countries).

Behaviour of the central bank:

We suppose that the central bank cancels the currency area's average inflation, that is:

$$\delta p + p^* = 0 \tag{11.6}$$

Inflation in the small country p weighs $\delta < 1$ times more than that of the large country p^*. (11.6) can be rewritten:

$$\delta y + y^* = \delta z + z^* \tag{11.6'}$$

Whether governments cooperate or not with one another to choose the tax burdens t and t^*, we suppose that the equilibrium between the central bank and the governments is a Stackelberg equilibrium with leader governments:

- The central bank takes fiscal policies as given (and the various levels of supply of goods that result from them).
- The governments know that the central bank's behaviour (equation (11.6)) consists in stabilizing inflation. In our opinion, this model best describes the way in which economic policy decisions are taken in the euro zone.

(11.6′) then leads to:

$$-\alpha r(1+\delta) = (\delta z + z^*)(1-\beta) \qquad (11.7)$$

with $1-\beta > 0$: a rise in the supply goods (weighted by the sizes of the countries) allows interest rates to fall since it reduces inflation, hence for production levels:

$$\begin{cases} y(1+\delta) = (\beta+\delta)z + z^*(1-\beta) \\ y^*(1+\delta) = (1+\beta\delta)z^* + \delta z(1-\beta) \end{cases} \qquad (11.8)$$

A rise in the supply of goods in a country increases production in the other country because of the decline in interest rates it leads to; this effect is smaller ($\delta < 1$) with regard to production y^* in the large country since the small country hardly weighs in the zone's average inflation. A rise in the supply of goods in a country y increases production directly (this implies a coefficient $\beta\,(1+\delta)$) and via the effect on the interest rate ($\delta\,(1-\beta)$ in the small country, $1-\beta$ in the large country). This effect is also larger for the large country than for the small country ($1+\beta\delta > \beta+\delta$).

Lastly, by identifying the levels of supply of goods z and z^*, we obtain:

$$\begin{cases} y(1+\delta) = -t[\gamma(\beta+\delta)+\lambda\beta(1+\delta)] + t^*[\lambda\beta(1+\delta)-\gamma(1-\beta)] \\ y^*(1+\delta) = -t^*[\gamma(1+\beta\delta)+\delta\lambda\beta(1+\delta)] + t[\lambda\beta\delta(1+\delta)-\gamma\delta(1-\beta)] \end{cases} \qquad (11.9)$$

We have:

$$\begin{aligned} \gamma(1+\beta\delta)+\delta\lambda\beta(1+\delta) &< \gamma(\beta+\delta)+\lambda\beta(1+\delta) \\ \text{si}\,\gamma(1-\beta) &< \lambda\beta(1+\delta) \end{aligned} \qquad (11.10)$$

$\gamma(1-\beta)$ represents the positive effect of a rise in the tax burden in the other country on the interest rate (hence a negative effect on production) via its direct negative effect on the gap between supply and demand for goods.

$\lambda\beta$ stands for the positive effect on the production of a country from capital transfers due to the increase in the tax burden in the other country.

If (11.11) $\lambda\beta(1+\delta) > \gamma(1-\beta)$, the effects that operate via capital transfers outweigh the effects that operate directly via the supply of goods. We suppose that (11.11) is verified.

This implies that:

- A rise in the tax burden in the other country increases production because of its effect on capital transfers; this is especially the case, via a size effect, for the small country (in (11.9), the coefficient of t in the equation that determines y^*, the production of the large country, is multiplied by $\delta < 1$ in relation to the coefficient of t^* in the equation that determines y).
- A rise in the tax burden in the small country reduces output in this country to a greater extent (in relative terms) than a rise in the tax burden in the large country, since the transfer of capital is larger, relative to production in the small country than in the larger one.

We are going to denote:

$$\begin{cases} D = [\gamma(1+\beta\delta) + \delta\lambda\beta(1+\delta)]/(1+\delta) \\ C = [\lambda\beta(1+\delta) - \gamma(1-\beta)]\,/(1+\delta) > 0 \end{cases} \tag{11.12}$$

We can then rewrite (11.9) as:

$$\begin{cases} y = -[D + (1+\delta)C]t + Ct^* \\ y^* = -Dt^* + \delta C t \end{cases} \tag{11.13}$$

and this clearly shows the stronger reaction of production in the small country both to its own tax burden and to the large country's tax burden.

Preferences of Governments

We write, for the loss functions of governments:

$$\begin{cases} L = (K-y)^2 + A(H-g)^2 & \text{(small country)} \\ L^* = (K-y^*)^2 + B(H-g^*)^2 & \text{(large country)} \end{cases} \tag{11.14}$$

K is the logarithm of full-employment production, $K-y$ the degree of under-employment; H is the logarithm of optimal government expenditure, $H-g$ the relative insufficiency of government expenditure.

A stands for the relative weight of the government expenditure target in the small country, and B in the large country.

We suppose that $B > A$: the large country has a spending bias, where A stands for the 'normal' weight of the spending target.

LACK OF COORDINATION BETWEEN GOVERNMENTS

The two governments will in this case choose their taxation rate, by taking that of the other country as given, to minimize their loss.

We can rewrite (11.14) as:

$$\begin{aligned} L &= (K + (D + (1-\delta)C)t - Ct^*)^2 \\ &\quad + A(H - \ell n(t) + (D + (1-\delta)C)t - Ct^*)^2 \\ L^* &= (K + Dt^* - \delta Ct)^2 + B(H - \ell n(t^*) + Dt^* - \delta Ct)^2 \end{aligned} \tag{11.15}$$

hence the optimality conditions.

Small country:

$$\begin{aligned} & t(1+A)(D+(1-\delta)C)^2 - Ct^*(1+A)(D+(1-\delta)C) \\ & + A\left(-\frac{1}{t}\right)(H - \ell n(t) + (D+(1-\delta)C)t - Ct^*) \\ & - A(D+(1-\delta)C)\ell n(t) + A(D+(1-\delta)C)H + K(D+(1-\delta)C) = 0 \\ & = (D+(1-\delta)C)(K-y) \\ & \qquad + A\left(-\frac{1}{t} + (D+(1-\delta)C)\right)(H-g) = 0 \end{aligned} \tag{11.16a}$$

Large country:

$$\begin{aligned} & t^*(1+B)D^2 - \delta DCt(1+B) + B\left(-\frac{1}{t^*}\right)(H - \ell n(t^*) + Dt^* - \delta Ct) \\ & \qquad - BD\ell n(t^*) + BDH + KD = 0 \\ & \qquad = D(K - y^*) + B(H - g^*)\left(-\frac{1}{t^*} + D\right) \end{aligned} \tag{11.16b}$$

This enables us to calculate the effects of our various hypotheses on the equilibrium.

Marked Preference for Government Expenditure in the Large Country

This is the hypothesis according to which $B > A$.

$$\begin{matrix} \frac{\partial g^*}{\partial t^*} > 0 \\ \frac{1}{t^*} - D > 0 \end{matrix} \quad \text{if:} \tag{11.17}$$

the rise in the taxation rate increases government expenditure in the large country if it is not merely offset by the contraction in production. We suppose that (11.17) is verified.

We then have by differentiating (11.16b):

$$dt^*\left[D^2 + B\left(\frac{1}{t^*} - D\right)^2 + \frac{B}{t^{*2}}(H - g^*)\right] = dB(H - g^*)\left(\frac{1}{t^*} - D\right)$$
$$+ dt \cdot \delta C\left[\frac{B}{t^*} - D(1 + B)\right] \tag{11.18}$$

there is a rise in t^* if B increases.

The differentiation of (11.16a) gives:

$$dt\left[(D + (1 - \delta)C)^2 + A\left(\frac{1}{t} - (D + (1 - \delta)C)\right)^2 + \frac{A}{t^2}(H - g)\right]$$
$$+ dt^* C\left[\frac{A}{t} - (D + (1 - \delta)C)(1 + A)\right] = 0 \tag{11.19}$$

A rise in t^* increases y (production of the small country), hence a fall in the cost, in this country, of increasing t; it increases g (government expenditure of the small country), hence a fall in the need, in the small country, to increase t. The sign of the total effect of t^* on $\partial L/\partial t$ (or of t on $\partial L^*/\partial t^*$) is therefore ambiguous.

(11.18) and (11.19) show that a rise in B (weight of the government expenditure target in the large country):

- increases the tax burden t^* in the large country
- has an ambiguous effect on the tax burden t of the small country.

If the small country is primarily concerned about its production y (small A), the small country's tax burden is increased (the rise in t^* increases y); if the small country is primarily concerned about its government expenditure, the small country's tax burden is reduced (the rise in t^* increases g).

Different Size of Countries

The derivative of the left-hand side member of (11.16a) in relation to δ, at point $\delta = 1$, is:

$$-C(K-y) - AC(H-g) + Ct\left(A\left(\frac{1}{t} - D\right) - D\right) \tag{11.20}$$

The derivative of the left-hand side member of (11.16b) in relation to δ is:

$$Ct\left[B\left(\frac{1}{t^*} - D\right) - D\right]$$
$$\text{with } \frac{\partial y}{\partial \delta} = \frac{\partial y^*}{\partial \delta} = Ct. \tag{11.21}$$

As we saw above, the smaller the size of the small country (δ), the more a rise in the tax burden in small country y reduces production y (in relative terms) since the transfer of capital is all the larger relative to production in the country. This explains why $\partial y/\partial\delta > 0$. The smaller the size of the small country, the less the small country's tax burden exerts influence on the large country, and this explains why $\partial y^*/\partial\delta > 0$. (if δ declines, a high value of t increases y^* to a lesser extent).

If t is sufficiently small, we can see that term (11.20) is negative, while term (11.21) is small: a smaller size for the small country (decline in δ), reduces the tax burden t in the small country, and hardly has an impact on the tax burden t^* in the large country. The smaller the country, the more the decline in the tax burden y increases production, hence this result.

The effect on the utility of the large country depends on:

$$\left[-t-\delta\frac{C(K-y)+AC(H-g)}{(D+(1+\delta)C)^2 + A\left(\frac{1}{t}-(D+(1-\delta)C)\right)^2 + \frac{A}{t^2}(H-g)}\right]d\delta \tag{11.22}$$

Since $\frac{\partial L^*}{\partial \delta} = (K - y^*)(-Ctd\delta - \delta Cdt) + B(H - g^*)(-Ctd\delta - \delta Cdt)$

and $\frac{\partial t}{\partial \delta} = \frac{C(K - y) + AC(H - g)}{(D + (1 - \delta)C)^2 + A\left(\frac{1}{t} - (D + (1 - \delta)C)\right)^2 + \frac{A}{t^2}(H - g)}$

a decline in the size δ of the small country without ambiguity reduces well-being in the large country:

- since it leads to a cut in the tax burden t of the small country
- since the decline in δ reduces the positive effect on production in the large country of the tax burden t of the small country.

COORDINATION OF TAX POLICIES

We suppose here that taxation policies (t and t^*) are chosen to minimize the loss of the currency area as a whole, that is $\delta L + L^*$, as the small country is naturally weighted by its weight δ. This leads to the following optimality conditions:

Relative to t (small country's tax burden):

$$(D + (1 - \delta)C)(K - y) + A\left(-\frac{1}{t} + (D + (1 - \delta)C)\right)(H - g) - C(K - y^*) - BC(H - g^*) = 0 \tag{11.23}$$

Relative to t^* (tax burden of the large country):

$$D(K - y^*) + B\left(-\frac{1}{t^*} + D\right)(H - g^*) - \delta C(K - y) - \delta AC(H - g) = 0 \tag{11.24}$$

At non-cooperative equilibrium t and t^* are such that:

$$\begin{cases} (D + (1 - \delta)C)(K - y) + A\left(-\frac{1}{t} + (D + (1 - \delta)C)\right)(H - g) = 0 \\ D(K - y^*) + B(H - g^*)\left(-\frac{1}{t^*} + D\right) = 0 \end{cases} \tag{11.25}$$

For the values t_0, t_0^* of the tax burdens corresponding to the non-cooperative equilibrium, we therefore have, at cooperative equilibrium:

$$\begin{cases} \dfrac{\partial(\delta L + L^*)}{\partial t}(t_0, t_0^*) = -\dfrac{1}{t_0^*}\dfrac{BC}{D}(H - g^*) < 0 \\ \dfrac{\partial(\delta L + L^*)}{\partial t^*}(t_0, t_0^*) = -\dfrac{1}{t_0}\dfrac{\delta AC(H - g)}{D + (1 - \delta)C} < 0 \end{cases} \tag{11.26}$$

The cooperative equilibrium thus corresponds to values of tax burdens t and t^* higher than the non-cooperative equilibrium, since each country, at cooperative equilibrium, takes into account the positive effect on the other country of the rise in its tax burden.

We can see that if the small country is very small ($\delta \approx 0$), coordination implies primarily a rise in the tax burden t of the small country since the overall loss ($\delta L + L^*$) hardly depends on that of the small country. Coordination therefore cancels the effects of the small size of this country, since we have seen above that the smaller the small country, the more it reduces its tax burden without that of the large country being significantly affected.

Without ambiguity therefore, coordination increases the welfare of the large country and reduces the welfare of the small country.

CAN THE LACK OF COORDINATION OFFSET THE LARGE COUNTRY'S EXCESSIVE TASTE FOR GOVERNMENT EXPENDITURE?

Let us continue to examine the case of a really small country (δ small). We have seen above that in this case:

- At non-cooperative equilibrium, the tax burden in the small country is low, the tax burden t^* of the large country is hardly affected by the small size of the small country.
- The coordination of taxation in the case where each country has a weight corresponding to its size results in driving the tax burden t of the small country upwards, without any major impact on the tax burden in the large country.
- The fact that the large country has an 'excessive' preference for government expenditure increases the large country's tax burden, and has an ambiguous effect on the small country's tax burden.

The lack of coordination of taxation policies reduces the small country's tax burden, and this increases the welfare of the small country and reduces the welfare of the large country. It is therefore absolutely not a way to correct the large country's excessive preference for government expenditure, as this would imply a reduction in the large country's tax burden.

Note that this result results from the fact that since each country has a weight in the currency area's single target corresponding to its size, the coordination of taxation does not change the taxation policy of the large country, since minimizing $\delta L + L^*$ or L^* is nearly equivalent when δ is small.

SYMMETRICAL COORDINATION

So far we have defined coordination as a situation where the tax burdens of the two countries are chosen in such a way as to maximize their common well-being, with each country having a weight corresponding to its size (or minimizing $\delta L + L^*$). We are now going to suppose that the coordination of taxation is symmetrical: each country has the same weight in the currency area's common target, regardless of its size (one minimizes $L + L^*$).

For the values t_0 and t_0^* of the tax burdens corresponding to the non-cooperative equilibrium, we then have instead of (11.26):

$$\begin{cases} \dfrac{\partial(L+L^*)}{\partial t}(t_0,t_0^*) = -\dfrac{1}{t_0^*}\dfrac{\delta BC}{D}(H-g^*) \\ \dfrac{\partial(L+L^*)}{\partial t}(t_0,t_0^*) = -\dfrac{1}{t_0^*}\dfrac{AC(H-g)}{D+(1-\delta)C} \end{cases} \tag{11.27}$$

If δ is small, the tax burden t of the small country is now the one that is not modified by (symmetrical) coordination, whereas the tax burden t^* of the large country is increased by coordination. The two countries have the same weight in the target. The result results from the fact that production of the large country ($y^* = -Dt^* + \delta Ct$) hardly depends, if δ is small, on the tax burden of the small country. We have seen above that this is due to the fact that the transfer of capital between countries is less significant relative to production in the large country than in the small country. Consequently, (symmetrical) coordination does not change the small country's tax policy, if it is very small in relation to the large one ($\delta \approx 0$) since the tax policy of the small country barely has any influence on the large country.

CONCLUSION

The lack of tax coordination could be a remedy for excessive government expenditure in European countries, provided the reference is symmetrical coordination between large and small countries.

We have seen above that:

- 'Weighted' coordination of tax policies (when each country has a weight corresponding to its size in the overall target of a currency area) leads to, in comparison with the lack of coordination of tax policies, a rise in the tax burden in the small countries of the currency area, without any major effect on the tax burden of large countries.
- 'Symmetrical' coordination of tax policies (when each country has an equal weight), in comparison with the lack of coordination of tax policies, leads to a rise in the tax burden of large countries, without any effect on that of small countries.

If the large EMU countries have an excessive preference for government expenditure, their tax burden is too high and must be reduced. The lack of coordination of tax policies is thus, from this point of view, preferable to symmetrical coordination (identical weight for all countries) but not asymmetrical coordination (the weight of countries corresponds to their size).

Furthermore asymmetrical coordination is unacceptable to the small countries, since it reduces without ambiguity their welfare.

What is the reference in the euro zone? It is asymmetrical coordination, except in the cases where there is a unanimous vote, and this corresponds more to a form of symmetrical coordination.

The lesson for currency areas is therefore as follows: if the coordination of tax policies gives a greater weight to large countries, tax competition (that is the free-rider behaviour of small countries) reduces well-being, without any favourable effect on the possible behaviour biases of large countries in favour of excessive spending.

REFERENCES

Artus, P. (1997), 'La concurrence sociale va-t-elle remplacer la concurrence par les taux de change?', *Annales d'Economie et de Statistiques*, **48**, 83–100.

Artus, P. (1998), 'Une guerre des productivités après l'unification monétaire?', CDC Working Paper, 1998-23-EI.

Artus, P. (2001), 'Fédéralisme, coordination ou compétition budgétaire dans la zone euro?', CDC Working Paper, 2001-50-EI.

Beetsma, R. and A.L. Bovenberg (1998), 'Monetary unification without fiscal coordination may discipline policymakers', *Journal of International Economics*, **45**, August, 239–58.

Newell, A. and J. Symons (1987), 'Corporatism, laissez-faire and the rise of unemployment', *European Economic Review*, **31** (3), 567–601.

Razin, A. and E. Sadka (1991), 'International fiscal coordination and competition: an exposition', NBER Working Paper 3797.

Sinn, H.W. (1990), 'Tax harmonisation and tax competition in Europe', *European Economic Review*, **34**, 489–504.

12. Comparing monetary and fiscal policies in Europe and in the United States: a strategic analysis

Pierre Faure

INTRODUCTION

According to some economists (Emerson et al., 1990), monetary unification in Europe should facilitate dialogue and cooperation with the rest of the world. Some others think on the contrary that the launch of the euro is likely to complicate international macroeconomic policy coordination (Goodhart, 1993; Kenen, 1993; Begg et al., 1997). The optimistic point of view in Emerson et al. (1990) mainly rests on the idea that the European currency union is likely to increase the costs of non-cooperative behaviour for the United States, because of the removal of the asymmetry linked to the small size and high degree of openness of European economies. The other countries should be more aware of those costs and therefore take into account the spillovers of their policies.

We think however that the analysis in the Emerson report oversimplifies many things, especially because it considers the European Monetary Union (EMU) as representing a single actor and, in this way, supposes the appearance of a G4 at the international level. It is true that the finance ministers agreed in 1998 upon a three-handed representation mode in the G8 meetings. But such a simplification does not make sense from a fiscal point of view (see in particular Goodhart, 1993). No treaty ensures the coordination of national fiscal policies or their consistency with the monetary strategy of the European Central Bank (ECB). In view of the fact that fiscal and monetary policies are closely interdependent in their effects on the exchange rate, it is rather difficult to see in the launch of the euro the start of a new international cooperation era with the United States.

Some other arguments justify our scepticism, among which are counted the very large weight that the ECB attaches to inflation in its loss function. The priority given to price stability in Europe might well complicate negotiation and informal agreements in international policy forums.[1] Why would European authorities not become as indifferent as the others to monetary spillovers (Kenen, 1993; Begg et al., 1997)?

The consequence of the coexistence of one central bank and of several governments defending their own interests, and therefore in a relatively weak strategic position *vis-à-vis* the common monetary policy-maker, is that the EMU is an original mosaic as regards economic policy, a complex architecture combining centralized and decentralized powers. In other words, the current European set-up raises a two-level coordination problem, between the ECB and the governments of the currency zone taken together, on the one hand, and among national authorities, on the other hand. The fact that national fiscal players do not share the same objectives or the same preferences leads us to think that the ECB is likely to be even more independent *de facto* than it is *de jure* (Johnson, 1994). From a strategic point of view, the monetary policy-making authority could take advantage of fiscal decentralization and impose its choices very easily. The fact that several governments face one central bank actually means that each national fiscal decision-maker taken separately has little incentive to internalize the monetary reaction to his own policy. Accordingly the modelling framework used to study the decision-making process inside the EMU has to take into account all the interactions among budgetary and monetary players.

In particular it seems to us important to consider the differences subsisting on both sides of the Atlantic in the internal economic policy design, and so in the strategic interdependencies among the various authorities. The institutional differences may have significant repercussions on welfare by affecting fiscal and monetary choices as well as the pay-off distribution in the case of cooperation. For instance the US fiscal policy-maker and European governments might react very differently after a common worldwide shock owing to decentralization in the EMU, that is, because of the additional non-cooperative game among European budgetary authorities. Another effect is that the intra-European fiscal conflict will also normally imply different monetary policies on the two sides of the Atlantic.

Our general objective in this chapter is to bring out the consequences of those institutional differences. More widely, we aim to explore, in a game-theoretic framework, the repercussions of the strategic interactions between the ECB and European governments on the world macroeconomic equilibrium, on the one hand, and the spillovers of foreign policies on European welfare, on the other. For this purpose we use the three-country model developed by Eichengreen and Ghironi (1997), in which two (European) countries, forming a monetary union, are economically interrelated with a third (representing the rest of the world) where fiscal powers are centralized. This framework is used to study on the basis of numerical simulations the policy-makers' responses to a negative global supply shock, producing both inflation and unemployment.

We compare in the first part the authorities' losses in a wholly non-cooperative setting by calculating the Nash and the Stackelberg solutions and the consistent conjectural equilibrium between the fiscal and monetary policy-makers of each area. The combination of two governments with their own objectives inside the monetary union and of a sole fiscal authority in the third (non-European) country allows us to underline some divergences relating to macroeconomic performance or the policy-makers' strategic incentives. It is shown that monetary leadership leaves governments worse off and harms social welfare; fiscal leadership is better and works like a second-best form of intra-zone cooperation.

The second part of the chapter is about policy coordination. The separation of fiscal and monetary powers inside each country enables us to distinguish intra-zone cooperation (between the fiscal and monetary authorities of the same economic area) from inter-country cooperation (among central banks or governments only) in international policy forums, such as the G8 meetings (Capoen et al., 1994; Villa, 1995; Capoen and Villa, 1996). Consequently we have not only to compare negotiated solutions with non-cooperative equilibria, but also to assess the potential benefits of the two types of cooperation. It appears that inter-country cooperation is always counterproductive, in the sense that there is at least one non-cooperative equilibrium for which social welfare is higher for all economies. Intra-zone cooperation is on the contrary the best solution, because the interest conflicts among the authorities of the same zone are stronger, and the combination of their instruments still more ineffective, as each player seeks to counteract the impact of the other's policy on the variable that is the most important for him. It therefore appears important to set up in Europe new institutional arrangements able to facilitate dialogue and cooperation between the ECB and the various national governments.

Taking into account the specificity of the European institutional arrangements as regards monetary policy is another way to highlight asymmetries between the two continents. We lastly study what happens if monetary policy in Europe is left to an ultraconservative central banker (that is, with a very great dislike for inflation). The results of our simulations are plain: appointing a governor with a high degree of inflation aversion leaves every decision-maker in the world worse off since it only exacerbates the policy conflicts. This points to the risk of an independent central bank weighting price stability too heavily.

A FEW REMARKS ABOUT THE MODEL

With the aim of illustration, the three countries of the model are the United States, Germany and France (denoted by the subscripts US, G and F, respectively). The two European countries form a monetary union. The dollar–euro exchange rate is free to float. The size of the German and French economies is half the size of the US economy. So Europe and the United States are symmetric to one another. Moreover the structural parameters for the three countries are equal.

The analytical tool we use here is the model of Eichengreen and Ghironi (1997); this is a standard three-country Mundell–Fleming model, in the tradition of Canzoneri and Henderson (1991), extended to include fiscal policy. For the sake of brevity, all the equations are written in the Appendix. In this section we present the budgetary and monetary authorities' loss functions.

The main change compared to Canzoneri and Henderson (1991) is that demand in each country also depends on public expenditure. We suppose that budgetary policy has standard Keynesian effects, that is, government spending cuts are contractionary (see Equations A.12a–A.12b in the Appendix).[2]

A second difference with the original Canzoneri–Henderson (1991) framework is that the demand for money depends on the domestic nominal interest rate too (see A.8 in the Appendix). The last two authors use a simpler condition for the money market equilibrium in which only income appears, so that employment in each country is directly explained by its money growth rate. Introducing the interest rate in the money market equilibrium equation allows us to highlight new strategic interdependencies since output in each country then depends on foreign budgetary and monetary policies too.

Thirdly, we follow Kébabdjian (1996) to consider the current account between Europe and the United States in addition. It essentially depends on the dollar–euro real exchange rate, and varies with the incomes of the two areas too (see A.9 in the Appendix).

Decision-makers set their policy instrument on the basis of a quadratic loss function (L) defined over inflation (q), employment (n), the current account value (d) and – for governments solely – public spending (g). Each variable is measured as a deviation from its desired value (equal to zero in the absence of any disturbance).

The Federal Reserve (Fed) and the European Central Bank control money supply (m) and want to minimize, respectively:

$$L_{Fed} = \frac{1}{2}\{\gamma_q q_{US}^2 + \gamma_n n_{US}^2 + \gamma_d d_{US}^2\} \qquad (12.1a)$$

$$L_{ECB} = \frac{1}{2}\{\theta_q q_{EU}^2 + \theta_n n_{EU}^2 + \theta_d d_{EU}^2\} \qquad (12.1b)$$

Welfare losses increase in the deviations of the consumer price index, employment (that is, output) and the current account value from the bliss points. The parameters γ_q, γ_n and γ_d measure the importance the Fed attaches to price stability, employment and external equilibrium (that is, real exchange rate stabilization), respectively. θ_q, θ_n and θ_d are the corresponding weights for the ECB.

We make the normative assumption according to which each country features a social welfare function that is shared by the government of that country. Hence fiscal authorities are benevolent. They control public spending and their preferences are represented by the following loss functions:

$$L_{US} = \frac{1}{2}\{\psi_q q_{US}^2 + \psi_n n_{US}^2 + \psi_d d_{US}^2 + \psi_g g_{US}^2\} \qquad (12.2a)$$

$$L_G = \frac{1}{2}\{\omega_q q_G^2 + \omega_n n_G^2 + \omega_d d_{EU}^2 + \omega_g g_G^2\} \qquad (12.2b)$$

$$L_F = \frac{1}{2}\{\omega_q q_F^2 + \omega_n n_F^2 + \omega_d d_{EU}^2 + \omega_g g_F^2\} \qquad (12.2c)$$

The presence of a term in g^2 in (12.2a)–(12.2c) plays the role of a budget constraint: taking into account the cost of the deviations of public expenditure is a way to capture the idea that fiscal policy is difficult to fine tune and cannot be adjusted as quickly as monetary policy (the higher the parameters ψ_g and ω_g, the less the degree of fiscal activism).

The reduced form of the model is too complicated to obtain analytical solutions, and we must assign numerical values to the different parameters in order to simulate the stabilization game. We have chosen the following values for the target weights: $\gamma_q = \theta_q = 5$, $\gamma_n = \theta_n = 0.5$ and $\gamma_d = \theta_d = 0.1$ for central banks; $\psi_q = \omega_q = \psi_d = \omega_d = 0.25$, $\psi_n = \omega_n = 2$ and $\psi_g = \omega_g = 5$ for governments. The weights are equal on both sides of the Atlantic in order to bring out the specific effects of the differences in the internal economic policy design. Central banks put relatively more weight on inflation, while governments care relatively more about output, as is commonly assumed in the policy coordination literature.

The substantial weight given to the deviations of public spending expresses the limits of fiscal activism (Eichengreen and Ghironi, 1997; Ghironi and Giavazzi, 1997)[3] and means that governments are reluctant to run very expansionary policies, in order not to aggravate their budget deficit, or very tight policies, in view of the attachment to public utility service. Moreover this large weight might illustrate the ceilings on public debt and fiscal deficits in Europe incorporated in the Maastricht Treaty, or a strict application of the Stability and Growth Pact, preventing each participating country from actively using the fiscal tool, and the desire of reducing public debt in the United States.[4]

Finally, as regards the weight placed on the achievement of external equilibrium, which can be directly interpreted as that given to the dollar–euro real exchange rate stabilization,[5] we follow the common idea that monetary unification in Europe is likely to bring about much more benign neglect *vis-à-vis* the exchange rate (Begg et al., 1997; Bénassy-Quéré et al., 1997): since the euro zone is larger and mechanically less open than its member states, it is natural to expect that the ECB will behave much more like the Fed, devoting far less attention to the exchange rate during normal periods. The implication of reciprocal benign neglect is that monetary and budgetary policies will be predominantly set with a view to domestic objectives everywhere in the world.

NON-COOPERATIVE EQUILIBRIA

In this section, every player is supposed to behave in a non-cooperative way and to set his policy on the basis of his sole objective function, without considering the consequences of his choice on the other players' welfare. The strategic interdependencies between Europe and the United States are always modelled with a Nash game. We successively calculate the Nash, the Stackelberg (with monetary and fiscal leadership) and the consistent conjectural equilibria to describe the relationship between fiscal and monetary policy-makers inside each currency area.

Worldwide Nash Equilibrium

We analyse the policy-makers' reactions to a symmetric adverse worldwide productivity shock (that is, $x > 0$ in the reduced-form equations). The monetary and fiscal best-response functions are found by routine analytics from the first-order conditions of the monetary and fiscal authorities' minimization problems:

$$m_{US} = 0.068m_{EU} - 0.731g_{US} - 0.646\frac{(g_G + g_F)}{2} - 1.810x \qquad (12.3a)$$

$$m_{EU} = 0.068m_{US} - 0.731\frac{(g_G + g_F)}{2} - 0.646g_{US} - 1.810x \qquad (12.3b)$$

$$g_{US} = -0.167m_{US} + 0.008m_{EU} - 0.093\frac{(g_G + g_F)}{2} + 0.042x \quad (12.3c)$$

$$g_G = -0.094m_{EU} + 0.005m_{US} - 0.052g_{US} - 0.041g_F + 0.024x \quad (12.3d)$$

Other things being equal, a reduction in the money supply and an increase in public expenditure in the European Union (the United States) force the Fed (the ECB) to conduct a more contractionary policy to damp down imported inflation. On average, monetary policymakers mainly react to domestic fiscal decisions (see 12.3a–12.3b). Likewise, fiscal policy is mainly dependent on domestic monetary choices because of their stronger impact on home employment (see 12.3c–12.3d). An increase in the money supply and public spending cuts in the EMU (the United States) restrain production abroad, because the dollar (the euro) appreciates against the euro (the dollar), and forces the US government (European governments) to increase spending in order to fight unemployment. Fiscal policies in Europe are strategic substitutes since any increase in public spending in a member state exerts beneficial effects in the neighbouring country, so that each government cuts its spending if the other raises its own.[6]

In the Nash equilibrium (N), each central bank tries to conduct a still more contractionary monetary policy than the other in the hope to export inflation abroad with a real appreciation, while governments increase spending to bolster activity (see the first column of Table 12.1). The fundamental point is that the US fiscal policy is twice as expansionary as European fiscal policies owing to the non-cooperative game between Germany and France. Each European budgetary player is aware of the beneficial effect of the other player's expansion on home employment, and internalizes the information by expanding less than he would in the absence

Table 12.1 Optimal policies and endogenous variables in wholly non-cooperative games

	1 (N)	2 (ML)	3 (FL)	4 (CCE)
m_{US}	$-2.4026x$	$-2.4554x$	$-2.0050x$	$-2.0113x$
m_{EU}	$-2.3867x$	$-2.4211x$	$-2.0028x$	$-2.0065x$
g_{US}	$+0.4048x$	$+0.4131x$	$+0.0551x$	$+0.0555x$
$g_G = g_F$	$+0.2069x$	$+0.2094x$	$+0.0278x$	$+0.0279x$
e_{EU}	$-0.0728x$	$-0.0813x$	$-0.0100x$	$-0.0111x$
z_{EU}	$-0.0809x$	$-0.0853x$	$-0.0112x$	$-0.0116x$
q_{US}	$+0.5070x$	$-0.4967x$	$+0.5118x$	$+0.5105x$
$q_G = q_F$	$+0.5151x$	$+0.5097x$	$+0.5130x$	$+0.5123x$
n_{US}	$-1.6004x$	$-1.6327x$	$-1.6162x$	$-1.6205x$
$n_G = n_F$	$-1.6273x$	$-1.6461x$	$-1.6199x$	$-1.6222x$
d_{US}	$-0.0659x$	$-0.0686x$	$-0.0091x$	$-0.0093x$

of the other player's response. And neither player takes into account the beneficial impact of his own policy on the other player. As a result the Nash solution does not exploit the positive externalities associated with fiscal policy in the euro zone enough.

Thus the European monetary policy is less contractionary than the US one, because the ECB sets its instrument according to public expenditure in Germany and France above all. It results from the differences in the internal economic policy design that the dollar appreciates against the euro, hence the external deficit of the United States. But internal stabilization is better in the United States than in the European Union: the more contractionary monetary policy and the more expansionary fiscal policy lead to lower inflation and unemployment rates.

Stackelberg Equilibria

Under the Stackelberg regime, fiscal and monetary authorities no longer act simultaneously. It is now assumed that one player (the Stackelberg leader) has a first-mover advantage when selecting his policy, and takes into account the response of the other player (the follower) to his measures. Hence the leader chooses his optimal strategy subject to the follower's reaction function, and the follower's committed response is to simply take the leader's policy as given and minimize his loss. We think that the leader–follower policy regime is interesting inasmuch as it allows the strategic aspects of the decision-making process to be highlighted, especially the consequences of the differences in the economic policy architecture on both sides of the Atlantic.

In the Stackelberg equilibrium, monetary leadership (ML) is a usual way to capture the notion of central bank independence (Petit, 1989; Hughes Hallett and Petit, 1990; Debelle, 1996). In the context of the EMU, an alternative interpretation for the Stackelberg leadership of the monetary player rests on the fact that the ECB deals with several national fiscal policymakers, which is likely to strengthen the strategic position of the common central bank against each government (van Aarle, 1996). However the opposite case of fiscal leadership (FL) is conceivable too, and does not call into question central bank independence, insofar as fiscal policy cannot be adjusted as quickly as monetary policy, so that choosing the level of public spending provides the government with a first-mover advantage (Beetsma and Bovenberg, 1998). In fact the latter equilibrium might be an even more appropriate description of fiscal–monetary interactions in practice than the standard Nash equilibrium, as fiscal policy is typically set on an annual basis, and even usually adopted for several years running. We shall consider the two possibilities in what follows.

Monetary leadership

Suppose in the first place that central bankers are Stackelberg leaders in the EMU and in the rest of the world. Thus the Fed moving first anticipates that the US government will respond to its policy according to the reaction function (12.3c), while the ECB internalizes the EMU-wide fiscal reaction function (see note 6). The new monetary best-response functions are then:

$$m_{US} = 0.072m_{EU} - 0.664\frac{(g_G + g_F)}{2} - 2.142x \qquad (12.4a)$$

$$m_{EU} = 0.070m_{US} - 0.655g_{US} - 1.978x \qquad (12.4b)$$

Compared to (12.3a) and (12.3b), the reaction coefficients for the productivity shock are higher. Monetary policies are more contractionary than in the Nash game (see the second column of Table 12.1). Each central bank knows that fiscal authorities are mainly concerned with employment, and internalizes the increase in public spending following any reduction in the money supply now. Since the fiscal reaction weakens the impact of monetary policy on prices, each governor is *ex ante* driven to adopt a more aggressive policy in order to control inflation, so that fiscal policies become more expansionary: thus, monetary leadership intensifies the policy conflict inside each currency zone.[7]

The US monetary policy is the most contractionary again because the US government reacts more than the German and French policy-makers (see 12.3c and note 6) $(\partial g_{US})/(\partial m_{US}) = -0.167$, whereas $(\partial g_{EU})/(\partial m_{EU}) = -0.090$ only). The difference is due to the lack of cooperation between the two national governments in the EMU that drives each of them to limit the increase in public expenditure. Accordingly, monetary leadership strengthens the appreciation of the dollar against the euro, and makes the US external deficit worse. The US and European rates of inflation are lower, but unemployment increases. Inflation and output stabilization remains better in the United States.

Fiscal leadership

Now consider the reverse case of fiscal leadership. The US government knows that the Fed will react to any change in fiscal policy according to the reaction function (12.3a), while European governments internalize the reaction function (12.3b) of the ECB. The best-response functions for the US and the German governments become:

$$g_{US} = -0.001m_{EU} + 0.007\frac{(g_G + g_F)}{2} + 0.053x \qquad (12.5a)$$

$$g_G = -0.001m_{US} + 0.004g_{US} - 0.002g_F + 0.027x \qquad (12.5b)$$

Compared to (12.3c) and (12.3d), the sign of the reaction coefficients concerning foreign policies is the opposite: at present, governments slightly reduce public spending after any monetary expansion or any budgetary contraction in the rest of the world. Such a change is due to the fact that fiscal players, when leading, worry less about the consequences of any deterioration in competitiveness on home employment, and care more about the spillovers of their instrument on consumer prices.

The main thing is that fiscal policies become much less expansionary (see the third column of Table 12.1): governments do not raise public spending as much as before, as they take into account *ex ante* the fact that monetary policy is less aggressive when their budget deficit is smaller, which in principle should make it possible to limit the fall in activity because monetary policy has a bigger impact than fiscal policy on home employment (see A.12a–A.12b in the Appendix). The reduction in the budget deficit with respect to the Nash solution is much greater in the United States than in Europe. Of course this is due to the institutional differences again. The potential gain of the monetary reaction as regards employment is higher in the rest of the world. The strategic incentive of each European government to reduce its budget deficit in order to alter the monetary strategy of the ECB is indeed limited because of the intra-zone non-cooperative game: *ex ante*, the German and French authorities solely consider the impact of a variation of the value of their own instrument on the EMU-wide money supply, instead of taking into account the effect of an EMU-wide budget deficit variation. In concrete terms, the fiscal inducement calculated by the US government corresponds to the partial derivative $(\partial m_{US})/(\partial g_{US}) = -0.731$ (see 12.3a), which is twice as big as the inducement calculated by each European player $((\partial m_{EU})/(\partial g_G) = (\partial m_{EU})/(\partial g_F) = -0.3655$ according to 12.3b). The Stackelberg game with fiscal leadership clearly illustrates what we said in the introduction: namely, each national authority in the EMU is likely to feel that the repercussions of its own choices on the trend in monetary policy will tend to be small.

The more pronounced curtailment in public expenditure in the United States limits the dollar's rise against the euro and the US external deficit. However compared to the Nash solution, the inflation and output stabilization measures in the United States turn out to be less effective *ex post*: as regards home inflation, the spending cuts in every country do not offset the less contractionary policy of the Fed; as regards home employment, the higher money supply does not counteract the initial reduction in public expenditure. This contrasts with the situation in the EMU, where the inflation and unemployment rates are lower under fiscal leadership than in the Nash equilibrium.

Consistent Conjectural Equilibrium

The usual Cournot–Nash solution does not really result from a rational behaviour of authorities. Under the Cournot assumption, each player assumes when calculating the value of his instrument that the other players will not react, which is hardly realistic. In fact in the Cournot game, each player is wrong in predicting the response of the others. For instance in the present model it is reasonable to expect that the Fed and the ECB know in advance that any monetary contraction will provoke an increase in public expenditure. In the same way, governments are likely to anticipate a monetary easing if public spending decreases. Therefore in the consistent conjectural equilibrium (CCE), it is assumed that each player, in choosing his own strategy, takes into account the reaction of the others.[8]

We consider here the CCE between the fiscal and monetary authorities of each economic area. The interesting point concerns the differences in the policy-makers' conjectures in Europe and in the United States induced by fiscal decentralization. For the Fed and the US government, the first-order conditions become $(\partial L_{Fed})/(\partial m_{US}) + (\partial L_{Fed})/(\partial g_{US}) \times (\partial g_{US})/(\partial m_{US}) = 0$ and $(\partial L_{US})/(\partial g_{US}) + (\partial L_{US})/(\partial m_{US}) \times (\partial m_{US})/(\partial g_{US}) = 0$, respectively, with $h_{Fed} \equiv (\partial g_{US})/(\partial m_{US})$ the Fed's conjecture relating to the fiscal reaction and $h_{US} \equiv (\partial m_{US})/(\partial g_{US})$ the US fiscal policymaker's conjecture relating to the Fed's reaction (the first-order conditions for European players are obtained from the same principle). Some calculus shows that the Fed and the US government make the conjectures $h_{Fed} = -0.024$ and $h_{US} = -0.730$: thus the Fed logically foresees that any increase in the money supply will involve a cut in public spending, and the US government expects a decrease in the money supply if the budget deficit goes up.[9] Fiscal decentralization in Europe imply different results: $h_{ECB} = -0.012$ and $h_G = h_F = -0.365$ (that is, the conjectured variations of monetary and fiscal tools are divided by two in the EMU). In concrete terms, the ECB estimates that increasing the money supply by 1 will induce each member state to cut public spending by (only) 0.012, while both the German and French authorities anticipate that cutting public expenditure by 1 will lead to a rise in the money supply by (only) 0.365. Thus the monetary reaction conjectured by the US government is twice as strong as the reaction expected by European governments because the latter neglect the impact of their partner's choices on the trend in monetary policy, as under the previous Stackelberg game. And the non-cooperative game between Germany and France means that the rise in public spending expected by the ECB after a monetary contraction is smaller than the rise expected by the Fed (since each European government would like to benefit from the fiscal stimulus undertaken in the rest of the union while containing its budget deficit).

Ex ante, anticipating the monetary reaction may lead the fiscal player either to increase public expenditure even more, in order to fight the adverse effect of the monetary contraction through the fiscal stimulus, or to reduce the budget deficit, because the central banker's response renders any budgetary expansion ineffective. *Ex post*, we are in the latter case. Governments indeed take into account the fact that employment depends more on monetary policy than fiscal policy; as a consequence they run less expansionary policies, as under the Stackelberg regime with fiscal leadership. On the other hand, central banks are now induced to contract more because they know that any decrease in the money supply will drive fiscal authorities to raise spending, thereby feeding inflation. In the end, monetary policies are slightly more contractionary than in the previous Stackelberg equilibrium, but remain less restrictive than in the Cournot–Nash game (the incentive to contract more in order to control inflation is eliminated by the cut in public spending).

Comparison of Losses: Fiscal Leadership as a Second-Best Form of Intra-zone Cooperation

Social welfare turns out to be higher in the EMU than in the rest of the world under the Nash and monetary leadership regimes (see Table 12.2). The decentralization of fiscal policy in Europe leads to a lesser degree of fiscal activism, hence a first-order gain: the better control of the public spending level in the EMU explains the most part of the loss difference between the two continents. The Fed is however better off than the ECB because the more contractionary US monetary policy stabilizes home inflation to a larger extent.

On the other hand, social welfare losses are very close when monetary policy is determined after the event and in the consistent conjectural equilibrium. The CCE between the fiscal and monetary decision-makers of each currency area gets closer to the fiscal leadership as regards its

Table 12.2 Losses in wholly non-cooperative games

	1 (N)	2 (ML)	3 (FL)	4 (ECC)
L_{Fed}	$1.2832x^2$	$1.2834x^2$	$1.3080x^2$	$1.3080x^2$
L_{ECB}	$1.3255x^2$	$1.3270x^2$	$1.3139x^2$	$1.3140x^2$
L_{US}	$3.0036x^2$	$3.1240x^2$	$2.6525x^2$	$2.6664x^2$
$L_{G=}L_F$	$2.7888x^2$	$2.8522x^2$	$2.6590x^2$	$2.6663x^2$

consequences. Under the Stackelberg regime with fiscal leadership, welfare is slightly better in the United States because European governments, playing Nash against one another, are not so able as the US government to take advantage of their first-mover situation.

The Stackelberg game in which central banks lead is the worst scenario: monetary leadership stabilizes inflation, but the employment loss is larger than under any other regime. Conversely, the Stackelberg equilibrium with fiscal leadership is the best non-cooperative solution from a social point of view: this sequential game can be understood as a second-best form of cooperation with the domestic monetary authority, in the sense that the fiscal player takes into account the consequences of his budget deficit on the monetary policy that will be chosen by the central banker. What the former has to do is to encourage the latter to pursue a less aggressive policy. The main credit of this Stackelberg game is that it strengthens fiscal discipline, that is, the deviations of public spending from zero become smaller.[10] This is notably the case for the United States, where the impact on welfare of the higher inflation and unemployment rates – compared to the Nash solution – is more than offset by the substantial decrease in the cost from adjusting the fiscal instrument (and by the reduction in trade deficit to a lesser extent).

COOPERATIVE SOLUTIONS

We explore in this section the welfare implications of economic policy coordination. We distinguish the *intra-zone* cooperation problem, between the fiscal and monetary authorities of each currency area, from the (usual) *inter-country* cooperation problem, among central banks or governments only, in international policy forums like the G8 meetings. Such a distinction seems to us very important in the discussion about coordination problems, in the sense that the bigger impact of policy instruments on domestic variables normally implies that the welfare losses resulting from a conflict between the decision-makers of the same zone are likely to be higher. Therefore in a normative perspective the main thing is to see if intra-zone cooperation matters more than dialogue and negotiation on the world scale.

In the first subsection, we examine some inter-country cooperation cases, between central banks or governments. In the second subsection, we study the effects of intra-zone cooperation, first in the United States only (in order to see if the European Union might benefit from policy coordination in the rest of the world), then inside the two areas simultaneously.[11]

Inter-country Cooperation

Cooperation between central banks

We first suppose that the Fed and the ECB cooperate (case C1) and jointly minimize, with respect to m_{US} and m_{EU} respectively, the average of the loss functions $1/2(L_{Fed}) + 1/2(L_{ECB})$ (setting the weights to 1/2, given that the two currency zones of the model are symmetric to one another). The US and European monetary policies are now defined according to:

$$m_{US} = 0.136 m_{EU} - 0.681 g_{US} - 0.597 \frac{(g_G + g_F)}{2} - 1.646x \quad (12.6a)$$

$$m_{EU} = 0.136 m_{US} - 0.681 \frac{(g_G + g_F)}{2} - 0.597 g_{US} - 1.646x \quad (12.6b)$$

Central bankers are now aware of the uselessness of competitive policies and no longer seek to export inflation by manipulating the exchange rate. Cooperation involves a greater increase in the money supply in response to any monetary expansion abroad (that is, central bankers no longer try to take advantage of foreign monetary policies). In the same way, the response to the productivity shock x is less aggressive, and the monetary contraction following any fiscal expansion is less strong than before (compare with 12.3a and 12.3b).

Therefore compared to the non-cooperative Nash solution, monetary policies on both sides of the Atlantic become less contractionary while fiscal authorities increase spending by less (see the first column of Table 12.3).

Table 12.3 Optimal policies and endogenous variables in cooperative games

	1 (C1)	2 (C2)	3 (C3)	4 (C4)	5 (C5)
m_{US}	$-2.3566x$	$-2.5469x$	$-2.9570x$	$-0.7180x$	$-0.5342x$
m_{EU}	$-2.3422x$	$-2.5469x$	$-2.9570x$	$-2.0377x$	$-0.5342x$
g_{US}	$+0.3978x$	$+0.4089x$	$+0.6864x$	$+0.0491x$	$+0.0458x$
$g_G = g_F$	$+0.2034x$	$+0.4089x$	$+0.6864x$	$+0.2008x$	$+0.0458x$
e_{EU}	$-0.0711x$	0	0	$+0.5134x$	0
z_{EU}	$-0.0793x$	0	0	$+0.2058x$	0
q_{US}	$+0.5155x$	$+0.5105x$	$+0.5091x$	$+0.8499x$	$+0.8371x$
$q_G = q_F$	$+0.5232x$	$+0.5105x$	$+0.5091x$	$+0.5038x$	$+0.8371x$
n_{US}	$-1.5732x$	$-1.6122x$	$-1.6077x$	$-0.5644x$	$-0.5552x$
$n_G = n_F$	$-1.6006x$	$-1.6122x$	$-1.6077x$	$-1.5898x$	$-0.5552x$
d_{US}	$-0.0647x$	0	0	$+0.1028x$	0

The appreciation of the dollar against the euro is less strong. Monetary cooperation leads to higher inflation rates (the spending cuts do not offset the less restrictive stance adopted by central banks), but unemployment is lower than under any non-cooperative regime in Europe as well as in the United States. The employment gain is due to the fact that monetary policy is altered more and has a greater impact on home activity than fiscal policy.

Cooperation between European governments

Consider the consequences of fiscal cooperation now, and suppose first that only European governments coordinate their measures (case C2) in the sense that they minimize the common loss function $1/2(L_G) + 1/2(L_F)$ (given that both member states are identical in all respects). The new European fiscal reaction function is found by symmetry with (12.3c).[12]

The German and French governments now internalize the fact that a public spending increase stimulates activity in the neighbouring country and so raise the budget deficit much more (see the second column of Table 12.3). Consequently, the conflict between the two national governments and the common central bank is exacerbated, since the great increase in public expenditure fuels inflation. Fiscal cooperation thus forces the ECB to pursue a more contractionary policy. The new European policy mix contributes to weakening the dollar against the euro, so that the Fed is induced to adopt a more restrictive stance too in order to fight imported inflation. The spillovers of the policy changes on US production tend to offset one another, so that the US fiscal policy is finally altered less.

Inflation in Europe is lower than under the Nash regime (the increase in public expenditure is offset by the more contractionary policy of the ECB), but the other countries suffer from higher inflation (since their currency no longer rises against the euro). Unemployment falls in Europe (the increase in public expenditure turns out to be enough to counteract the harsher policy adopted by the ECB), whereas the further monetary tightening undertaken by the Fed strengthens the destabilizing impact of the supply shock on output and employment in the United States.

Global fiscal cooperation

When all three fiscal policymakers cooperate (case C3), they minimize the sum, with weights equal to 1/2, of the US player's objective function and of the average of the German and French governments' losses, $1/2(L_{US}) + 1/4(L_G + L_F)$. The fiscal reaction functions become:

$$g_{US} = -0.150m_{US} - 0.101m_{EU} - 0.173g_{EU} + 0.064x \qquad (12.7a)$$

$$g_{EU} = -0.150m_{EU} - 0.101m_{US} - 0.173g_{US} + 0.064x \qquad (12.7b)$$

Governments react more to any change in foreign economic policies. The increase in public spending following the productivity shock is also bigger than in the non-cooperative case.

Compared to the previous scenario, the increase in public expenditure is dramatically greater because fiscal authorities now internalize the positive spillovers of their pump-priming measures on activity in the rest of the world (see the third column of Table 12.3). Global fiscal cooperation thus forces the ECB and the Fed to pursue extremely restrictive policies in order to fight the inflationary consequences of budget deficits. The stabilization of endogenous variables is improved: inflation turns out to be lower, and employment higher.

Intra-zone Cooperation

We are now interested in the welfare implications of policy coordination between the fiscal and monetary authorities of the same currency zone. At first glance, given the close interactions of fiscal and monetary policies, a good case can be made for the cooperative setting of money supply and public spending, which is not incompatible with central bank independence.[13]

Cooperation between the Fed and the US government

First of all, consider the outcome of a cooperative process between the US fiscal decision-maker and the Federal Reserve (case C4). We suppose that the Fed and the US government now minimize the average loss $1/2(L_{Fed}) + 1/2(L_{US})$ with respect to m_{US} and g_{US}. The US monetary and fiscal best-response functions become, respectively:

$$m_{US} = 0.058m_{EU} - 0.802g_{US} - 0.604\frac{(g_G + g_F)}{2} - 0.439x \quad (12.8a)$$

$$g_{US} = -0.227m_{US} + 0.012m_{EU} - 0.129\frac{(g_G + g_F)}{2} - 0.063x \quad (12.8b)$$

On the one hand, cooperating with the budgetary decision-maker requires the Fed's governor to take the spillovers of his policy instrument on home employment more into account. Therefore, his reaction to the productivity shock is far less strong, and any decrease in the budget deficit g_{US} entails a bigger monetary relaxation now. For the same reason, the Fed weights imported inflation less heavily following any monetary contraction or any budgetary expansion in the EMU (compare with 12.3a). On the other hand, the US government must care more about the inflationary effect of its budget deficit. This is why the US fiscal policy-maker now curtails spending in response to the supply shock x (given that it has a bigger impact

Table 12.4 Losses in cooperative games

	1 (C1)	2 (C2)	3 (C3)	4 (C4)	5 (C5)
L_{Fed}	$1.2834x^2$	$1.3014x^2$	$1.2942x^2$	$1.8861x^2$	$1.8290x^2$
L_{ECB}	$1.3249x^2$	$1.3014x^2$	$1.2942x^2$	$1.2669x^2$	$1.8290x^2$
L_{US}	$2.9043x^2$	$3.0497x^2$	$3.7950x^2$	$0.4162x^2$	$0.4010x^2$
$L_G = L_F$	$2.7000x^2$	$3.0497x^2$	$3.7950x^2$	$2.6613x^2$	$0.4010x^2$

on prices than on employment). The same rationale implies that the curtailment in public expenditure following a monetary relaxation is stronger than in the non-cooperative game, and that the US government weights imported inflation more following any monetary contraction or any fiscal expansion in the EMU (compare with 12.3c).

The consequences of cooperation between the two US authorities appear to be very clear (see the fourth column of Table 12.3). The new US monetary policy is considerably less contractionary, and the US budget deficit is widely cut down. Thus cooperation with the central bank allows stronger government discipline. The new US policy mix automatically contributes to a depreciation of the dollar, which gives the ECB the opportunity to adopt a less restrictive stance too. The French and German fiscal policies are altered to a lesser extent, since the spillovers on home employment of the euro's rise and of the new common monetary policy tend to offset one another.

The US price index is the highest in this scenario (the positive impact of the spending cut on inflation is counteracted by the much less contractionary policy adopted by the Fed), but in return the unemployment rate is considerably reduced by comparison with all the previous games (given that monetary policy has a greater effect on output); and the US current account now shows a surplus. European economies benefit from cooperation on the other side of the Atlantic: the euro's rise allows inflation to be contained, while the less restrictive policy pursued by the ECB permits better output stabilization to be achieved than in all non-cooperative cases. This is an important result: monetary and fiscal policy coordination in the rest of the world is welfare enhancing from the European standpoint (as is shown in Table 12.4).

Cooperation between all authorities within each currency area

We lastly assume that the German and French governments jointly define their fiscal policy and bargain at the same time in an equal position with the European Central Bank for the common monetary policy (case C5). We therefore minimize the sum $1/2(L_{ECB}) + 1/4(L_G + L_F)$ with respect to m_{EU}, g_G and g_F, so that the new monetary and fiscal reaction functions for the EMU are analogous to the previous ones for the United States (see 12.8a and 12.8b).

Monetary and fiscal policies are obviously the same on both sides of the Atlantic again (see the fifth column of Table 12.3). On the one hand, the cooperative process among European governments implies that they raise spending in order to exploit the positive externalities associated with fiscal policy; on the other hand, taking the common central banker's objective function into account leads each budgetary decision-maker to cut spending in order to contain inflation. *Ex post*, the latter effect gets the upper hand over the former: the German and French budget deficits are widely reduced when compared with the other solutions (except for the fiscal leadership case and the CCE). And the ECB adopts a much less restrictive policy, given that it weights employment more heavily now. These policy changes facilitate price stabilization in the United States, which allows the Federal Reserve to opt for a still less contractionary policy than before, so that the US government cuts spending. From the US standpoint, cooperation within the EMU is obviously beneficial: it automatically stops the euro's rise, and so imported inflation, and thus increases the US central banker's leeway, providing the possibility to protect home employment more. In the EMU the employment gain is huge, but the cooperative process causes a sharp price increase in return.

Comparison of Losses: Intra-zone Cooperation as the Best Solution

It emerges from our simulations that cooperation between fiscal and monetary authorities in each currency area matters much more than international dialogue on the occasion of the G8 meetings because the problems due to an intra-zone policy conflict are more serious than those due to the lack of cooperation with the rest of the world.

Intra-zone cooperation brings the highest social welfare gains owing to the bigger impact of policy instruments on home variables (see Table 12.4). In fact only governments take advantage of fiscal and monetary policy coordination, since it allows them both to achieve better output stabilization and to improve fiscal discipline significantly, whereas central banks sustain much larger losses due to the price upsurge and so prefer other solutions. The monetary player indeed prefers a Nash game against fiscal authorities combined with cooperation abroad, as suggested in the penultimate scenario (case C4): the ECB's loss is then the lowest because the cooperative game between the Fed and the US government contributes towards price stabilization in the EMU. Since governments and central banks do not share the same preferences, the problem of process implementation comes up: the fact that the monetary authority suffers larger losses when coordinating monetary and fiscal policies might well complicate dialogue and negotiation. This points to the risk of conflicting priorities between an independent governor, who worries about inflation above all, and society.

The outcomes of inter-country cooperation are not so good. The coordination of monetary or fiscal policies alone turns out to be counterproductive, in the sense that there is always at least one non-cooperative equilibrium for which social welfare is higher for all economies. Transatlantic cooperation among governments is clearly the worst scenario, because it encourages them to pursue much more expansionary policies that compel central banks to respond with sharp contraction. Thus fiscal cooperation aggravates the inefficiency of the policy mix. The danger here is of being confronted with an overly restrictive monetary policy coupled to a too lax fiscal policy. Although the deviations of inflation and employment are lower than when only European governments cooperate, the weakening of fiscal discipline is so marked that each fiscal player is far worse off.

Social loss within each currency area turns out to be lower with monetary cooperation when compared with the Nash equilibrium: governments are better off since unemployment and public expenditure are then lower. Although inflation goes up, the ECB is also better off, and therefore induced to cooperate with the Fed, but the latter would gain nothing since its losses are practically equal in the two situations (that is, the inflation loss offsets the employment gain and the reduction in external deficit).

WHO BENEFITS FROM A CONSERVATIVE CENTRAL BANKER?

The theoretical arguments in favour of a central banker attaching a larger weight to price stability than society are well known and are mainly due to considerations that are absent in the model. Delegating the control of monetary policy to an independent governor, with his own inflation–output trade-off, is one of the most important recommendations of the literature on time inconsistency and commitment problems (Rogoff, 1985). This literature has had in an incontestable way a great influence on the institutional arrangements for monetary policy in the EMU. We explore in this section the consequences of an increase in the ECB's level of inflation aversion on the world macroeconomic equilibrium.

It is now assumed that the control of the common monetary policy in the euro zone is left to a governor whose dislike for inflation is still greater than before. We recalculate the different equilibrium values for the worldwide Nash game with the weights 20, 50 and 100 for price stability in the ECB's loss function. Thus, the limiting case of $\theta_q = 100$ fits the situation in which the European monetary decision-maker would be ultraconservative. Moreover it is assumed that the progressive increase in the weight θ_q does not affect the Fed's output–inflation trade-off.

The larger the weight θ_q, the stronger the European monetary contraction (see Table 12.5). Any increase in the degree of inflation aversion intensifies the effect of the supply shock on employment and so compels the German and French governments to pursue still more expansionary fiscal policies. In fact the appointment of a central banker whose inflation aversion is higher amounts in a way to giving a first-mover advantage to the monetary player, as in a Stackelberg game, in the sense that he can impose a tighter policy on fiscal authorities. The combination of a more and more restrictive monetary policy and of more and more expansionary national budgetary policies in Europe – as θ_q rises gradually – fuels inflation in the United States, and so forces the Federal Reserve to run a more and more contractionary policy too. On the other hand, the more the European Central Bank penalizes inflation in its objective function, the more the European policy mix stimulates activity in the United States. The US government reacts far less to any increase in the ECB's degree of conservativeness, because the spillovers of the European policy mix and of the Fed's policy on home employment tend to offset one another.

When the ECB becomes more conservative than the Fed (that is, as from $\theta_q = 20$ in our simulations), the euro rises against the dollar, even if the US

Table 12.5 Optimal policies and endogenous variables for several degrees of conservatism of the ECB

	1 $\theta_q = 5$	2 $\theta_q = 20$	3 $\theta_q = 50$	4 $\theta_q = 100$
m_{US}	$-2.4026x$	$-2.5825x$	$-2.6477x$	$-2.6734x$
m_{EU}	$-2.3867x$	$-3.7751x$	$-4.2775x$	$-4.4764x$
g_{US}	$+0.4048x$	$+0.4119x$	$+0.4144x$	$+0.4154x$
$g_G = g_F$	$+0.2069x$	$+0.3309x$	$+0.3758x$	$+0.3936x$
e_{EU}	$-0.0728x$	$+0.3899x$	$+0.5573x$	$+0.6236x$
z_{EU}	$-0.0809x$	$+0.0988x$	$+0.1638x$	$+0.1896x$
q_{US}	$+0.5070x$	$+0.5137x$	$+0.5162x$	$+0.5171x$
$q_G = q_F$	$+0.5151x$	$+0.2053x$	$+0.0932x$	$+0.0488x$
n_{US}	$-1.6004x$	$-1.6225x$	$-1.6305x$	$-1.6337x$
$n_G = n_F$	$-1.6273x$	$-2.5928x$	$-2.9421x$	$-3.0805x$
d_{US}	$-0.0659x$	$+0.0210x$	$+0.0525x$	$+0.0649x$

budgetary policy remains more expansionary, and the European current account shows a growing deficit. Of course the appointment of a governor with a very high degree of inflation aversion allows far better price stabilization to be achieved in Europe, despite the significant increase in public expenditure in each member state, but such a result is obtained to the detriment of employment. The more expansionary fiscal policies in Germany and France cannot counteract the monetary tightening implemented by the ECB, so the unemployment rate grows fast with the degree of Rogoff-conservativeness. The US inflation and unemployment rates increase with the ECB's weight on inflation. The Fed does not manage to offset the adverse spillovers of the European policy mix on consumer prices, although it runs a more and more contractionary policy, so that the United States imports more and more inflation as θ_q rises gradually. Besides, the tighter US monetary policy produces more unemployment, even if the European policy mix improves competitiveness abroad, and the US government's policy is not expansionary enough to counteract the destabilizing effect on output.

Thus, any increase in the degree of inflation aversion of the European monetary authority makes things worse (see Table 12.6). Indeed every player suffers larger losses. Putting a still larger weight on price stability is harmful, not only from the standpoint of governments, but also from the standpoint of central banks. In particular, the loss for a European central banker endowed with a rather progressive temperament, who follows a pragmatic approach (that is, a balance between price stability and employment), is smaller than that of a governor worrying about inflation only. In fact the less conservative the ECB, the better economic performance will be, because the policy mix will then be closer to the one achieved under the assumption of intra-zone cooperation. The clear conclusion is that the European Central Bank cannot disregard employment, and that it should be inspired by the Federal Reserve's behaviour, which allows the latter to enjoy considerable credibility.

Table 12.6 Losses for several degrees of conservatism of the ECB

	1 $\theta_q = 5$	2 $\theta_q = 20$	3 $\theta_q = 50$	4 $\theta_q = 100$
L_{Fed}	$1.2832x^2$	$1.3180x^2$	$1.3309x^2$	$1.3360x^2$
L_{ECB}	$1.3255x^2$	$1.7860x^2$	$2.1858x^2$	$2.3785x^2$
L_{US}	$3.0036x^2$	$3.0897x^2$	$3.1216x^2$	$3.1344x^2$
$L_{G} = L_F$	$2.7888x^2$	$7.0016x^2$	$9.0105x^2$	$9.8774x^2$

CONCLUSION

In this chapter we have addressed the issue of monetary and fiscal policy interactions between the European Union and the rest of the world. The responses of central banks and governments to an adverse supply shock have been simulated by means of a game-theoretic three-country model. Taking fiscal policy into account allowed us to focus on the consequences of the coexistence of several national governments defending their own interests within the EMU on the game with foreign countries, and thus to highlight the welfare disparities across the world due to the maintenance of fiscal sovereignty for each participating country. The separation of budgetary and monetary authority also enabled us to compare the outcomes of intra-zone cooperation with those of inter-country cooperation.

We have first calculated several equilibria in a wholly non-cooperative setting. Fiscal decentralization in Europe involves not inconsiderable differences concerning economic performance as well as the decision-makers' strategic incentives. In particular it has been shown under the Stackelberg regime with fiscal leadership – which might be a more realistic depiction of the relationship between authorities – that the lack of cooperation among national authorities in the EMU leads to the weakening of each government's influence on monetary policy. The additional non-cooperative game between European governments is then all the more harmful since fiscal leadership is the best solution when central banks act in isolation and take the fiscal policy choices as given. This Stackelberg regime is a second-best form of intra-zone cooperation: once the central bank's reaction function is known to the fiscal player, the latter can anticipate that a less expansionary policy will lead to a looser monetary policy. Thus fiscal leadership allows government discipline, thereby producing a gain in welfare. Conversely the Stackelberg game with monetary leadership is the worst scenario, because it strengthens the conflict with the fiscal player and entails a still more inefficient policy mix.

Several cooperative situations have next been analysed. Our numerical simulations support the idea of fostering intra-zone cooperation between fiscal and monetary authorities rather than international dialogue in the G8 meetings, since welfare losses are then much lower. The coordination of monetary and fiscal policies yields a first-order gain in welfare, by disciplining governments (that is, by reducing the expansionary bias of fiscal policies) and stabilizing the employment level simultaneously, even if inflation is higher *ex post*. Such a solution however raises the issue of its implementation (especially in the EMU, owing to the numerous decision-makers), as the ensuing price upsurge leaves central banks worse off, but the problem goes beyond the scope of the present chapter, that fits into a normative perspective.

Conversely, cooperation among governments or central banks solely turns out to be always counterproductive, because there remain other externalities not taken into account: the problem is that a cooperative process between a subset of players (that is, when the monetary and fiscal authorities of each currency area play Nash against one another) entails still more aggressive reactions from the other players that finally harm welfare. The counterproductivity of fiscal cooperation in the EMU notably suggests that institutional arrangements for fiscal policy alone might make things worse: in this model, *setting up a federal fiscal authority makes sense only if it enables monetary and fiscal authorities to act cooperatively in the management of economic policy.*

We have lastly explored how the appointment of an ultra-conservative central banker in the EMU affects welfare. The conclusion is plain: delegating the control of monetary policy to a governor *à la* Rogoff, who is extremely attached to price stability, is clearly suboptimal and has negative consequences all over the world, because it violently exacerbates the policy conflict with fiscal authorities.

APPENDIX

The model used here is that of Eichengreen and Ghironi (1997) in the standard Keynesian case (that is, there are no supply-side distortions due to taxes). This Appendix only contains the main equations describing the three economies and the reduced form. We refer to their paper for the technical derivations and the other mathematical details concerning the resolution of the model.

All variables represent deviations from zero-disturbance equilibrium values and are expressed in logarithms (except for interest rates and public expenditure). The subscripts *US*, *G* and *F* refer to the US, German and French economies, respectively. *EU* denotes average European variables.

Output (y) in the country j (j = *US*, *G*, *F*) is an increasing function of employment (n) and a decreasing function of a world productivity shock x, which is identically and independently distributed with zero mean (a positive value for x is an adverse shock, producing both inflation and unemployment):

$$y_j = (1 - \alpha)n_j - x \tag{A.1}$$

Labour demand is derived from the standard profit maximization condition. Denoting the nominal wage as w and the product price as p, and omitting unimportant constants, we have:

$$n_j = \frac{p_j - w_j - x}{\alpha} \tag{A.2}$$

Consumer price indices (q) are weighted averages of the prices of US, German and French goods:

$$q_{US} = (1 - \beta)p_{US} + \frac{\beta(p_G + e_G)}{2} + \frac{\beta(p_F + e_F)}{2} \tag{A.3a}$$

$$q_G = \frac{(1 - \beta)p_G}{2} + \frac{(1 - \beta)(p_F + e_F - e_G)}{2} + \beta(p_{US} - e_G) \tag{A.3b}$$

$$q_F = \frac{(1 - \beta)p_F}{2} + \frac{(1 - \beta)(p_G + e_G - e_F)}{2} + \beta(p_{US} - e_F) \tag{A.3c}$$

The nominal exchange rates e_G and e_F are the dollar prices of the Deutschmark and the French franc (an increase in e_G or e_F means that the dollar depreciates against one of the other currencies). z_G and z_F are the dollar–Deutschmark and the dollar–franc real exchange rates:

$$z_G = e_G + p_G - p_{US} \tag{A.4a}$$

$$z_F = e_F + p_F - p_{US} \tag{A.4b}$$

Demand for all goods depends on output, competitiveness (real exchange rates), real interest rates (r) and government spending (g):

$$2y_{US} = 2(1 - \beta)\varepsilon y_{US} + \beta\varepsilon(y_G + y_F) + \delta(z_G + z_F) - 2(1 - \beta)\upsilon r_{US} - \beta\upsilon(r_G + r_F) + 2\eta g_{US} + (1 - \eta)(g_G + g_F) \tag{A.5a}$$

$$y_G = \frac{(1 - \beta)\varepsilon(y_G + y_F)}{2} + \beta\varepsilon y_{US} - \delta z_G - \frac{\delta(z_G - z_F)}{2} - \frac{(1 - \beta)\upsilon(r_G + r_F)}{2} - \beta\upsilon r_{US} + \frac{\eta(g_G + g_F)}{2} + (1 - \eta)g_{US} \tag{A.5b}$$

$$y_F = \frac{(1 - \beta)\varepsilon(y_G + y_F)}{2} + \beta\varepsilon y_{US} - \delta z_F + \frac{\delta(z_G - z_F)}{2} - \frac{(1 - \beta)\upsilon(r_G + r_F)}{2} - \beta\upsilon r_{US} + \frac{\eta(g_G + g_F)}{2} + (1 - \eta)g_{US} \tag{A.5c}$$

The real interest rate in the country j ($j = US, G, F$) is (with i the nominal interest rate, and the subscript '+ 1' indicating the expected value of a variable tomorrow on the basis of information available today):

$$r_j = i_j - q_{j_{+1}} + q_j \tag{A.6}$$

Uncovered interest parity holds:

$$i_{US} = i_G + e_{G_{+1}} - e_G \tag{A.7a}$$
$$i_{US} = i_F + e_{F_{+1}} - e_F \tag{A.7b}$$

The demand for money balances increases with the level of output and falls with the interest rate in each country (j = *US, G, F*):

$$m_j - p_j = y_j - \lambda i_j \tag{A.8}$$

where m is the money supply.

We consider in addition the trade balance (d) between the European Union and the United States. Following Kébabdjian (1996), it depends on incomes and on the dollar-euro real exchange rate ($d_{EU} < 0$ representing a European trade deficit):

$$d_{US} = -d_{EU} = \beta\varepsilon(y_{EU} - y_{US}) + \delta z_{EU} \tag{A.9}$$

with $y_{EU} = \frac{y_G + y_F}{2}$ and $z_{EU} = \frac{z_G + z_F}{2}$.

The values we assign to the structural parameters in order to simulate the stabilization game are the following: $\alpha = 0.3$, $\beta = 0.1$, $\varepsilon = 0.8$, $\delta = 0.8$, $\upsilon = 0.4$, $\eta = 0.9$ and $\lambda = 0.6$ (with $1 - \alpha$ the elasticity of output with respect to employment, β the propensity to import, ε the marginal propensity to consume, δ the elasticity of demand with respect to real exchange rates, υ the elasticity of demand with respect to *ex ante* real interest rates, η the fraction of its expenditure that each government devotes to goods produced in its own region, and λ the elasticity of money demand with respect to the interest rate).

The reduced-form equations are:

$$e_{EU} = 0.35(m_{US} - m_{EU}) - 0.34\left(g_{US} - \frac{g_G + g_F}{2}\right) \tag{A.10a}$$

$$z_{EU} = 0.11(m_{US} - m_{EU}) - 0.40\left(g_{US} - \frac{g_G + g_F}{2}\right) \tag{A.10b}$$

$$q_{US} = 0.24m_{US} - 0.02m_{EU} + 0.15g_{US} + 0.17\left(\frac{g_G + g_F}{2}\right) + 0.94x \tag{A.11a}$$

$$q_{EU} = q_G = q_F = 0.24m_{EU} - 0.02m_{US} + 0.15\left(\frac{g_G + g_F}{2}\right) + 0.17g_{US} + 0.94x \tag{A.11b}$$

$$n_{US} = 0.76m_{US} - 0.04m_{EU} + 0.64g_{US} + 0.44\left(\frac{g_G + g_F}{2}\right) - 0.22x \tag{A.12a}$$

$$n_{EU} = n_G = n_F = 0.76m_{EU} - 0.04m_{US} + 0.64\left(\frac{g_G + g_F}{2}\right) + 0.44g_{US} - 0.22x \quad \text{(A.12b)}$$

$$d_{US} = -d_{EU} = 0.04(m_{US} - m_{EU}) - 0.33\left(g_{US} - \frac{g_G + g_F}{2}\right) \quad \text{(A.13)}$$

We find the standard spillovers between the two currency zones of an increase in the money supply or of a spending cut through the exchange rate channel (that is, an appreciation of the foreign currency, which leads to disinflation and restrains activity). Notice that monetary policy has a bigger impact than fiscal policy both on prices and employment in each continent. As explained in Eichengreen and Ghironi (1997), locking the nominal exchange rate between the Deutschmark and the French franc implies the equalization *ex ante* of the inflation and unemployment rates in the two member states because the pattern of public spending is identical across the EMU.

NOTES

1. Even if the Council and the ECB have theoretically to share the management of the euro exchange rate, the latter will always have the possibility to stray from general orientations formulated by the former if price stability is called into question.
2. Eichengreen and Ghironi (1997) also consider the opposite case in which a fiscal contraction increases output by reducing distortionary taxes, as in Alesina and Tabellini (1987).
3. See Mélitz (1997) and Wyplosz (1999) for some econometric evidence on this point in Europe.
4. The various games considered here have been simulated with lower values of Ψ_g and ω_g. Quite similar results were obtained; in particular, the ranking of welfare losses under the cooperative and non-cooperative scenarios was the same. We have then chosen this large value for Ψ_g and ω_g because it seems to us more suitable to describe the fiscal decision-making process and the emphasis on balanced budgets nowadays.
5. As the European Union and the United States are two relatively closed economic areas (with a degree of openness around 10 per cent), the current account effectively depends much more on the real exchange rate than on incomes.
6. Equation (12.3d) is the approximation of the German government's reaction function. The French best-response function is directly recovered by symmetry. The EMU-wide reaction function is derived knowing that $g_G = g_F$ *ex post* (with $g_{EU} = (g_G + g_F)/2$); one obtains:

$$g_{EU} = -\ 0.090m_{EU} + 0.004m_{US} - 0.050g_{US}\ 0.023x.$$

7. Note that such a reasoning from monetary authorities might be questioned if their objective function also included the deviations of public spending. In fact central bankers might well become less restrictive if budget deficit stabilization was heavily weighted in their loss function (see for instance Artus, 1999).

8. Nevertheless the CCE is not necessarily better than the Cournot–Nash solution as regards welfare, because anticipating the response of the opponent may weaken or aggravate the interest conflict, according to the values of the parameters and target weights in the loss functions.
9. The variation conjectured by the Fed is smaller in absolute value because of the cost endured by the fiscal player when adjusting the level of public spending.
10. We can establish a connection between our result and the analysis in Beetsma and Bovenberg (1998), who show in a model incorporating commitment problems in the tradition of Barro and Gordon (1983) that monetary unification may reduce the inflation bias and the spending bias when fiscal policy remains decentralized and is chosen before monetary policy.
11. In every case, the decision-makers who do not cooperate always choose their strategy according to their reaction function under the Nash assumption (see 12.3a–12.3d).
12. Now, the optimal values of the policy instruments of the model are equal in Europe and in the rest of the world, as the cooperative process between the French and German governments amounts to considering a federal fiscal architecture in the EMU, so that the institutional differences among the two currency zones are eliminated.
13. As far as we are concerned, we think that defining a specific objective function for the central bank is already a way to capture the notion of its independence, apart from the nature of the policy game. If the central banker was really in a weak strategic position *vis-à-vis* the fiscal decision-maker, or completely dependent, there would be no reason to make such a distinction, and the monetary–fiscal mix would be fully determined according to just the government's loss function, exactly as if there was only one policy-maker.

REFERENCES

Alesina, A. and G. Tabellini (1987), 'Rules and discretion with noncoordinated monetary and fiscal policies', *Economic Inquiry*, **25** (4), 619–30.

Artus, P. (1999), 'Indépendance des banques centrales et conflits portant sur les politiques monétaire et budgétaire', *CDC Working Paper*, 1999-39/MA.

Barro, R.J. and D.B. Gordon (1983), 'Rules, discretion and reputation in a model of monetary policy', *Journal of Monetary Economics*, **12** (1), 101–21.

Beetsma, R. and A.L. Bovenberg (1998), 'Monetary union without fiscal coordination may discipline policymakers', *Journal of International Economics*, **45** (2), 239–58.

Begg, D.K., Giavazzi F. and C. Wyplosz (1997), 'Options for the future exchange rate policy of the EMU', *CEPR Occasional Paper*, No 17.

Bénassy-Quéré, A., B. Mojon and J. Pisani-Ferry (1997), 'The euro and exchange rate stability', *CEPII Working Paper*, 97-12.

Canzoneri, M.B. and D.W. Henderson (1991), *Monetary Policy in Interdependent Economies: A Game-Theoretic Approach*, Cambridge, MA: MIT Press.

Capoen, F., H. Sterdyniak and P. Villa (1994), 'Indépendance des banques centrales, politiques monétaire et budgétaire : une approche stratégique', *Revue de l'OFCE*, **50**, 65–102.

Capoen, F. and P. Villa (1996), 'La coordination interne et externe des politiques économiques: une analyse dynamique', *CEPII Working Paper*, 96-13.

Debelle, G. (1996), 'Central bank independence: a free lunch?', *IMF Working Paper*, 96-1.

Eichengreen, B. and F. Ghironi (1997), 'How will transatlantic policy interactions change with the advent of EMU?', *CEPR Discussion Paper*, 1643.

Emerson, M., D. Gros, A. Italianer, J. Pisani-Ferry and H. Reichenbach (1990), 'One market, one money', *European Economy*, **44**.

Ghironi, F. and F. Giavazzi (1997), 'Out in the sunshine? Outsiders, insiders and the United States in 1998', *CEPR Discussion Paper*, 1547.

Goodhart, C. (1993), 'The external dimension of EMU', *Louvain Economic Review*, **59** (1–2), 65–80.

Hughes Hallett, A. and M.L. Petit (1990), 'Cohabitation or forced marriage? A study of the costs of failing to coordinate fiscal and monetary policies', *Weltwirtschaftliches Archiv*, **126** (4), 662–90.

Johnson, C. (1994), 'Fiscal and monetary policy in economic and monetary union', in A. Duff, J. Pinder and R. Price (eds), *Maastricht and Beyond: Building the European Union*, London: Routledge, 71–83.

Kébabdjian, G. (1996), 'Les implications macro-économiques extérieures d'une monnaie unique en Europe', *Louvain Economic Review*, **62** (2), 155–89.

Kenen, P.B. (1993), 'EMU, exchange rates and the international monetary system', *Louvain Economic Review*, **59** (1–2), 257–81.

Mélitz, J. (1997), 'Some cross-country evidence about debt, deficits and the behaviour of monetary and fiscal authorities', *CEPR Discussion Paper*, 1653.

Petit, M.L. (1989), 'Fiscal and monetary policy coordination: a differential game approach', *Journal of Applied Econometrics*, **4** (2), 161–79.

Rogoff, K. (1985), 'The optimal degree of commitment to an intermediate monetary target', *Quarterly Journal of Economics*, **100** (4), 1169–89.

van Aarle, B. (1996), *Essays on Monetary and Fiscal Policy Interaction: Applications to EMU and Eastern Europe*, PhD Dissertation, Centre for Economic Research, Tilburg University, No. 24.

Villa, P. (1995), 'Policy-mix et indépendance des banques centrales', *Economie internationale*, **61**, 71–97.

Wyplosz, C. (1999), 'Economic policy coordination in EMU: strategies and institutions', *CEPII Working Paper*, 99-04.

13. Fiscal policy and war of attrition: the case of Latin American countries

Jean-Pierre Allégret and Marie-Noëlle Cales

INTRODUCTION

If monetary policy credibility has been the object of a large debate in the literature, it is not the case for fiscal policy credibility. Yet the analysis of the conduct of fiscal policy has been renewed in two directions. On the one hand, the Stability and Growth Pact in the European Union has showed the importance of the policy mix in a monetary union. On the other hand, studies on stabilization plans in Latin America – for instance Ter-Minassian and Schwartz (1997); Calvo and Végh (1998) – have stressed that the control of fiscal balances is an essential condition in the success of these plans. Monetary policy is not the only factor of inflation control. Indeed as demonstrated in numerous empirical studies, there is a long-term relationship between fiscal unbalances and inflation. To stabilize the expectation of inflation by the private agents, the authorities have to stabilize fiscal balances.

In this chapter we study fiscal policy credibility by focusing on the stabilization of the fiscal balance. Since the early 1990s, Latin American countries have displayed strong fiscal consolidation. But as noticed by Ter-Minassian and Schwartz (1997, p. 10), the common characteristic of these countries 'is perhaps the fact that they all failed to signal convincingly a fundamental change of the economic policy regime and therefore lacked credibility'. The main implication of the fiscal adjustment is to induce pro-cyclical fiscal policies which destabilize output. From our point of view such behaviour by authorities results from the necessity for governments to obtain reputation gains. Indeed past fiscal policies had been marked by a bias in favour of public spending. From this perspective, fiscal authorities have to convince the private agents, which don't know the type of these authorities ('weak' or 'strong') in the economy, that they have changed their behaviour. Taking into account past behaviours, the private agents are prone to disbelieve the commitment of the fiscal authorities. Pro-cyclical policies are interpreted as follows: the fiscal authorities want to show their degree of commitment in favour of fiscal stabilization. The question is then to determine this level of commitment by considering the trade-off between reputation gains and output loss. Otherwise it seems to us that the main problem is to determine if the fiscal authorities will renounce first, that is to say will abandon the fiscal adjustment, or if the private agents will change their inflation expectations in a consistent direction with the new government behaviour.

The remainder of the chapter is organized as follows. The first section analyses the main fiscal indicators in Latin American countries. The next section shows that the main difficulty encountered by the fiscal authorities is their credibility. The third section presents a credibility model of fiscal policy based on the interaction between the authorities and the private agents behaviours. This model allows us to study the previous trade-off.

FISCAL INDICATORS IN LATIN AMERICA AND INDUSTRIALIZED COUNTRIES

Firstly, the evolution of fiscal balances is analysed. Secondly, the pro-cyclical characteristic of fiscal policy in Latin American countries is stressed.

Main Fiscal Balances Indicators[1]

As shares of GDP, Table 13.1 shows that the fiscal situation in Latin American countries is not worse than in industrialized countries. This is due to the fiscal consolidation working since the end of the 1980s. The improvement of fiscal situation in the first group of countries contrasts with the worsening observed in the second group.

A better indicator of fiscal situation is the ratio of surplus total to total revenue. This ratio refers to the ability of a country to service its debt. As a share of tax revenues, fiscal unbalances appear more important in Latin America than in industrialized countries. Latin American economies have a limited capacity to raise revenues over a long period: in percentage of GDP, tax revenues evolved from 20.4 per cent over the 1970–79 period to 23.2 per cent over the 1990–95 period. In industrialized countries, the ratio evolved from 39.5 per cent to 49.6 per cent respectively. Such situation suggests a long-run vulnerability of Latin American countries in case of negative macroeconomic shocks.

The volatility of fiscal indicators in Latin American economies is a significant difference relative to industrialized countries (Table 13.2). Is such volatility the result of a fiscal composition tilted towards more volatile

Table 13.1 Main fiscal indicators in Latin America and industrialized countries (%)

		1970–95	1970–79	1980–89	1990–95
Total surplus / GDP	*Latin America*	−1.4	−1.3	−2.4	0.5
	Industrialized Countries	−2.5	−0.8	−3.3	−4.1
Total surplus / Total revenue	Latin America	−10.6	−9.5	−17.3	1.4
	Industrialized Countries	−6.5	−3.1	−8.5	−9.2
Primary surplus / GDP	*Latin America*	1.3	−0.3	1.0	3.6
	Industrialized Countries	−0.4	−0.0	−0.5	−0.8
Primary surplus / Total revenue	*Latin America*	1.1	−3.2	−2.1	14.0
	Industrialized Countries	−1.3	−0.8	−1.7	−1.7

Source: Gavin and Perotti (1997), p. 19.

Table 13.2 Volatility of fiscal indicators in Latin America and industrialized countries (Average standard deviation (%))*

		1970–95	1970–79	1980–89	1990–95
Total surplus	*Latin America*	3.3	2.0	3.8	2.4
	Industrialized Countries	1.6	1.5	1.5	1.3
Primary surplus	*Latin America*	3.3	2.0	3.7	2.9
	Industrialized Countries	1.6	1.5	1.5	1.4
Total revenue	*Latin America*	12.2	9.8	12.9	9.1
	Industrialized Countries	3.6	3.4	2.8	3.5
Total expenditures	*Latin America*	12.8	9.0	14.9	9.0
	Industrialized Countries	3.1	3.0	2.3	2.5

Note: * Total surplus and primary surplus: standard deviation of first differences of GDP shares.

Source: Gavin and Perotti (1997), p. 23.

components? The answer is negative: industrialized countries spend more on a highly volatile component, transfers, than Latin American countries (48.2 per cent and 27.8 per cent respectively).

From the viewpoint of fiscal policy credibility, the important point is to determine if this volatility is due to the macroeconomic volatility. This latter is two or three times higher in Latin America than in industrialized countries (Gavin et al., 1996). Despite the difficulty in obtaining precise tests, Gavin and Perroti (1997) consider that the volatility of fiscal indicators is more than a passive response to macroeconomic fluctuations.[2] Thus fiscal policy is the object of a high volatility which does not only result from the intrinsic instability of Latin American economies. In this context, can fiscal policy exert a stabilizing effect on the economy?

A Pro-cyclical Fiscal Policy in Latin America

From a neoclassical perspective, the intertemporal budget constraint is enforced when the path of public spending is consistent with the path of revenues. More precisely, the sequence of present values of the former must be equal to the sequence of the present values of the latter. In order to avoid suboptimal distortions, taxes must be constant during the business cycle. Thus the respect of the intertemporal budget constraint and optimal taxation rule imply that fiscal unbalances must evolve in concert with the cycle: increasing during recession periods and decreasing during expansion periods. As a result, co-movements between fiscal indicators and business cycles are weak.[3] In fact, as shown in Table 13.3, fiscal indicators in Latin American economies have a pro-cyclical behaviour.

In OECD countries, fiscal surpluses exert a stabilizing effect in the economy: a one percentage point increase in the GDP growth rate is associated with an increase in the fiscal surplus of 0.25 percentage points of GDP.[4] In Latin American countries, the response is weaker: the primary surplus increases four times less. This result suggests a weak stabilizing effect of fiscal policy. Table 13.3 shows that the weak stabilizing effect of fiscal policy does not result from a smaller sensitivity of total revenue. It is due to the stronger pro-cyclical response of public spending to a rise of GDP (0.61 points) than in OECD countries. In the long run, we observe that fiscal policy in Latin America exerts a destabilizing macroeconomic influence. This point is very clear when we compare the responses of fiscal surplus during expansion and recession periods (Table 13.4).

Table 13.3 Cyclical response of fiscal indicators in Latin America and OECD

Impact of real GDP growth:	OECD	Latin America
Total surplus (% of GDP)	0.25	0.08
Primary surplus	0.22	0.05
Total revenue (% change)	0.84	1.32
Total expenditures (% change)	0.09	0.61

Source: Gavin et al. (1996), p. 13.

Table 13.4 Responses of fiscal balance to GDP growth in good times and bad

	High growth periods		Low growth periods	
	OECD	*Latin America*	*OECD*	*Latin America*
Total surplus	0.174	0.154	0.611	−0.022
Primary surplus	0.136	0.123	0.580	−0.049

Source: Gavin et al. (1996), p. 14.

Table 13.4 exhibits the impact of a one percentage point increase in real GDP on surplus balance in percentage of GDP. A positive number means that fiscal policy exerts a stabilizing effect. In OECD countries it appears that the fiscal response is higher in recession periods than in expansion. An opposite tendency emerges in Latin American countries: fiscal policy is pro-cyclical in recession periods. The pro-cyclical characteristic of fiscal policy is stronger if we consider only major recession periods.[5] While in OECD major recessions lead to high fiscal deficit, it is not the case in Latin America. More precisely, a cumulative decline in real GDP of 3.3 per cent is associated with a change in total surplus (as share of GDP) of –3 per cent (–2.3 per cent for the primary surplus) in OECD countries. In Latin American economies, a cumulative decline in real GDP of 10.7 per cent leads to a change in total surplus of 1.6 per cent (1.8 per cent for the primary surplus).

Overall, as noticed by Gavin and Perotti (1997, p. 35), 'recessions are associated with exaggerated collapses in public spending'. Such a reaction by fiscal authorities is linked to the lack of credibility of fiscal policy.

FISCAL POLICY CREDIBILITY IN LATIN AMERICAN COUNTRIES

Calvo and Vegh (1998) recalled that Latin American countries with stabilization plans experienced accommodative economic policies. As a consequence, temporary inflation shocks became permanent shocks. Past reactions – for example before the 1990s – of fiscal policy played a decisive influence on these inflationary pressures. More precisely, economic policy is time inconsistent if the government cannot control its public debt. Indeed in such situations government is tempted to repudiate its debt (Calvo, 1988). This strategic behaviour is due to the costs for the government associated with an increase in tax. When public debt is not indexed on inflation, any inflation surprise engendered by the central bank is equivalent to a repudiation of debt: its real value is lower than its nominal value.[6] The credibility problem of fiscal policy in Latin America is explained by two main factors: on the one hand, the access constraint of these countries to international capital markets; on the other hand, institutional constraints.

The Pro-cyclical Fiscal Policy: A Signal Towards International Capital Markets

The pro-cyclical fiscal policy is a reaction of authorities to the unstable access of their economy to international capital markets. According to Gavin et al. (1996, p. 7), this unstable access is the reflection of the fragility of their creditworthiness. On the one hand, since the early 1980s international capital flows have been marked by massive boom-and-bust cycles. Capital flows to Latin American countries are particularly sensitive to US interest rates changes. The changes in country-risk evaluations by credit rating agencies are a good approximation of the difficulties encountered by Latin American countries in international capital markets. Indeed major currency devaluation and currency crises are followed by a downgrade of the score in emerging economies slightly higher than for developed countries. According to Calvo and Reinhart (2000), this downgrade is about five times greater than for industrialized countries. The differences between the post-crisis scores are higher between the two groups of countries than before. This result suggests a strong difference between them to access to international capital markets. On the other hand, short-run effects of currency depreciations in emerging economies are very different than those in developed countries. In the first group, they are followed by a sudden stop of capital inflows which induces official reserves losses and brutal current account adjustment. As a result, aggregate demand falls to allow this adjustment.

In such a context, any economic policy susceptible to decreasing the confidence of international investors, for instance a fiscal deficit to stabilize the economy after a negative shock, is rejected by the authorities, even if this policy could be optimal from the short-term stabilization viewpoint. In 1995, Mexican and Argentinean reactions were a good illustration of such behaviour. They adopted pro-cyclical fiscal policy despite the recession in order to safeguard the confidence of international investors.

The Pro-cyclical Fiscal Policy: A Consequence of Institutional Constraints

In the 1990s, numerous studies dedicated to fiscal policy in Latin America have suggested that fiscal outcomes depend on an institutional framework

Table 13.5 Current account adjustments and GDP growth before and after a currency crisis

Country group	T−1	T, currency crisis year	T+1	Change from T−1 to T+1
Current account deficit as % of GDP				
Emerging markets	−1.46	−3.97	−1.39	3.47
Developed countries	−2.84	−3.06	−2.10	0.74
Difference	−1.62	−0.91	0.71	2.73**
% change in real GDP				
Emerging markets	3.61	1.27	1.62	−1.99
Developed countries	1.73	1.49	1.58	−0.15
Difference	1.88**	−0.22	0.04	−1.84**

Note: ** Significance at the 5% level.

Source: Calvo and Reinhart (2000), p. 18.

tilted towards chronicle fiscal deficits. As a consequence, in this group of countries, the stake is to elaborate an institutional architecture promoting fiscal authorities discipline. Thus budget procedures[7] exert a significant influence on fiscal outcomes.

Three main institutional arrangements should be more conducive to fiscal discipline. First, law could be implemented to establish *ex ante* constraints on deficits. We can refer here to balanced budget rules and to legislative ceilings on borrowing capacity of the government imposed *ex ante*. The main drawback of such rules is to limit the capacity of reaction of the authorities when major negative shocks occur. It is then possible to propose a contingent budget rule which includes an escape clause linked to bad states of nature. But the complexity of such arrangement limits its credibility (simple rules are better).[8] A second potential means to promote fiscal discipline is hierarchical procedures by opposition to collegial procedures. These two institutional frameworks concern, on the one hand, the respective role of central government and parliament to take fiscal decisions; and on the other hand the weight of the Finance Ministry in the definition of fiscal orientations. In this perspective, the fiscal discipline is stronger the more the Finance Ministry has significant power and the more the central government exerts an influence on fiscal decision to the detriment of the legislative power. Third, transparency should favour fiscal discipline. According to the theory of fiscal illusion, private agents overestimate the benefits of public spending and, at the same time, underestimate the current and future costs of taxation. The lack of fiscal procedures transparency has two consequences. On the one hand, the fiscal illusion of private agents increases. On the other hand, the government has an incentive to increase the deficit bias.

Empirical studies which include institutional variables to estimate fiscal deficits confirm the theoretical relationship between budget procedures and budget balances (Alesina et al., 1999). Overall it appears that fiscal policy credibility, as for monetary policy credibility, must be built over time. The question is now to identify how authorities could convince private agents to adopt a new behaviour.

THE CHANGE IN REGIME OF THE FISCAL POLICY

We interpret the new fiscal strategy in Latin America as a change in regime where authorities have to build their credibility. The important point is to explain why authorities conduct pro-cyclical fiscal policy in recession periods. It seems to us that strategic interactions between them and private agents are the main justification explaining such behaviour. More precisely, authorities must convince private agents about their resolution to fight inflation in reducing fiscal imbalances. In this context restrictive policies, particularly in recession times, can be interpreted by the proof that the degree of commitment of authorities is high. The problem is that such behaviour is suboptimal in the long run because the social costs are high. The question is then to explain why private agents do not immediately believe authorities and how the game between the two actors ends. In fact we interpret pro-cyclical fiscal policies as a result of war of attrition between authorities and private agents. After briefly reviewing the relevant literature we consider the Argentine crisis in 2000–2002 as a case of war of attrition. We present a model which explains this situation.

Change in Regime and War of Attrition: A Brief Review of the Literature

Our model is based on two main literatures: on the one hand, a change in regime, and on the other, war of attrition.

Backus and Driffill (1985) study disinflationary monetary policies following a change in regime. Very often, the authorities who adopt such policies follow brutal and painful strategies – costly in terms of macroeconomic stabilization – instead of more gradual policies. According to Backus and Drifill, the authorities' strategy is due to the interaction between monetary policy credibility and wage demands in the private sector. More precisely, when an inflationary bias was strong in the past, there is no reason for the private agents to believe the new and sudden commitment of the authorities to fight inflation. So they continue to demand wage increases in nominal terms. As a result the authorities have to conduct more restrictive policies in order to convince the private agents about the credibility of the new monetary policy. This game describes both a change in regime and a war of attrition between public authorities and private agents. The final outcome of this game depends on the capacity of authorities to resist inflationary pressures by private agents. Such a situation is well adapted to the Latin American case where private agents hesitate to believe in the new fiscal policy. They test authorities over several periods, in maintaining high inflation expectation, because of the high weight of public debt and the temptation for authorities to sustain output in recession times.

The canonical war of attrition model was put forward by Alesina and Drazen (1991). The authors describe an economy in which large fiscal deficits are such that they imply an explosive path of the public debt and an increase in inflation. Thus the current policy is unsustainable. In this context the authorities have to bring in a stabilization plan immediately. Indeed the sooner the country adopts an adjustment plan – increasing taxes – the lower the cost of this plan. Even if delays in stabilization are inefficient, the authorities do not adopt reforms immediately. Why? According to Alesina and Drazen, the main explanation is the heterogeneity of the population. More specifically, a fiscal reform implies distributional conflicts between different socio-economic groups which wage a war of attrition between them. Both groups will improve their welfare after the reform, but they disagree about how the burden of the policy change is to be shared between them. Each group has an incentive to wait, because the group which concedes first will shoulder the major share of the burden. At the same time, fighting is costly.

The model describes a game of incomplete information. Thus each group must choose a time to concede if the opposing group has not already done so. For a particular group, the choice of the moment to concede depends on its costs and pay-offs (its type), on the distribution of its opponent's possible type, and on knowing that its opponent is solving the same problem of choice. The fighting cost changes over time. At the beginning of the war of attrition, it is low because there is some probability that the opponent's type is such that he will concede first.

If the opponent does not concede, it provides information on how strong he is. Thus the cost of fighting increases for the other group, which reconsiders its beliefs about the interest the opponent might have in adopting the reform. In equilibrium, the time for concession occurs when the cost of remaining in the fight for longer is just equal to the gain expected from remaining in it. When a group concedes, a change in policy is implemented. Such war of attrition model has been extended in several directions.

Casella and Eichengreen (1996) study the importance of timing foreign aid for the expected time of stabilization. They show that the earlier the foreign aid is transferred, the earlier the stabilization plan. But if the aid is only announced and not transferred, stabilization reform can be postponed. Carré (2000) considers a model of fiscal reform in which there is an exogenous date – a deadline – at which the reform must be adopted. If no reform is adopted at this date, both groups will bear an extra cost. It appears that the higher the extra cost is, the higher the probability of stabilizing before that date will be. Allsopp (2000) uses a war of attrition framework to explain the duration of the exchange rate crisis of the European Exchange Rate Mechanism in 1992. When a speculative attack is launched, governments[9] endure pre-stabilization losses which are functions of the costs imposed by sterilization policy. The attack can be stopped only if one of the governments undertakes a fundamental change in policy. This government will bear a utility loss in excess. Thus, as in the Alesina and Drazen's model, each government has an incentive to wait if it expects that the opponent will concede first. The timing of the collapse of an exchange rate regime depends on the optimal time of concession for each government.

Is Argentina a War of Attrition Situation?

In December 2001, the currency board arrangement which fixed a parity between the Argentine peso and the US dollar collapsed. For the Argentine economy, it appeared to face the threat of the return of hyperinflation. How to explain this apparently brutal and unpredictable collapse?

In April 1991, in order to stop hyperinflation, Argentina established a Convertibility Plan which strictly limited domestic money creation under a currency board. As usual with exchange rate stabilization, inflation decreased dramatically. The Convertibility Plan was a success: on the one hand, the Argentine economy recovered immediately after the Plan; on the other, the currency board resisted the Tequila crisis in 1995.

In fact, the Convertibility Plan has been only a part of the stabilization process of the Argentine economy. Indeed the Argentine authorities have to control the evolution of fiscal balance in order to avoid any inflationary financing of public spending. If inflation has been stabilized since 1991, Table 13.6 shows that it is not the case for public sector operations. The overall balance of the consolidated public sector went from a deficit of – 2.1 per cent of GDP in 1997 to a deficit of – 3.6 per cent in 2000. Public debt in percentage of GDP rose from 38.1 per cent in 1997 to 49.7 per cent in 2000 while external public debt increased from 25.5 per cent of GDP

Table 13.6 Argentine public sector operation: some indicators (in % of GDP)

	1991	1992	1993	1994	1995	1996	1997	1998	1999	2000
Federal government										
Primary balance	0.2	1.2	2.0	0.7	0.1	−0.8	0.4	0.9	0.4	0.9
Interest payments	2.6	1.5	1.1	1.2	1.5	1.2	2.0	2.2	2.9	3.4
Overall balance	−2.5	−0.2	0.9	−0.5	−1.4	−2.5	−1.6	−1.3	−2.5	−2.4
Provincial governments										
Primary balance	−0.6	−0.1	−0.6	−0.6	−1.0	−0.3	−0.1	−0.4	−1.1	−0.5
Interest payments	0.1	0.2	0.2	0.2	0.3	0.4	0.4	0.4	0.5	0.6
Overall balance	−0.8	−0.2	−0.8	−0.9	−1.3	−0.7	−0.5	−0.8	−1.6	−1.2
Public sector debt										
Total	35.8	30.8	30.1	32.1	36.3	38.5	38.1	41.3	47.3	49.7

Source: International Monetary Fund.

to 32.0 per cent over the same period. In August 1999, Argentina enacted a Fiscal Responsibility Law which has been interpreted by the International Monetary Fund as the second pillar of the stabilization programme.[10]

This law sets limits to the government debt and aligns the growth of current public expenditure with that of the GDP. The Fiscal Responsibility Law establishes penalties on civil servants that fail to implement the budget and calls for mid-year congressional hearings on its implementation. The law also improves fiscal transparency by prohibiting the creation of extra budgetary funds and by requiring a detailed published account of the implementation of the budget.

The Fiscal Responsibility Law has been strengthened by two complementary measures. In November 2000 the government established a federal pact with the provinces over the years 2001–2005. The pact contains federal transfers to the provinces and keeps primary spending in the provinces in deficit, at a level no higher than in 2000. Primary spending is frozen until budget balance is reached. The pact also commits the provinces to introduce their own fiscal responsibility laws. This federal pact is a response to the inability of the central government to control the provincial governments' operations. Indeed the provinces have the initiative for public spending, but it is the central government that is in charge of raising revenue and repaying debt. Under such a regime of fiscal irresponsibility, the provincial governments have a structural deficit (Table 13.6). Then in July 2001 the Argentine authorities enacted a zero-deficit law with a view to reaching equilibrium in 2003. In fact, these new fiscal laws were unable to prevent the collapse of the peso in 2002 because of their lack of credibility.

Figure 13.1 exhibits that the fiscal laws were implemented in a context of recession linked both to external shocks (the Tequila crisis in 1995; the Asian crisis in 1997 and the 1999 devaluation of the Brazilian real) and domestic reasons. As a result, the authorities faced an impossible trade-off between avoiding a significant contractionary fiscal impulse and meeting the announced fiscal targets. In 2001, the Argentine authorities decided on an important spending cuts package reinforcing the pro-cyclical impulse of fiscal policy. Investment contracted by 23 per cent over the years 2000–2001. The essential question is to determine if the fiscal situation in Argentina is the result of a significant loosening of fiscal policy or not. More precisely, are fiscal pacts credible?

According to Weisbrot (2002), the Argentine fiscal situation results from a succession of external shocks which increased interest rates. Indeed, Table 13.6 shows that the interest payments in percentage of GDP increased dramatically during the 1990s. At the same time, government spending, excluding interest, were stable throughout the period at around 20 per cent of GDP. On the revenue side, the economic slowdown reduced the tax revenue. It is difficult to ignore such developments. Table 13.6 reveals that the primary balance of the federal government deteriorates less than the overall balance which includes interest payments.

At the same time, as stressed by Figure 13.1, it appears that Argentine authorities were unable to improve the fiscal balance during expansion periods. Despite the recession due to the 1995 Tequila crisis, Argentina's real GDP progressed at an annual average rate of almost 4.4 per cent between 1993 and 1998. Over the same period the overall balance of the federal government does not improve significantly.

Overall, the Argentine fiscal policy during the 1990s is characterized by a deficit bias. As a consequence any fiscal pact aimed at reaching fiscal balance could not be credible immediately. This lack of credibility exerts an increasing pressure on interest rates, downgrading the fiscal situation.

In the following paragraph, we suggest that the Argentine situation, and more generally the pro-cyclical fiscal policy in Latin America, can be explained in the spirit of Backus and Drifill (1985) and Alesina and Drazen (1991).

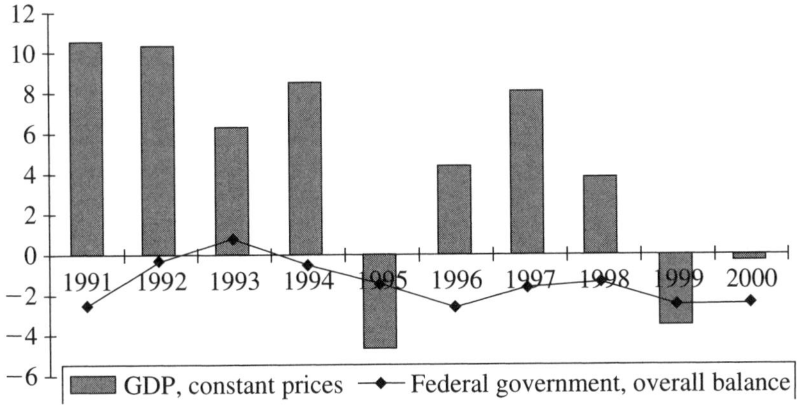

Source: International Monetary Fund.

Figure 13.1 Argentina: consolidated public sector balance in % of GDP and real GDP, 1991–2000

The Model

We interpret a game with incomplete information. Private agents do not know if authorities intend to follow a restrictive or an expansionary fiscal policy. Authorities do not know the intransigence degree of private agents when they bargain their nominal wages. Such a game is based on different preferences between actors. Authorities have an aversion to inflation and wishes to reduce fiscal imbalances, but at the same time they could stabilize the output in generating inflation surprise. Private agents are only averse to inflation.

Assumptions

The framework of the model is the following:

1. the authorities have a quadratic loss function with three targets: inflation rate (π_t), growth (y_t), and public spending (g_t) (equation 13.1);
2. the authorities take care of the public finance balance (g_t) but they are averse to an increase in taxes ($\tau_t = \bar{\tau}$) (equation 13.3);
3. the supply function is an expectations-augmented Phillips curve (equation 13.2);
4. public spending has a partial effect on the output level which is measured by δ.

Three equations are deduced from these hypotheses:

$$l_t^G = \frac{a_t}{2}\pi_t^2 + \frac{b}{2}(y_t - y^*)^2 + \frac{1}{2}g_t^2 \tag{13.1}$$

$$y_t = \pi_t - \pi_t^e + \delta g_t - \bar{\tau} \tag{13.2}$$

$$g_t + d_{t-1}(1 + i_t - \pi_t) = d_t + \pi_t + \bar{\tau} \tag{13.3}$$

The loss function of private agents is as follows:

$$l_t^P = \frac{1}{2}(\pi_t - \pi_t^e)^2 + \frac{A_t}{2}\pi_t^2 \tag{13.4}$$

At each period, authorities choose α_t, the norm of progression of debt at t, and the inflation rate. The debt at t can then be written as: $d_t = \alpha_t d_{t-1}$, and $d_t = \alpha_t d$. Authorities choose debt at t in order not only to reimburse debt of the preceding period but also to finance public spending in the current period.[11] The budget constraint is rewritten as:

$$g_t + d(1 + r_t - \pi_t + \pi_t^e) = \alpha_t d + \pi_t + \bar{\tau} \tag{13.5}$$

with $i_t = r_t + \pi_t^e$, the Fisher equation.

The behaviours of agents

Four cases are distinguished according to the interaction between the behaviours adopted by actors:

- the authorities follow, or not, restrictive monetary and fiscal policies;
- the private agents believe, or not, in the authorities commitment to fight inflation in the long run.

	Authorities concede	Authorities do not concede
Private agents do not concede	$l(D,d)$	$l(R,d)$
Private agents concede	$l(D,r)$	$l(R,r)$

where D and R represent discretionary or rigorous policies respectively; d and r are expectations formed by the private agents.

Thus private agents' expectations constitute an estimate of the credibility of the policies and of the authorities' reputation, that is their determination to follow rigorous policies.

The following equations present the government's (l^G) and the private agents (l^P) loss functions according the four previous cases:

Case 1: The authorities concede – the private agents do not concede

$$l^G(D,d) = \frac{b}{2}[\delta^2(\Delta + B)^2 + \tau^2(\delta - 1)^2 + y^{*2} + 2\delta(\Delta + B)\tau(\delta - 1) - 2\delta(\Delta + B)y^*$$
$$- 2\tau(\delta - 1)y^*] + \frac{1}{2}[(\Delta + B)^2 + \tau^2 + 2(\Delta + B)\tau] + \frac{a}{2}B^2 \qquad (13.6)$$

$$l^P(D,d) = \frac{A}{2}B^2 \qquad (13.6')$$

Case 2: The authorities concede – the private agents do not concede

$$l^G(D,r) = \frac{a}{2}B^2 + \frac{b}{2}[l^G(D,r) = \frac{a}{2}B^2 + \frac{b}{2}[B^2 + \delta^2(\Delta + dB + B)^2$$
$$+ \tau^2(\delta - 1)^2 + y^{*2} + 2B\delta(\Delta + dB + B) + 2B\tau(\delta - 1) - 2By^*$$
$$+ 2\delta(\Delta + dB + B)\tau(d - 1) - 2\delta(\Delta + dB + B)y^* - 2\tau(\delta - 1)y^*]$$
$$+ \frac{1}{2}[(\Delta - dB + B)^2 + \tau^2 + 2\tau(\Delta - dB + B)] \qquad (13.7)$$

$$l^P(D,r) = \frac{B^2}{2}(1 + A) \qquad (13.7')$$

Case 3: The authorities do not concede – the private agents concede

$$l^G(R,d) = \frac{b}{2}[B^2 + \delta^2(D - dB)^2 + \tau^2(\delta - 1)^2 + y^{*2} - 2B\delta(D - dB)$$
$$- 2B\tau(\delta - 1) + 2By^* + 2\delta(D - dB)\tau(\delta - 1) - 2\delta(D - dB)y^*$$
$$- 2\tau(\delta - 1)y^*] + \frac{1}{2}[(D - dB)^2 + \tau^2 + 2(D - dB)\tau] \qquad (13.8)$$

$$l^P(R,d) = \frac{B^2}{2} \qquad (13.8')$$

Case 4: The authorities do not concede – the private agents do not concede

$$l^G(R,r) = \frac{b}{2}[\delta^2 D^2 + \tau^2(\delta - 1)^2 + y^{*2} + 2\delta D\tau(\delta - 1) - 2\delta Dy^*$$
$$- 2\tau y^*(\delta - 1)] + \frac{1}{2}[D^2 + \tau^2 + 2D\tau] \qquad (13.9)$$

$$l^P(R,r) = 0 \tag{13.9'}$$

with $B = \dfrac{b(y^* + \tau)}{a(b\delta^2 + 1)}$, $D = d(\alpha_D - 1 - i)$ and $\Delta = d(\alpha_R - 1 - i)$

The resolution of the model

Following Alesina and Drazen's approach, we calculate the intertemporal utility function of the two agents in function of the optimal time for concession T. The agent who concedes first is called 'loser', the opponent 'winner'. The lost functions of the private agents are:

$$L^{PW}(T) = \int_0^T l^P(R,d)(x)e^{-rx}dx + e^{-rT}l^P(R,r)(T) \tag{13.10}$$

$$L^{PL}(T) = \int_0^T l^P(R,d)(x)e^{-rx}dx + e^{-rT}l^P(D,d)(T) \tag{13.11}$$

Equation (13.12) is the expected utility as of time zero as a function of one's chosen concession time T. It is the sum of L^{GL} multiplied by the probability of one's opponent conceding at t for $t < T_i$ and L^{GW} multiplied by the probability of one's opponent not having conceded by T.

$$EL(T) = [1 - H(T)]L^{PL}(T) + \int_0^T L^{PW}(x)h(x)dx \tag{13.12}$$

$$EU(T) = [1 - H(T)] \times \left[\int_0^T l^P(R,d)(x)^{-rx}dx + e^{-rT}L^P(R,r)(T)\right]$$

$$+ \int_0^T \left[\int_0^x l^P(R,d)(z)e^{-rz}dz + e^{-rx}L^P(R,r)(x)\right]h(x)dx$$

where $H(T)$ is the distribution of an opponent's optimal time for concession and $h(T)$ the associated density function.

Then, by substitution of (13.10) and (13.11) in (13.12), we obtain the following equation:

$$\frac{dEU}{dT} = e^{-rT}\begin{Bmatrix} \frac{h(T)}{r}[l^P(R,r)(T) - l^P(D,d)(T)] + [1 - H(T)] \\ \left[l^P(R,d)(T) - l^P(D,d)(T) + \frac{dl^P(D,d)(T)}{dT} \right] \end{Bmatrix} \quad (13.13)$$

Equations (13.10), (13.11), (13.12) and (13.13) can be rewritten for the government.

It is possible to find optimal time for concession for the private agents by finding the value of T, that maximizes equation (13.13). Differentiating (13.13) with respect to T and setting the resulting expression equal to zero gives:

$$\frac{dEU}{dT} = e^{-rT}h(T)\left[-\frac{A}{2r}B^2 \right] + e^{-rT}[1 - H(T)]\left[\frac{B^2}{2} - \frac{A}{2}B^2 \right] = 0 \quad (13.14)$$

Differentiating with respect to A gives:

$$\frac{d^2EU}{dTdA} = e^{-rT}\left[h(T)\left(-\frac{1}{2}B^2 \right) + (1 - H(T))\left(-\frac{1}{2}B^2 \right) \right] < 0 \quad (13.15)$$

The optimal concession time T is monotonically decreasing in A, so it defines the relationship between $H(T)$ which is unknown and $F(A)$ which is known:

$$1 - H(T) = F(A) \quad (13.16)$$

Differentiating this gives:

$$-h[T(A)]T'(A) = f(A) \quad (13.17)$$

The optimal conceding time function is then given by:

$$-\frac{f(A)}{F(A)T'(A)}\left[\frac{AB^2}{2\ r} \right] = \left[\frac{B^2}{2} - \frac{AB^2}{2} \right] \quad (13.18)$$

We can now understand the nature of the optimal strategy for the private agents. The right-hand side is the cost of waiting another period to concede.

The left-hand side denotes the expected gain of waiting another period to concede. Equation (13.18) may be rewritten:

$$-\frac{f(A)}{F(A)T'(A)}\left[\frac{A}{r}\right]=[1-A] \tag{13.19}$$

For simplicity, the distribution of A is assumed to be uniform between $\underline{A}$ and $\bar{A}$, so that $\dfrac{f(A)}{F(A)}=\dfrac{1}{A-\bar{A}}$. We obtain one differential equation which determines private agents attitude:

$$T'(A)=\frac{1}{r(A-\underline{A})(A-1)} \tag{13.20}$$

By solving the differential equation, we can find $T(A)$:

$$T(A)=\frac{1}{2r}\left[\ln(A-\underline{A})(A-1)+\frac{A+1}{\underline{A}-1}\ln\left[\frac{A-\underline{A}}{A-1}\right]\right] \tag{13.21}$$

The optimal time of concession only depends on A, the private agents' aversion to inflation. By using the same method, it is possible to determine the condition which gives the government optimal time for concession. After some calculations and simplifications, we obtain:

$$\frac{-f(a)}{F(a)T'(a)r}\left[\frac{\beta}{a}L+G\right]=\frac{\beta}{a}M+K \tag{13.22}$$

and then we solve this differential equation:

$$T(a)=\frac{-G}{2Kr}\left\{\left[\frac{{}^{2\beta L}/_{G}+{}^{\beta M'}/_{K}+\underline{a}}{{}^{\beta M'}/_{K}-\underline{a}}\right]\ln\frac{a-{}^{\beta M'}/_{K}}{a-\underline{a}}+\ln(a-{}^{\beta M 4}/_{K})(a-\underline{a})\right\} \tag{13.23}$$

where,

$$L=\frac{\beta}{a}(b\delta^2+1)\left(\frac{1}{d^2}+1-\frac{2}{d}\right)$$

$$G=\beta+(b\delta^2+1)\left[\frac{2\beta\delta+2\tau}{d^2}+2\frac{\beta\delta-\tau}{d}\right]-2\left(\frac{1}{d}-1\right)[b\delta(\tau-y^*)+\tau]$$

$$M = \left[(b\delta^2 + 1)\left(d^2 - \frac{1}{d^2} - 1 + \frac{2}{d}\right) + b(1 + 2\delta d)\right)\right]$$

$$K = -\beta + (b\delta^2 + 1)\left\{-2(\beta\delta - \tau) - \left[\frac{2\beta\delta + 2\tau}{d^2} + 2\frac{\beta\delta - \tau}{d}\right]\right\}$$

$$+ 2\left(\frac{1}{d} - d - 1\right)(b\delta(\tau(\delta - 1) - y^*) + \tau) + b[-2\delta D - 2(\tau(\delta - 1) - y^*)]$$

and $B = \beta/a$.

This equation determines the optimal strategy for the government. Then the model is simulated by choosing values as parameters of loss functions: $\delta = 0{,}2$; $\tau = 0{,}40$; $y^* = 1$; $d = 0{,}50$; $r = 0{,}10$; $b = 0{:}80$. By choosing $\underline{a} = 1$ and $\underline{A} = 1{,}5$, we can determine the optimal time for concession for every player:

$$T(A) = 5\ln\left[\frac{(A - 1.5)^6}{(A - 1)^4}\right] \text{ for the private agents.} \tag{13.24}$$

$$T(a) = 5\ln\left[\frac{(a - 1)^{5.6}}{(a - 0.088)^{1.48}}\right] \text{ for the government.} \tag{13.25}$$

Interpretations of the model

During the period when nobody concedes, every player bear costs. But when somebody concedes, the share of the burden becomes smaller for the other player. When there are fiscal deficits implying strong pro-cyclical policies, the agents and the authorities wage a war of attrition. They know that if somebody concedes first they will have the better part of the burden to bear. The authorities have an incentive to wait and resist because they want to gain credibility and reputation. That is why they do not change their fiscal policy during a recession. But their choice depends on the agents' behaviour because they do not know when the agents will concede.

We have simulated the model in Figure 13.2.[12] The horizontal axis represents the degree of aversion to inflation and the vertical axis the number of periods of resistance.

Figure 13.2 shows that under conditions of similar aversion to inflation, the authorities resist longer than the private agents. For example, when aversion to inflation is five for the two groups of agents, the private agents concede after nine periods, and the authorities after 27 periods. But in general, the aversion to inflation is different for both private agents and authorities.

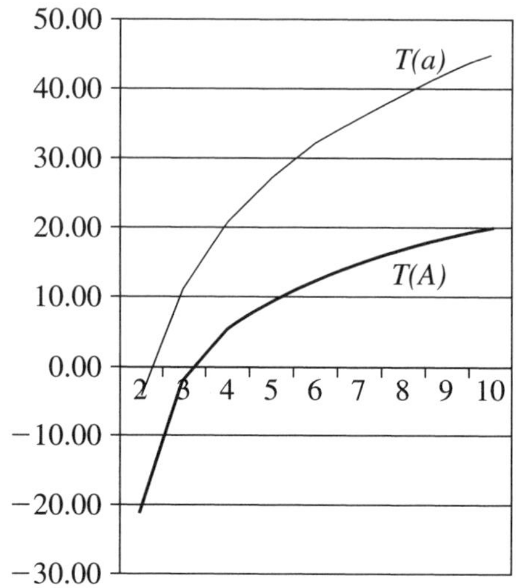

Figure 13.2 Simulation of the model

As for the private agents, the ability to resist depends on two parameters: on the one hand, their preference parameter for inflation, and on the other, their beliefs about the authorities' aversion to inflation. When the private agents have no aversion to inflation far higher than the authorities they intend to concede before: $T(A) < T(a)$. But when the private agents believe that the authorities' aversion to inflation is low, they resist, and test the authorities' resistance level. Thus our model suggests that the private agents' beliefs about the authorities' aversion to inflation is a decisive variable explaining the war of attrition.

The decisive role of the private agents' beliefs implies that history does matter. Indeed when past economic records show how chronic inflation is linked to a fiscal deficit bias, the private agents interpret the authorities' inability to respect their fiscal commitment as a decrease in their aversion to inflation. This interpretation, in turn, increases the resistance degree of the private agents. For the authorities, the costs of the war of attrition increase because they must convince the private agents that they do not renounce their commitment against inflation despite fiscal deficits. As a result, interest rates increase. If there is a strong uncertainty about the true type of the authorities, weak or strong, the private agents do not modify their beliefs and continue to resist. They do not concede during the war of attrition. So the economic situation worsens and the authorities must concede first.

CONCLUSION

In this chapter, we have modelled a war of attrition situation between private agents and authorities to explain the pro-cyclical fiscal policy observed in Latin American countries. The change in regime could be very costly because private agents doubt the credibility of the new authorities' commitment. This cost is higher the longer is the war of attrition. In such a situation, it is important to stress that both groups of agents are in a better situation if they accept the new commitment, that is a regime of low inflation. But if authorities cannot demonstrate their ability to reduce fiscal unbalances, the new commitment could be counterproductive via the war of attrition process. Our model and the stylized facts recalled in this chapter about Argentina suggest that the peso collapse at the end of 2001 can be interpreted in this manner.

APPENDIX: NUMERICAL RESULTS

	a,A	2	3	4	5	6	7	8	9	10
	T(A)	−20.79	−1.70	5.52	9.86	12.93	15.31	17.24	18.86	20.26
C=0	T(a)	−4.80	11.71	21.00	27.45	32.40	36.40	39.76	42.66	45.21
C=0.05	T(a)	−4.65	11.67	20.86	27.25	32.14	36.11	39.44	42.31	44.83
c=0.1	T(a)	−4.54	11.57	20.66	26.97	31.81	35.73	39.02	41.86	44.36
c=0.2	T(a)	−4.33	11.40	20.28	26.46	31.19	35.02	38.24	41.02	43.46
c=0.3	T(a)	−4.14	11.24	19.93	25.98	30.61	34.37	37.52	40.24	42.63

NOTES

1. In this paragraph, our comments are based on the database by Gavin and Perotti (1997). Contrary to the International Monetary Fund, they provide a more relevant estimation of the fiscal position by not focusing exclusively on the central government. Their database covers 13 countries (Argentina, Bolivia, Brazil, Chile, Columbia, Costa Rica, Ecuador, Mexico, Panama, Paraguay, Peru, Uruguay, Venezuela) over the 1968–95 period.
2. They provide indirect evidence by regressing, country by country, the log change of each fiscal variable in real terms on a constant, the rate of growth of output, and the rate of change in the terms of trade. Their main result is the following: the average standard deviation of the residuals of these regressions displays identical patterns to those displayed in Table 13.2.
3. From a Keynesian perspective, this weak co-movement results from the stabilization of output by authorities.
4. Due to a large increase in taxes and a small spending response.
5. A major recession is characterized by a cumulative decline of the real GDP of more than 4 per cent for Latin America and 1.5 per cent for OECD. See Gavin et al.(1996), p. 14.
6. The cost is low because inflation is like a lump-sum tax.
7. Following Alesina and Perotti (1996, p. 6), we define budget procedures as a three-phase process: (1) formulation of a proposal within the executive; (2) the presentation and

approval of the budget in the legislature; and (3) the implementation of the budget by the bureaucracy.
8. Recall that complexity reduces the transparency of budget process by inciting opportunistic behaviour.
9. The model is composed of two governments: Germany and the United Kingdom.
10. On the IMF position about Argentina, see Mussa (2002).
11. The debt at $t-1$ is reimbursed during the following period and represents a spending at t, so: $d_{t-1}=d$.
12. Precise values of Figure 13.1 are presented in the Appendix.

REFERENCES

Alesina, A. and A. Drazen (1991), 'Why is stabilization delayed?', *American Economic Review*, **81**, 1170–88.

Alesina, A. and R. Perotti (1996), 'Budget deficits and budget institutions', *NBER Working Paper Series*, 5556, May.

Alesina, A., R. Hausmann, R. Hommes and E. Stein (1999), 'Budget institutions and fiscal performance in Latin America', *IADB, Office of the Chief Economist, Working Paper Series*, 394.

Allsopp, L. (2000), 'A model to explain the duration of a currency crisis', *International Journal of Finance and Economics*, **5**(4), 331–7.

Backus, D. and J. Driffill (1985), 'Rational expectations and policy credibility following a change in regime', *Review of Economic Studies*, **52**, 211–21.

Calvo, G.A. (1988), 'Servicing the public debt: the role of expectations', *The American Economic Review*, **78**, 647–61.

Calvo, G.A. and C.M. Reinhart (2000), 'Fixing for your life', May, www.puaf.umd.edu/papers/reinhart.htm.

Calvo, G.A. and C.A. Végh (1998), 'Inflation stabilization and BOP crises in developing countries', *NBER Working Paper Series*, 6925, February.

Carré, M. (2000), 'Debt stabilization with a deadline', *European Economic Review*, **44**, 71–90.

Casella, A. and B. Eichengreen (1996), 'Can foreign aid accelerate stabilization?', *Economic Journal*, **106**, 605–19.

Gavin, M. and R. Perotti (1997), 'Fiscal policy in Latin America', *NBER Macroeconomic Annual*, 11–72.

Gavin, M., R. Hausmann, R. Perotti and E. Talvi (1996), 'Managing fiscal policy in Latin America and the Caribbean: volatility, pro-cyclicality, and limited creditworthiness', *IADB, Office of the Chief Economist, Working Paper Series*, 326.

Mussa, M. (2002), 'Argentina and the Fund: from triumph to tragedy', Institute for International Economics, March, http://www.iie.com/papers/mussa0302-1.htm.

Ter-Minassian, T. and G. Schwartz (1997), 'The role of fiscal policy in sustainable stabilization: evidence from Latin America', *IMF Working Paper*, WP/97/94, August.

Weisbrot, M. (2002), 'Hearing on the state of the Argentine economic crisis and the role of the International Monetary Fund', testimony before the Subcommittee on International Monetary Policy and Trade Committee on Financial Services, US House of Representatives, Washington, DC.

14. Are there benefits to a monetary policy rule in the EMU?

Jean-Jacques Durand, Nathalie Payelle and Virginie Traclet

INTRODUCTION

Recent years have been characterized by a flourishing literature on the 'rules versus discretion' debate in monetary policy. In this context, the European Central Bank (ECB) had to adopt a clear position on this subject.

The ECB has logically rejected discretionary stimulating monetary surprises, since it is widely recognized that they create an inflationary bias in economy (Kydland and Prescott, 1977; Barro and Gordon, 1983). Furthermore the ECB has clearly announced a strategy consistent with the Maastricht Treaty which states that 'the primary objective of the European System of Central Banks (ESCB) shall be to maintain price stability'. The ECB has therefore adopted a price stability goal for the long run[1] like the main central banks around the world.

However, while choosing a 'two-pillar' strategy to satisfy its price stability goal, the ECB has adopted a strategy which can be viewed as less transparent than a rule. Effectively these two pillars include a wide variety of indicators which are used by monetary authorities to evaluate the risks to price stability. These indicators include monetary growth (M3) as the first pillar, and several monetary, financial and real indicators as the second pillar. It is worth underlining here that these various variables can give contradictory information about future price developments (what may not be the case with a precise rule). This two-pillar strategy, considered representative of central bank's pragmatism, has been recently justified by a severe criticism of policy rules, which are considered by the ECB as much too inflexible, fragile and, ultimately, inefficient (ECB, 2001).

The ECB has then retained only the price stability goal from the debate on monetary policy rules. Will it be sufficient to insure both the credibility of its primary goal and the stability of the euro? More generally, the institutional framework of the euro area is frequently viewed as potentially unsustainable because of persistent real asymmetries, against which national fiscal policies are certainly unable to fight. This situation conducts international markets to a certain mistrust, with weakness of the euro in face of the dollar as a corollary.

In this context it is interesting to see whether or not European monetary authorities give up a potential useful tool with this systematic rejection of monetary policy rules. Our study supplies the current discussion and tries to answer these questions. Is the nominal convergence of the euro area's member states sufficient to insure an efficient unique monetary policy, that is a unique reaction function applied to economies with still heterogeneous real structures? In this context, is a monetary policy rule always conceivable? Does it contain advantages in comparison with another monetary policy procedure? If so, under which conditions?

We first show that a particular form of McCallum monetary base rule is able to reproduce fairly the effective monetary policies which have been conducted in the three main European countries (France, Germany and Italy) since 1984. We can therefore retain this rule as the reaction function of these national central banks. We next aggregate these three economies and we calculate a common reaction function, based on this particular monetary rule. We then show with counterfactual simulations that applying this common rule would have given results at least as good as the ones obtained with historical monetary policy, despite structural heterogeneities in these economies. Therefore the costs of this rule would have been weak in comparison with its potential benefits in terms of credibility, contrary to the criticism made by the ECB. Moreover these results can be compared with the results previously obtained with a similar study including the Taylor rule as the common monetary reaction function (Durand et al., 1999). This comparison enables us to deduce some implications for the conduct of monetary policy in the euro area.

The remainder of the chapter is organized as follows. We first remind ourselves of the traditional arguments in favour of monetary policy rules and we comment on the ECB's point of view in this regard. Moreover we justify our choice of a particular form of the nominal GDP rule proposed by McCallum (1987). We next present our empirical analysis and its practical implications, in each country individually and in a 'fictive euro area' (obtained from aggregation of these three countries) in the second and third parts of this chapter respectively.

MONETARY POLICY RULES AND UNCERTAINTY

This section first explains the ECB's point of view about policy rules and criticizes its arguments. It next shows that a particular form of McCallum rule may be used to represent accurately effective monetary policy aiming at price stability in the long run.

The ECB and Monetary Policy Rules

The ECB recognizes the merits of rules in order to stabilize expectations, since the use of a rule induces a more foreseeable monetary policy, but rejects them afterwards. 'The challenge for monetary policy in practice is to retain the virtues of rule-based policy-making, while taking into account the complex, uncertain and constantly evolving environment facing monetary policy-makers' (ECB, 2001, p. 38). All its rationale lies then on this uncertainty, and the ECB concludes that in this context a rule would reduce decision processes too much.

With such a reasoning, McCallum rule is immediately rejected by the ECB, first because it manipulates a monetary base instrument while in practice central banks use an interest rate instrument, and second because it includes a nominal GDP goal to satisfy the long-run price stability goal, which can induce a certain 'confusion' (ECB, 2001, p. 40). The Taylor rule receives a little more consideration from the ECB, since it is subject to a long criticism. We can however underline the fact that this criticism is general and also concerns the McCallum rule. It is then very interesting to assess the scope of the arguments of the ECB.

The ECB uses two main arguments to justify its rejection of monetary policy rules. The first argument concerns the lack of information given by the variable(s) included in the rule. The ECB effectively indicates that a nominal GDP target (McCallum) or a 'two faces' target including inflation and output gap separately (Taylor) does not include all the relevant information necessary for monetary policy. Furthermore output gap, which requires assessment of potential output, and inflation expectations, which are included in the generalized form of the Taylor rule, are not observable. Is it sufficient to reject the relevance of a monetary rule? These objective variables are indeed 'global', but they precisely represent the objectives of central banks aiming at price stability in the long run.[2] Of course, these variables are unobservable, but there exists a vast literature on the measurement of potential GDP (St-Amant and van Norden, 1997, and *Economie Internationale*, 1997, **69**, for instance) and on inflation expectations.[3] In any case, these variables have a 'true meaning', which the ECB tries to recover with a wide variety of indicators (deviation of M3 growth from its reference value, prices and costs indicators, asset prices, and so on). Since these various indicators sometimes evolve in opposite directions, the ability of monetary authority to correctly anticipate inflation can be affected, which can consequently weaken policy transparency.

The second argument of the ECB concerns the results given by the simulation of a rule in a particular model of economy. As there is no consensus about the 'good' model of the economy, the simulated performance of any rule must be considered with caution. We agree with this reservation. However, it is not a sufficiently strong reason to discard the use of models and to give up the benefits of rules. This argument developed by the ECB to justify its rejection of rules is all the more fallacious in that the ECB itself employs a number of models to analyse information given by its different indicators.[4] Moreover, testing for the robustness of any rule is a current practice in the literature: a monetary rule can be viewed as robust when its simulation gives similar results in competitive models of economy (McCallum, 1988).

Finally, the ECB's criticism towards rules asks fundamental and relevant questions, which cannot be answered on an a priori basis. In this context, experience – that means simulated results – is the only way of improving this debate. The 'two-pillar' alternative chosen by the ECB lies then on a priori justifications and is characterized by a significant complexity which damages transparency of policy decisions. Furthermore this complexity may throw doubt in the public mind on a possible comeback of more or less discretionary practices, which are not easy to interpret for market participants.

It is therefore interesting to see whether central banks' practice, and the ECB's in particular, may be illustrated by a simple rule. (The following two sections try to prove it.)

In Search of a Common Rule

This first requires us to retain a rule which is compatible with the overriding long-run price stability goal imposed by the Maastricht Treaty. We choose to turn down the Taylor rule since it includes the output gap in addition to an inflation target; what could be interpreted as a real growth goal implying trade-offs between price stability and real growth. We prefer to retain a well-adapted nominal GDP McCallum rule. Effectively the nominal GDP target included in this rule can be assimilated to an implicit inflation target since it is the sum of the potential growth rate of economy and a quantitative inflation rate representative of an 'acceptable' inflation.

McCallum (1987) proposes a rule which sets monetary base quarterly growth rate (Δb_t) in order to allow nominal GDP to grow at a non-inflationary rate, which is equal to the long-run growth rate of economy (Δy_t^f), plus an acceptable inflation rate, Δp_t^*.

A McCallum-type rule is written as:

$$\Delta b_t = [\Delta y_t^f + \Delta p_t^*] - (1/16)\,[(x_{t-1} - b_{t-1}) - (x_{t-17} - b_{t-17})] + \lambda\,(x_{t-1}^* - x_{t-1}) \qquad (14.1)$$

where b, y, p and x are the logarithms of monetary base, real GDP, price level and nominal GDP respectively.

The first term – $[\Delta y_t^f + \Delta p_t^*]$ – represents the long-run non-inflationary target path of nominal GDP, equal to potential growth (Δy_t^f) and an acceptable inflation (Δp_t^*), which represents the fact that authorities can accept a higher inflation in some circumstances (this is the case in the beginning of our sample for instance). The second term represents the average growth rate of base velocity over the previous four years.[5] The third term – $\lambda.(x_{t-1}^* - x_{t-1})$ – represents monetary response to past departures of nominal GDP (x) from its target path (x^*). The value of the monetary feedback coefficient λ should be large enough to conduct base growth to respond adequately to target misses, while avoiding dynamic instability.

We choose here a nominal GDP target expressed in growth rate in order to take real disturbances persistence into account (McCallum, 1993). This growth rate target is expressed as:

$$x_t^* = x_t + \Delta y_t^f + \Delta p_t^* \tag{14.2}$$

Past shocks are then treated as bygones. In this case, at each period, monetary authorities aim at obtaining a nominal GDP growth equal to the sum of potential growth and the inflation goal, whatever the nominal GDP growth rate was in the previous period.

It is next necessary to choose the long-run real growth rate (Δy_t^f) and the numerical inflation goal (Δp_t^*). As for potential growth estimation, we choose here the most widespread method: we apply the Hodrick–Prescott filter to effective series of real GDP in order to obtain potential GDP series. The quantitative inflation target is not problematic today since inflation is already low and stable, which enables central banks to choose an inflation target representative of price stability (generally, the inflation target is between 0 and 3 per cent per annum). However our study covers the 1984–99 sample, which has been characterized by very different inflationary situations. In particular, France and Italy suffered from high inflation rates at the beginning of this sample. These rates have next been progressively reduced along the considered period. Therefore we formulate for each country an evolutionary inflation target representative of its historical inflationary experience (the construction of these national evolutionary inflation targets series is detailed in the second section of this chapter). The nominal GDP target evolves then over time.

We then use this rule to represent monetary policies which have effectively been conducted by the central banks of the three European countries considered in our study (France, Germany and Italy). The monetary base has not indeed been used as a monetary policy instrument, but this 'adapted' rule seems coherent with the monetary objectives[6] used in this sample, or with the reference value for M3 growth which is computed by the ECB.[7] The next two sections are favourable to this rule formulation.

EMPIRICAL STUDY IN EACH COUNTRY

The first purpose of our empirical study is to see whether a McCallum monetary base rule including a nominal GDP growth target is able to represent accurately the effective monetary policies conducted by the French, German and Italian central banks in the 1984–99 sample. This sample is particularly interesting since it is the one during which the main European countries, which adopted the EMS (European Monetary System) in 1979, began to try to fight inflation. Effectively, the adoption of the EMS was the signal of their willingness to progressively reduce their inflation and to keep closer to German inflationary rigour.[8]

The aim of our simulation exercises is to compare the economic performance obtained with these historical national monetary policies with simulated performance under the McCallum rule.

The Nominal GDP Target

As previously noticed, the nominal GDP target is the sum of potential GDP growth (measured by applying a Hodrick–Prescott filter) and an implicit inflation target. Before running simulation exercises, we have to determinate this inflation target. Effectively, since national inflation rates were very different in our sample (in particular, inflation was much higher in France and Italy than in Germany at the beginning of the sample), it would be unrealistic to consider that the goal of monetary policy in these three countries was an inflation target representative of the price stability goal as is now the case at the European level. Therefore we formulate an inflation target path representative of this reality and representative of the willingness of national monetary authorities to progressively reduce inflation.

In the German case, this task is not difficult since the monetary growth targeting effectively used by the Bundesbank lies on an implicit inflation target path: we then use this implicit inflation target series (Bernanke and Mihov, 1996). In the French case, we use announcements made by the Banque de France,[9] which enable us to construct an evolutionary inflation target. The Italian case is more problematic since there are no elements in the Bank of Italy's announcements which could be used to construct such an evolutionary inflation target able to represent its willingness to progressively diminish its national inflation rate. As inflation was particularly high at the beginning of the sample, it would be totally unrealistic to adopt a fixed inflation target. We then choose to apply a simple mathematical formulation to represent the evolutionary inflation target in Italy. According to this formula, the inflation target progressively decreases in the period and attains 1 per cent at the end of the sample.[10] For each of these three countries, the nominal GDP target series is then obtained by adding the evolutionary inflation target series of each country and its potential GDP growth rate series.

Simulation Methodology

We choose here to adopt VAR models to represent the functioning of each economy, in order to make no hypotheses about the 'good' model of economy on account of no agreement on this model. We use quarterly series on 1984:1–1998:4. Each national VAR includes Δy, Δp, Δe, Δb, and Δi, where y is the real GDP, p the price level, e the nominal effective exchange rate, b the monetary base and i the monetary market interest rate. All these variables are expressed in first differences in order to have good stationary properties. Moreover all variables except interest rates are expressed in logarithm form. Lags in regression equations are chosen to satisfy the Akaike criterion.

The simulation methodology for each country is the following. First, we estimate the national VAR on our sample and we save estimated residual series (except those of the monetary policy instrument regression) which are then assimilated to historical shocks. We then replace the monetary base equation by the well-adapted McCallum rule in the estimated system. We next reintroduce the historical residuals into this system including the rule. This gives us the simulated path for all the variables of the model.

The optimal monetary feedback coefficient (λ^*) is the one for which simulated RMSE[11] – measuring the gap between simulated nominal GDP and its target – is the lowest one. We then compare this simulated RMSE with historical RMSE, which measures the gap between effective nominal GDP and the target. If simulated RMSE is lower than its historical counterpart, this indicates that the McCallum rule would have given a better result than effective monetary policy in terms of nominal GDP. However, this is not a sufficient criterion to assess the performance of the rule. It is also necessary to see whether this rule gives results compatible with European priorities, namely price stability (which is the long-run objective of the ECB), a sustained real growth, and reasonable interest rates. These last two variables are effectively frequently cited by the ECB as justifying its rejection of rules.[12]

We then report simulated inflation, simulated real growth and simulated interest rates in order to compare them with their historical values (see Table 14.1). A graphical analysis of simulated and effective series gives a good global vision to assess the performance of McCallum base rule more easily (see Appendix 1).

Simulation Results

Table 14.1 reports optimal monetary feedback coefficient (λ^*), corresponding simulated RMSE and historical RMSE. It also reports average and standard-error of simulated real growth, inflation rate and short rate, and of their effective counterparts, for each country. Figures 14.1a, b and c reported in Appendix 1 make it easier to compare effective with simulated performance in each European country.

Previous results indicate that a well-adapted McCallum rule seems to reproduce quite faithfully historical monetary policy in each of these three countries:

- Simulated and historical RMSE are quite similar, but simulated RMSE is however lower, which indicates a potentially higher efficiency of the rule in comparison with historical practice.
- In France and Italy, simulated inflationary performance is better than the effective one (simulated average inflation rates are lower for similar volatility). This result is particularly interesting since inflation in both these countries was very high at the beginning of the sample. In the German case, simulated and historical inflation are very similar.
- Simulated interest rates are similar, on average, to their historical levels in Germany and Italy, with an identical or even lower volatility. In France, average simulated interest rate is slightly higher than historically, but is less volatile.
- There are no real costs in Germany and these costs are very moderate in Italy. In the French case, improvement of real growth with the rule can be explained, in part by less volatile interest rates, and also by our simulation method.

Finally, these results indicate that a well-adapted McCallum rule seems able to reproduce fairly reaction functions of these national central banks in our sample (the German case is the most obvious example). However disparity in national optimal feedback coefficients (λ^*) illustrates the persistent structural heterogeneity of these economies. Therefore even if a unique policy in a monetary union constituted by these countries seems feasible since their national reaction functions have the same form (a monetary base

Table 14.1 Simulation of the McCallum rule in France, Germany and Italy (1984–98)

	France	Germany	Italy
λ^*	0.30	0.98	4.44
Simulated RMSE	**0.00462**	**0.01402**	**0.00779**
Historical RMSE	0.00547	0.01498	0.00839

	France				Germany				Italy			
	Simulated series		Historical series		Simulated series		Historical series		Simulated series		Historical series	
	Average	Standard-error	Average	Standard-error	Average	Standard-error	Average	Standard-error	Average	Standard-error	Average	Standard-error
Δy	0.0070	0.0041	0.0051	0.0048	0.0073	0.0144	0.0072	0.0155	0.0044	0.0064	0.0047	0.0059
Δp	0.0057	0.0050	0.0067	0.0046	0.0059	0.0042	0.0059	0.0048	0.0123	0.0062	0.0130	0.0060
i	8.3318	1.3019	7.5801	2.6263	5.1649	1.6710	5.5346	2.0684	11.207	3.1752	11.209	3.1392

Note: Bold face indicates that McCallum base rule would have given a better result than effective monetary policy in terms of nominal GDP growth.

rule including a growth rate nominal GDP target), their very different monetary feedback coefficients illustrate the difficulty of finding a common optimal coefficient, both for the monetary union and for each country individually. The lack of real convergence among European economies consequently implies a risk of asymmetric effects if a common monetary policy is adopted.

In the current context of theoretical knowledge, and as it is too early to assess definitively the functioning of the euro area, an empirical approach is the only way for us to estimate the consequences of a common feedback coefficient. This is the aim of the third part of this chapter.

EMPIRICAL STUDY IN A FICTIVE EMU

We use here a two-step approach to assess the consequences of a monetary rule including a common feedback coefficient in a 'fictive euro area' in our sample period (1984–98). We first simulate a well-adapted McCallum rule in our fictive euro area. We next introduce the 'optimal' European monetary feedback coefficient in individual VARs representing each European economy in order to assess the effects of a common monetary feedback coefficient.

Monetary Rule for the EMU

We constitute a fictive euro area by aggregation of national series. European GDP and monetary base series are obtained by a simple summation of national series. European inflation rate and interest rate series are a weighted sum of national series, where national weights are equal to the ratio of national real GDP to European real GDP. The VAR model used to represent the European economy excludes exchange rate since there is no external constraint any more. We then include a well-adapted McCallum rule in this system instead of its base regression equation, and we use the same simulation method as for each country individually to find the optimal European feedback coefficient (λ^*_{EURO}).

The quantitative inflation goal to include in nominal GDP growth target is 'problematic' since considered countries have experienced various inflationary situations in our sample. A fixed inflation target is indeed feasible today since France, Germany and Italy have attained low and stable inflation rates, but it would be unrealistic for the whole sample. Therefore we have to formulate an evolutionary inflation target series for the euro area. We choose here to follow Gerlach and Svensson (2001) in order to compute this series, which is based on German implicit inflation targets.

Simulation results are reported in Table 14.2. Figure 14.2 (see Appendix 1) illustrates these results graphically.

European monetary feedback coefficient (λ^*_{EURO}) takes an 'intermediate' value in comparison with individual coefficients. Previous results bear out that a well-adapted McCallum rule is effectively able to represent the effective monetary policy in our fictive euro area.

Overall, simulated results are very similar to historical evolutions:

- Simulated RMSE is slightly lower than effective RMSE, which indicates that the rule produces a better performance in terms of nominal GDP growth than historical monetary policy.
- The main improvement given by the rule concerns volatility in the economy. Effectively, simulated averages of real growth, inflation and short-term interest rate are almost identical to their historical averages. Simulated volatility of these three variables is a little lower, which is particularly interesting since it enables a better decision-making process.

Using a well-adapted monetary base rule as common reaction function for our fictive Euro area therefore seems justified since its simulated performance is quite similar to historical performance (with a slight improvement). However as European monetary feedback coefficient is different from individual coefficients (presented above), it is particularly important to

Table 14.2 Application of a common monetary rule in our fictive EMU

	Fictive Euro area
λ^*_{EURO}	2.45
Simulated RMSE	**0.00756**
Historical RMSE	0.00888

	Simulated series		Historical series	
	Average	Standard-error	Average	Standard-error
Δy	0.0059	0.0075	0.0059	0.0077
Δp	0.0077	0.0032	0.0078	0.0036
i	7.2578	1.9182	7.5319	2.2486

Note: Bold face indicates that McCallum base rule would have given a better result than effective monetary policy in terms of nominal GDP growth.

assess the consequences of such a common feedback coefficient on each individual country.

Application of the European Common Feedback Coefficient to Individual Countries

Table 14.3 and Figure 14.3 (Appendix 1) report results from simulation exercises in each country where national 'optimal' feedback coefficients are replaced by the common one (Table 14.2).

While we feared that a common feedback would have induced harmful consequences on each country because of structural heterogeneity, above results indicate that a 'common monetary policy', in which feedback coefficient is defined at aggregated level, would have given a macroeconomic performance similar to the one obtained with effective monetary policies.

It is interesting to study each country separately in order to see whether any of them is more sensitive to this common feedback coefficient. We then compare simulated results obtained with the application of the common coefficient in each country (Table 14.3) and simulated results obtained with national optimal feedback coefficients (Table 14.1) in order to assess the consequences of a common coefficient instead of an 'optimal' national coefficient.

As for Germany, it is worth underlining that results are similar in both cases (national and common coefficients). Moreover these simulated performances are also quite similar to the historical one, which indicates that German monetary policy is well described by this policy rule. Given that the European feedback coefficient is higher than the national one, simulated performance logically 'suffers' from a slightly increased variability with the European rule. The application of the common feedback coefficient would also have anticipated (and limited) the interest rate increase which has been conducted to counter German reunification (see Figure 14.3).

In Italy, as the European feedback coefficient is lower than the national one (2.45 and 4.44 respectively), real costs are reduced on the whole sample, whereas simulated inflationary performance is similar to effective inflation in both cases (simulated inflation with European coefficient is logically higher than simulated inflation with national coefficient since European monetary response is less 'aggressive').

Application of the European coefficient in France, which is more restrictive than the national one (λ^*_{Euro} equals 2.45, whereas the French coefficient is only 0.30), gives a simulated performance which is more similar to the historical one. The simulated performance with 'optimal'

Table 14.3 Application of the common European monetary feedback coefficient in France, Germany and Italy (1984–98)

	France				Germany				Italy			
$\lambda^*_{Euro}/\lambda^*_{each\ country}$	2.45 / 0.30				2.45 / 0.98				2.45 / 4.44			
Simulated RMSE	**0.00468**				**0.01452**				**0.00797**			
Historical RMSE	0.00547				0.01498				0.00839			
	Simulated series		Historical series		Simulated series		Historical series		Simulated series		Historical series	
	Average	Standard-error	Average	Standard-error	Average	Standard-error	Average	Standard-error	Average	Standard-error	Average	Standard-error
Δy	0.0066	0.0043	0.0051	0.0048	0.0073	0.0152	0.0072	0.0155	0.0046	0.0061	0.0047	0.0059
Δp	0.0058	0.0049	0.0067	0.0046	0.0058	0.0041	0.0059	0.0048	0.0127	0.0059	0.0130	0.0060
i	7.9584	1.5423	7.5801	2.6263	4.9519	1.9428	5.5346	2.0684	11.1881	3.1306	11.209	3.1392

Note: Bold face indicates that McCallum base rule would have given a better result than effective monetary policy in terms of nominal GDP growth.

national rule effectively gives better results in terms of real growth, with a similar inflationary situation, than the European rule simulation. This tends to reinforce a widespread idea according to which French monetary policy in the 1990s was much too restrictive comparative to the French economic situation. Our simulations show that a monetary rule would have induced a more favourable sharing between quantity and price effects than effective monetary policy: simulated real growth is higher at the end of the sample, whereas simulated inflation is lower than its historical counterpart and simulated interest rate is less volatile.

It is particularly interesting to compare these simulation results with those obtained with a similar study in which monetary policy is represented by a Taylor rule (Durand et al., 1999). The Taylor rule has led to a vast literature since it is supposed to better represent monetary authorities' strategy (first because it uses an interest rate instrument, second because it includes both inflation and real production).

This previous study, based on similar methods, has led to the following conclusions: First, the Taylor rule is not able to represent correctly the effective reaction functions of national central banks (this study concerns Germany, France, Italy, Spain and the Netherlands). Next, simulation of a common Taylor rule, including two 'optimal' feedback coefficients (on inflation deviation from its target, and on output gap), induces asymmetric effects in national economies. In particular there are some important real costs in the main euro area countries (France, Germany and Italy).

Confrontation of previous conclusions and conclusions of our present study tends therefore to be more favourable to a well-adapted McCallum rule to represent accurately effective national monetary policies, than to the Taylor rule.

CONCLUSION

Rules used here to represent the behaviour of monetary authorities are not conceived to reproduce the very short-term reactions of these authorities. Effectively, day to day monetary rate adjustments are explained by a variety of monetary and financial factors, which are not necessary relevant for a medium- to long- run price stability objective. But a long-run policy seems to be fairly represented by a well-adapted McCallum rule. It is particularly interesting to see that effective national monetary policies since 1984 are relatively well reproduced by a particular form of McCallum rule in Germany, France and Italy. This is particularly true for Germany, which is appealing since German monetary policy is famous for its price stability success, and since it is considered to be very influential on the European one.

Moreover it must be underlined that a common well-adapted McCallum rule would have given a slightly better performance that the historical one in our fictive EMU. This leads us to ask why the ECB rejects rules, while they could be included as an additional tool. Our investigations indicate that a monetary base rule including a nominal GDP target expressed in growth rate would certainly constitute an interesting 'ally' to help economic agents in their expectation formulation for the long run. This empirical study constitutes then an appealing response to the ECB's negative attitude towards monetary rules.

APPENDIX 1: SIMULATION RESULTS

FRANCE, Nominal GDP

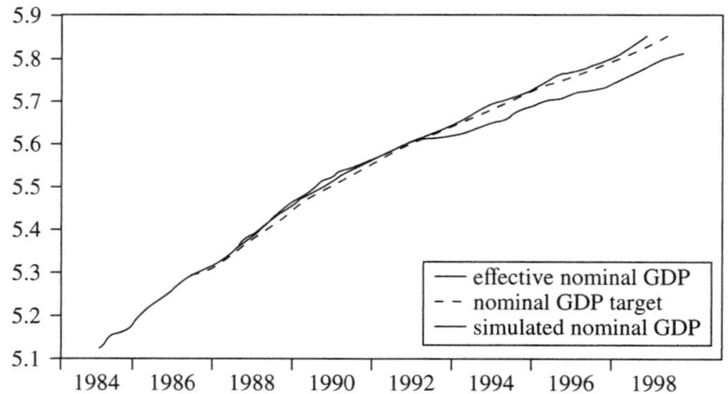

FRANCE, Inflation

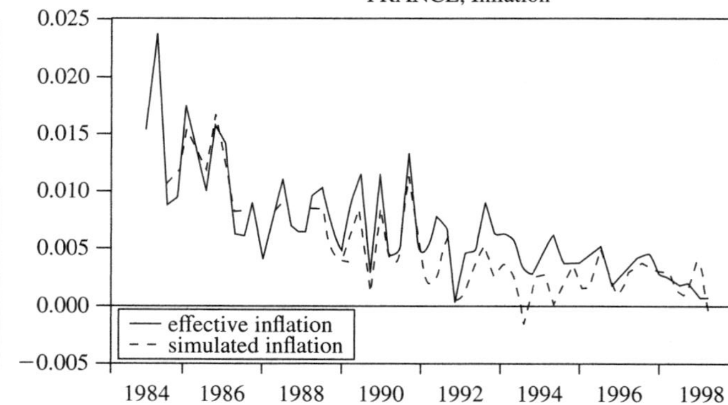

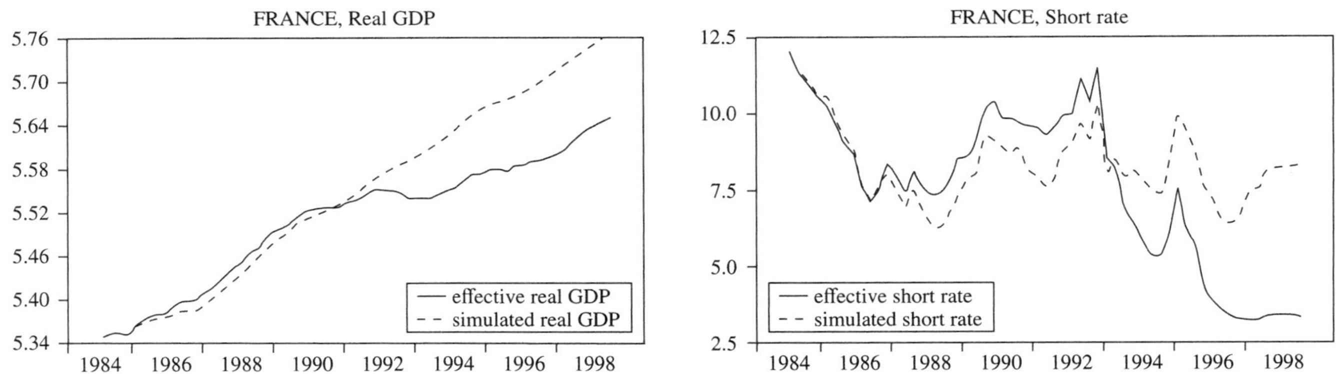

Figure 14.1a France

Figure 14.1 Simulation in each European country with its own 'optimal' feedback coefficient

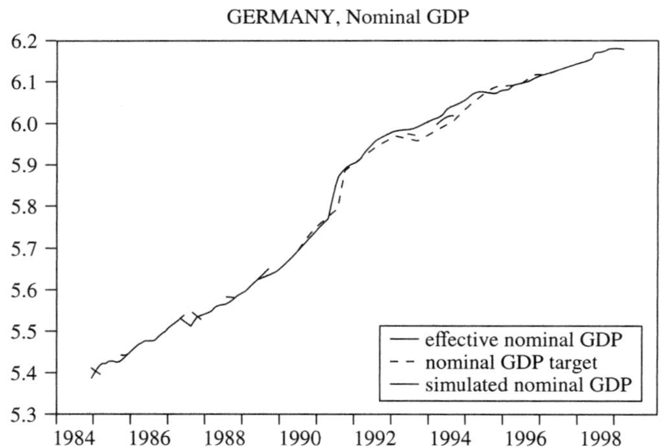

GERMANY, Nominal GDP
6.2
6.1
6.0
5.9
5.8
5.7
5.6
5.5
5.4
5.3
1984
1986
1988
1990
1992
1994
1996
1998
effective nominal GDP
nominal GDP target
simulated nominal GDP

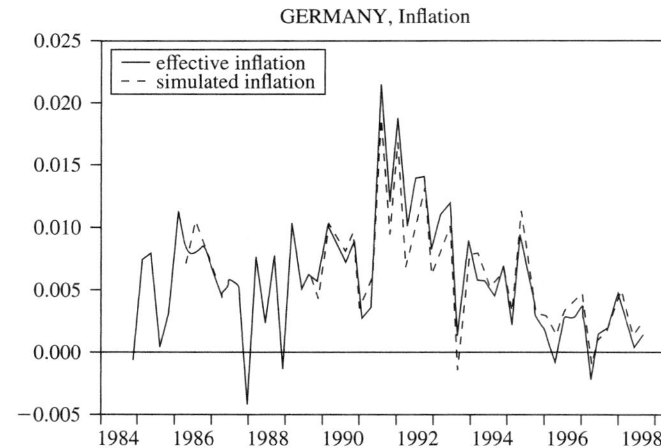

GERMANY, Inflation
0.025
0.020
0.015
0.010
0.005
0.000
−0.005
1984
1986
1988
1990
1992
1994
1996
1998
effective inflation
simulated inflation

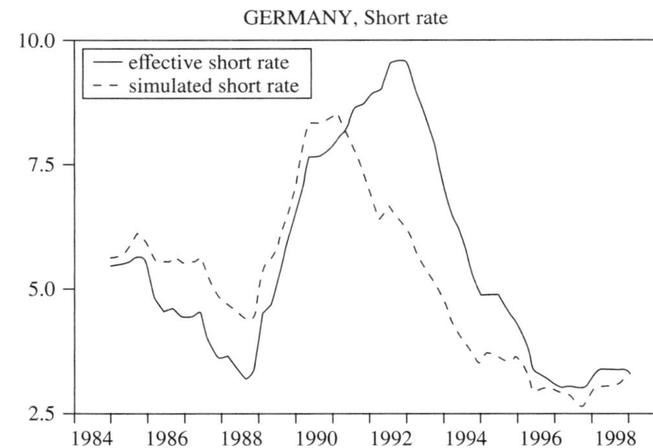

Figure 14.1b *Germany*

Figure 14.1 *(continued)*

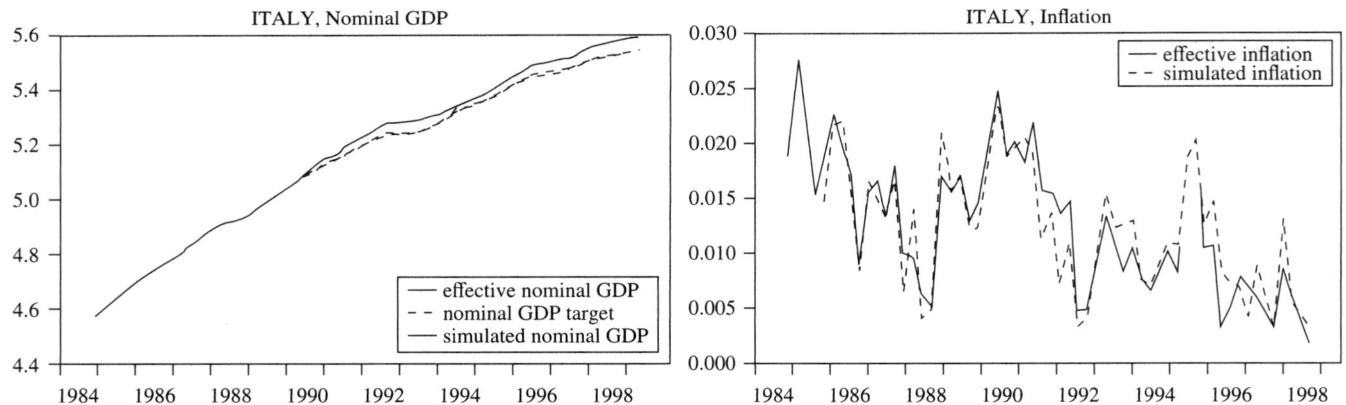
ITALY, Nominal GDP
5.6
5.4
5.2
5.0
4.8
4.6
4.4
1984
1986
1988
1990
1992
1994
1996
1998
effective nominal GDP
nominal GDP target
simulated nominal GDP
ITALY, Inflation
0.030
0.025
0.020
0.015
0.010
0.005
0.000
1984
1986
1988
1990
1992
1994
1996
1998
effective inflation
simulated inflation

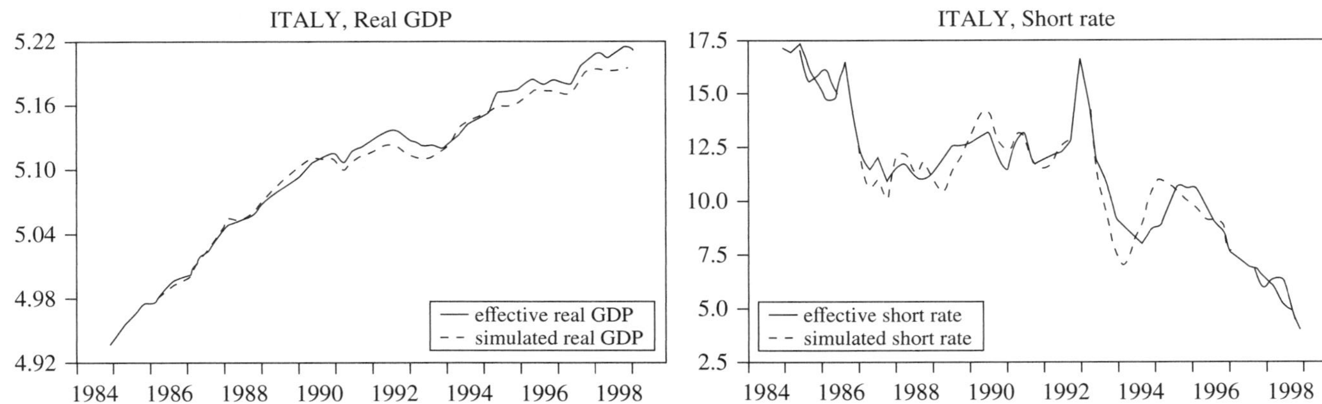

Figure 14.1c *Italy*

Figure 14.1 *(continued)*

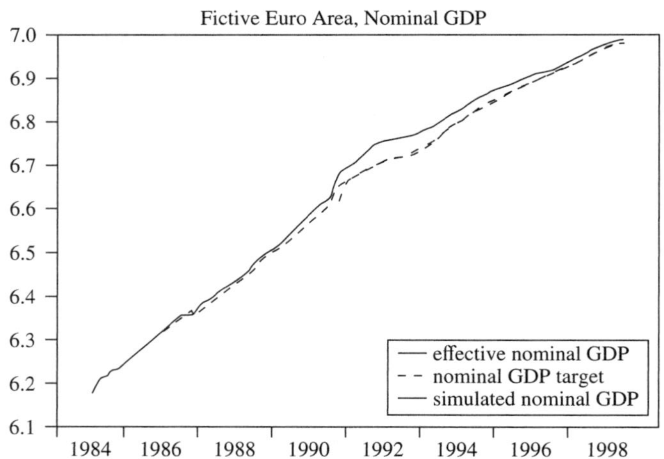
Fictive Euro Area, Nominal GDP
7.0
6.9
6.8
6.7
6.6
6.5
6.4
6.3
6.2
6.1
1984
1986
1988
1990
1992
1994
1996
1998
effective nominal GDP
nominal GDP target
simulated nominal GDP

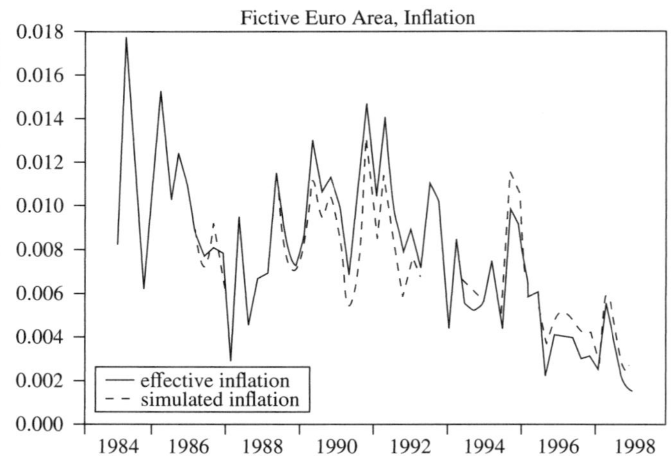
Fictive Euro Area, Inflation
0.018
0.016
0.014
0.012
0.010
0.008
0.006
0.004
0.002
0.000
1984
1986
1988
1990
1992
1994
1996
1998
effective inflation
simulated inflation

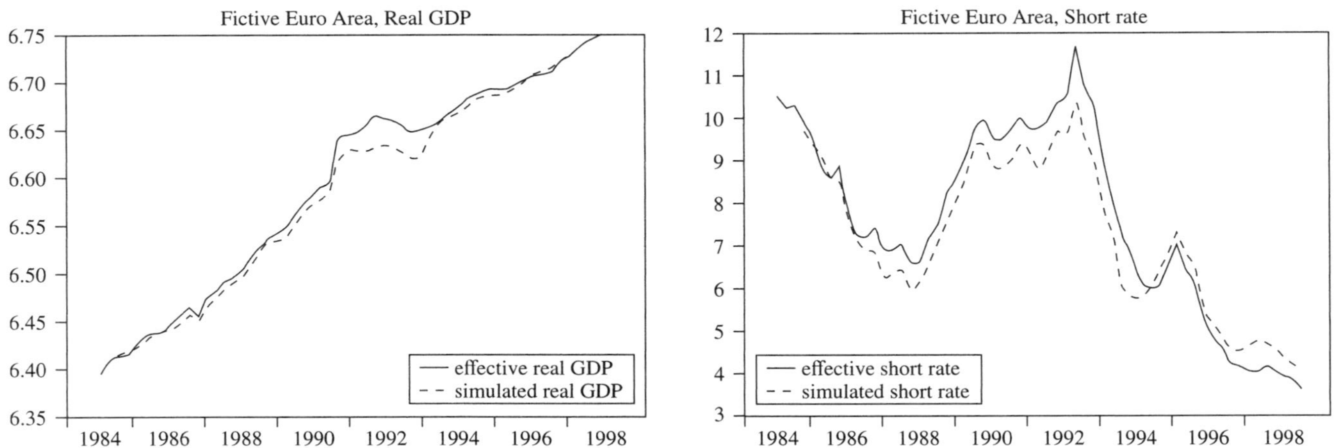

Figures 14.2 Simulation in our 'fictive' Euro area with European optimal monetary coefficient

FRANCE, Nominal GDP
Euro area monetary coefficient

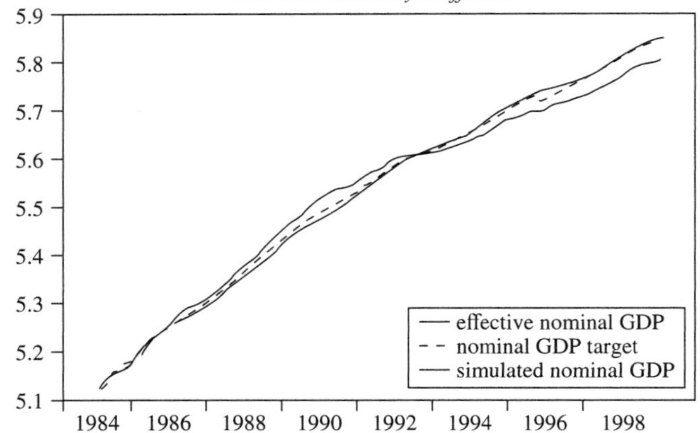

FRANCE, Inflation
Euro area monetary coefficient

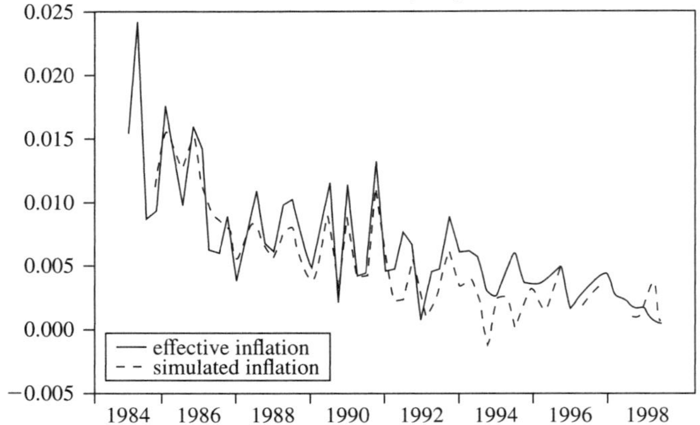

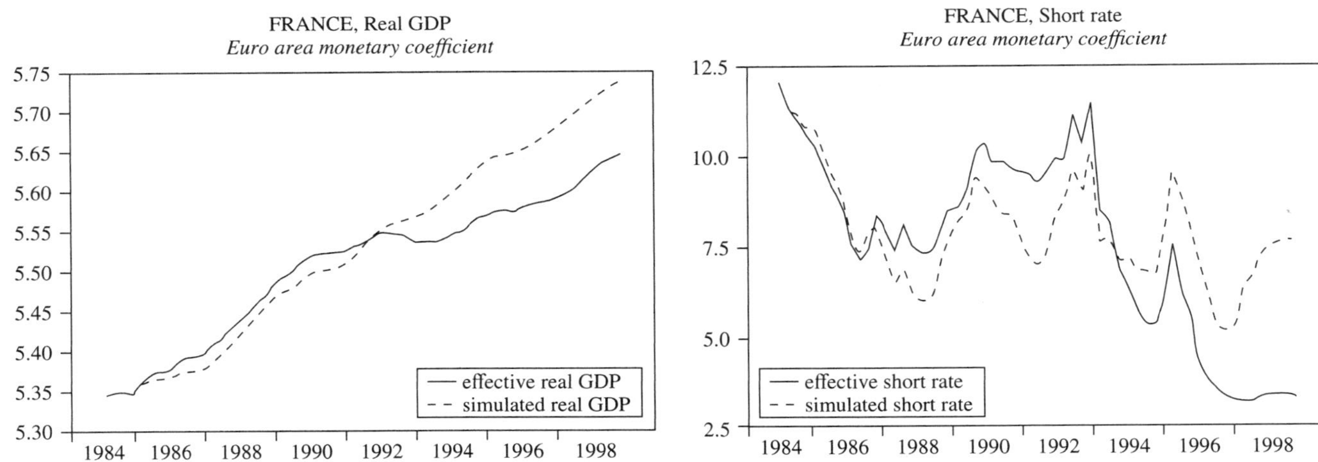

Figure 14.3a *France with Euro area coefficient*

Figure 14.3 *Simulation in each country with the European 'optimal' feedback coefficient*

GERMANY, Nominal GDP
Euro area monetary coefficient

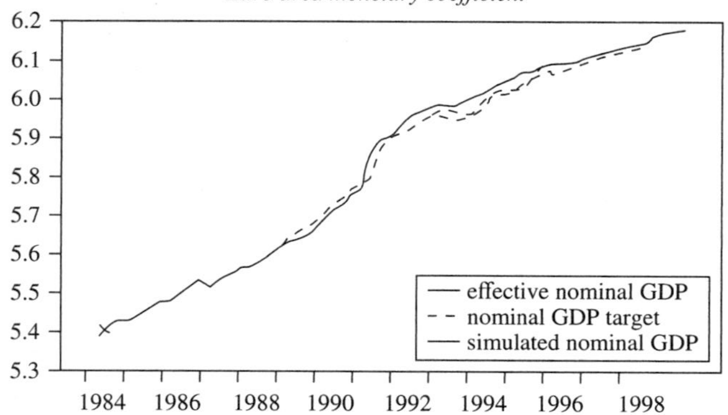

GERMANY, Inflation
Euro area monetary coefficient

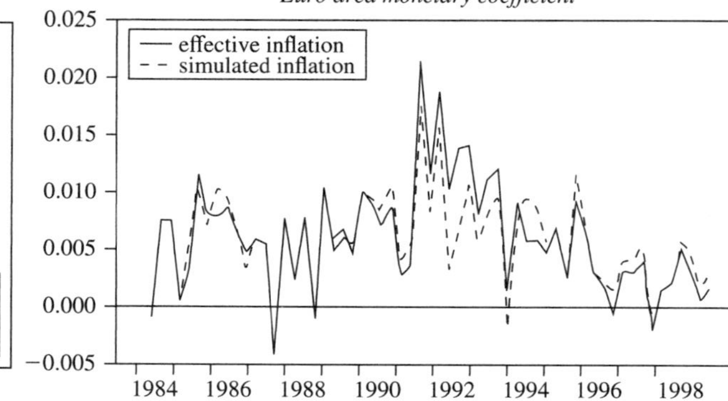

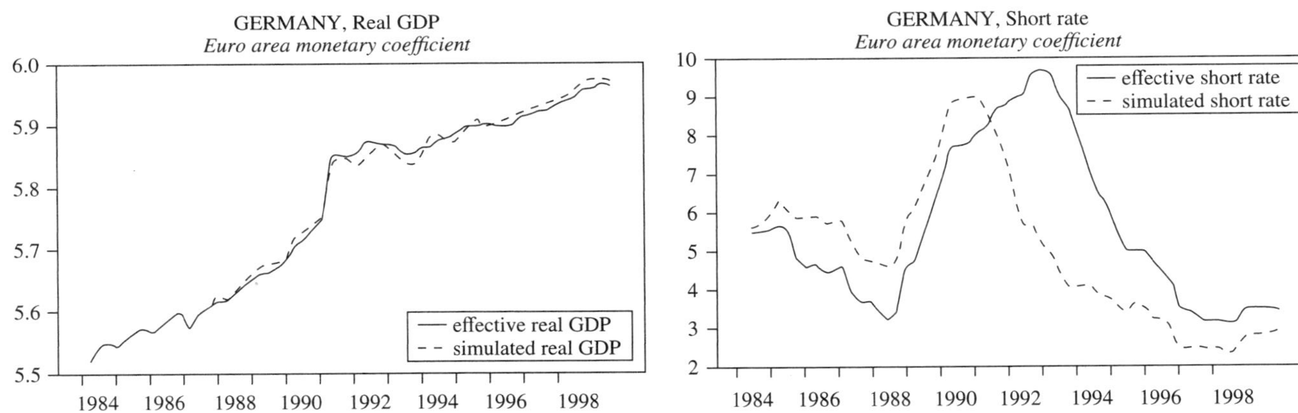

Figure 14.3b Germany with Euro area coefficient

Figure 14.3 (continued)

ITALY, Nominal GDP
Euro area monetary coefficient

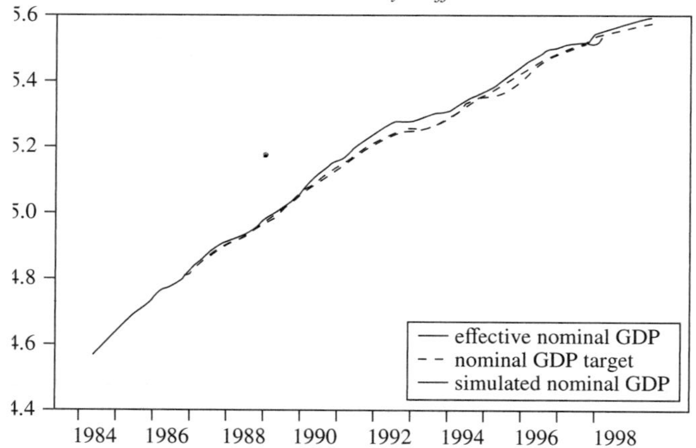

ITALY, Inflation
Euro area monetary coefficient

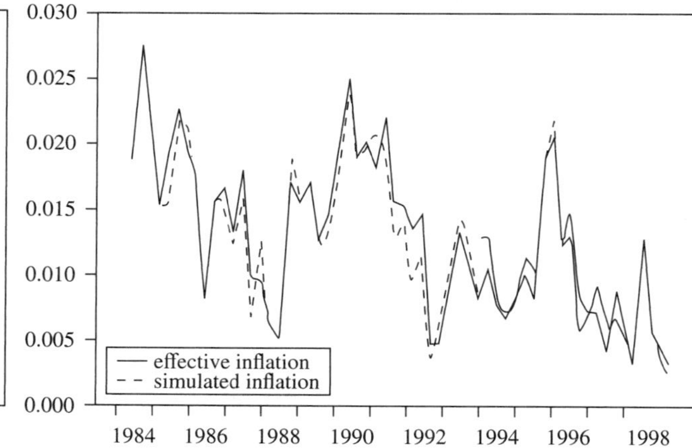

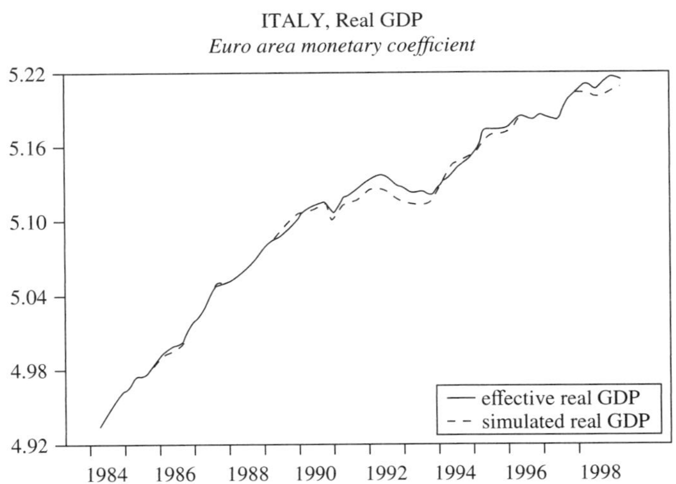

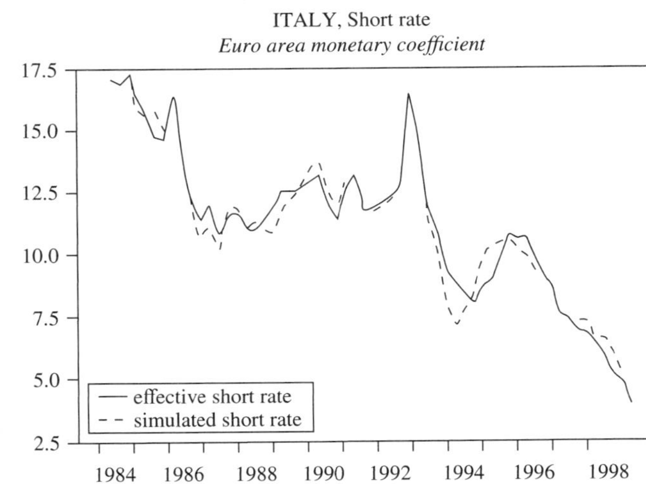

Figure 14.3c Italy with Euro area coefficient

Figure 14.3 (continued)

APPENDIX 2: SERIES (SOURCE AND TREATMENT)

We use quarterly series which are corrected for seasonal effects. They are expressed in logarithm form, except in the case of interest rates.

All the series are taken from the database DATASTREAM (OECD). In order to test their stationary properties, we apply Augmented Dickey-Fuller tests (ADF). All the series are I(1), we then use them in first differences in our VAR models.

Symbols and Mathematical Expressions used in the Text

$$\Delta b_t = [\Delta y_t^f + \Delta p_t^*] - (1/16)\,[(x_{t-1} - b_{t-1}) - (x_{t-17} - b_{t-17})] + \lambda\,(x_{t-1}^* - x_{t-1}) \quad (1)$$

$$x_t^* = x_t + \Delta y_t^f + \Delta p_t^* \quad (2)$$

Δ	p_t^*
λ	x_t^*
b_t	x_{t-1}^*
b_{t-1}	x_t
b_{t-17}	x_{t-1}
y_t^f	x_{t-17}

$$RMSE = \sqrt{\frac{\sum_{t=0}^{T} (x_t^s - x_t^*)}{T}}$$

$\sum_{t=0}^{T}$	x_t^s
$\sqrt{-}$	x_t^*

NOTES

1. Price stability is defined as an increase in the HCPI (Harmonised Consumption Price Index) of below 2 per cent per annum (ECB, 1999).
2. It must be remembered here that price stability is the overriding goal of monetary policy in the long run. However this does not mean that central banks do not pay attention to real output. On the contrary, stabilization of output fluctuations remains a short-run goal of monetary policy, as long as it does not endanger price stability. See Mishkin (2000) for instance.

3. This does not constitute the most important problem for central banks. Effectively the most serious difficulty central banks face with these rules is the availability of real time data (it is particularly true for GDP which is often and sizeably revised). This constitutes one of the most important challenges for future research in the monetary policy area (see ECB Workshop: *Monetary Analysis: Tools and Applications*, November 2000).
4. We consider that this is particularly problematic insofar as indicators of the second pillar are relevant only for the short-run dynamics of inflation. Therefore they are not compatible with the medium-term horizon of monetary policy. For more details on this point, see ECB (2000), p. 46.
5. The purpose of this term is to take account of possible changes in velocity growth because of regulatory and technological sources, which is the case in the middle of the 1980s with financial deregulation and innovations. We can notice here that this simple modelling of velocity changes gives as good results as more complex modelling (see Dueker, 1993).
6. The German case is particularly relevant. Effectively, monetary targets announced by the Bundesbank are tied to projections of inflation, potential output growth and velocity adjustment through the quantity equation relationship (see Bernanke and Mihov, 1996; von Hagen, 1995, 1999).
7. The reference annual growth rate for M3 (4.5 per cent per annum) is the sum of three components: (1) the numerical price stability goal in the euro area, which has been defined as an increase of the HCPI of below 2 per cent per annum, (2) the medium-term trend in real GDP growth for the euro, which is generally estimated at 2–2.5 per cent per annum, and (3) the trend decline in the velocity of circulation of M3, which is in a range of 0.5 to 1 per cent per annum. The Governing Council of the ECB has preferred to announce a single reference for money growth (whereas several of its components are expressed in the form of a range) in order to make it easier for the public to assess the inflationary situation by comparing this unique reference value with effective monetary growth rate.
8. The Bundesbank has successfully followed a monetary growth targeting strategy in 1975–98 in order to insure its price stability objective.
9. We use the announcements made in *La Monnaie en . . .* , which is published every year by the Banque de France.
10. The Italian inflation target can be written as: $\pi_t = \alpha / t + \beta$. We choose to take the average inflation in 1983 as the initial value and a 1 per cent target for the end of the period, since it is the middle of the inflation target interval announced by the ECB.
11. $RMSE = \sqrt{\sum_{t=0}^{T} (x_t^s - x_t^*)/T}$ where x_t^s is the simulated nominal GDP and x_t^* the targeted nominal GDP (everything is expressed in logarithms).
12. The ECB considers that a monetary rule would induce less good results in terms of real output and interest rates than its own monetary strategy. It is then interesting to see whether our simulated results support this point of view.

REFERENCES

Banque de France (1983–2000), *La Monnaie en . . .* , Paris.

Barro, R.J. and D.B Gordon (1983), 'Rules, discretion and reputation in a model of monetary policy', *Journal of Monetary Economics*, **12** (2), 101–21.

Bernanke, B. and A. Mihov (1996), 'What does the Bundesbank target?', *NBER Working Paper*, 5764, September.

Dueker, M. (1993), 'Can nominal GDP targeting rules stabilise the economy?', *Federal Reserve Bank of Saint Louis Review*, May–June, 15–29.

Durand, J-J., F. Martin and N. Payelle (1999), 'La convergence des degrés de sensibilité à la politique monétaire', in C. Tavéra (ed.), *La Convergence des Economies Européennes*, Economica, pp. 53–91.

Economie Internationale, 'Croissance potentielle et écart de production' (1997), **69.**

European Central Bank (1999), 'Euro area monetary aggregates and their role in the Eurosystem's monetary policy strategy', *ECB Monthly Bulletin*, February, 29–46.

European Central Bank (2000), 'The two pillars of the ECB monetary policy strategy', *ECB Monthly Bulletin*, November, 37–48.

European Central Bank (2001), 'Issues related to monetary policy rules', *ECB Monthly Bulletin*, October, 37–50.

Gerlach, S. and L. Svensson (2001), 'Money and inflation in the euro area: a case for monetary indicators?', Bank for International Settlements, *Working Paper*, 98, January.

von Hagen, J. (1995), 'Inflation and monetary targeting in Germany', in L. Leiderman and L.E.O. Svensson (eds), *Inflation Targets*, London: CEPR, pp. 107–21.

von Hagen, J. (1999), 'Money growth targeting by the Bundesbank', *Journal of Monetary Economics*, **43**, 681–701.

Kydland, F.E. and E.C. Prescott (1977), 'Rules rather than discretion: the inconsistency of optimal plans', *Journal of Political Economy*, **85** (June), 473–91.

McCallum, B. (1987), 'The case for rules in the conduct of monetary policy: a concrete example', *Federal Reserve Bank of Richmond Economic Review*, September/October, 10–18.

McCallum, B. (1988), 'Robustness properties of a rule for monetary policy', *Carnegie-Rochester Conference Series on Public Policy*, **29**, 173–204.

McCallum, B. (1993), 'Specification and analysis of a monetary policy rule for Japan', *Bank of Japan Monetary and Economic Studies*, **11** (2), November, 1–45.

Mishkin, F. (2000), 'What should central banks do?', *Federal Reserve Bank of St Louis Review*, November/December, 1–14.

Pill, H. (2000), 'Monetary analysis: tools and applications (summary)', *ECB Workshop: Monetary Analysis: Tools and Applications,* November, pp. 11–30.

St-Amant, P. and S. van Norden (1997), 'Measurement of the output gap: a discussion of recent Research at the Bank of Canada', *Bank of Canada, Technical Report*, 79.

Taylor, J.B. (1993), 'Discretion versus policy rules in practice', *Carnegie-Rochester Conference Series on Public Policy*, **39**, 195–214.

Index